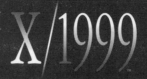

X/1999™

VOL. 11

INTERLUDE

Shōjo Edition

STORY & ART BY CLAMP

ENGLISH ADAPTATION BY FRED BURKE

Translation/Lillian Olsen
Touch-Up Art & Lettering/Stephen Dutro
Cover Design/Yuki Ameda
Graphic Design/Carolina Ugalde
Supervising Editor/Julie Davis
Editor/P. Duffield

Managing Editor/Annette Roman
Editor in Chief/William Flanagan
Director of Licensing & Acquisitions/Rika Inouye
VP of Sales & Marketing/Liza Coppola
Sr. VP of Editorial/Hyoe Narita
Publisher/Seiji Horibuchi

X/1999 is rated "T+" for Older Teens. It may contain violence, language, alcohol or tobacco use, or suggestive situations.

Printed in Canada

Published by VIZ, LLC
P.O. Box 77010 • San Francisco, CA 94107

Shōjo Edition
10 9 8 7 6 5 4 3 2 1
First printing, September 2003

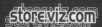

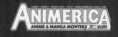

X/1999 ™

Vol. 11
INTERLUDE
Shōjo Edition

Story and Art by
CLAMP

X/1999
THE STORY THUS FAR

The End of the World has been prophesied …and time is running out. Kamui Shiro is a young man who was born with a special power—the power to decide the fate of the Earth itself.

Kamui had grown up in Tokyo, but had fled with his mother after the suspicious death of a family friend. Six years later, his mother too, dies under suspicious circumstances, engulfed in flames. Her last words to him are that he should return to Tokyo…that his destiny awaits.

Kamui obeys his mother's words, but almost immediately upon his arrival, he's challenged to a psychic duel—a first warning that others know of his power, and of his return.

Kamui is also reunited with his childhood friends, Fuma and Kotori Monou. Although Kamui attempts to push his friends away, hoping to protect them, they too are soon drawn into the web of destiny that surrounds him.

Meanwhile, the two sides to the great conflict to come are being drawn. On one side is the dreamseer Hinoto, a blind princess who lives beneath Japan's seat of government, the Diet Building. On the other side is Kanoe, Hinoto's dark sister with similar powers, but a different vision of Earth's ultimate future. Around these two women gather the Dragons of Heaven and the Dragons of Earth, the forces that will fight to decide the fate of the planet. The only variable in the equation is Kamui, whose fate it will be to choose which side he will join.

And Kamui finally does make a choice. He chooses to defend the Earth as it stands now. But by making this choice, he pays a terrible price. For fate has chosen his oldest friend to be his "twin star".—the other "Kamui" who will fight against him. And in this first battle, the gentle Kotori is the first casualty.

Now Kamui must face the consequences of his decision…and try to come to terms with not only his ultimate fate, but that of the Earth….

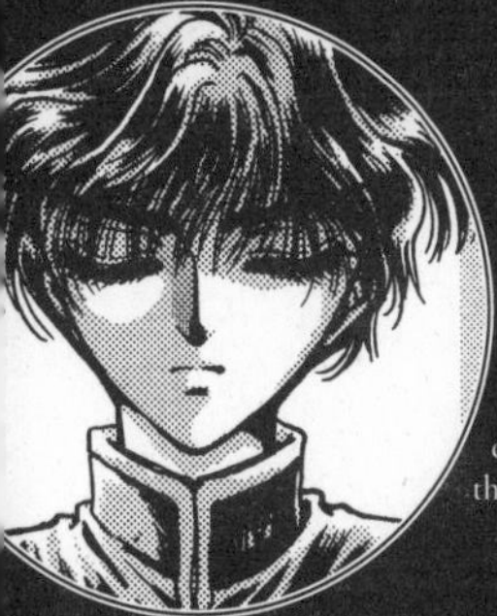

Kamui Shiro
A young man with psychic powers whose choice of destiny will decide the fate of the world.

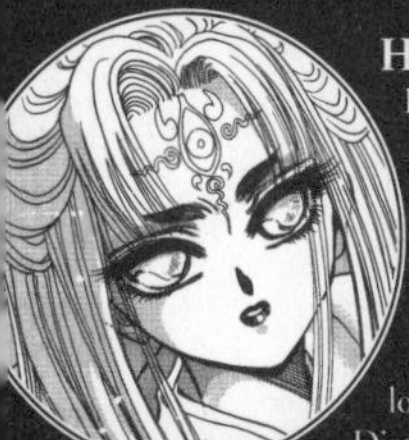

Hinoto
Blind, unable to speak or walk, Hinoto is a powerful prophetess, far older than she looks, who communicates with the power of her mind alone. She lives in a secret shrine located beneath Tokyo's Diet Building.

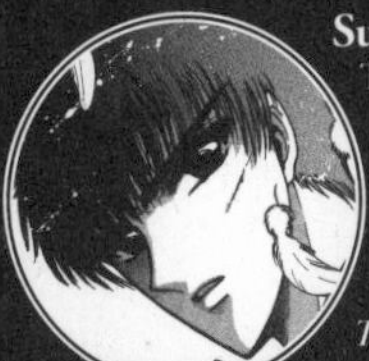

Subaru Sumeragi
The 13th family head of a long line of spiritualists and a powerful medium and exorcist. He is the lead character of another Clamp manga series, *Tokyo Babylon*.

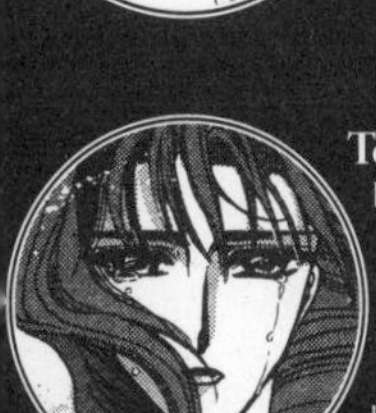

Toru
Kamui's mother was heir to the Magami clan, an ancient family of "Shadow Sacrifices," people who absorb the misfortunes of others.

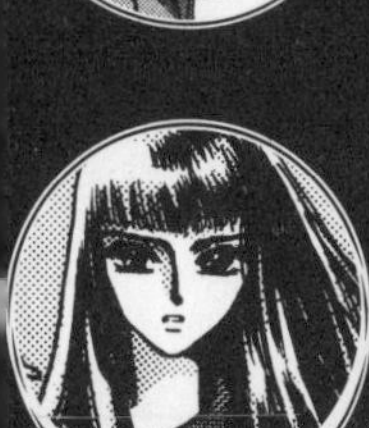

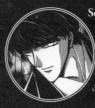

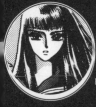

Arashi Kishu
Priestess of the Ise Shrine, Arashi can materialize a sword from the palm of her hand.

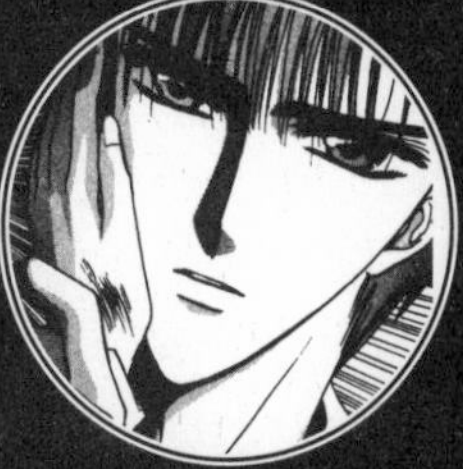

Fuma Monou
Kamui's childhood friend. When Kamui made his choice, Fuma was chosen by fate to become his "Twin Star" — the other "Kamui."

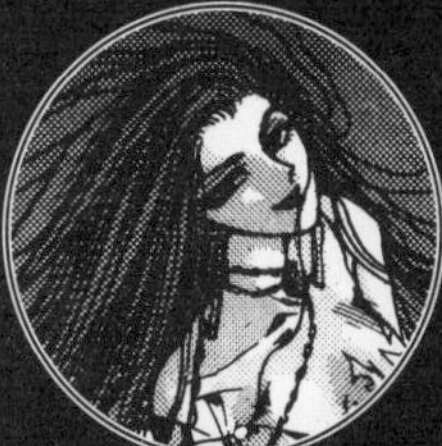

Kanoe
Hinoto's sister shares her ability to see the future… but Kanoe has predicted a different final result.

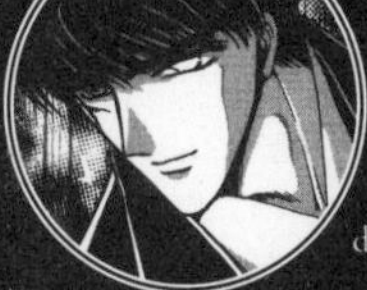

Seishiro Sakurazuka
Also called *Sakurazukamori*, the mysterious Seishiro is a crossover character from *Tokyo Babylon*. He lost his sight in one eye during that series. He shares a deep rivalry with Subaru.

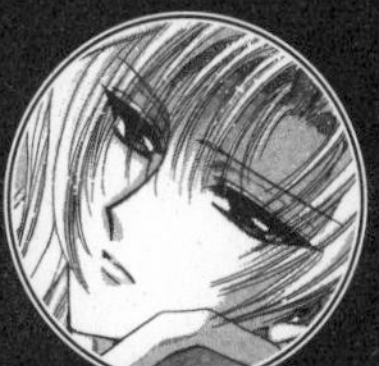

Kakyo Kuzuki
A dreamseer like Hinoto, Kakyo is a hospital-bound invalid kept alive by machines.

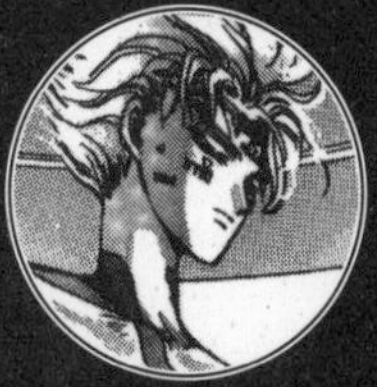

Nataku
A genetically engineered human, Nataku wields a ribbonlike piece of cloth.

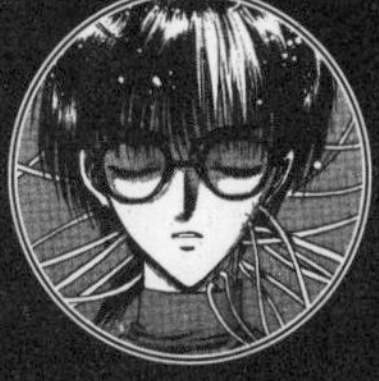

Satsuki Yatoji
A computer expert, Satsuki can interface directly with her personal machine, "The Beast."

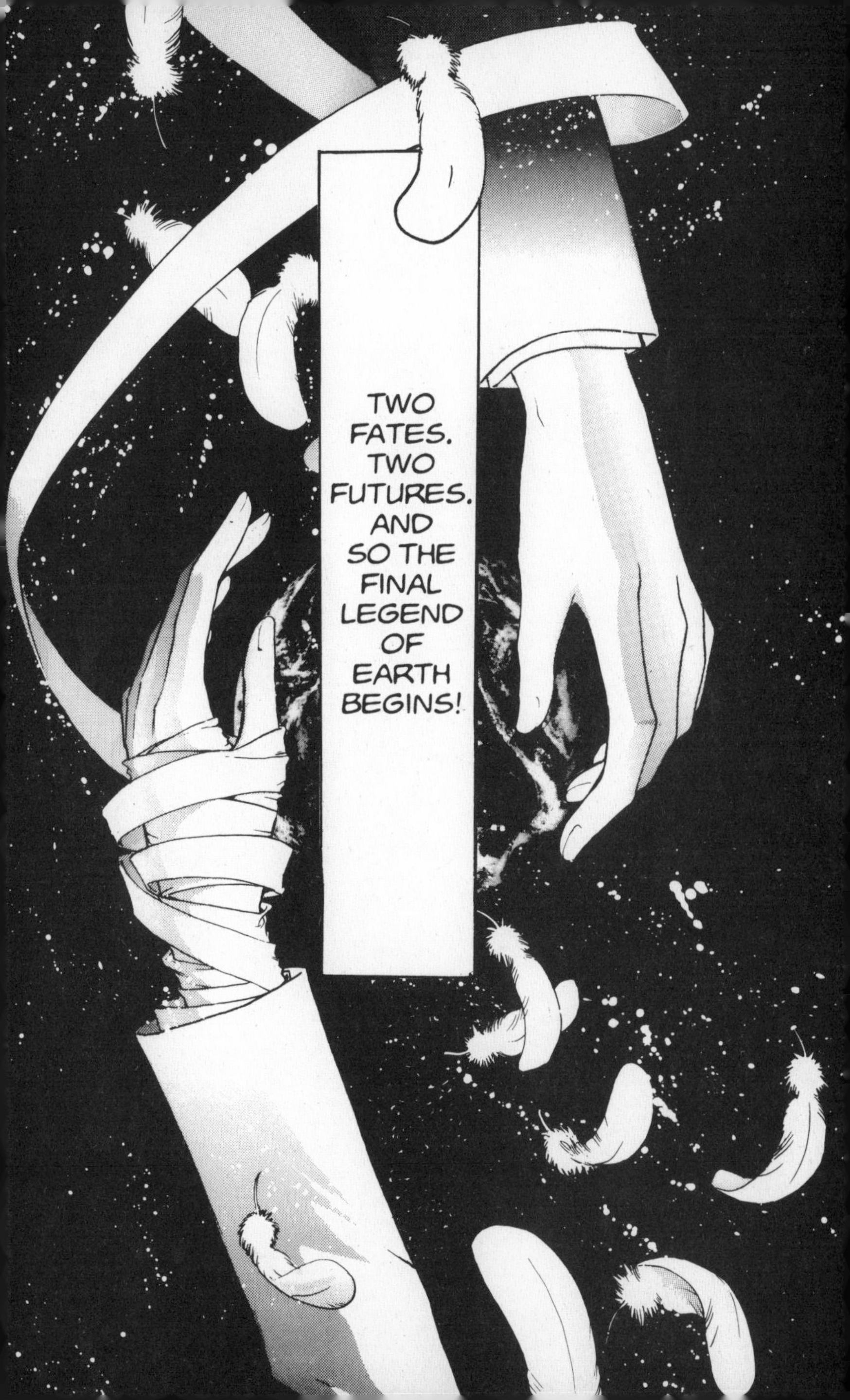
TWO FATES. TWO FUTURES. AND SO THE FINAL LEGEND OF EARTH BEGINS!

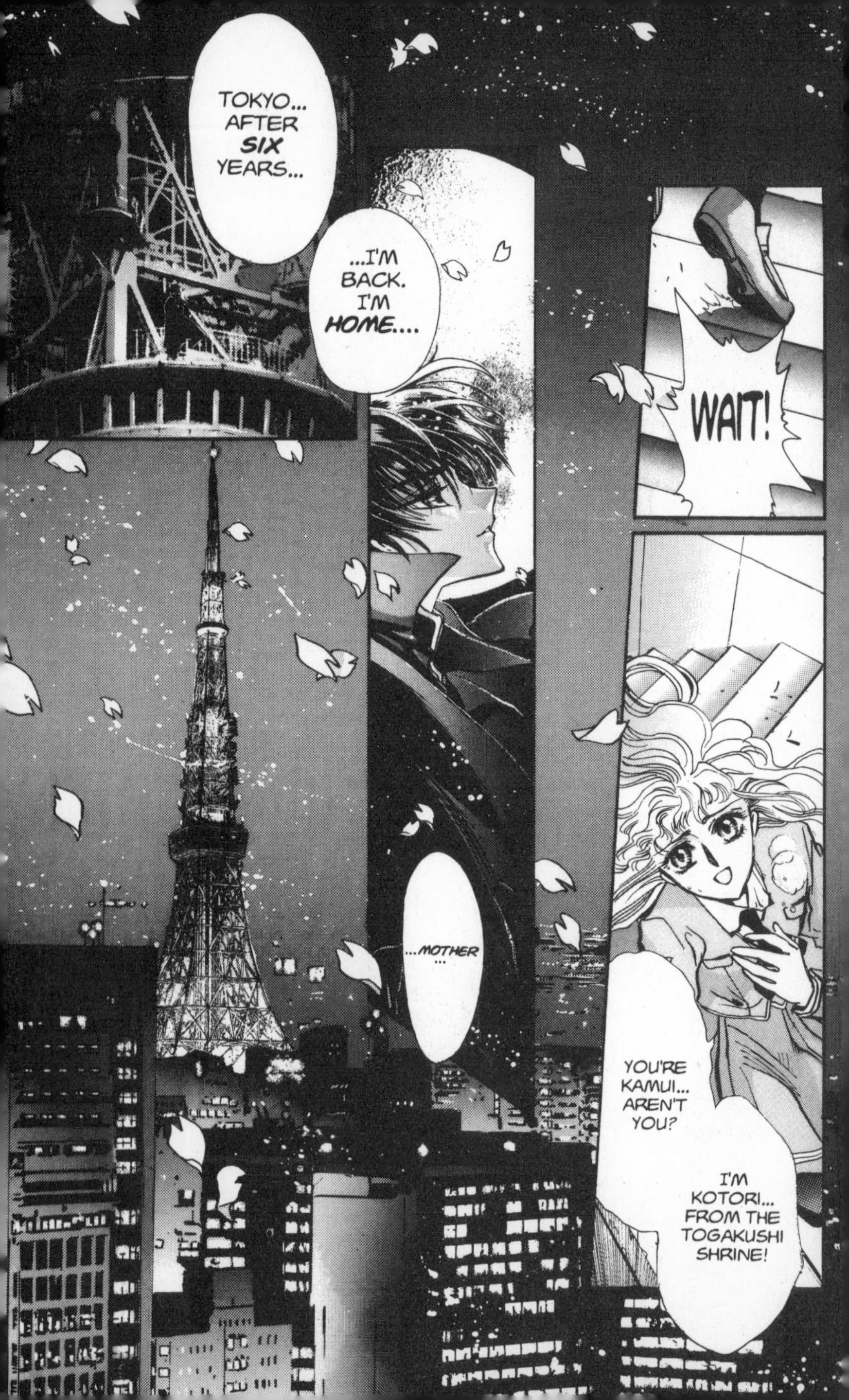
TOKYO... AFTER SIX YEARS...
...I'M BACK. I'M HOME....
...MOTHER ...
WAIT!
YOU'RE KAMUI... AREN'T YOU?
I'M KOTORI... FROM THE TOGAKUSHI SHRINE!

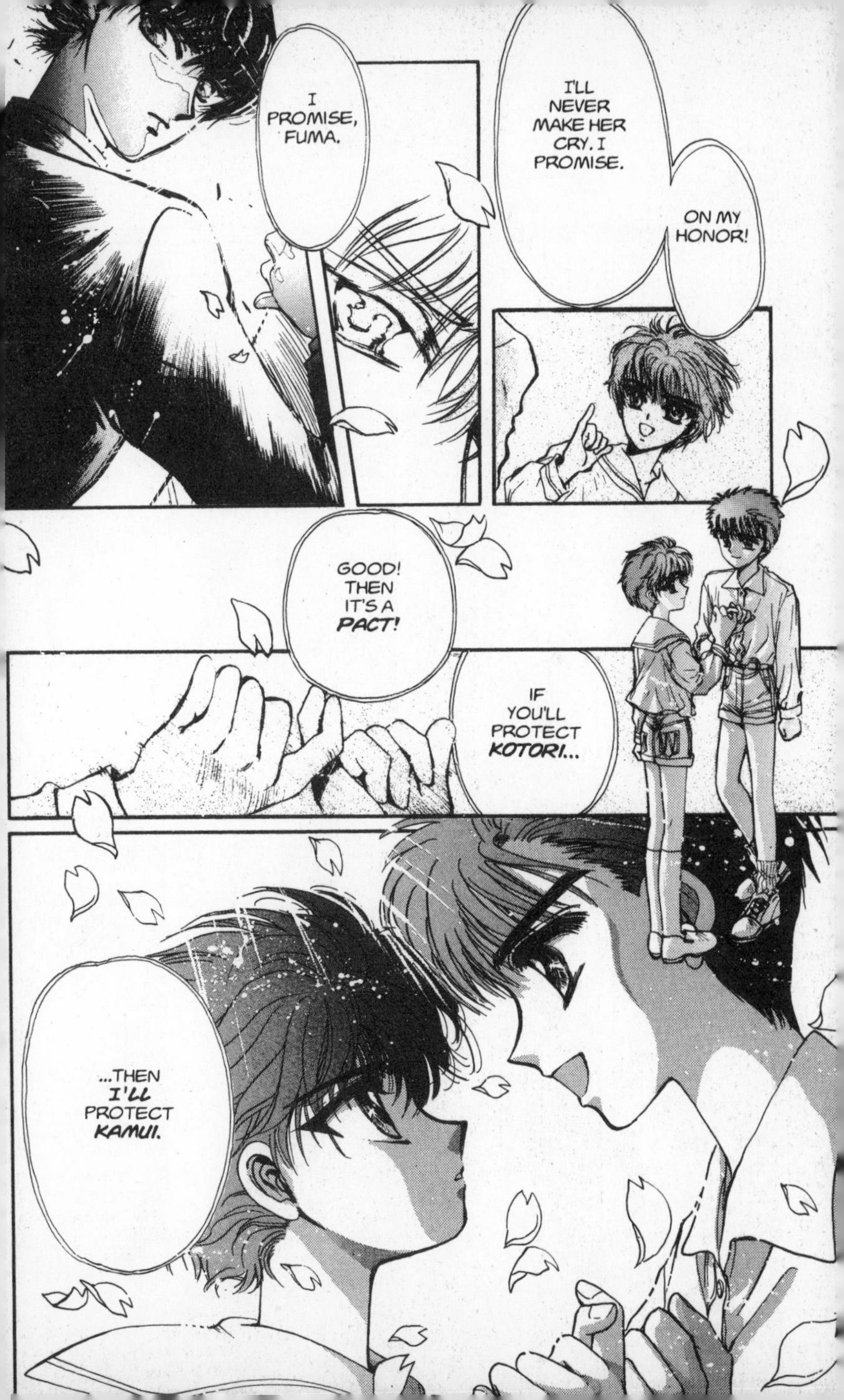
I PROMISE, FUMA.
I'LL NEVER MAKE HER CRY. I PROMISE.
ON MY HONOR!
GOOD! THEN IT'S A ***PACT!***
IF YOU'LL PROTECT ***KOTORI...***
...THEN ***I'LL*** PROTECT ***KAMUI.***

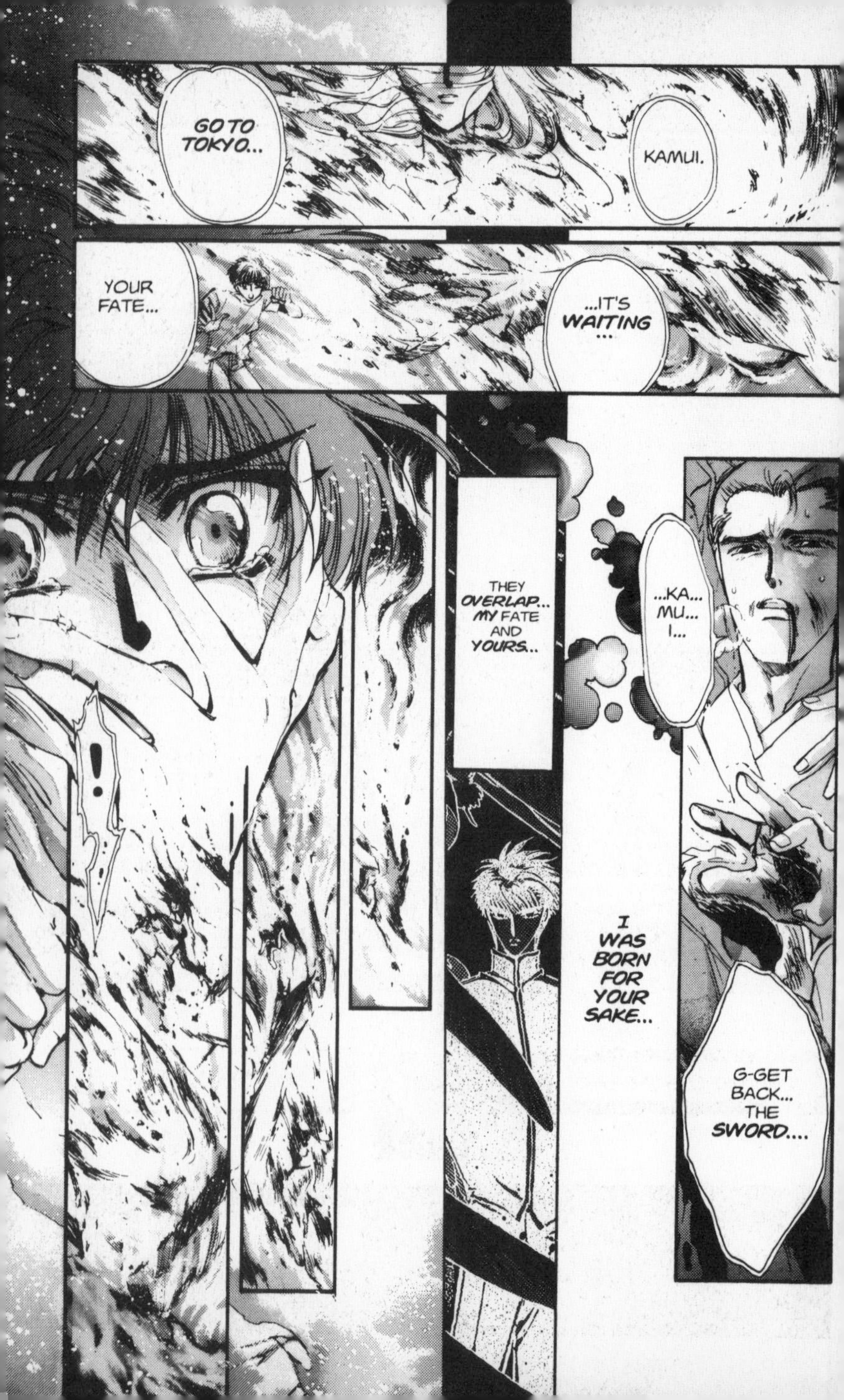
GO TO TOKYO...
KAMUI.
YOUR FATE...
...IT'S WAITING ...
THEY OVERLAP... MY FATE AND YOURS...
I WAS BORN FOR YOUR SAKE...
...KA... MU... I...
G-GET BACK... THE SWORD....

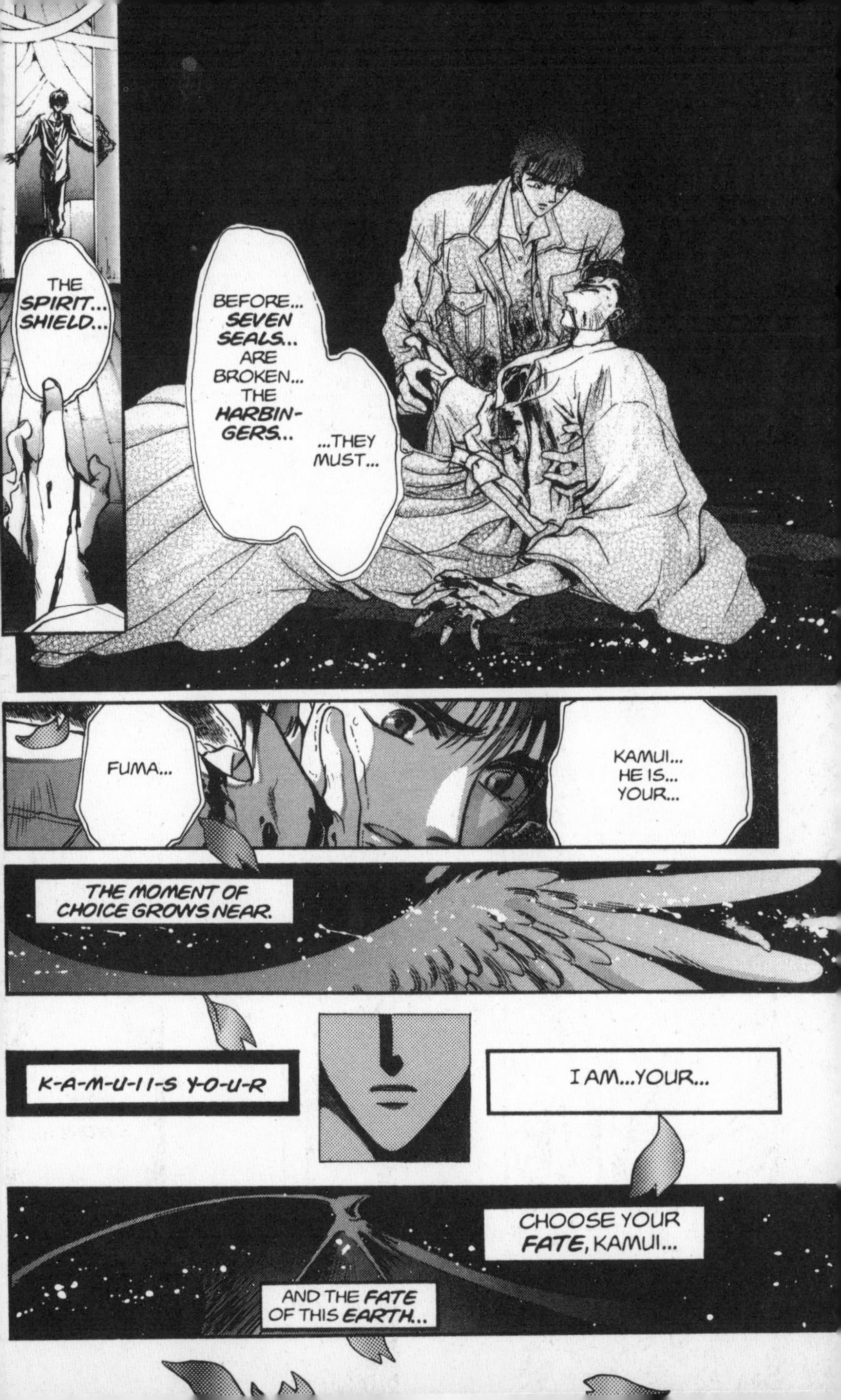
THE SPIRIT... SHIELD...
BEFORE... SEVEN SEALS... ARE BROKEN... THE HARBINGERS...
...THEY MUST...
FUMA...
KAMUI... HE IS... YOUR...
THE MOMENT OF CHOICE GROWS NEAR.
K-A-M-U-I I-S Y-O-U-R
I AM...YOUR...
CHOOSE YOUR FATE, KAMUI...
AND THE FATE OF THIS EARTH...

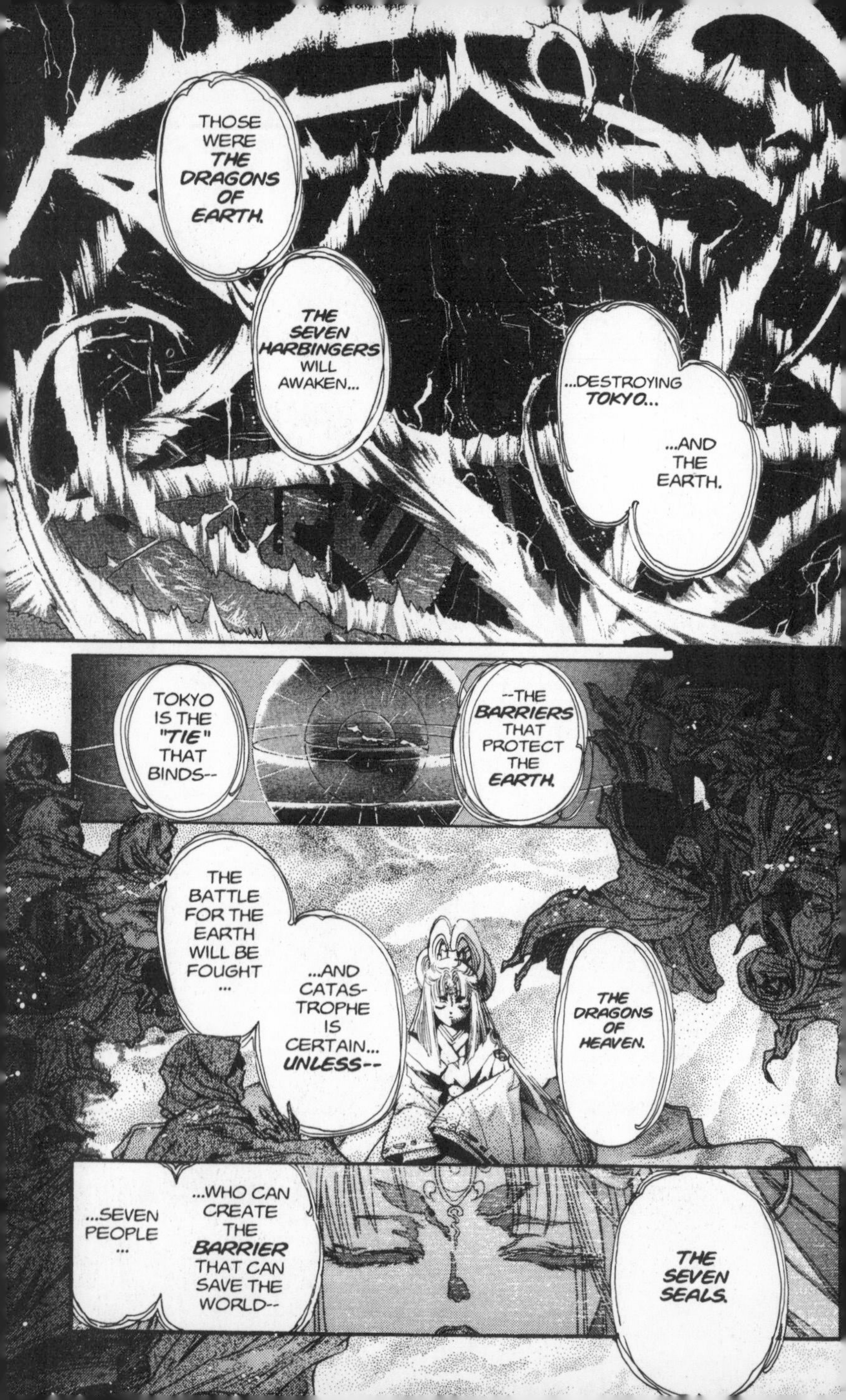
THOSE WERE THE DRAGONS OF EARTH.
THE SEVEN HARBINGERS WILL AWAKEN...
...DESTROYING TOKYO... ...AND THE EARTH.
TOKYO IS THE "TIE" THAT BINDS--
--THE BARRIERS THAT PROTECT THE EARTH.
THE BATTLE FOR THE EARTH WILL BE FOUGHT ...
...AND CATASTROPHE IS CERTAIN... UNLESS--
THE DRAGONS OF HEAVEN.
...SEVEN PEOPLE ...
...WHO CAN CREATE THE BARRIER THAT CAN SAVE THE WORLD--
THE SEVEN SEALS.

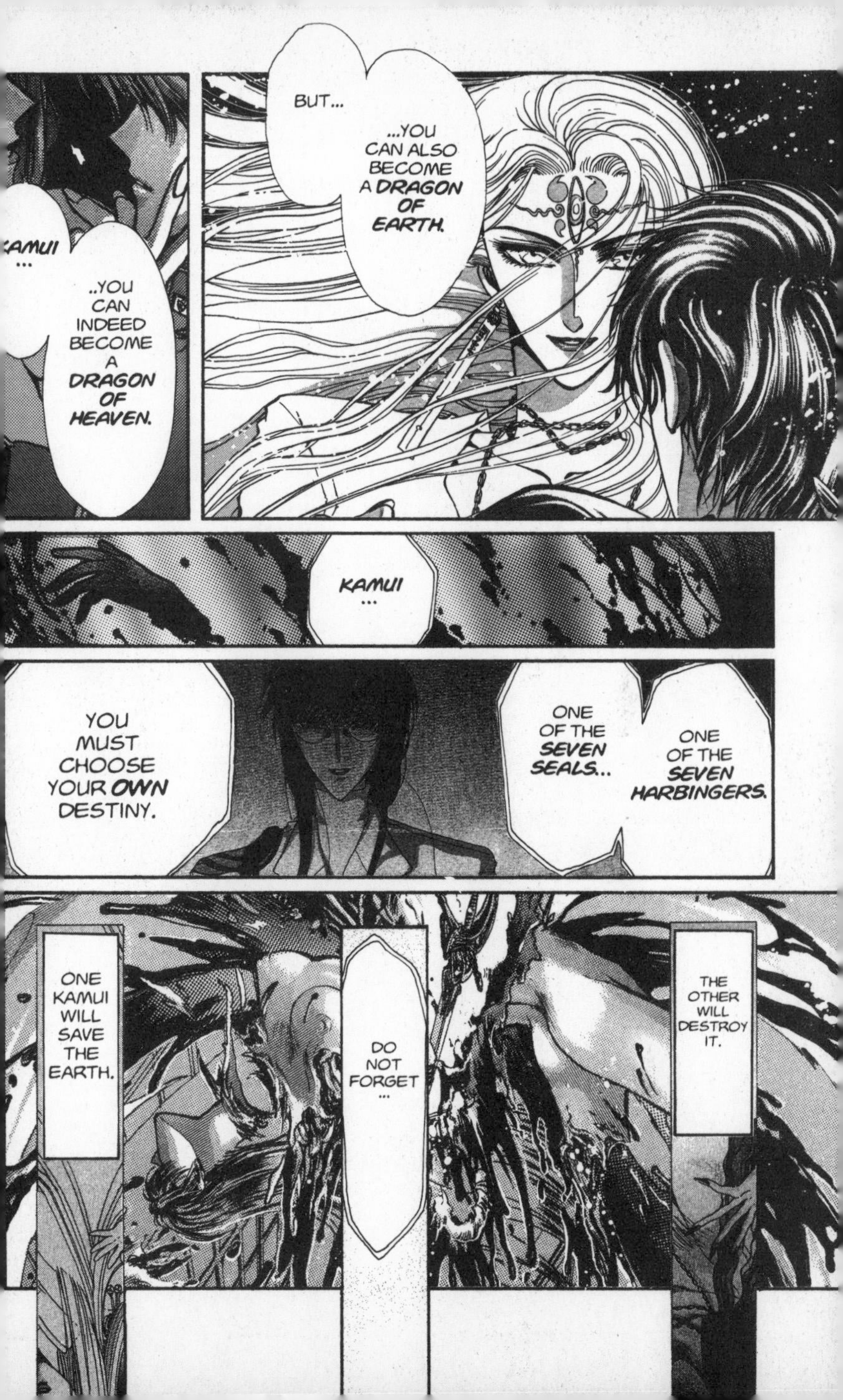

KAMUI ...
..YOU CAN INDEED BECOME A DRAGON OF HEAVEN.
BUT...
...YOU CAN ALSO BECOME A DRAGON OF EARTH.
KAMUI ...
YOU MUST CHOOSE YOUR OWN DESTINY.
ONE OF THE SEVEN SEALS...
ONE OF THE SEVEN HARBINGERS.
ONE KAMUI WILL SAVE THE EARTH.
DO NOT FORGET ...
THE OTHER WILL DESTROY IT.

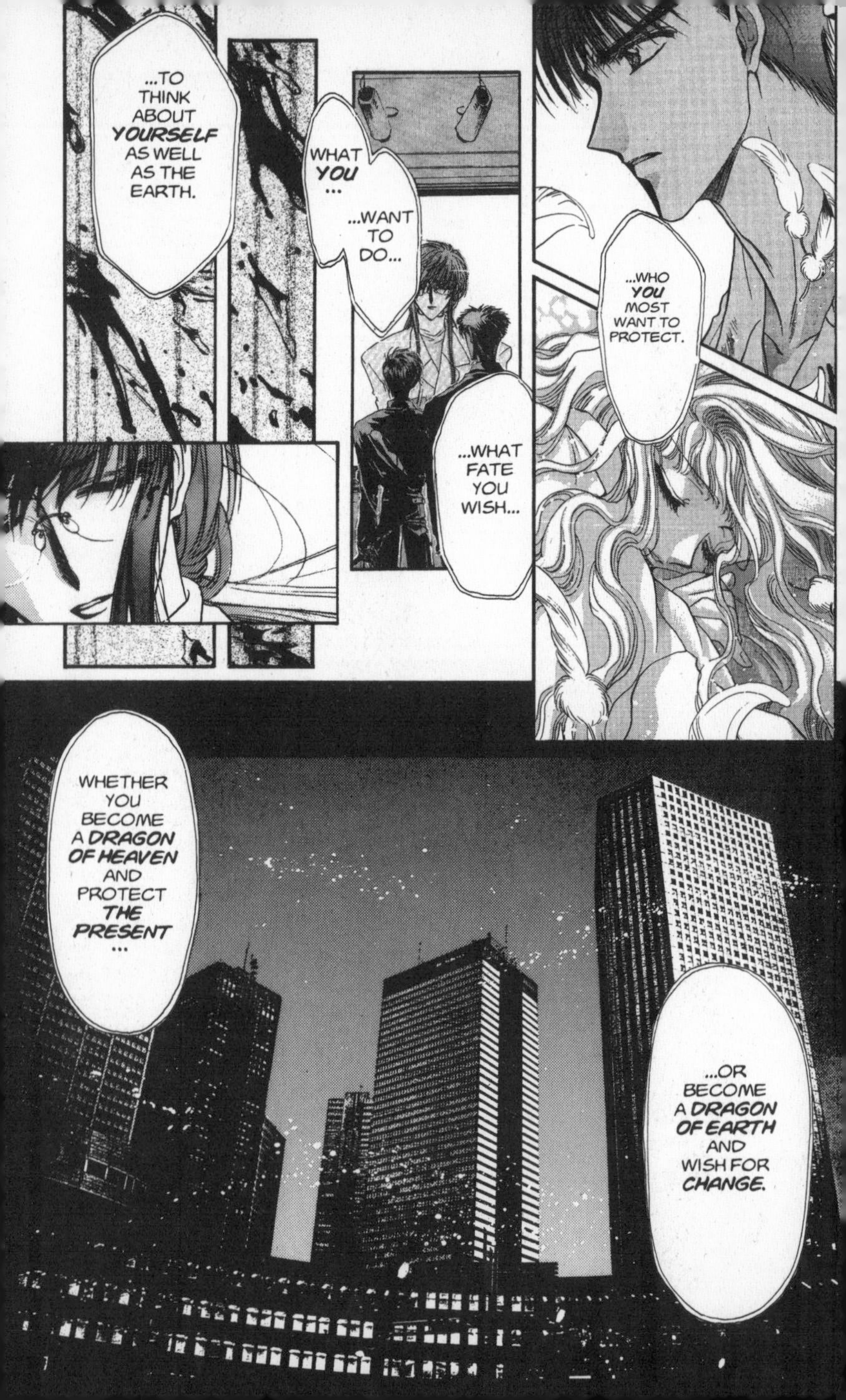

...TO THINK ABOUT YOURSELF AS WELL AS THE EARTH.
WHAT YOU ...
...WANT TO DO...
...WHAT FATE YOU WISH...
...WHO YOU MOST WANT TO PROTECT.
WHETHER YOU BECOME A DRAGON OF HEAVEN AND PROTECT THE PRESENT ...
...OR BECOME A DRAGON OF EARTH AND WISH FOR CHANGE.

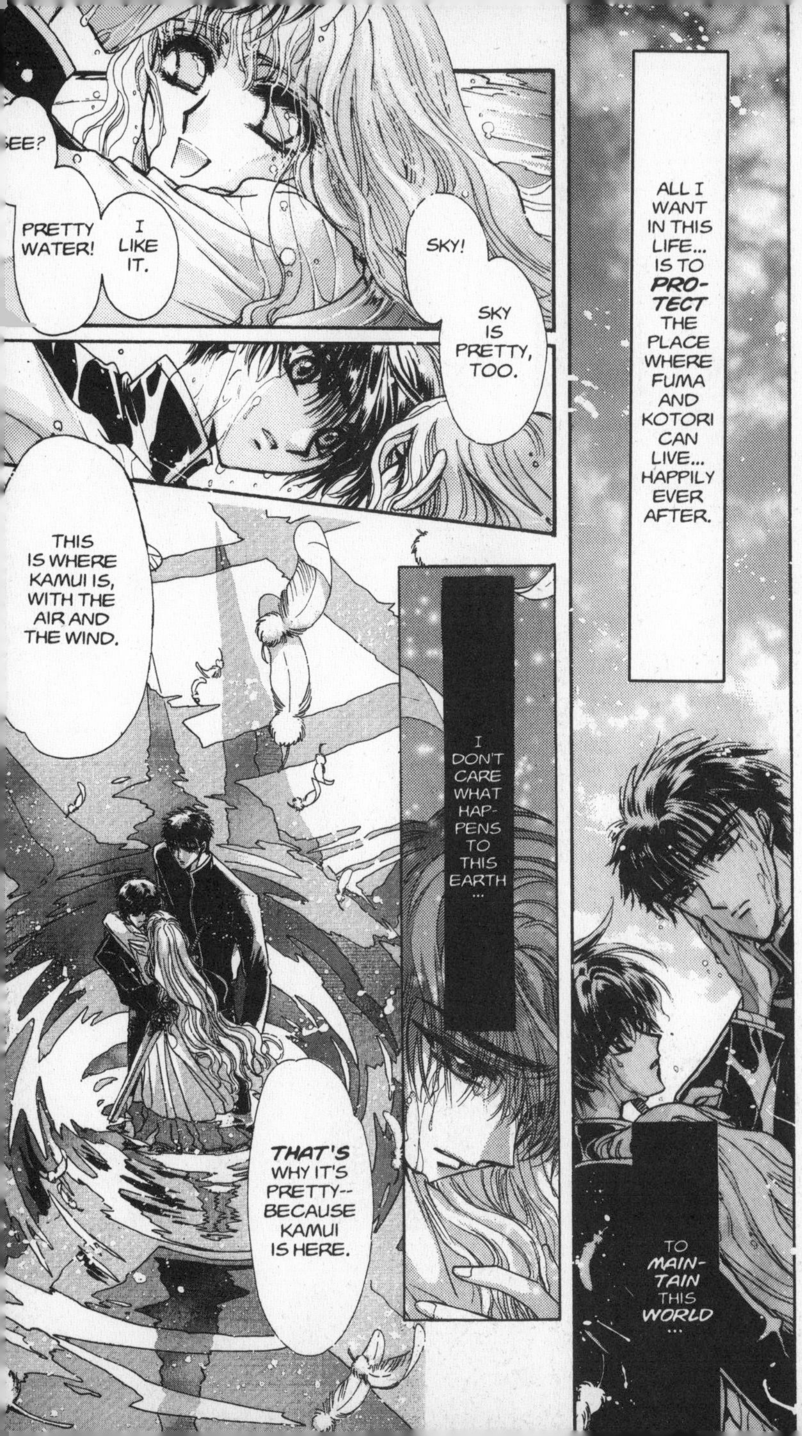
SEE?
PRETTY WATER!
I LIKE IT.
SKY!
SKY IS PRETTY, TOO.
THIS IS WHERE KAMUI IS, WITH THE AIR AND THE WIND.
THAT'S WHY IT'S PRETTY-- BECAUSE KAMUI IS HERE.
I DON'T CARE WHAT HAP-PENS TO THIS EARTH...
ALL I WANT IN THIS LIFE... IS TO PRO-TECT THE PLACE WHERE FUMA AND KOTORI CAN LIVE... HAPPILY EVER AFTER.
TO MAIN-TAIN THIS WORLD...

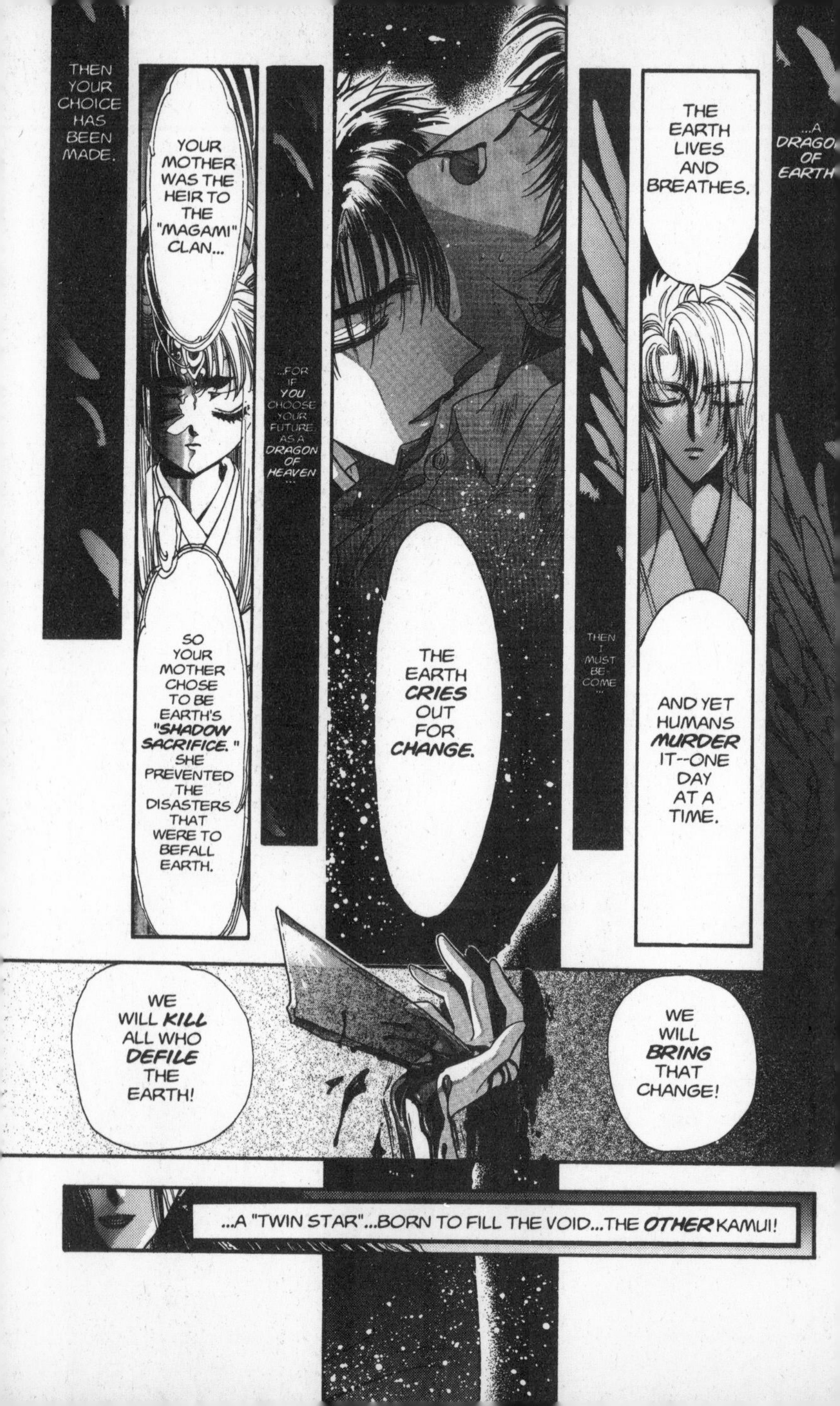

THEN YOUR CHOICE HAS BEEN MADE.
YOUR MOTHER WAS THE HEIR TO THE "MAGAMI" CLAN...
SO YOUR MOTHER CHOSE TO BE EARTH'S "SHADOW SACRIFICE." SHE PREVENTED THE DISASTERS THAT WERE TO BEFALL EARTH.
...FOR IF YOU CHOOSE YOUR FUTURE AS A DRAGON OF HEAVEN...
THE EARTH CRIES OUT FOR CHANGE.
THEN I MUST BECOME...
THE EARTH LIVES AND BREATHES.
AND YET HUMANS MURDER IT--ONE DAY AT A TIME.
...A DRAGO OF EARTH
WE WILL KILL ALL WHO DEFILE THE EARTH!
WE WILL BRING THAT CHANGE!
...A "TWIN STAR"...BORN TO FILL THE VOID...THE OTHER KAMUI!

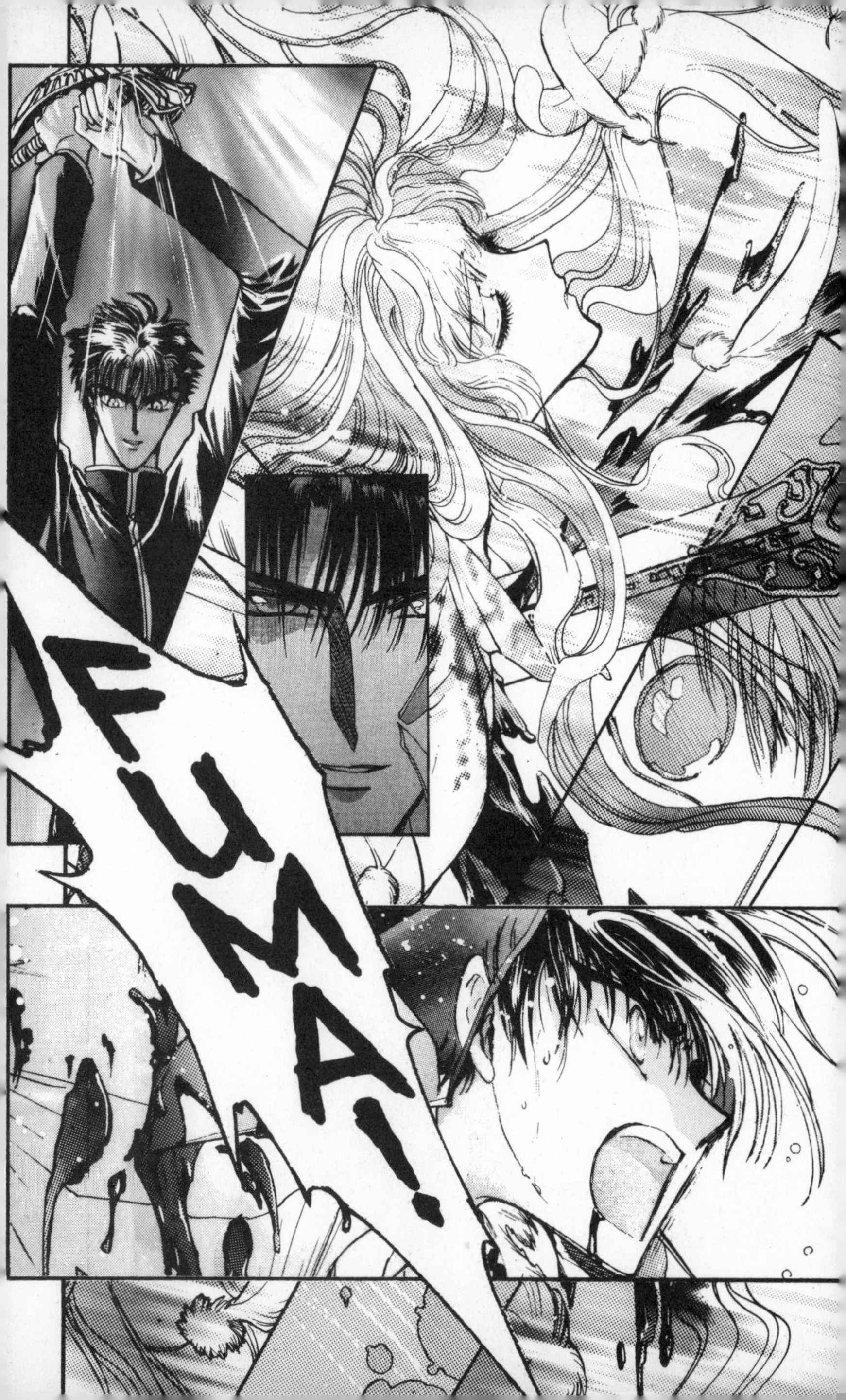
FUMA!!

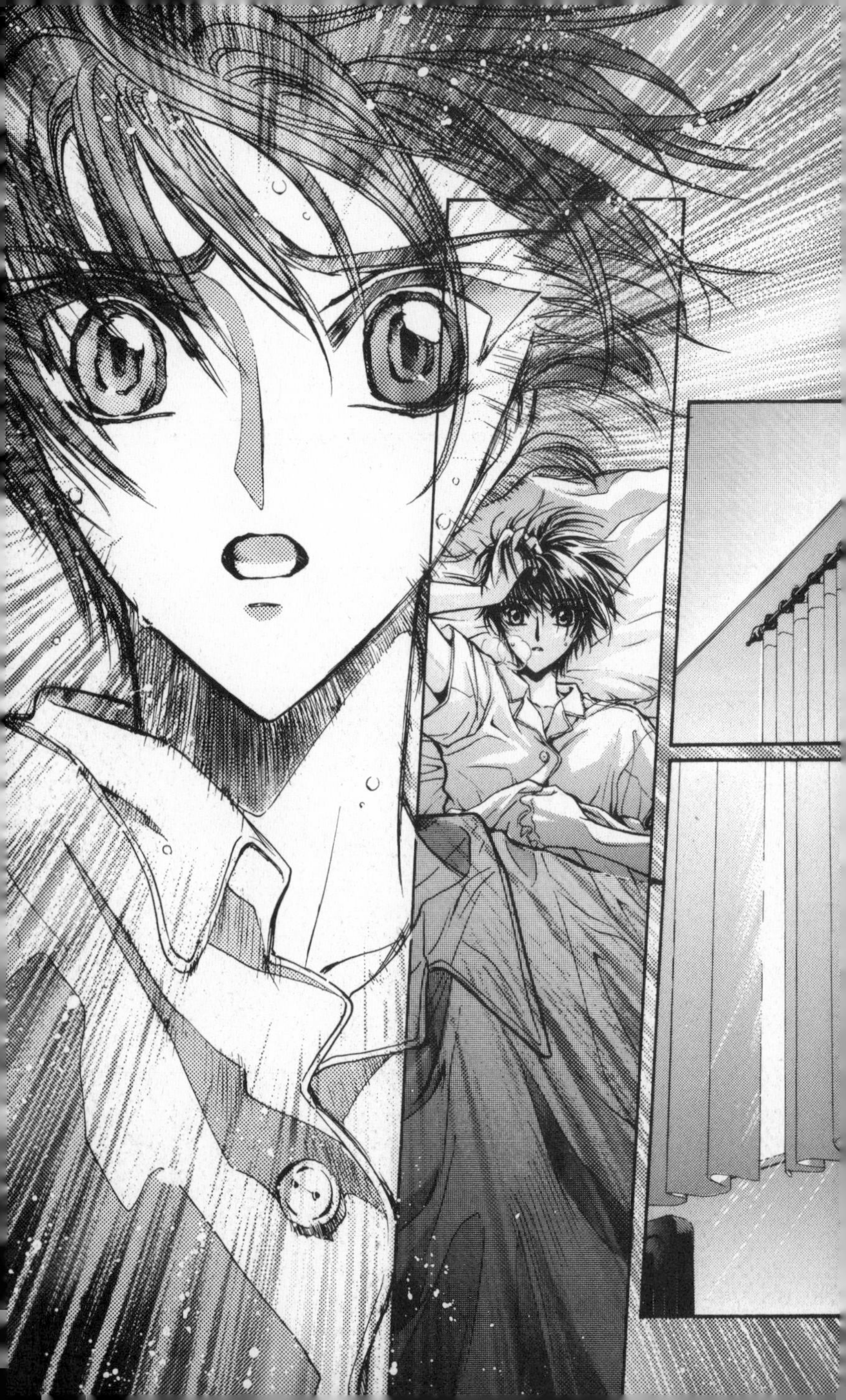

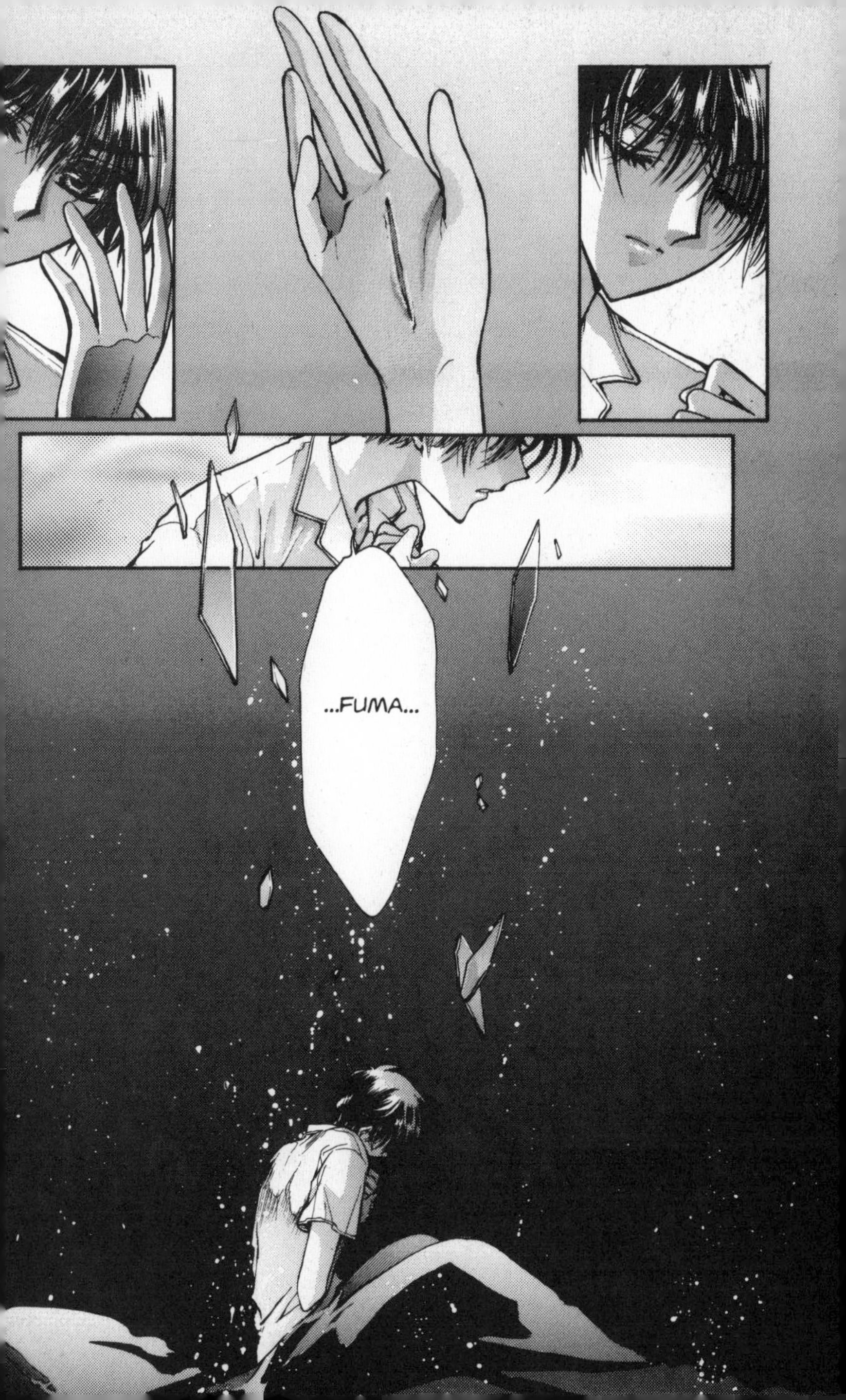
...FUMA...

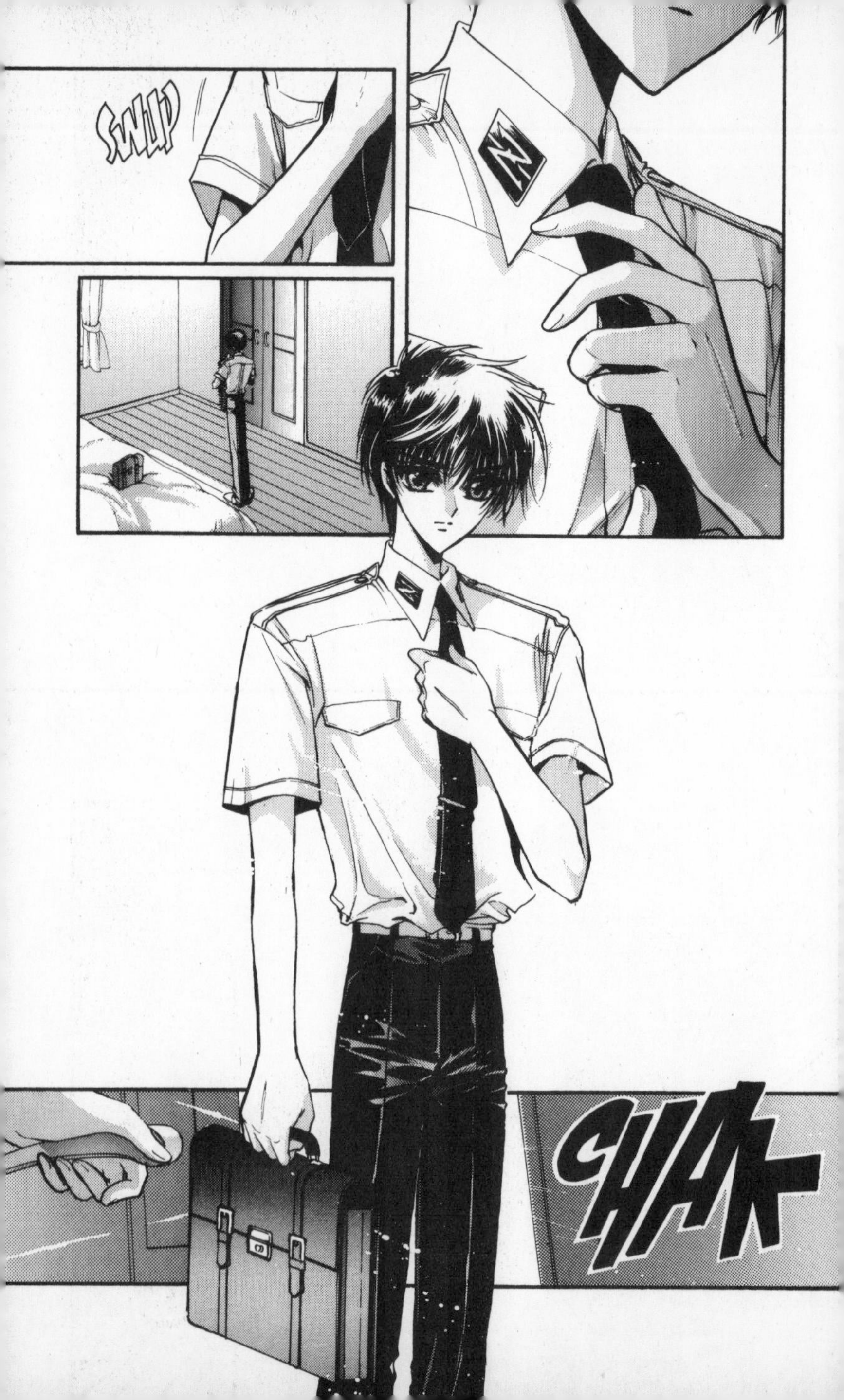
SWIP
CHAK

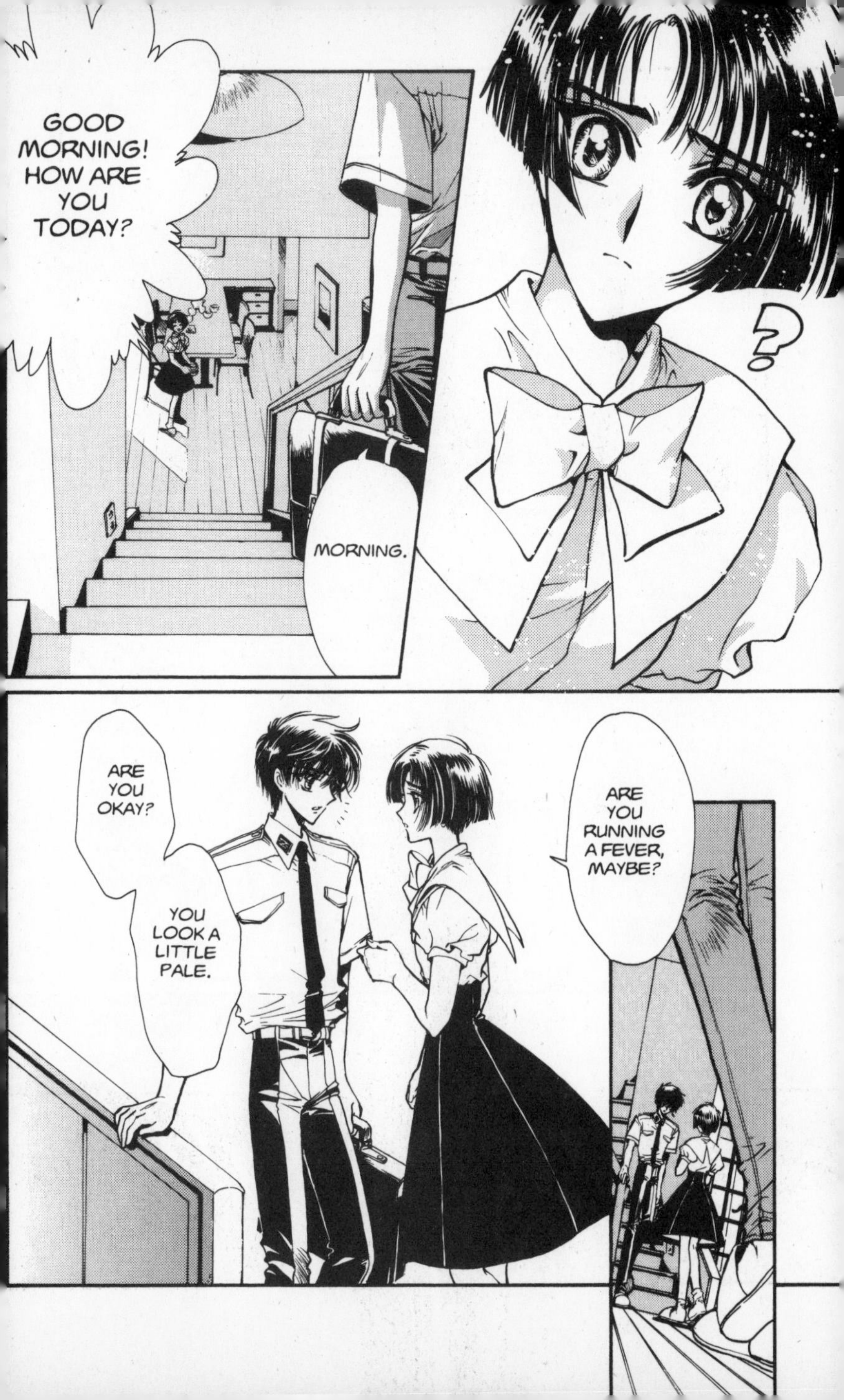
GOOD MORNING! HOW ARE YOU TODAY?
MORNING.
?
ARE YOU OKAY?
YOU LOOK A LITTLE PALE.
ARE YOU RUNNING A FEVER, MAYBE?

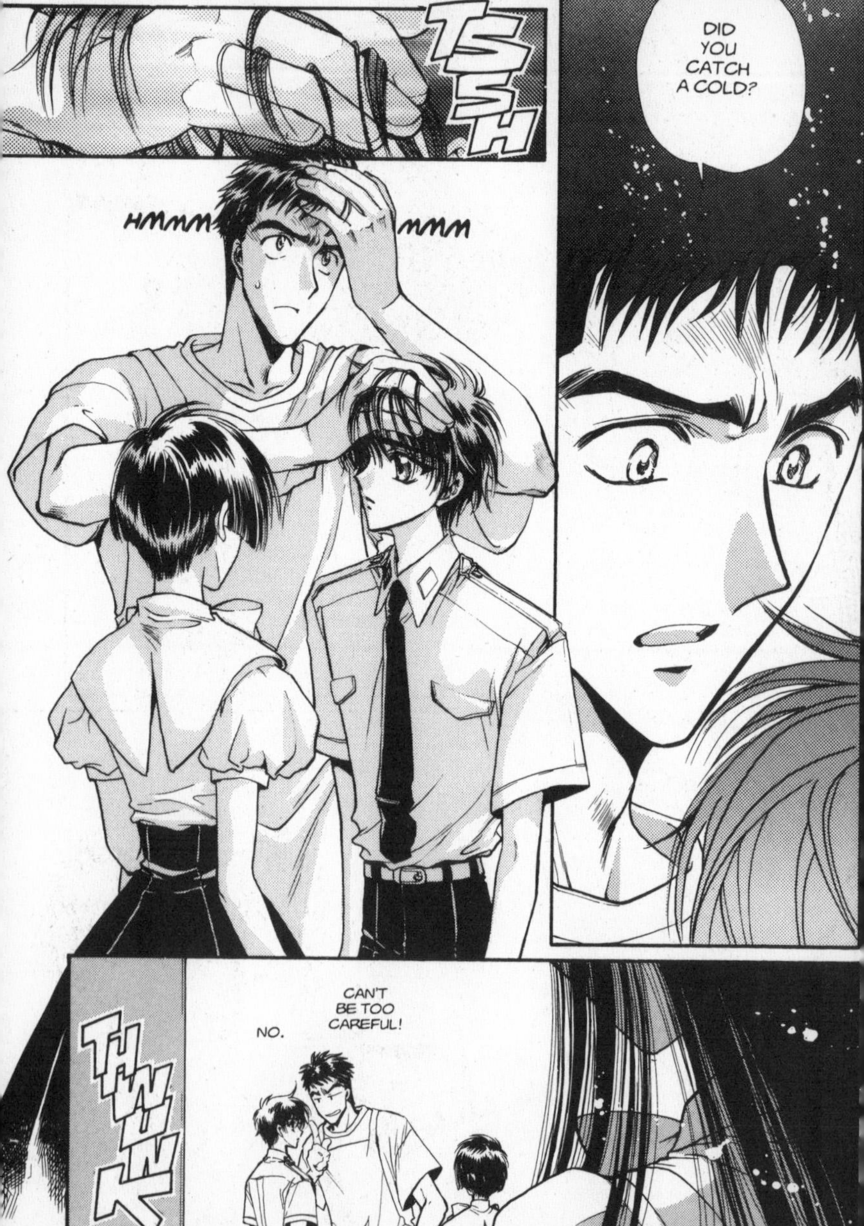
TSSH
HMMMM
MMM
DID YOU CATCH A COLD?
THUNK
NO.
CAN'T BE TOO CAREFUL!

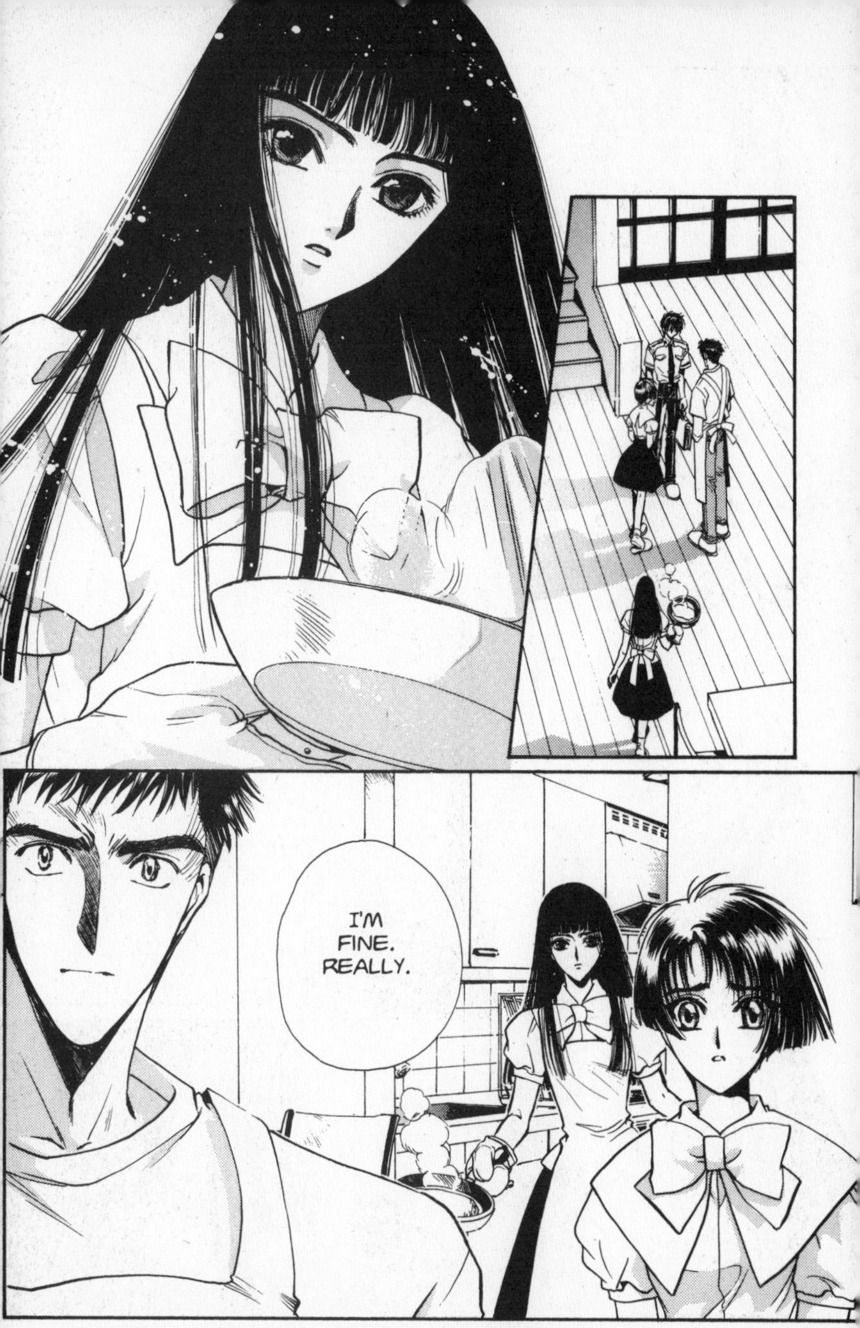
I'M FINE. REALLY.

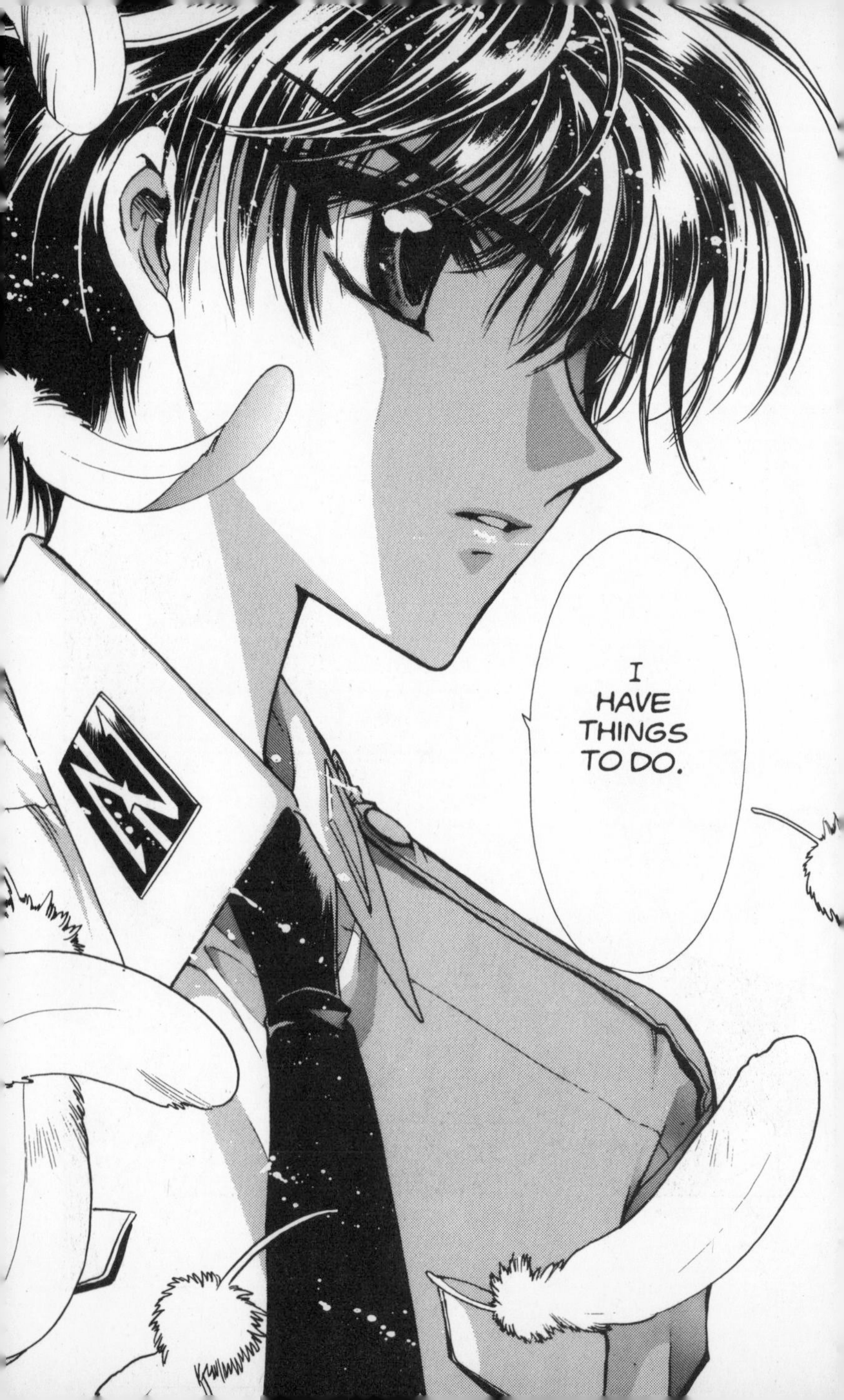
I HAVE THINGS TO DO.

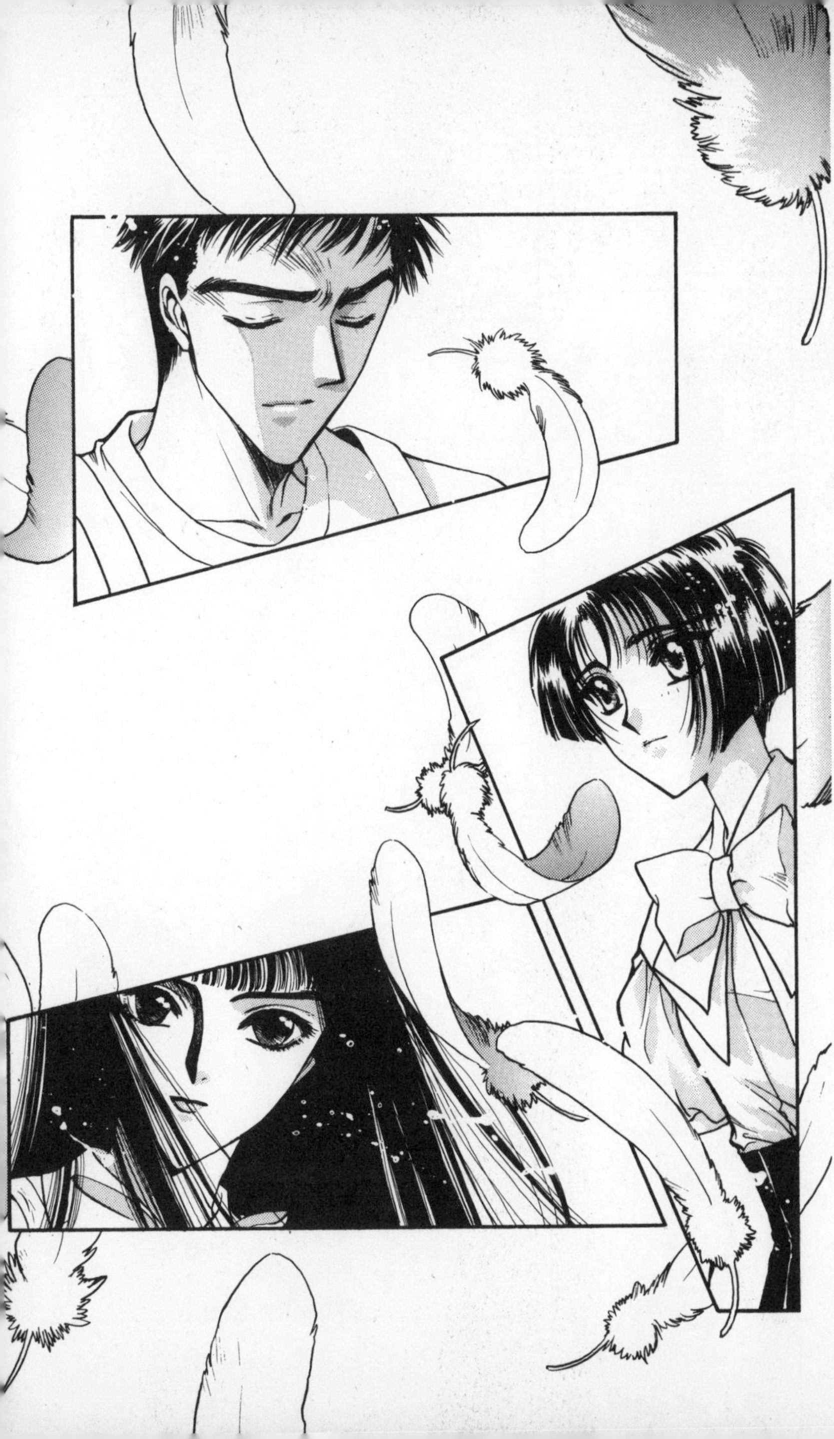

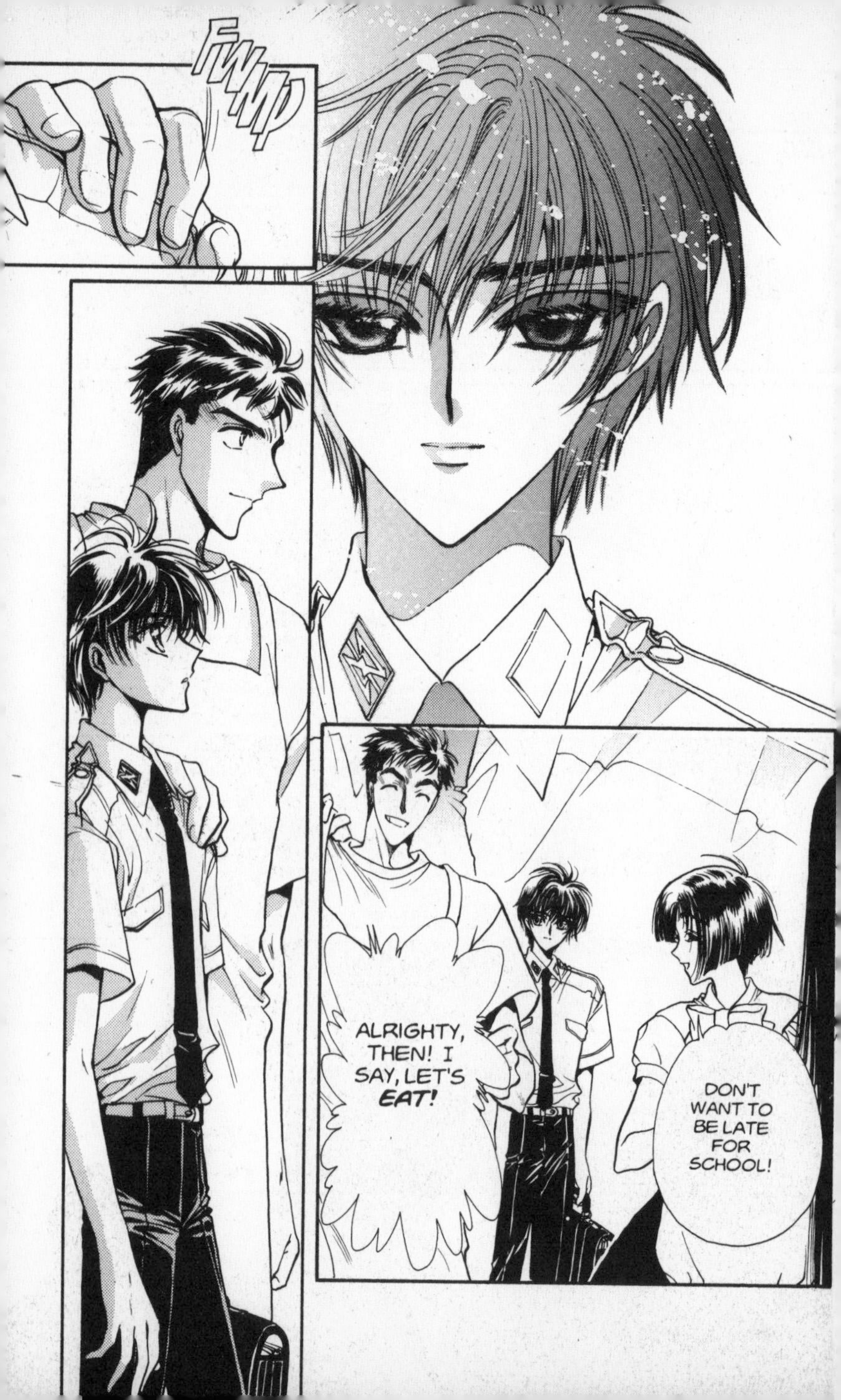
FWMP
ALRIGHTY, THEN! I SAY, LET'S EAT!
DON'T WANT TO BE LATE FOR SCHOOL!

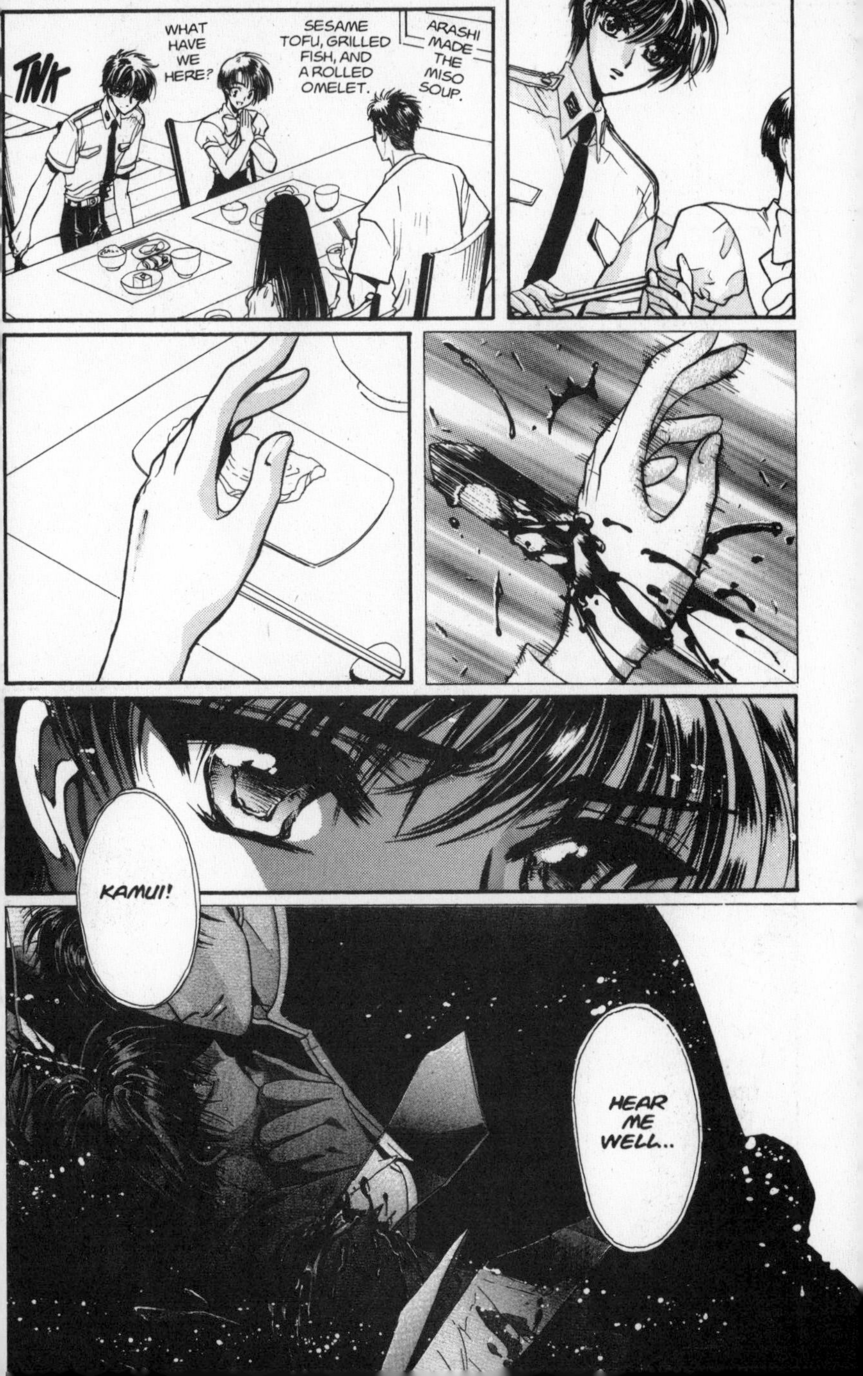
TNK
WHAT HAVE WE HERE?
SESAME TOFU, GRILLED FISH, AND A ROLLED OMELET.
ARASHI MADE THE MISO SOUP.
KAMUI!
HEAR ME WELL...

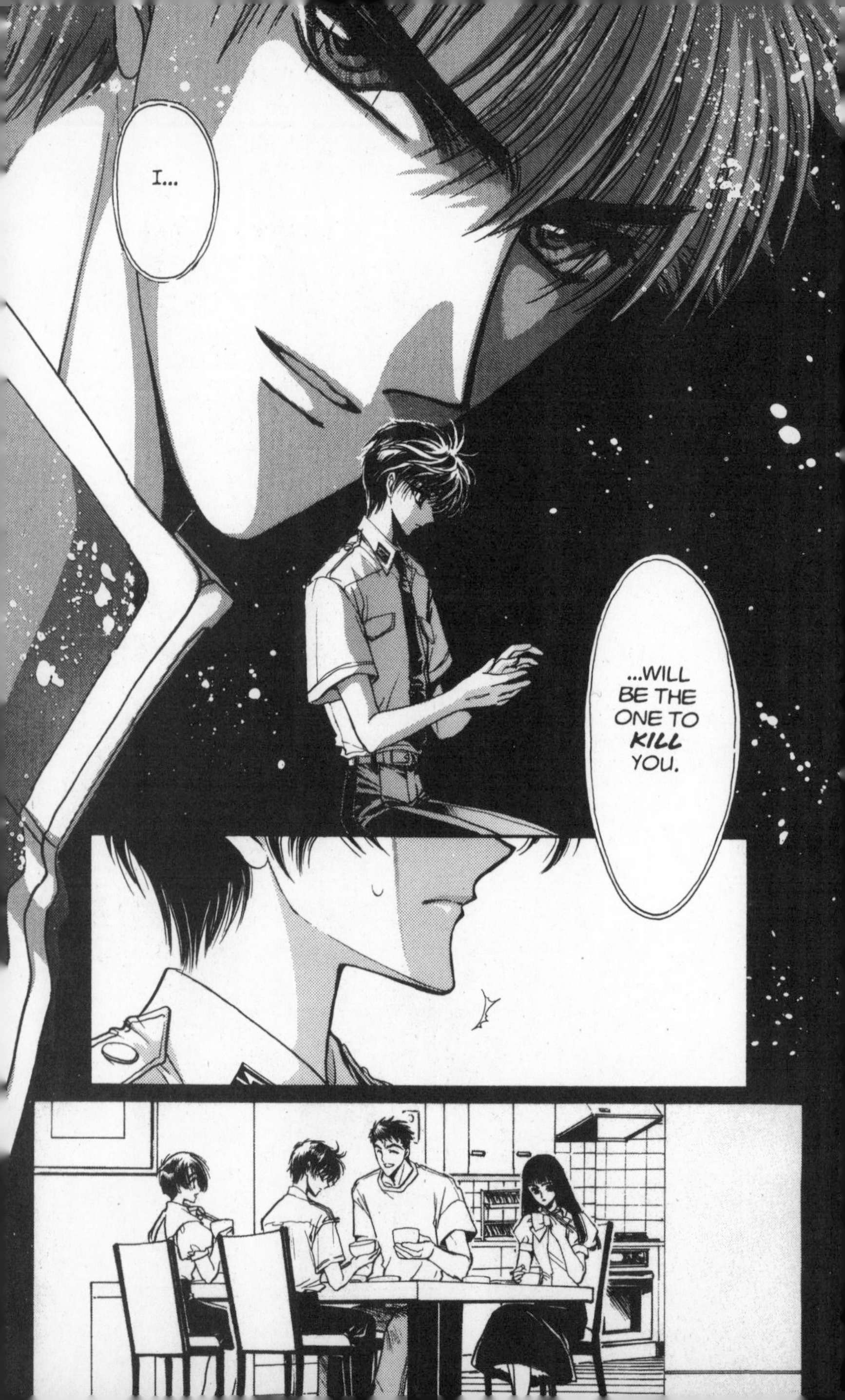
I...
...WILL BE THE ONE TO KILL YOU.

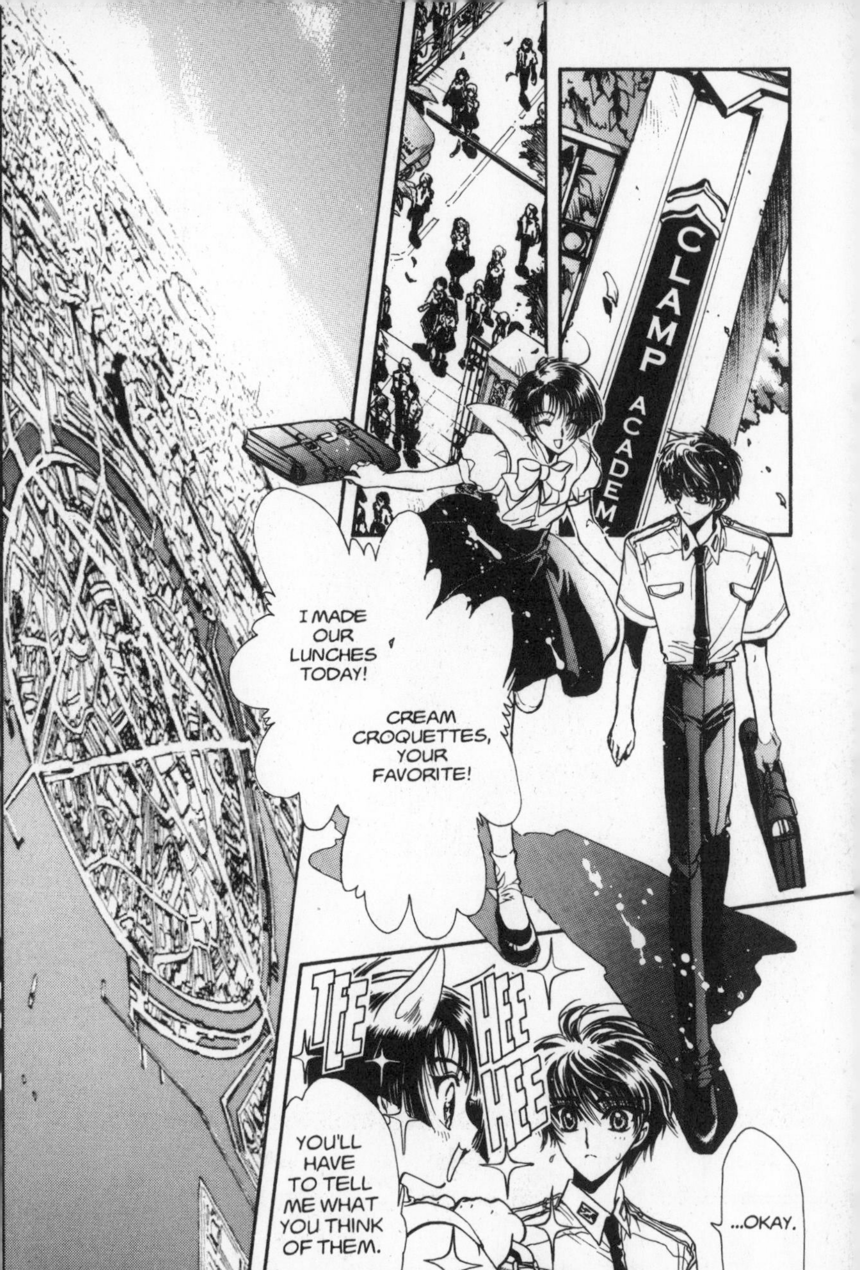
CLAMP ACADEM
I MADE OUR LUNCHES TODAY!
CREAM CROQUETTES, YOUR FAVORITE!
TEE
HEE HEE
YOU'LL HAVE TO TELL ME WHAT YOU THINK OF THEM.
...OKAY.

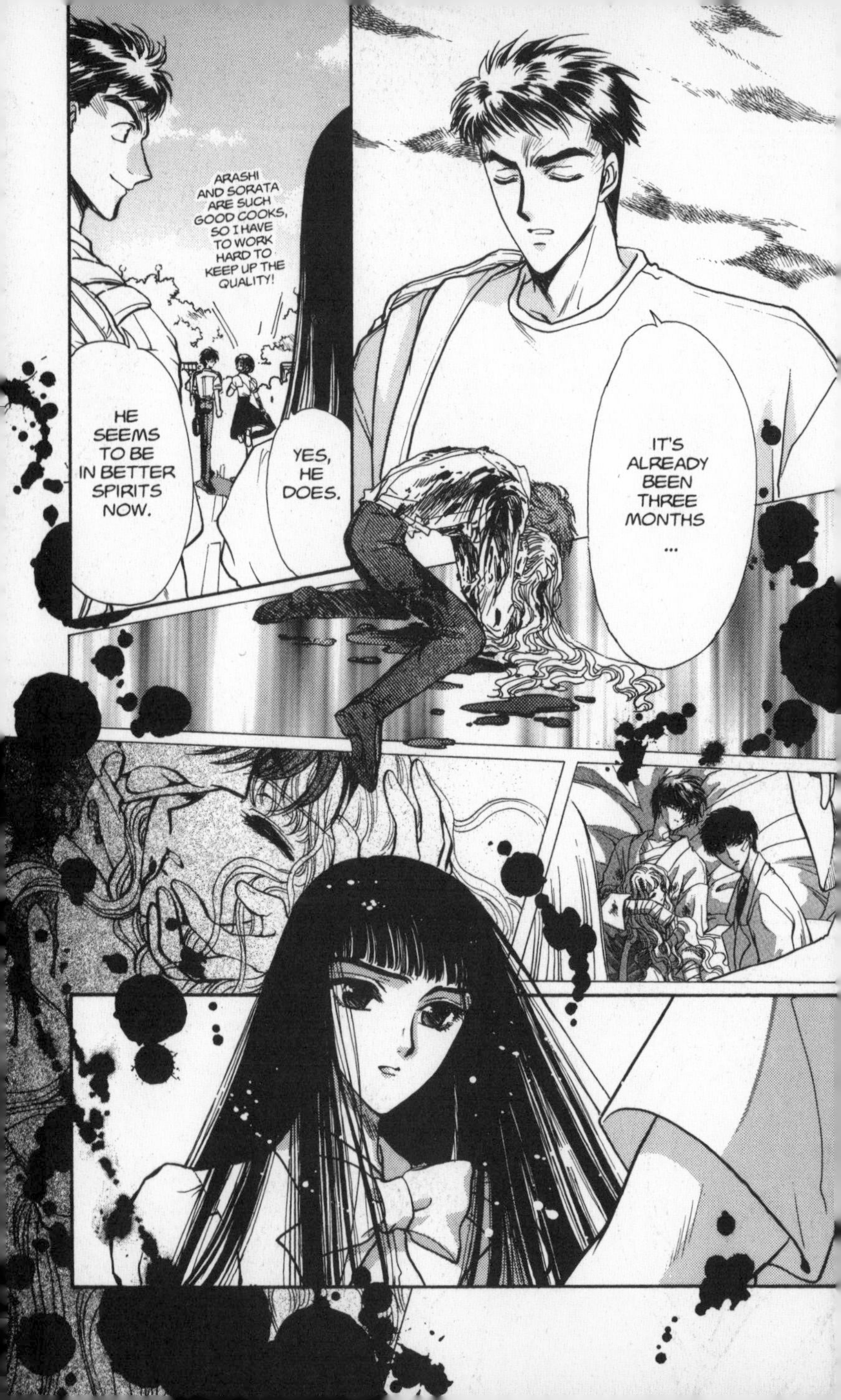
ARASHI AND SORATA ARE SUCH GOOD COOKS, SO I HAVE TO WORK HARD TO KEEP UP THE QUALITY!
HE SEEMS TO BE IN BETTER SPIRITS NOW.
YES, HE DOES.
IT'S ALREADY BEEN THREE MONTHS ...

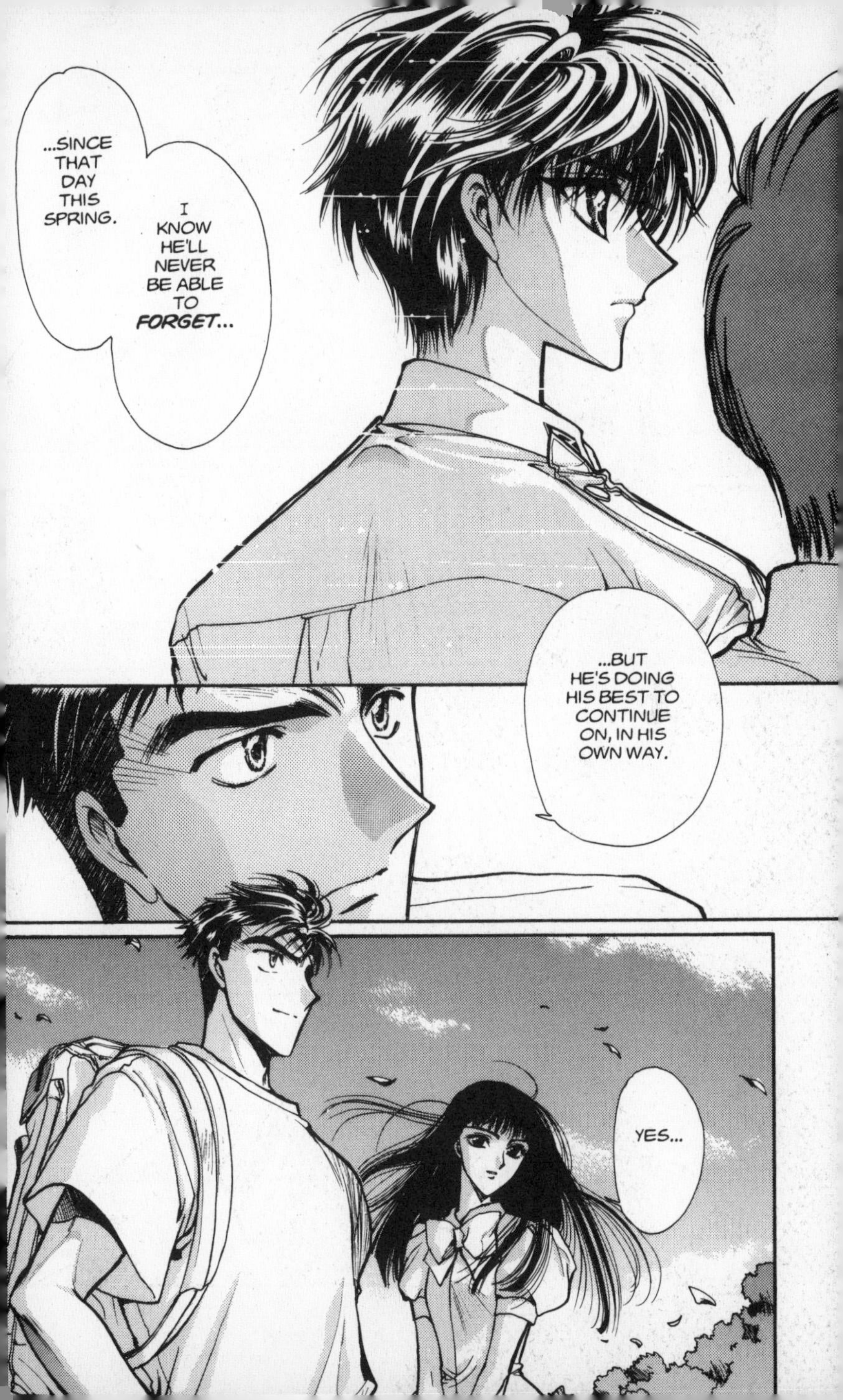
...SINCE THAT DAY THIS SPRING.
I KNOW HE'LL NEVER BE ABLE TO FORGET...
...BUT HE'S DOING HIS BEST TO CONTINUE ON, IN HIS OWN WAY.
YES...

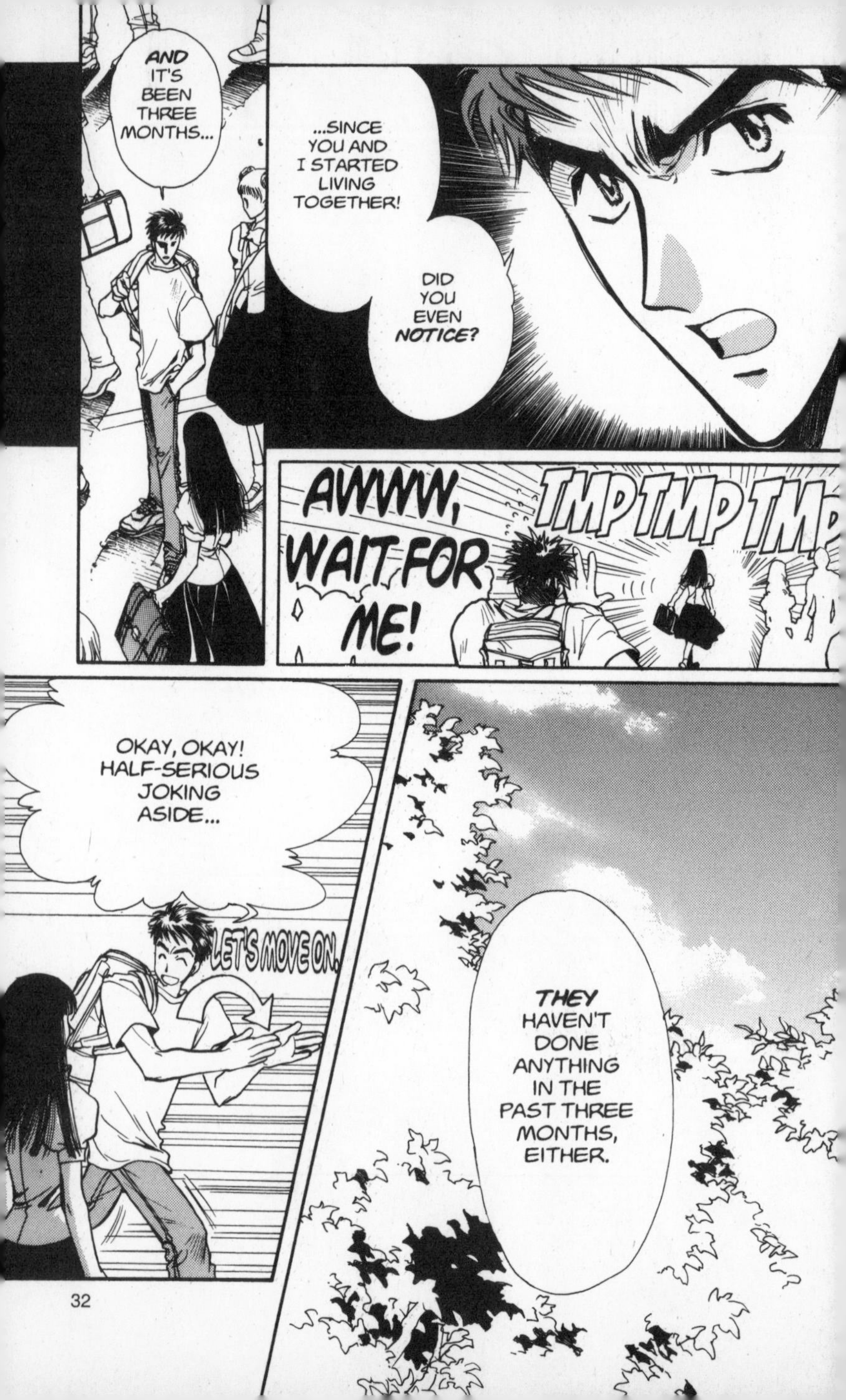
AND IT'S BEEN THREE MONTHS...
...SINCE YOU AND I STARTED LIVING TOGETHER!
DID YOU EVEN NOTICE?
AWWW, WAIT FOR ME!
TMP TMP TMP
OKAY, OKAY! HALF-SERIOUS JOKING ASIDE...
LET'S MOVE ON.
THEY HAVEN'T DONE ANYTHING IN THE PAST THREE MONTHS, EITHER.

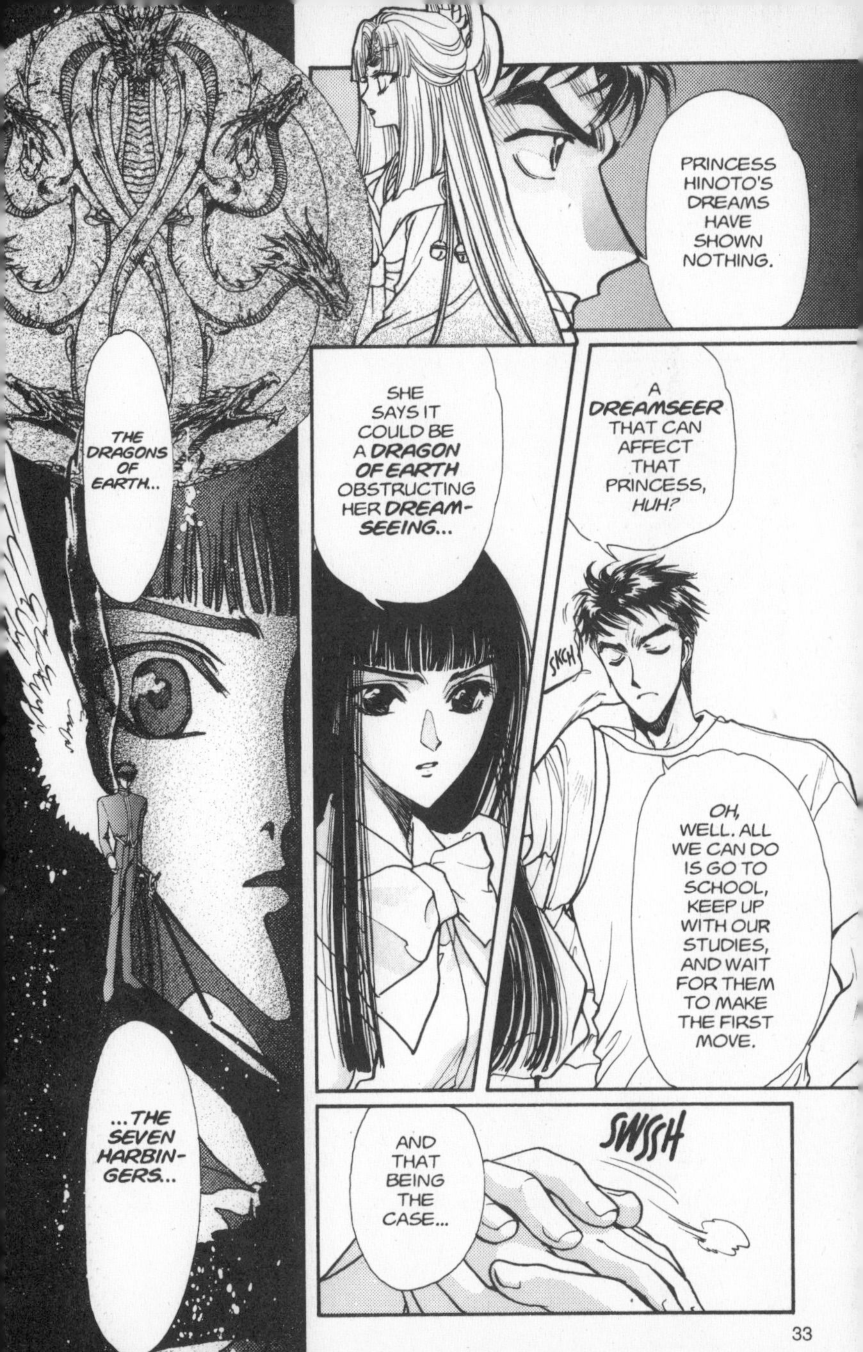
THE DRAGONS OF EARTH...
...THE SEVEN HARBINGERS...
PRINCESS HINOTO'S DREAMS HAVE SHOWN NOTHING.
SHE SAYS IT COULD BE A DRAGON OF EARTH OBSTRUCTING HER DREAM-SEEING...
A DREAMSEER THAT CAN AFFECT THAT PRINCESS, HUH?
SKCH
OH, WELL. ALL WE CAN DO IS GO TO SCHOOL, KEEP UP WITH OUR STUDIES, AND WAIT FOR THEM TO MAKE THE FIRST MOVE.
AND THAT BEING THE CASE...
SWSSH

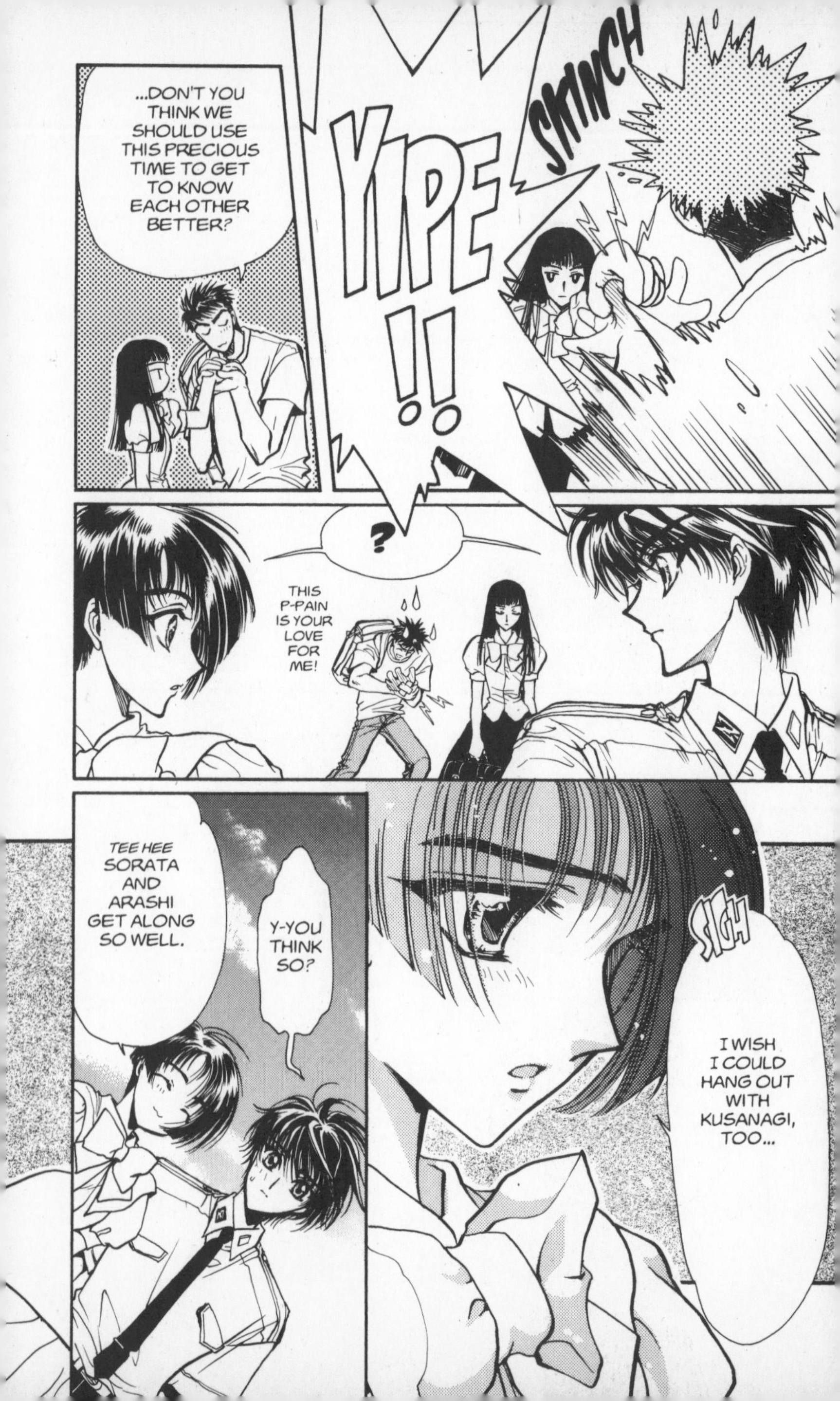
...DON'T YOU THINK WE SHOULD USE THIS PRECIOUS TIME TO GET TO KNOW EACH OTHER BETTER?
YIPE!!
SKINCH
?
THIS P-PAIN IS YOUR LOVE FOR ME!
TEE HEE SORATA AND ARASHI GET ALONG SO WELL.
Y-YOU THINK SO?
SIGH
I WISH I COULD HANG OUT WITH KUSANAGI, TOO...

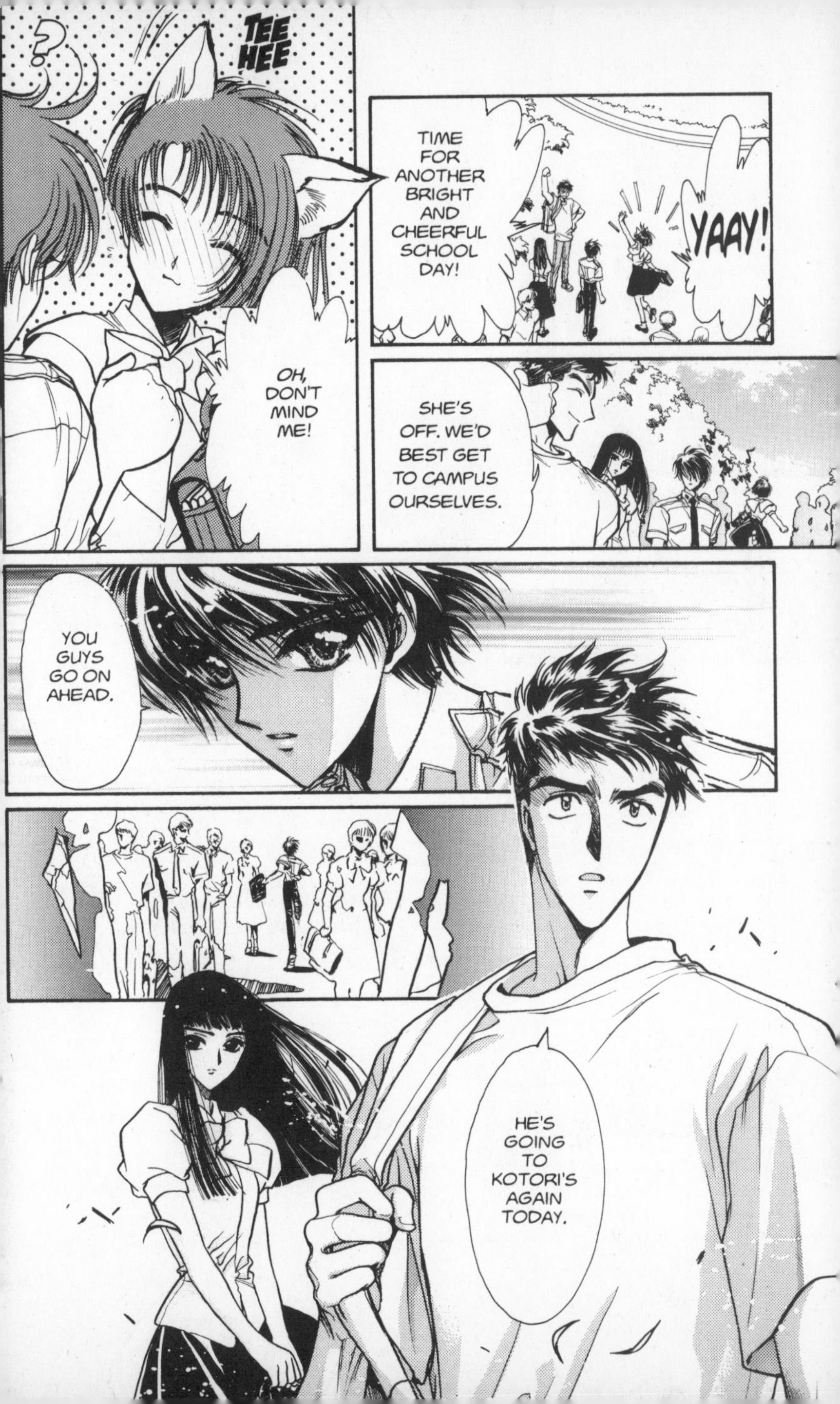
?
TEE HEE
OH, DON'T MIND ME!
TIME FOR ANOTHER BRIGHT AND CHEERFUL SCHOOL DAY!
YAAY!
SHE'S OFF. WE'D BEST GET TO CAMPUS OURSELVES.
YOU GUYS GO ON AHEAD.
HE'S GOING TO KOTORI'S AGAIN TODAY.

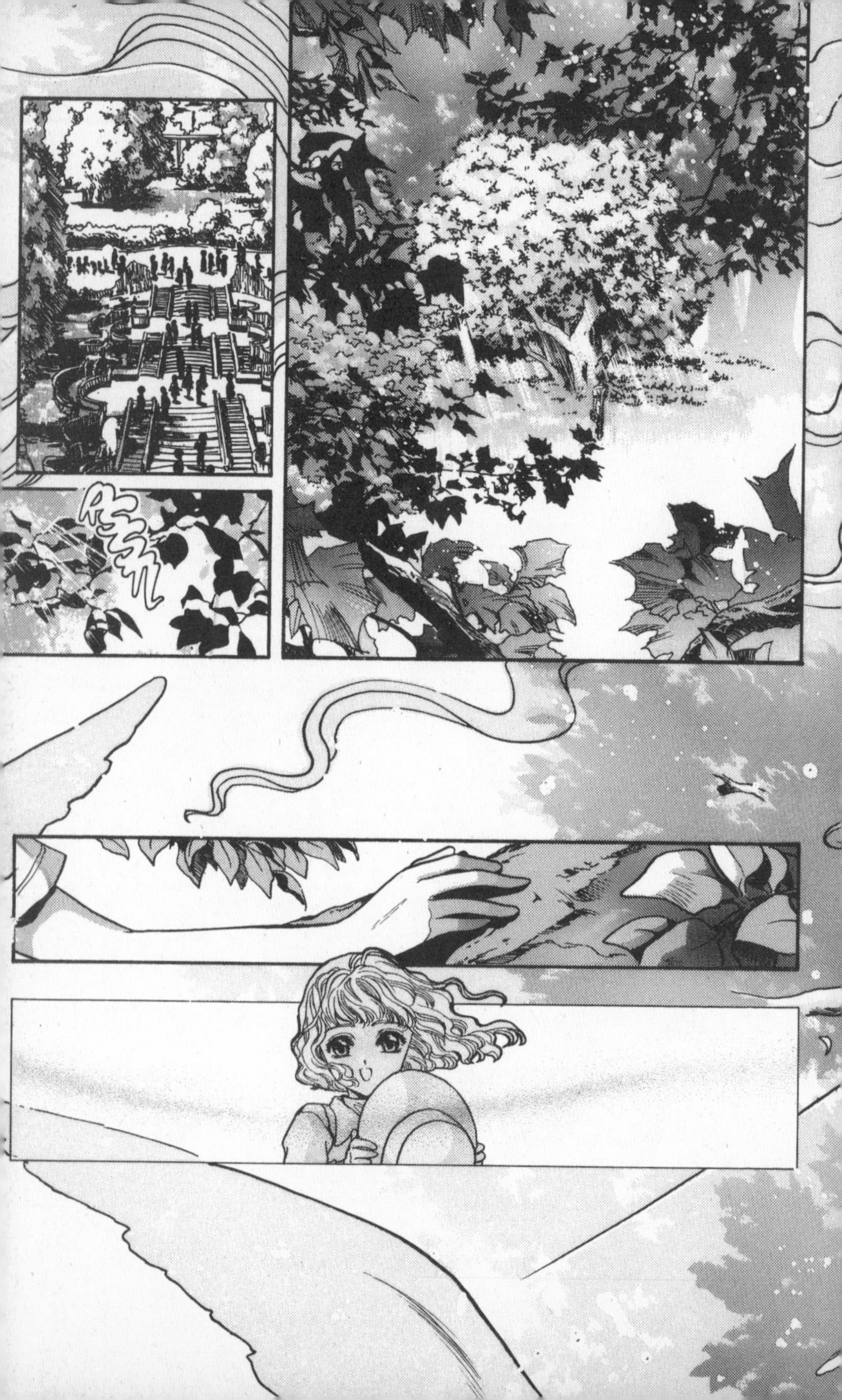

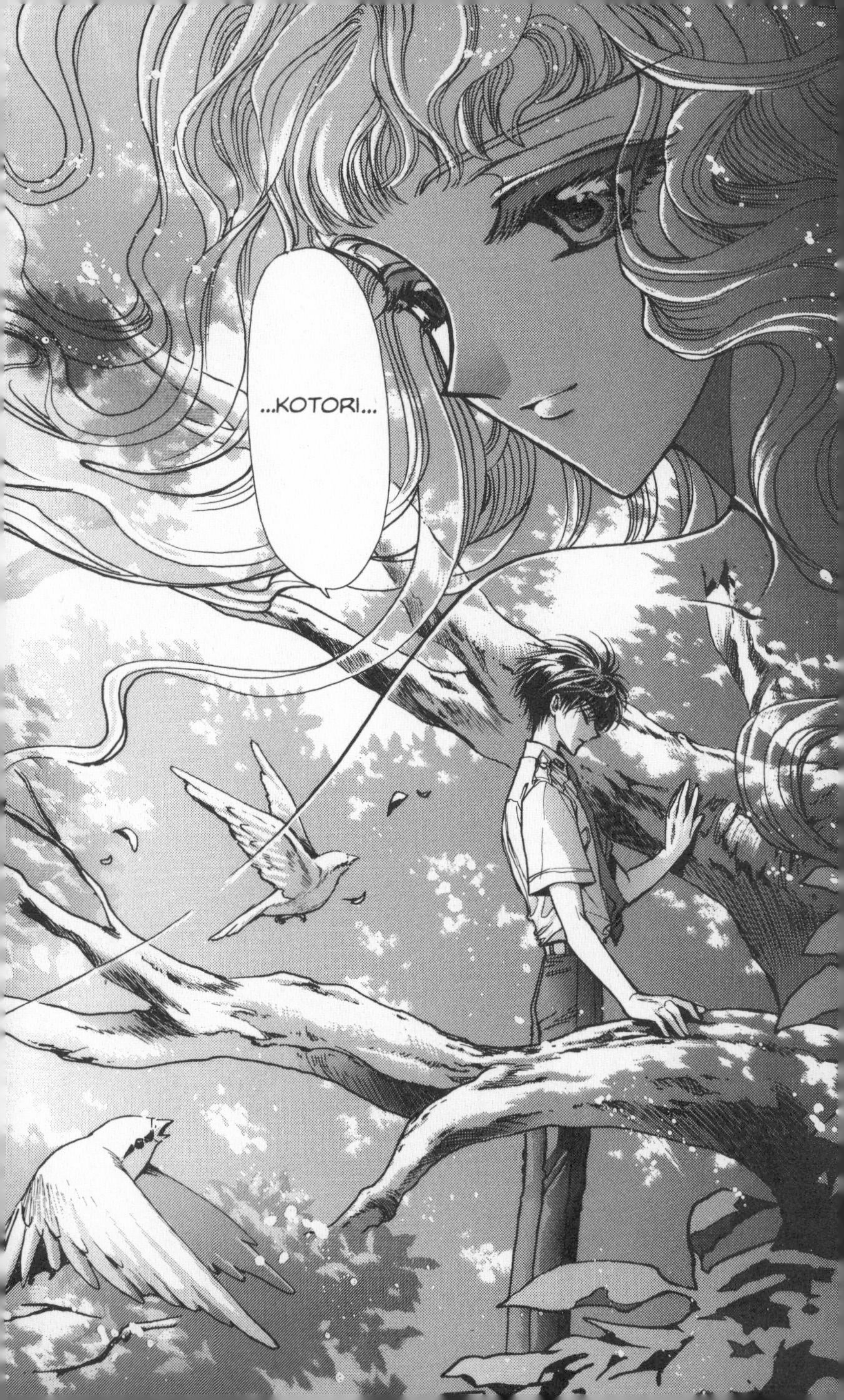
...KOTORI...

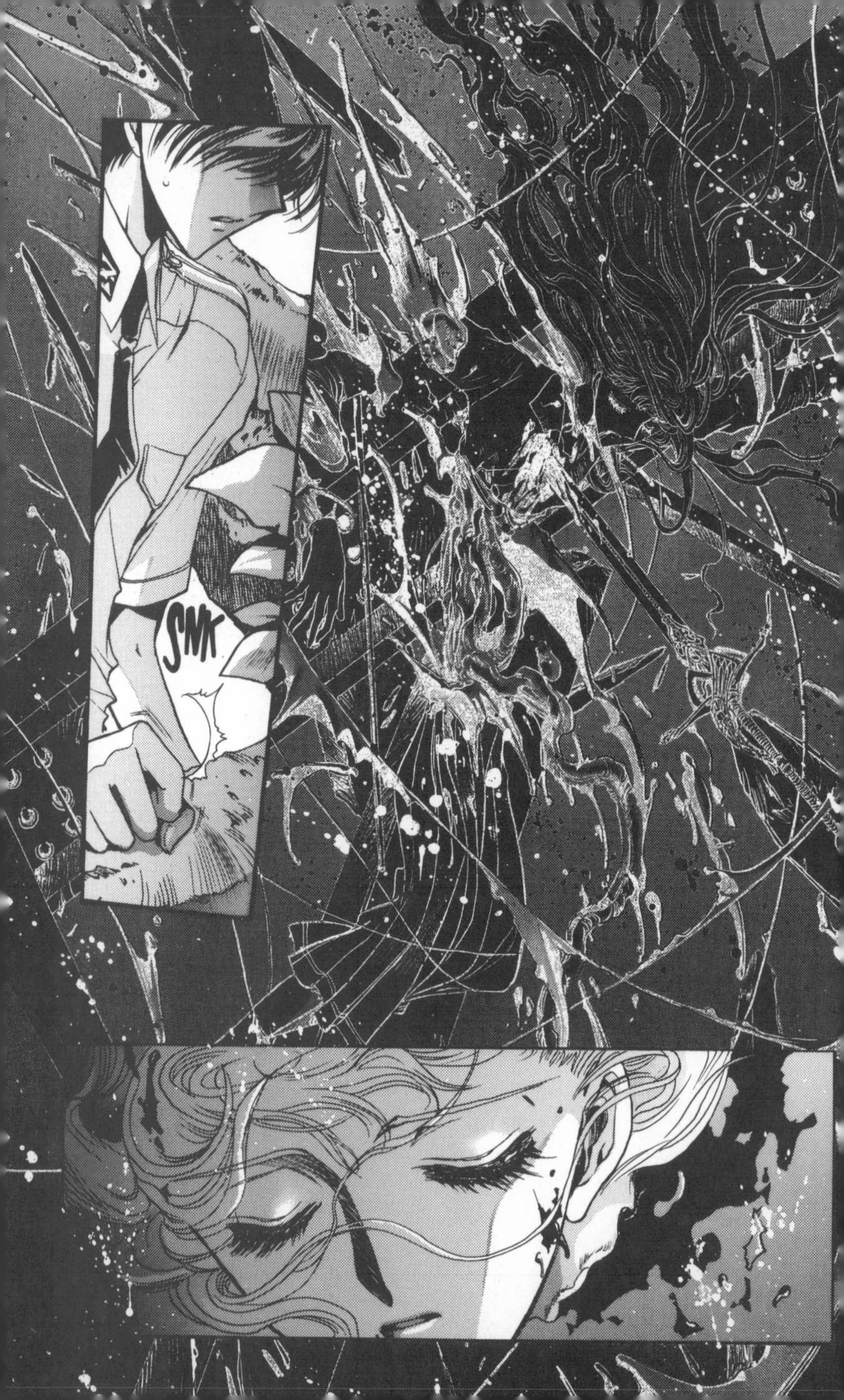
SNK

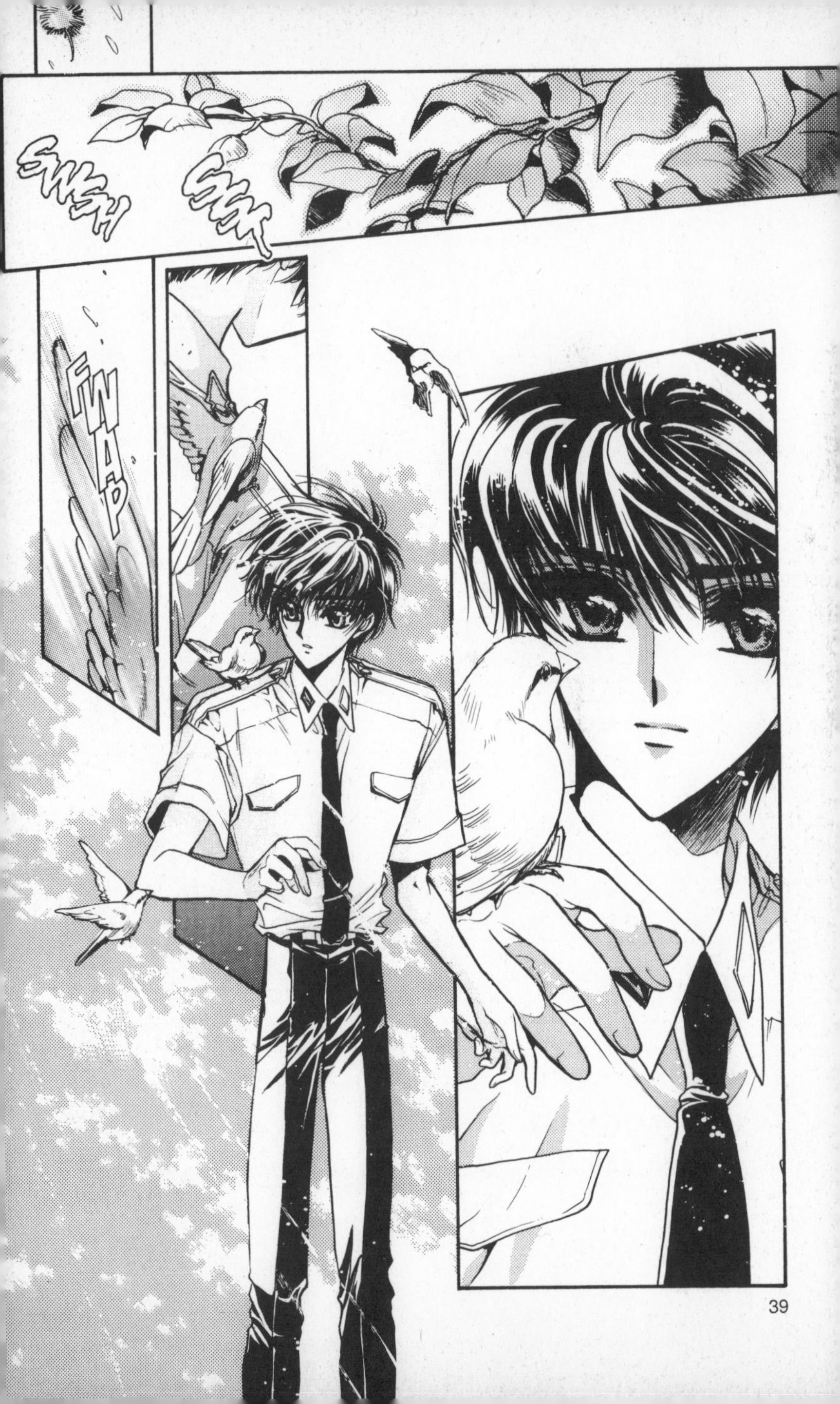
SWISH
SWISH
FWAP

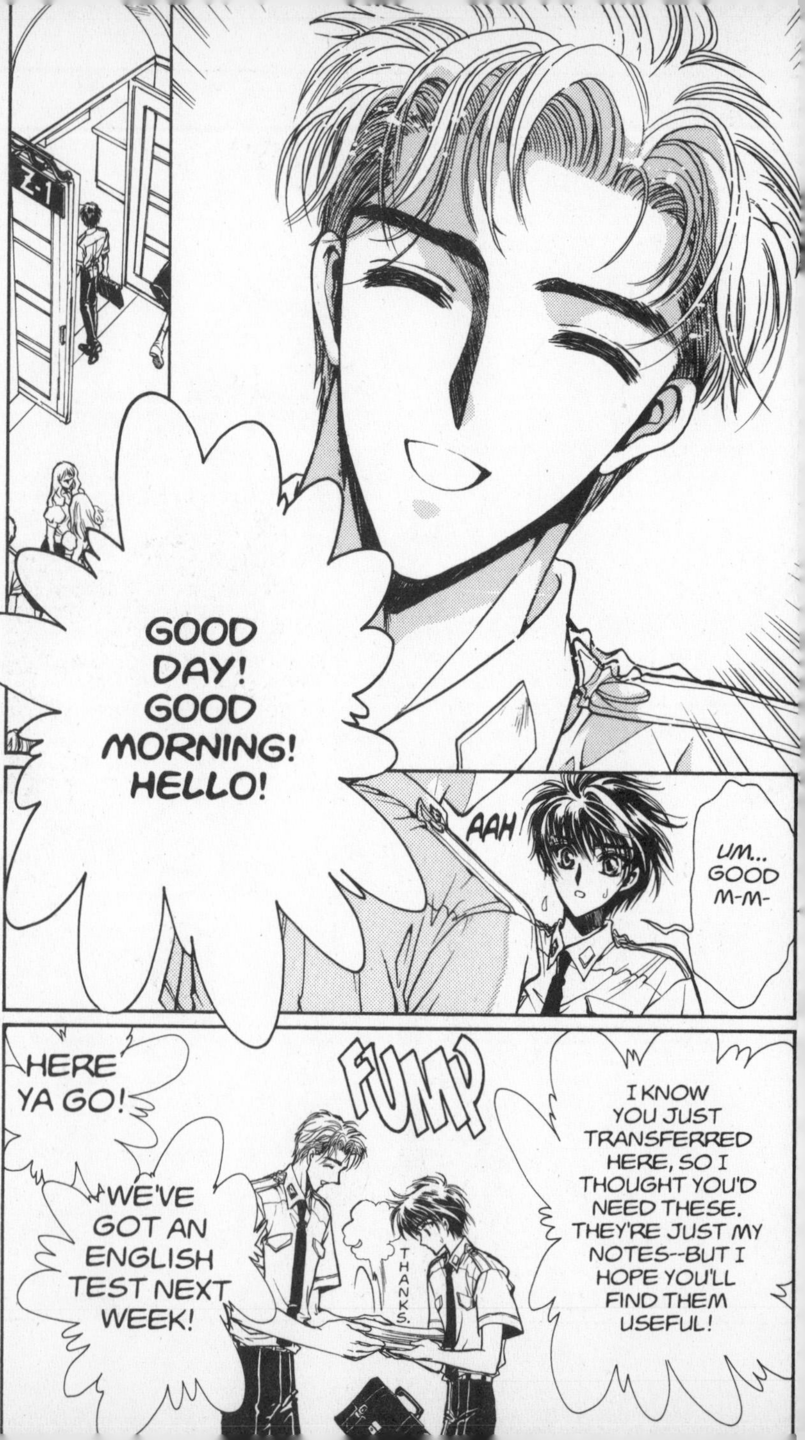
Z-1
GOOD DAY! GOOD MORNING! HELLO!
AAH
UM... GOOD M-M-
HERE YA GO!
FUMP
WE'VE GOT AN ENGLISH TEST NEXT WEEK!
THANKS.
I KNOW YOU JUST TRANSFERRED HERE, SO I THOUGHT YOU'D NEED THESE. THEY'RE JUST MY NOTES--BUT I HOPE YOU'LL FIND THEM USEFUL!

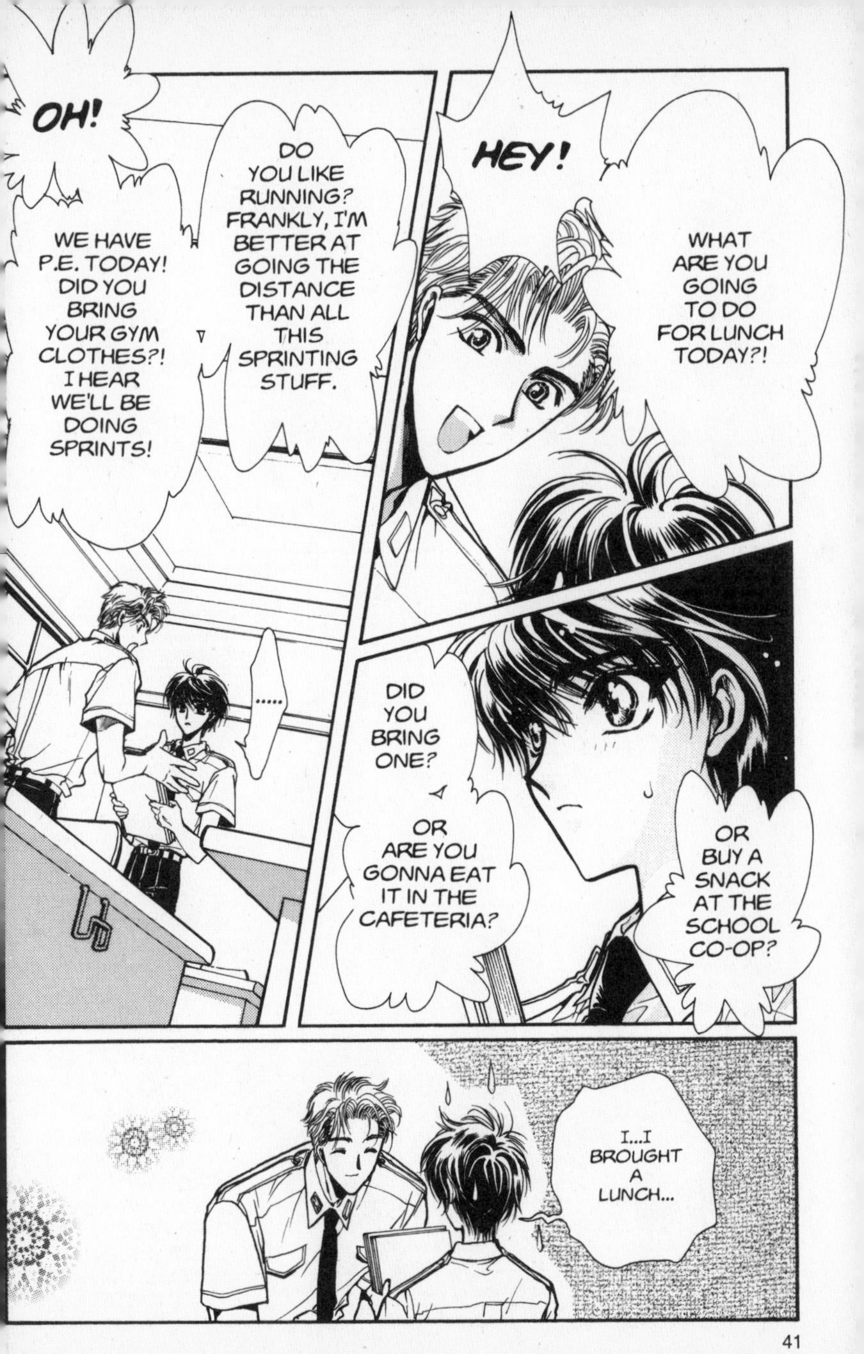
OH!
WE HAVE P.E. TODAY! DID YOU BRING YOUR GYM CLOTHES?! I HEAR WE'LL BE DOING SPRINTS!
DO YOU LIKE RUNNING? FRANKLY, I'M BETTER AT GOING THE DISTANCE THAN ALL THIS SPRINTING STUFF.
.....
HEY!
WHAT ARE YOU GOING TO DO FOR LUNCH TODAY?!
DID YOU BRING ONE?
OR ARE YOU GONNA EAT IT IN THE CAFETERIA?
OR BUY A SNACK AT THE SCHOOL CO-OP?
I...I BROUGHT A LUNCH...

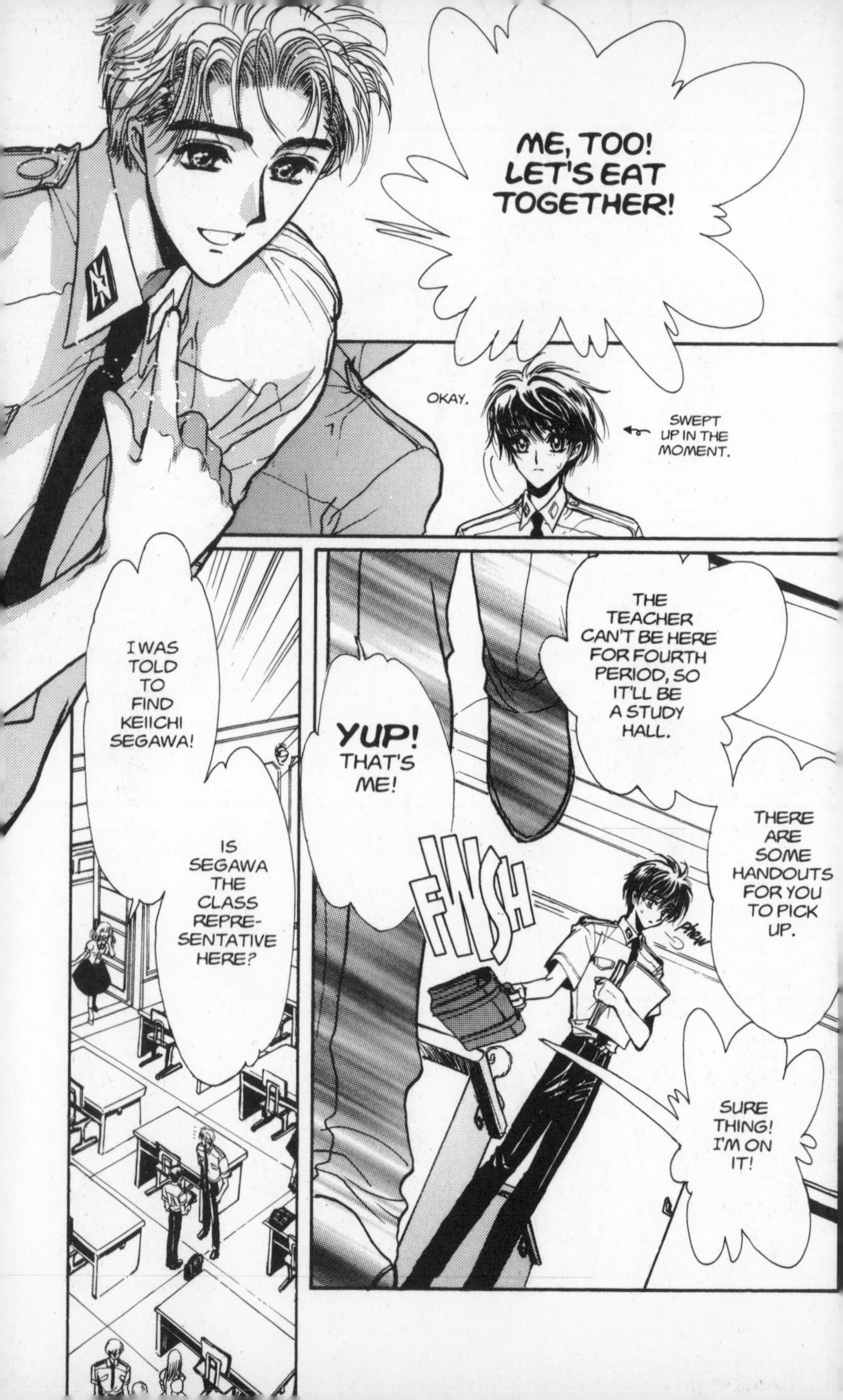
ME, TOO! LET'S EAT TOGETHER!
OKAY.
SWEPT UP IN THE MOMENT.
I WAS TOLD TO FIND KEIICHI SEGAWA!
IS SEGAWA THE CLASS REPRESENTATIVE HERE?
YUP! THAT'S ME!
THE TEACHER CAN'T BE HERE FOR FOURTH PERIOD, SO IT'LL BE A STUDY HALL.
FWSH
THERE ARE SOME HANDOUTS FOR YOU TO PICK UP.
phew
SURE THING! I'M ON IT!

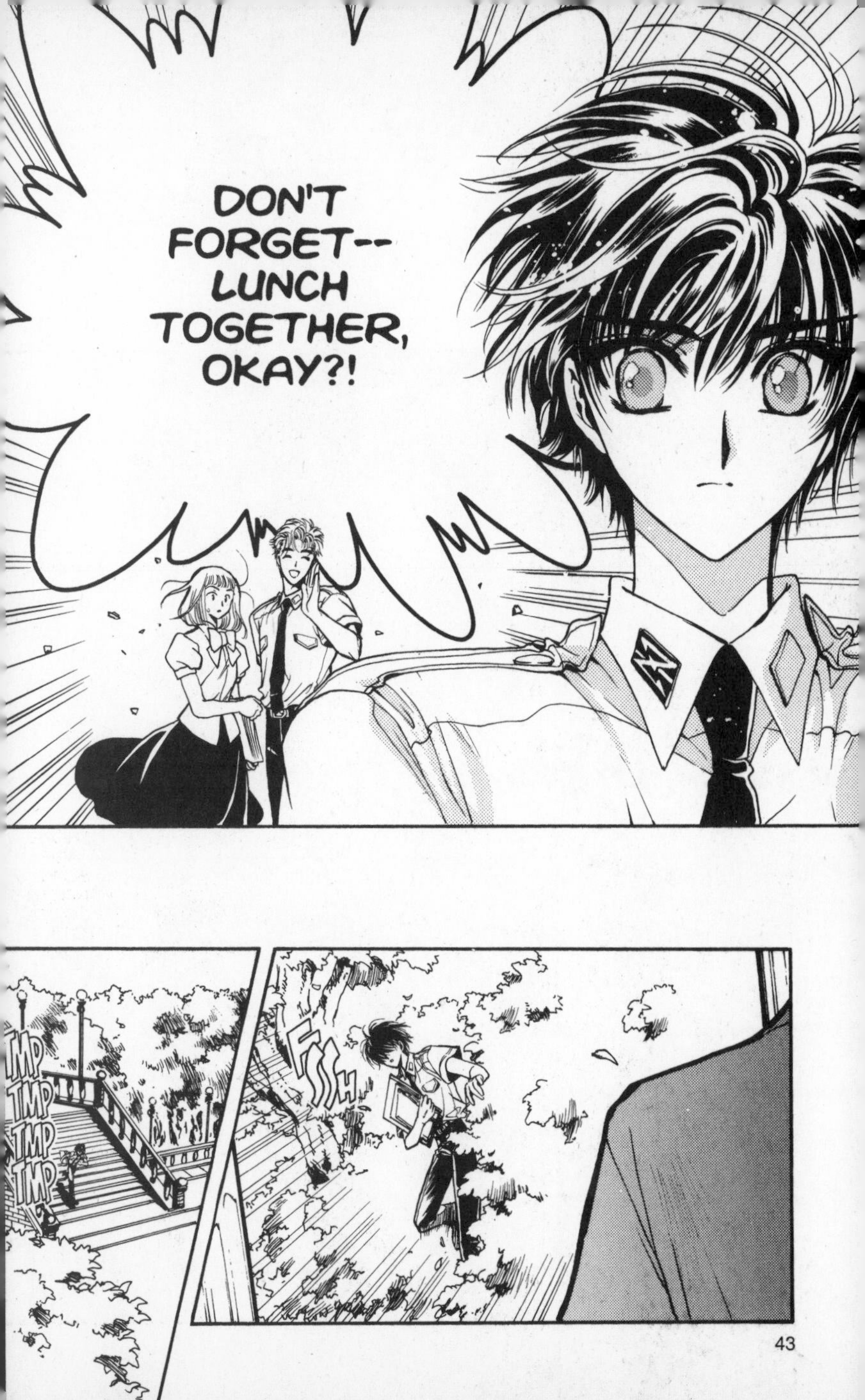
DON'T FORGET-- LUNCH TOGETHER, OKAY?!
TMP TMP TMP TMP
FSSH

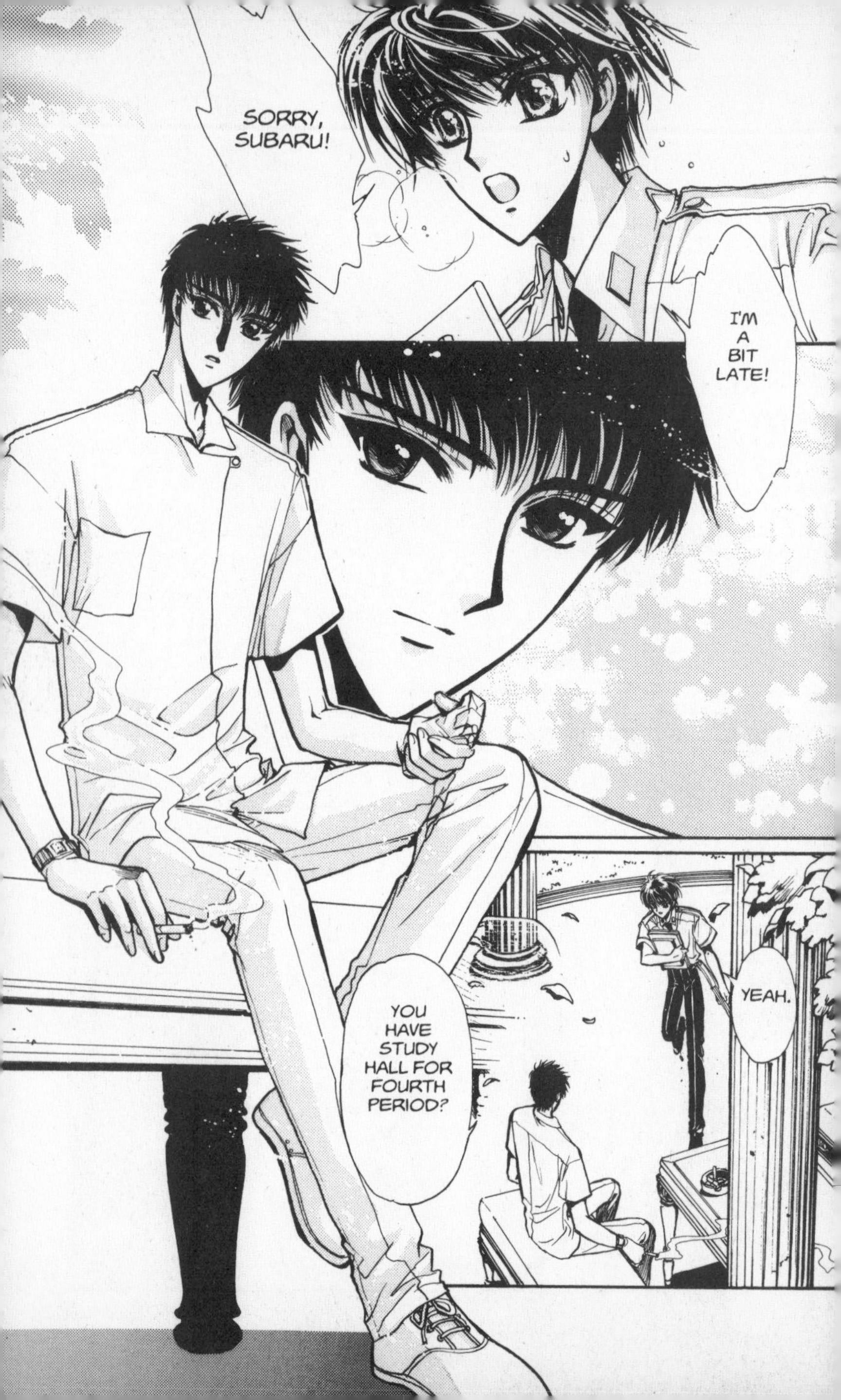
SORRY, SUBARU!
I'M A BIT LATE!
YOU HAVE STUDY HALL FOR FOURTH PERIOD?
YEAH.

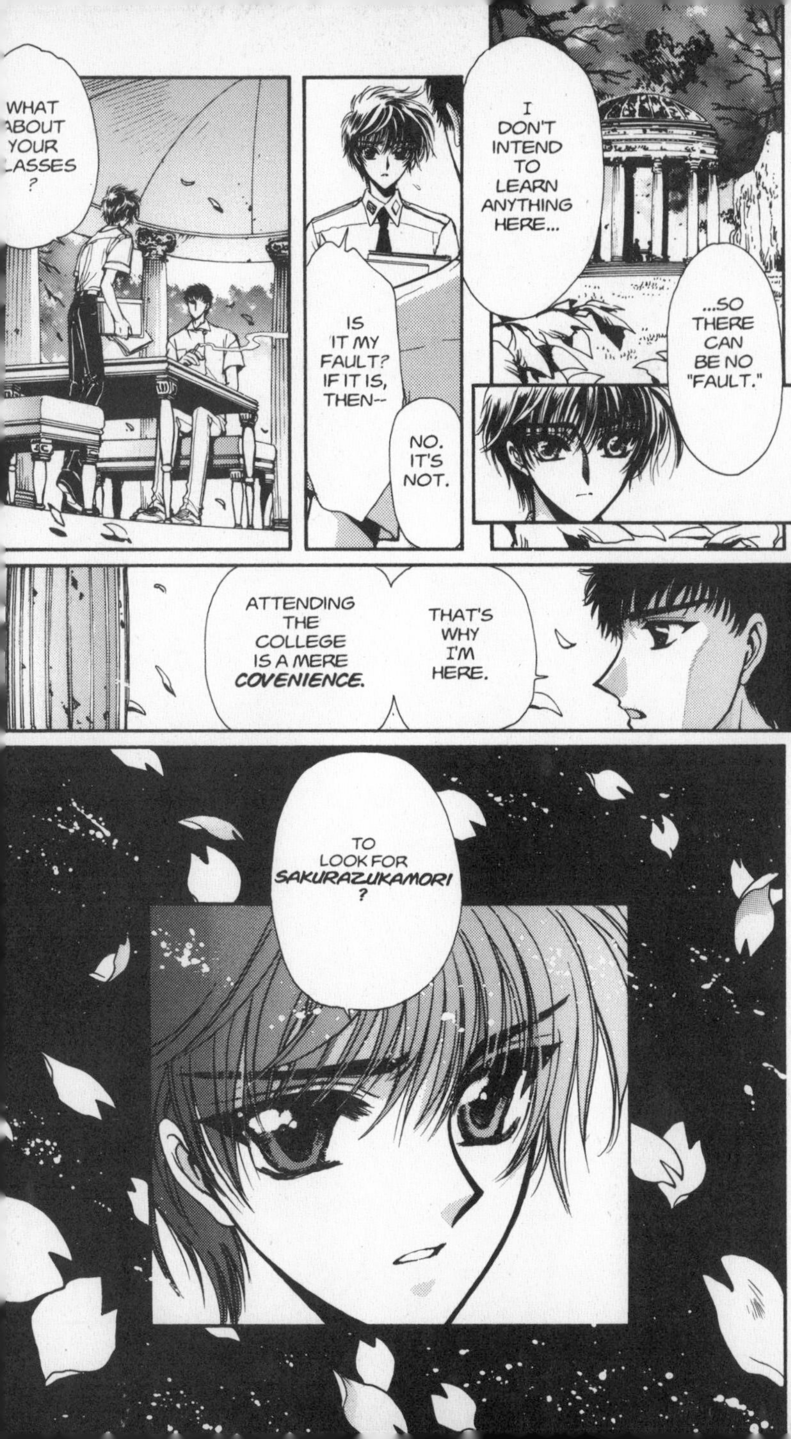
WHAT ABOUT YOUR LASSES ?
IS IT MY FAULT? IF IT IS, THEN--
NO. IT'S NOT.
I DON'T INTEND TO LEARN ANYTHING HERE...
...SO THERE CAN BE NO "FAULT."
ATTENDING THE COLLEGE IS A MERE COVENIENCE.
THAT'S WHY I'M HERE.
TO LOOK FOR SAKURAZUKAMORI ?

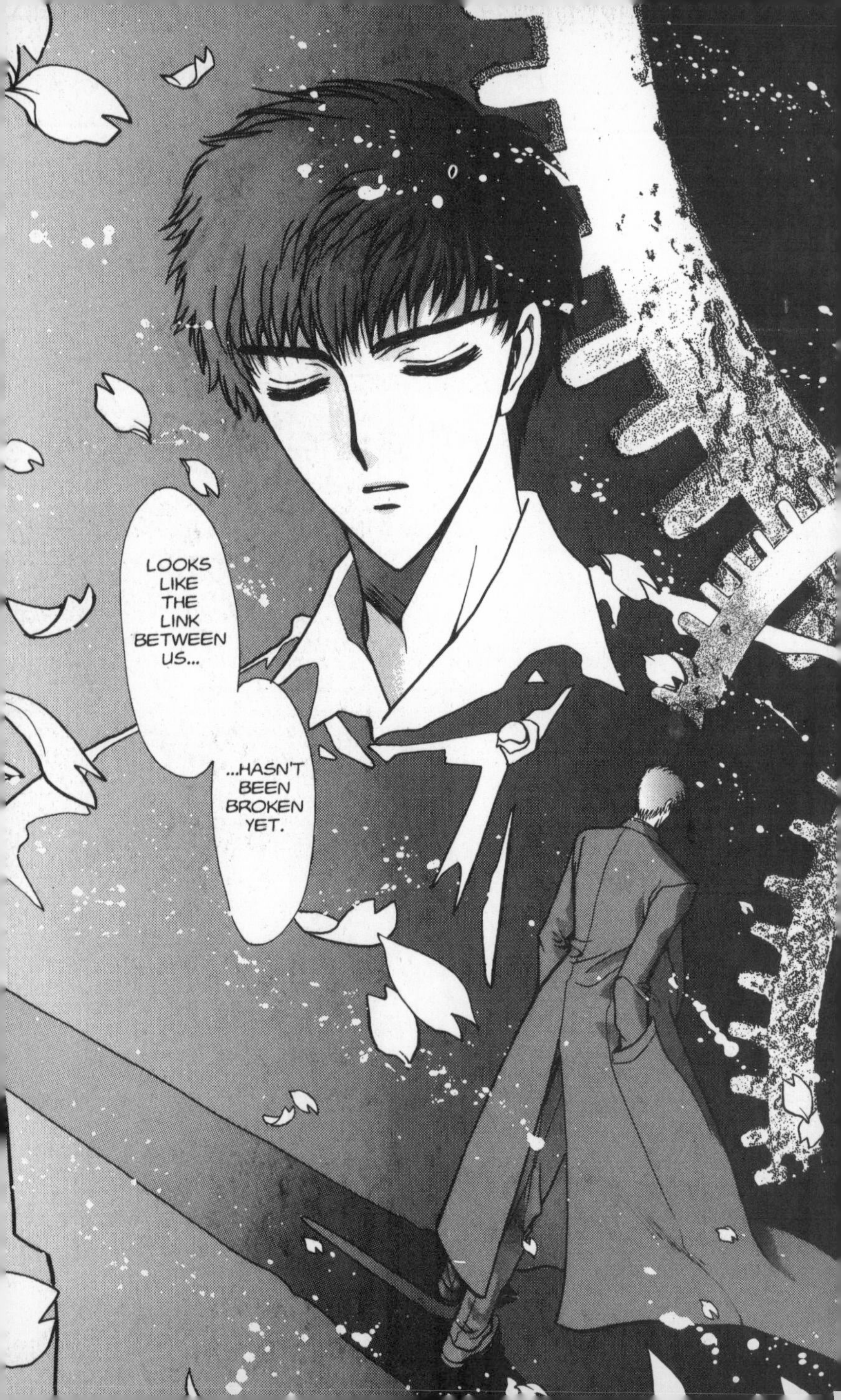
LOOKS LIKE THE LINK BETWEEN US...
...HASN'T BEEN BROKEN YET.

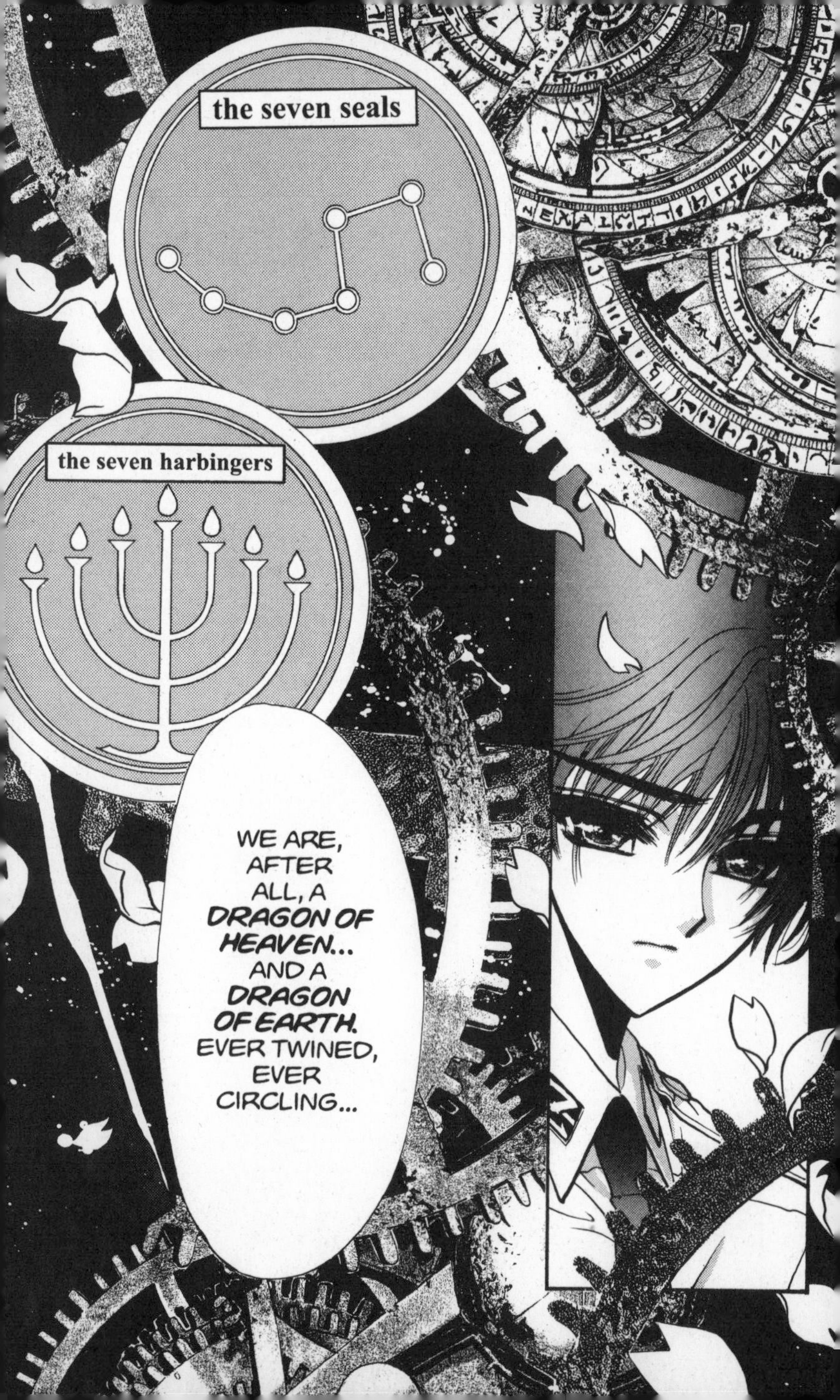
the seven seals
the seven harbingers
WE ARE, AFTER ALL, A DRAGON OF HEAVEN... AND A DRAGON OF EARTH. EVER TWINED, EVER CIRCLING...

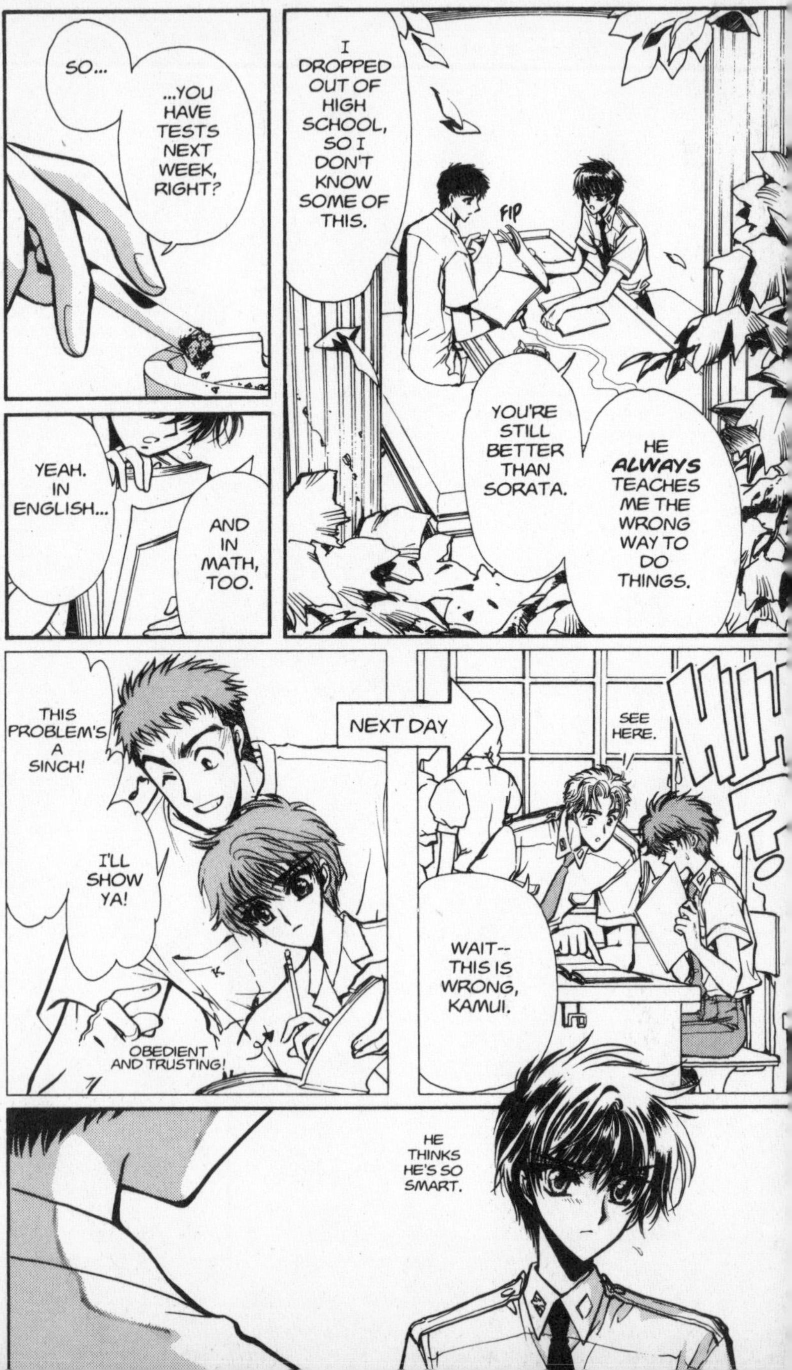
SO...
...YOU HAVE TESTS NEXT WEEK, RIGHT?
YEAH. IN ENGLISH...
AND IN MATH, TOO.
I DROPPED OUT OF HIGH SCHOOL, SO I DON'T KNOW SOME OF THIS.
FIP
YOU'RE STILL BETTER THAN SORATA.
HE **ALWAYS** TEACHES ME THE WRONG WAY TO DO THINGS.
THIS PROBLEM'S A SINCH!
I'LL SHOW YA!
OBEDIENT AND TRUSTING!
NEXT DAY
SEE HERE.
WAIT-- THIS IS WRONG, KAMUI.
HE THINKS HE'S SO SMART.

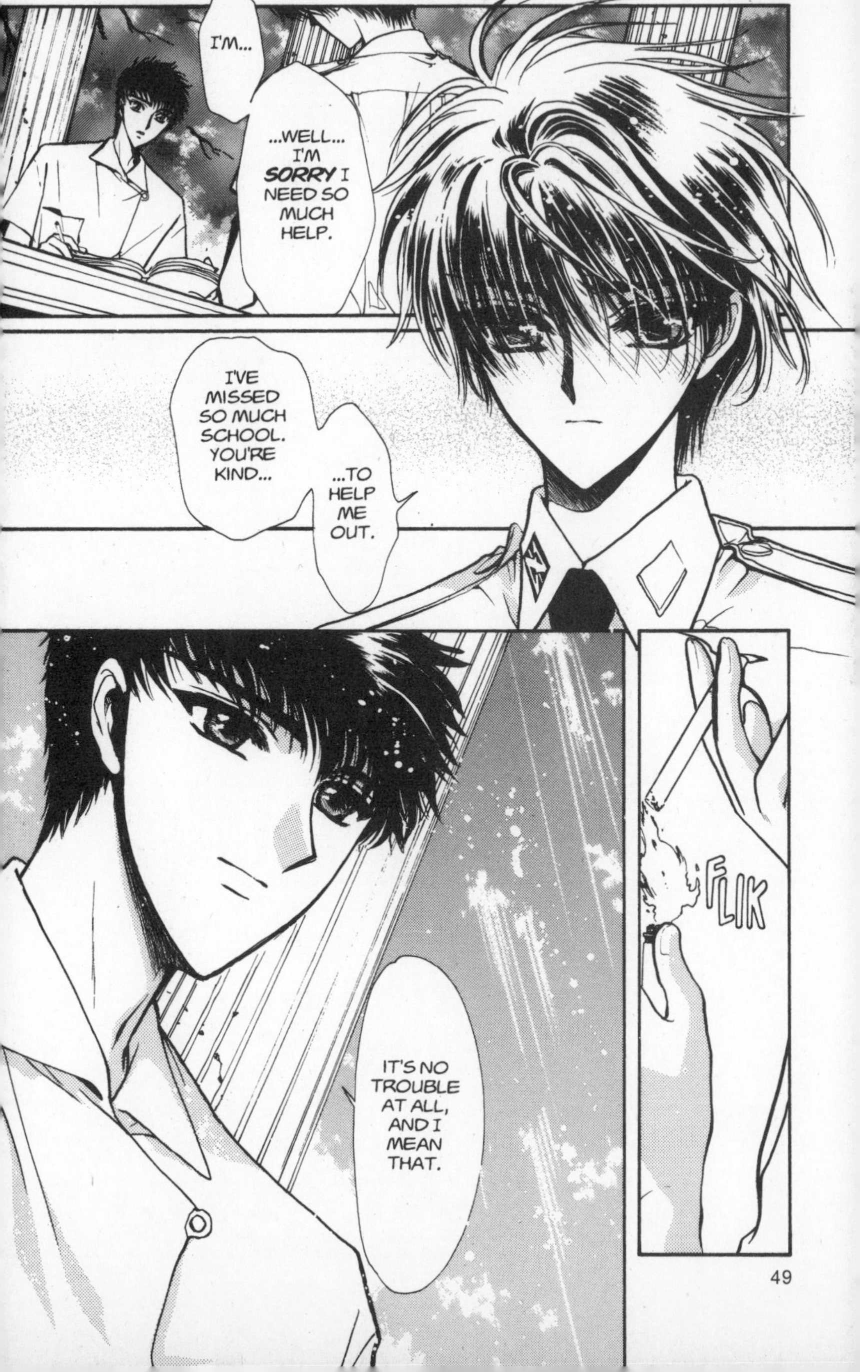
I'M...
...WELL... I'M **SORRY** I NEED SO MUCH HELP.
I'VE MISSED SO MUCH SCHOOL. YOU'RE KIND...
...TO HELP ME OUT.
IT'S NO TROUBLE AT ALL, AND I MEAN THAT.
FLIK

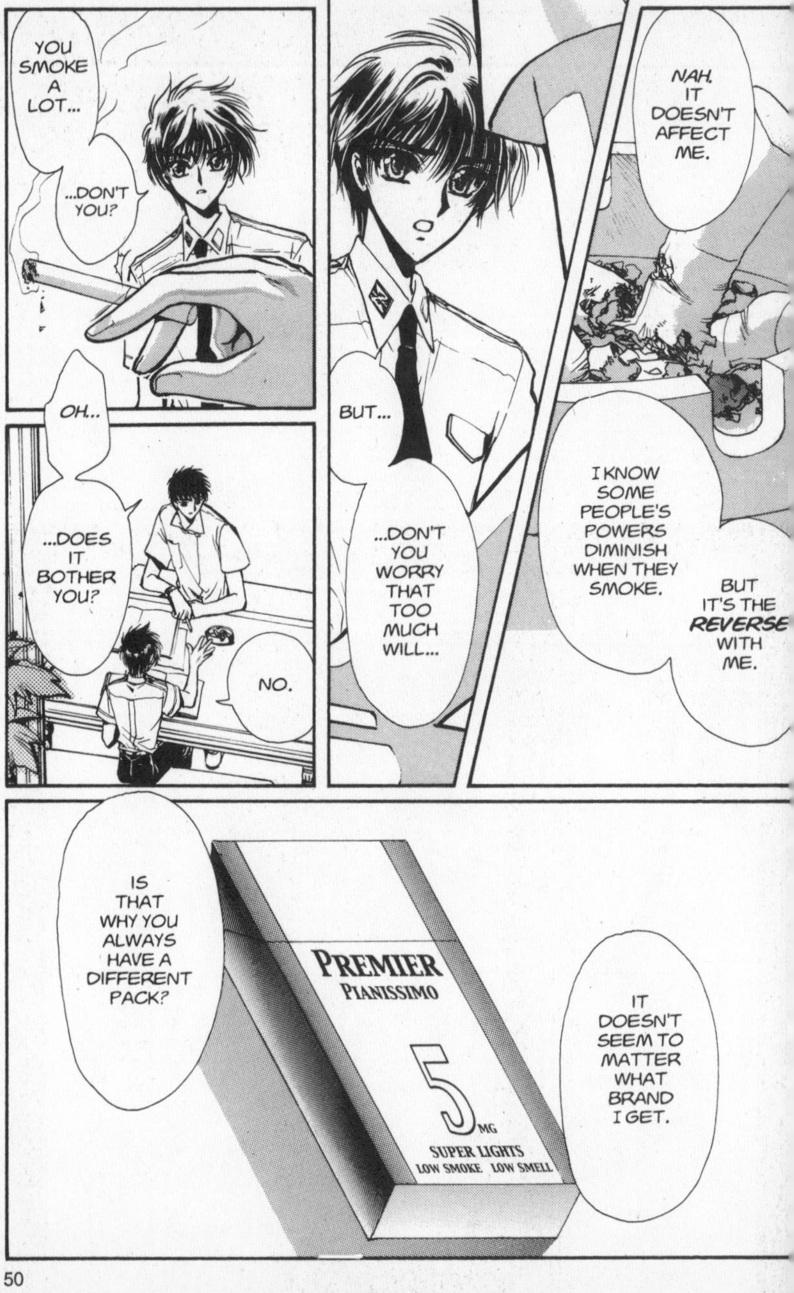
YOU SMOKE A LOT...
...DON'T YOU?
OH...
...DOES IT BOTHER YOU?
NO.
BUT...
...DON'T YOU WORRY THAT TOO MUCH WILL...
NAH. IT DOESN'T AFFECT ME.
I KNOW SOME PEOPLE'S POWERS DIMINISH WHEN THEY SMOKE.
BUT IT'S THE *REVERSE* WITH ME.
IS THAT WHY YOU ALWAYS HAVE A DIFFERENT PACK?
PREMIER
PIANISSIMO
5 MG
SUPER LIGHTS
LOW SMOKE LOW SMELL
IT DOESN'T SEEM TO MATTER WHAT BRAND I GET.

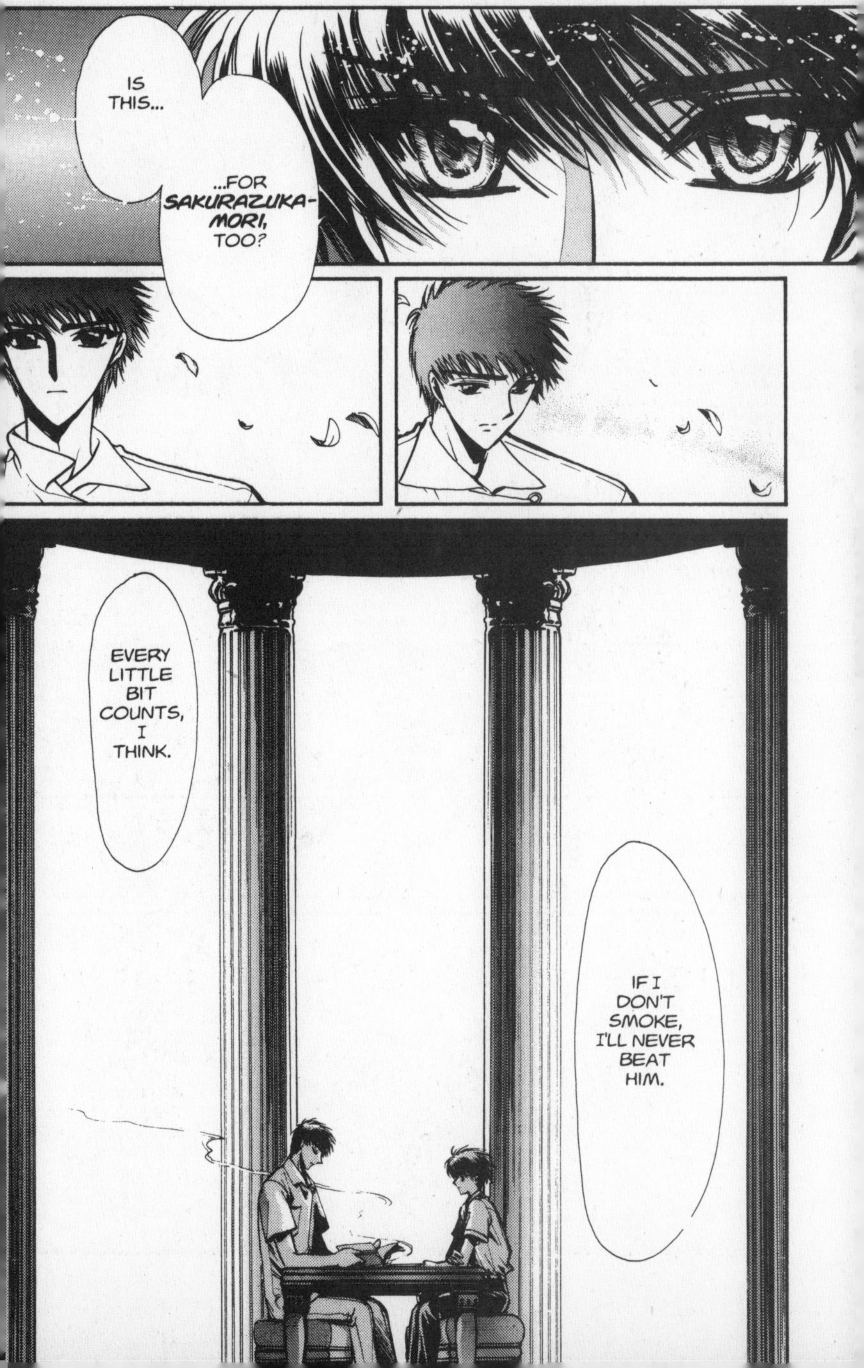
IS THIS...
...FOR SAKURAZUKA-MORI, TOO?
EVERY LITTLE BIT COUNTS, I THINK.
IF I DON'T SMOKE, I'LL NEVER BEAT HIM.

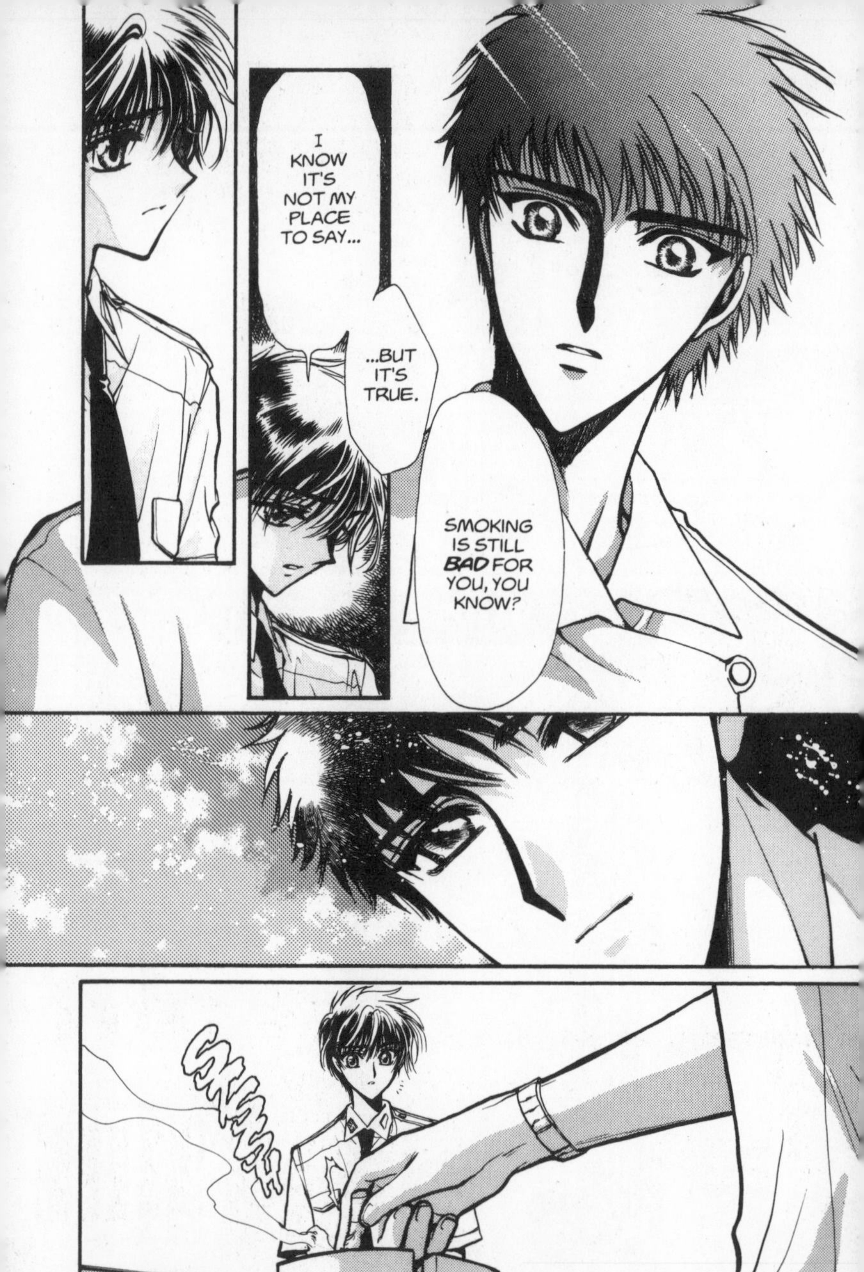
I KNOW IT'S NOT MY PLACE TO SAY...
...BUT IT'S TRUE.
SMOKING IS STILL **BAD** FOR YOU, YOU KNOW?
SKWSH

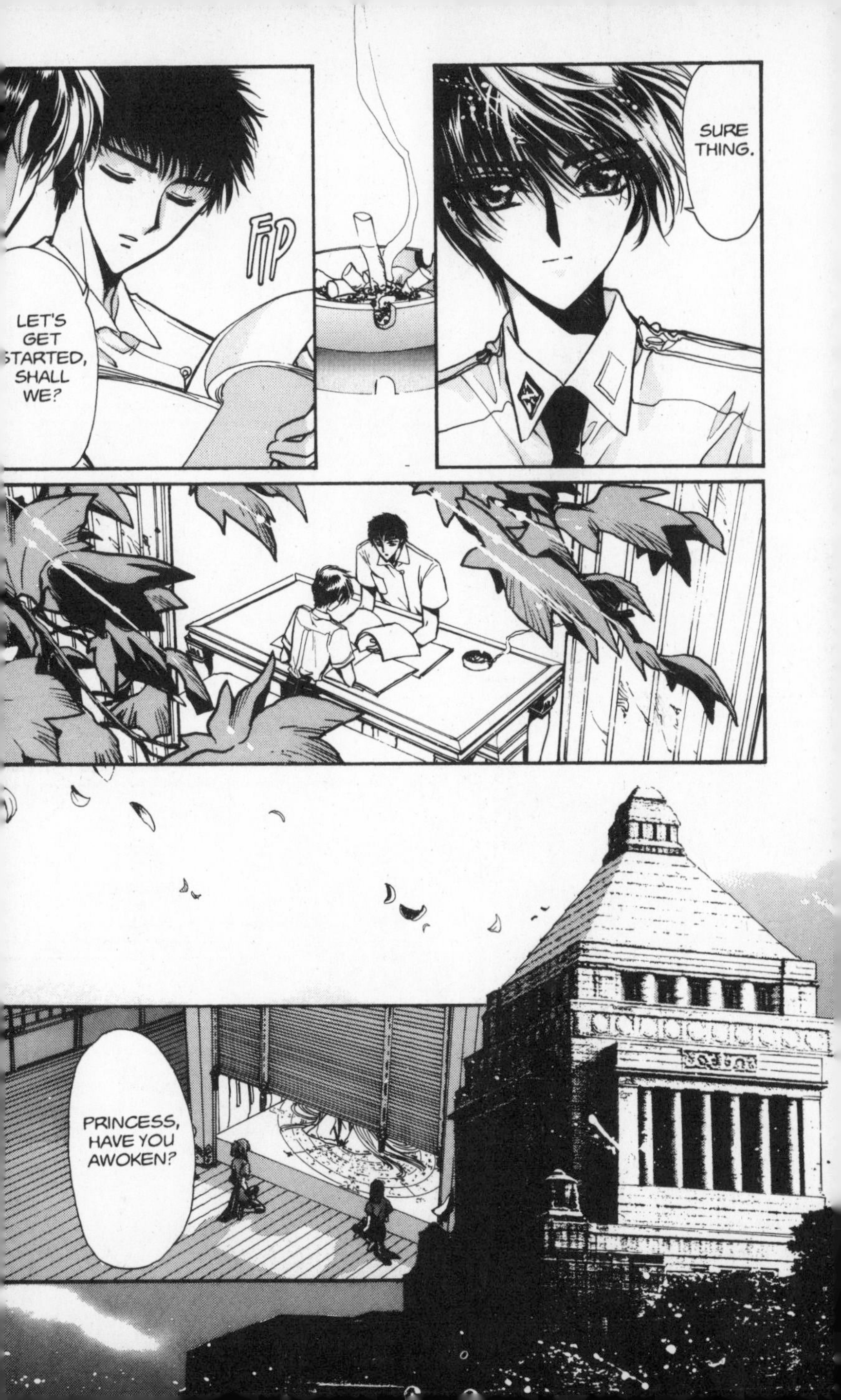
FIP
LET'S GET STARTED, SHALL WE?
SURE THING.
PRINCESS, HAVE YOU AWOKEN?

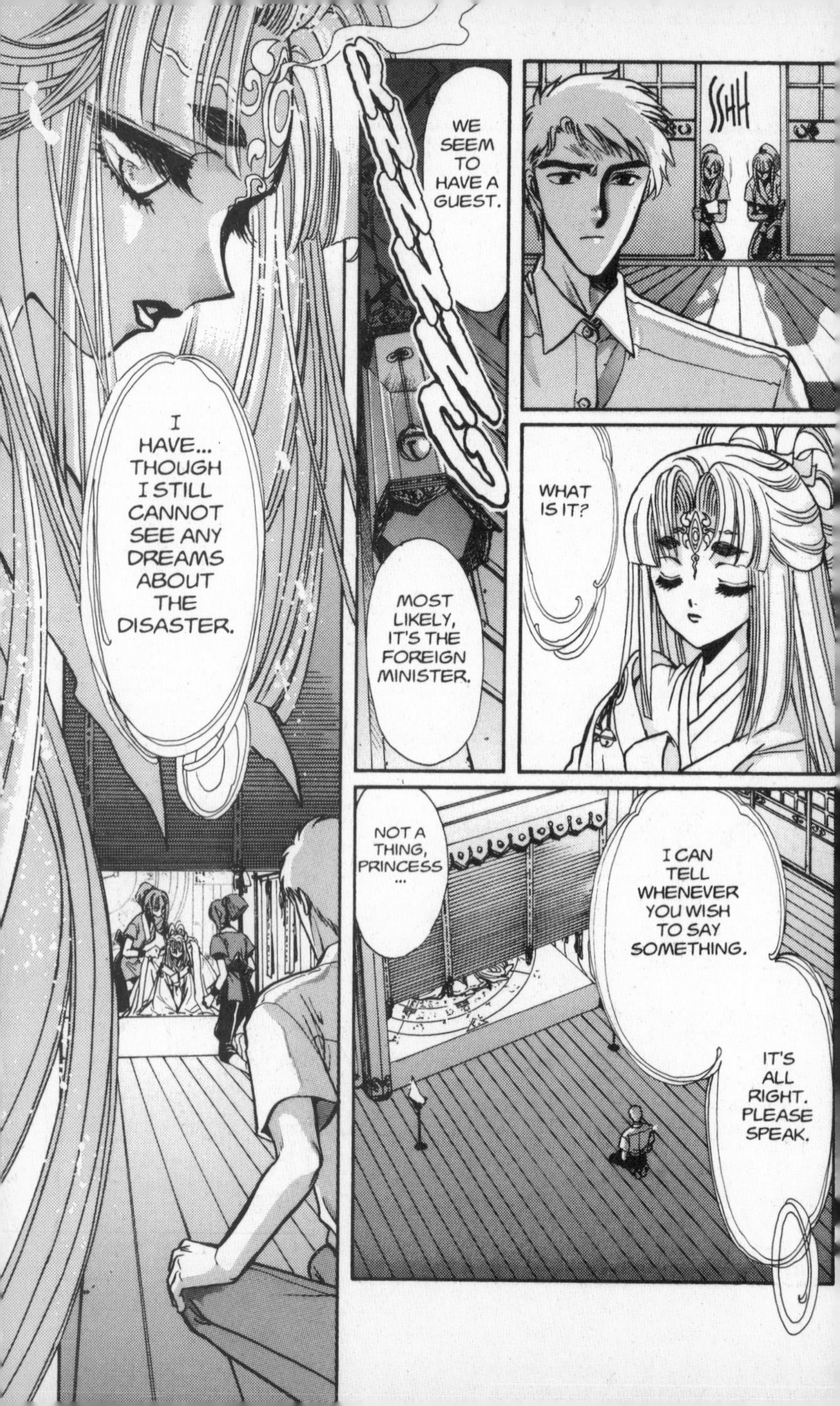
I HAVE... THOUGH I STILL CANNOT SEE ANY DREAMS ABOUT THE DISASTER.
RINNG
WE SEEM TO HAVE A GUEST.
MOST LIKELY, IT'S THE FOREIGN MINISTER.
SSHH
WHAT IS IT?
NOT A THING, PRINCESS...
I CAN TELL WHENEVER YOU WISH TO SAY SOMETHING.
IT'S ALL RIGHT. PLEASE SPEAK.

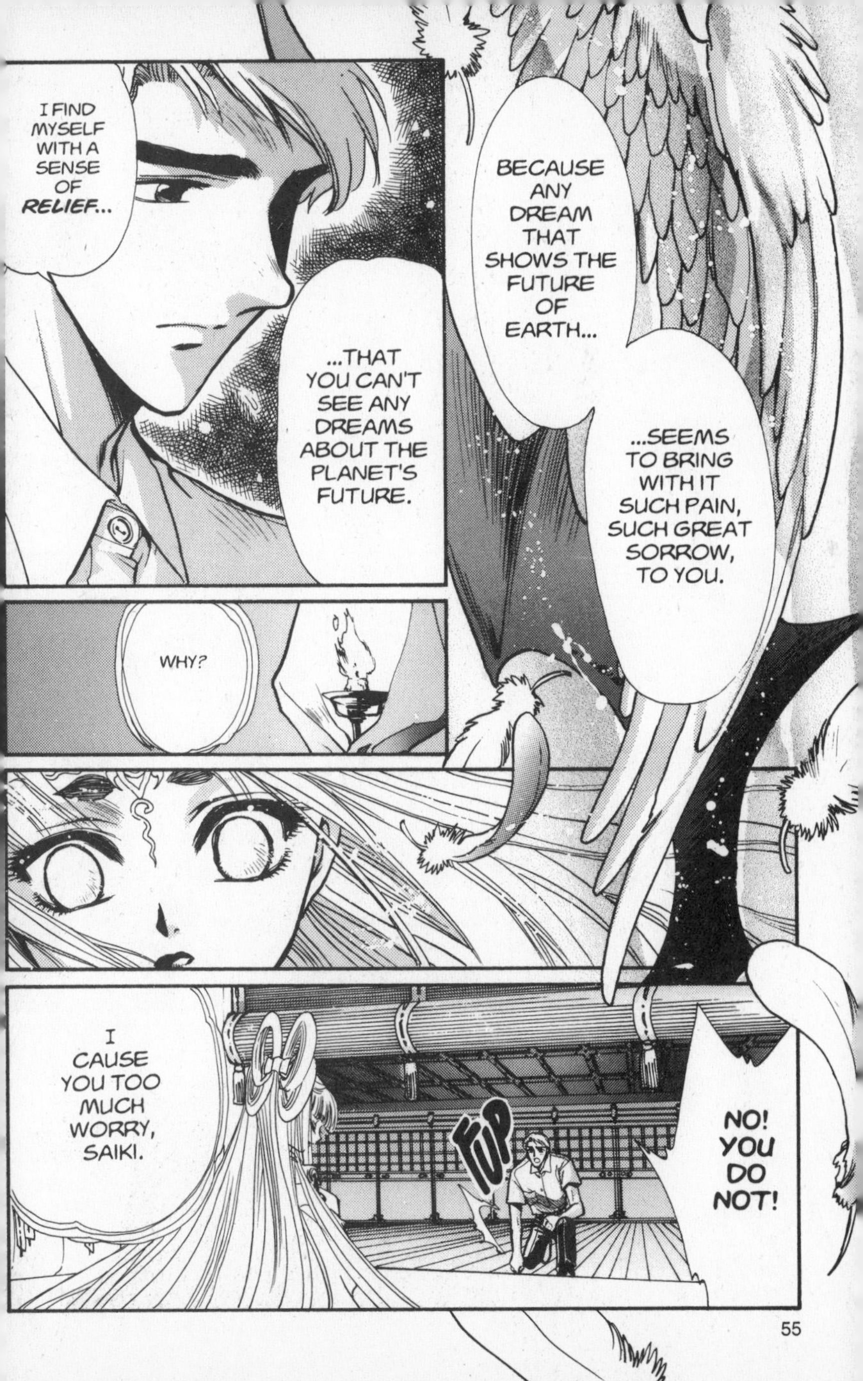
I FIND MYSELF WITH A SENSE OF RELIEF...
...THAT YOU CAN'T SEE ANY DREAMS ABOUT THE PLANET'S FUTURE.
WHY?
BECAUSE ANY DREAM THAT SHOWS THE FUTURE OF EARTH...
...SEEMS TO BRING WITH IT SUCH PAIN, SUCH GREAT SORROW, TO YOU.
I CAUSE YOU TOO MUCH WORRY, SAIKI.
FUP
NO! YOU DO NOT!

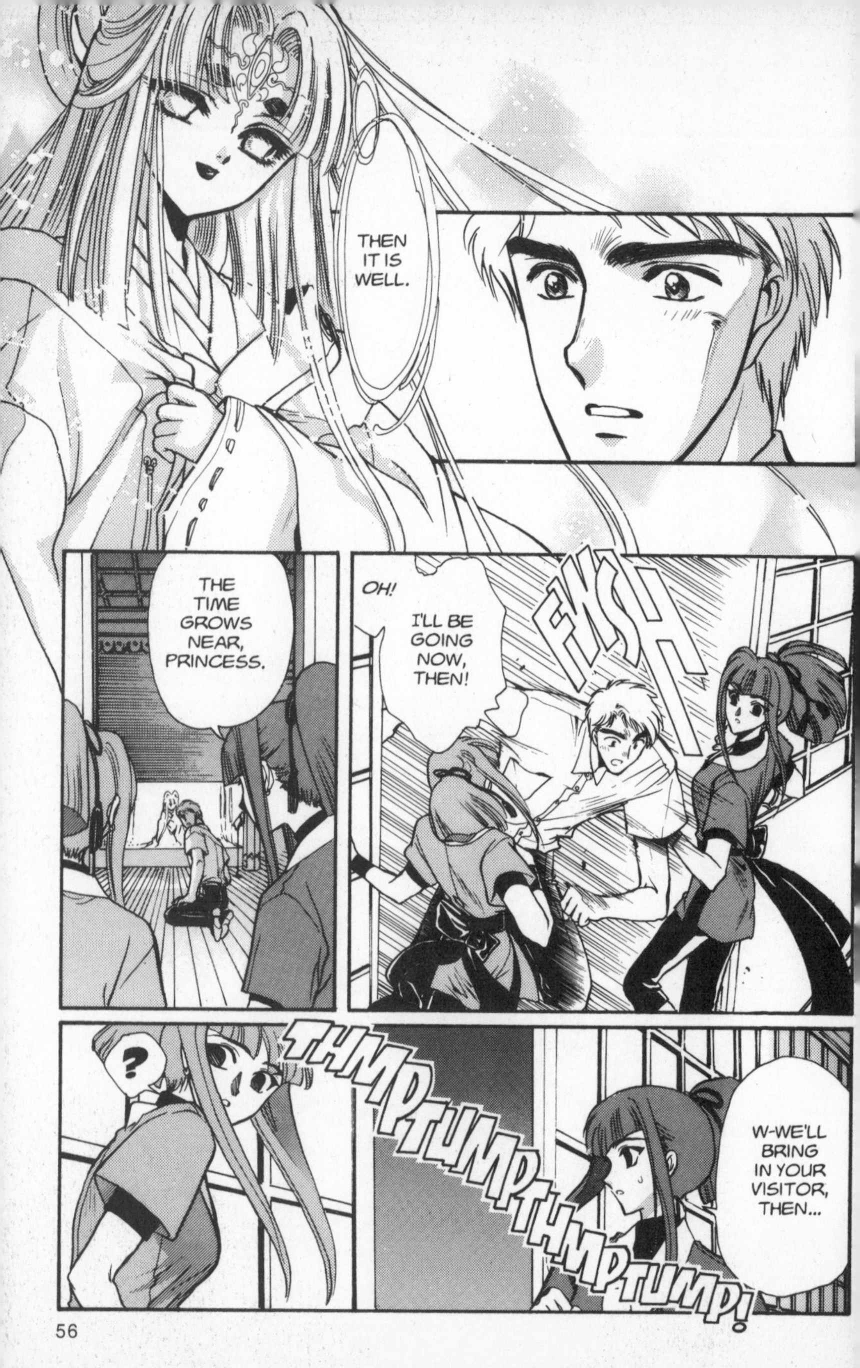
THEN IT IS WELL.
THE TIME GROWS NEAR, PRINCESS.
OH!
I'LL BE GOING NOW, THEN!
FWSH
?
THMPTUMPTHMPTUMP!
W-WE'LL BRING IN YOUR VISITOR, THEN...

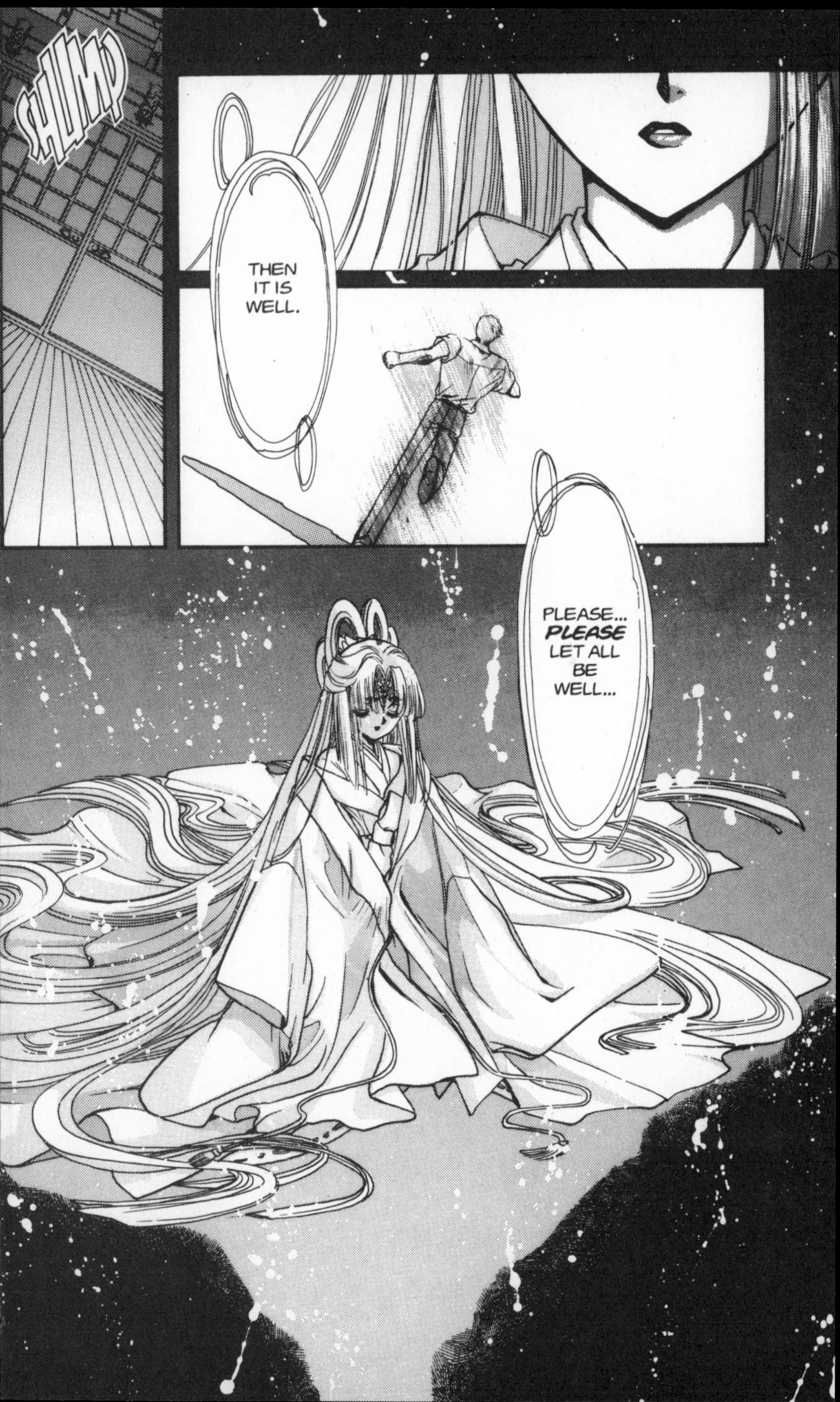
SHUMP
THEN IT IS WELL.
PLEASE... *PLEASE* LET ALL BE WELL...

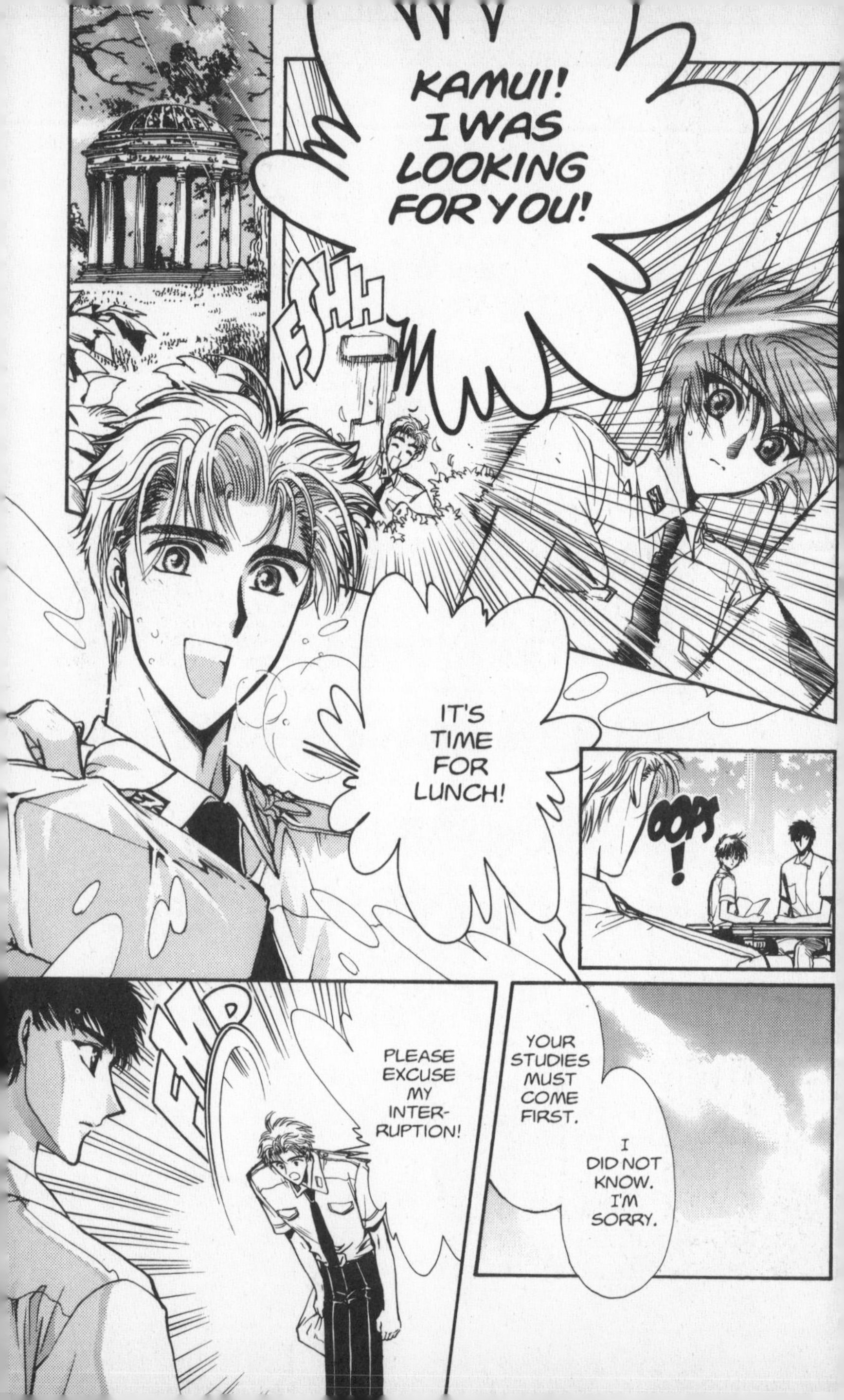
KAMUI! I WAS LOOKING FOR YOU!
FSHH
IT'S TIME FOR LUNCH!
OOPS!
PLEASE EXCUSE MY INTER-RUPTION!
YOUR STUDIES MUST COME FIRST.
I DID NOT KNOW. I'M SORRY.

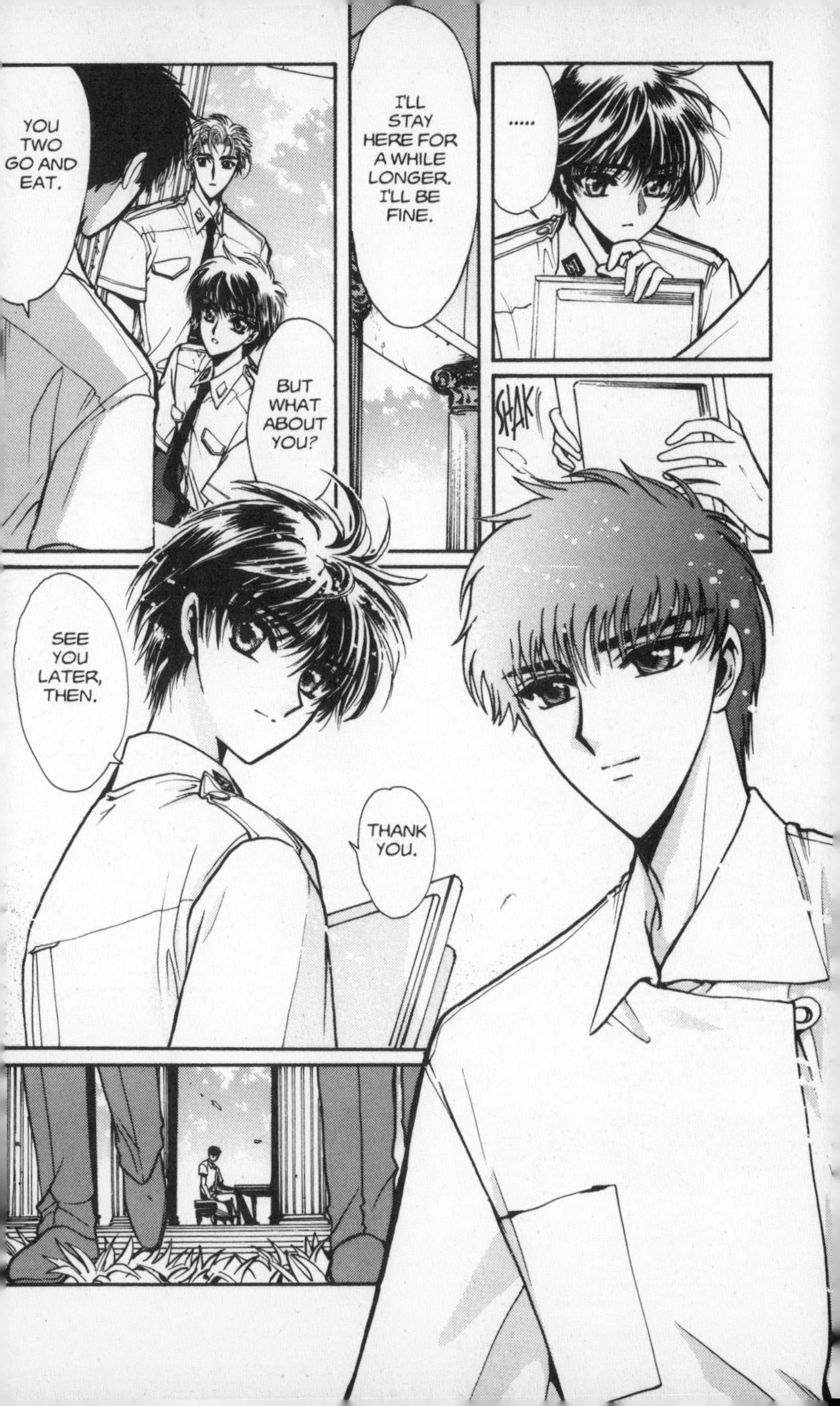
YOU TWO GO AND EAT.
BUT WHAT ABOUT YOU?
I'LL STAY HERE FOR A WHILE LONGER. I'LL BE FINE.
.....
SHAK
SEE YOU LATER, THEN.
THANK YOU.

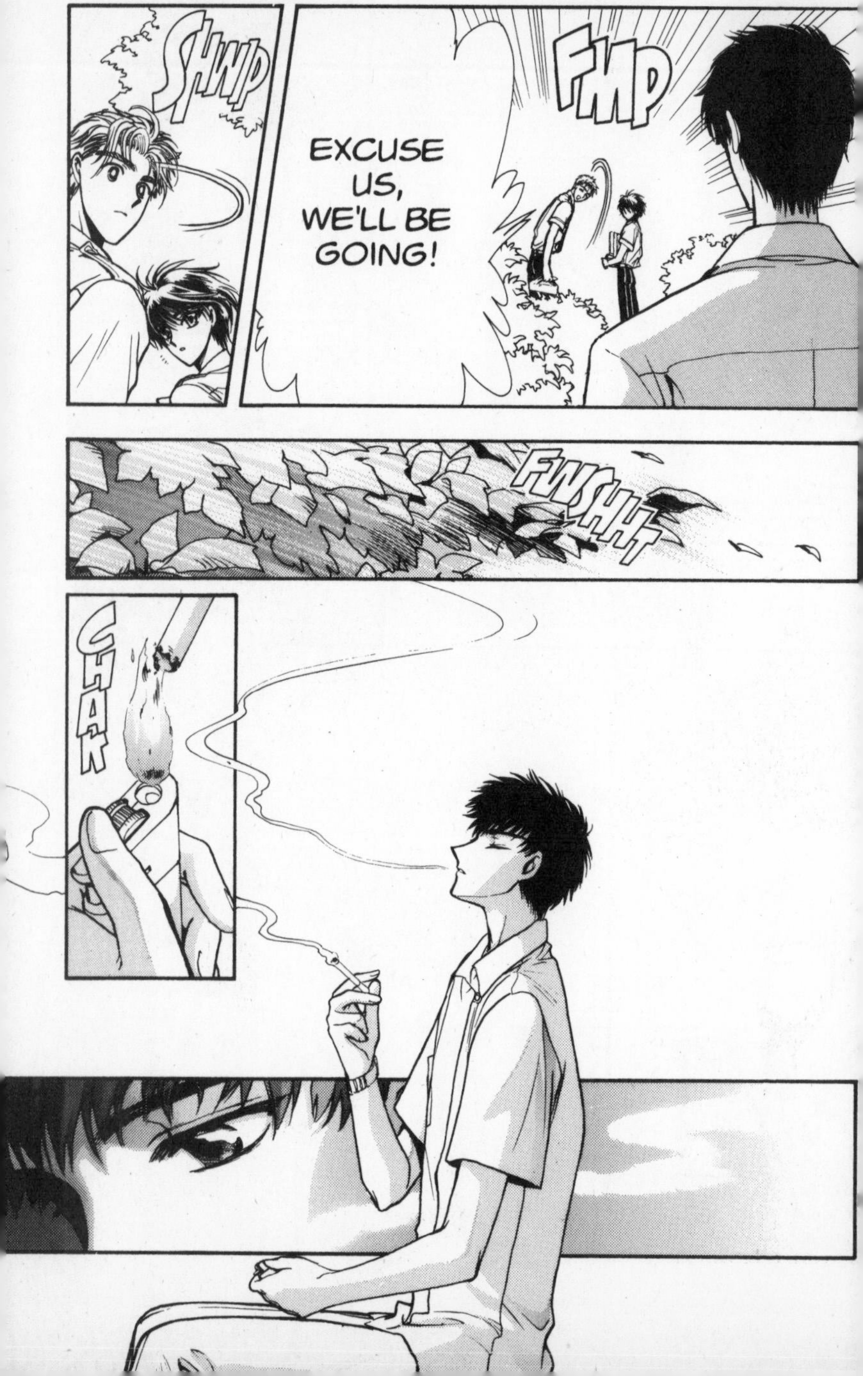
SHWIP
EXCUSE US, WE'LL BE GOING!
FWP
FWSHHT
CHAK

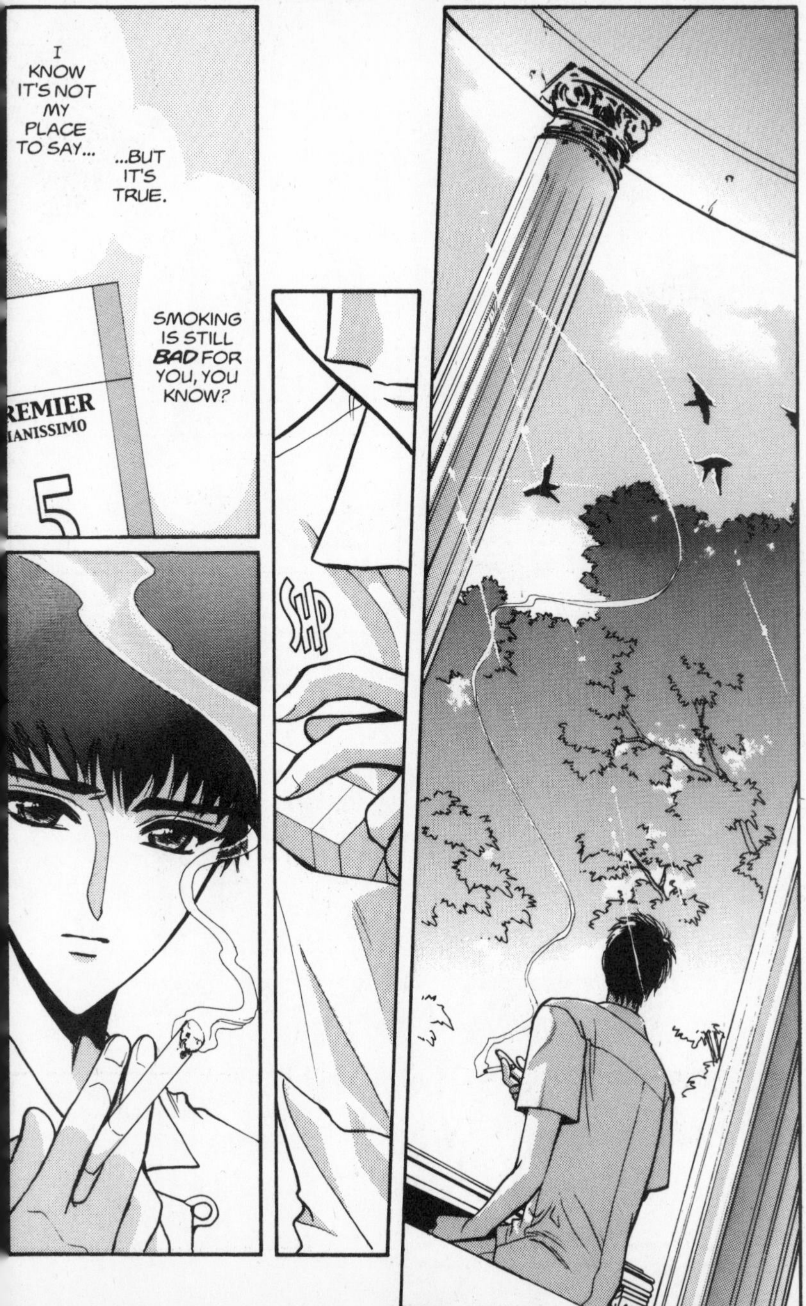
I KNOW IT'S NOT MY PLACE TO SAY...
...BUT IT'S TRUE.
SMOKING IS STILL BAD FOR YOU, YOU KNOW?
SHP

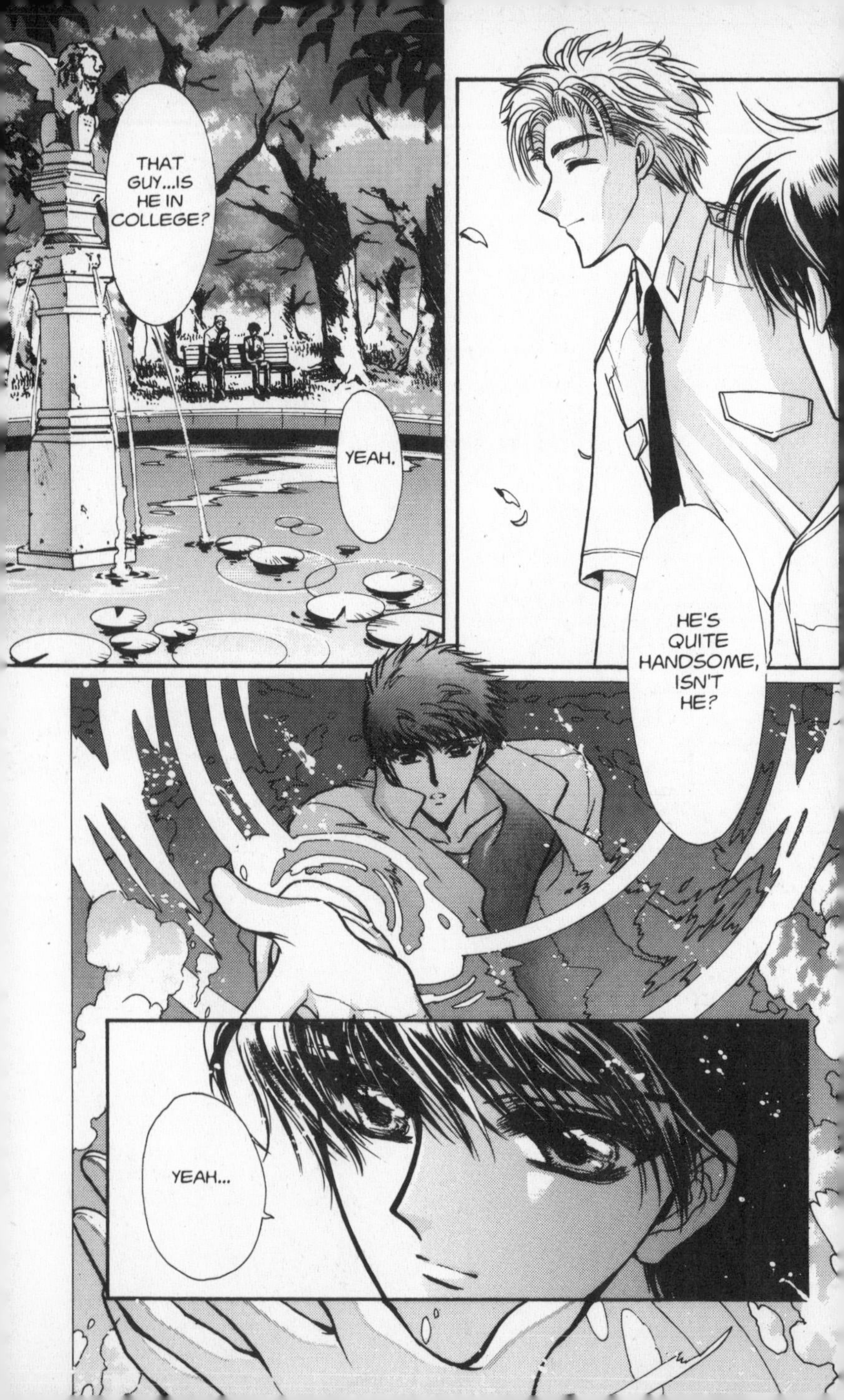
THAT GUY...IS HE IN COLLEGE?
YEAH.
HE'S QUITE HANDSOME, ISN'T HE?
YEAH...

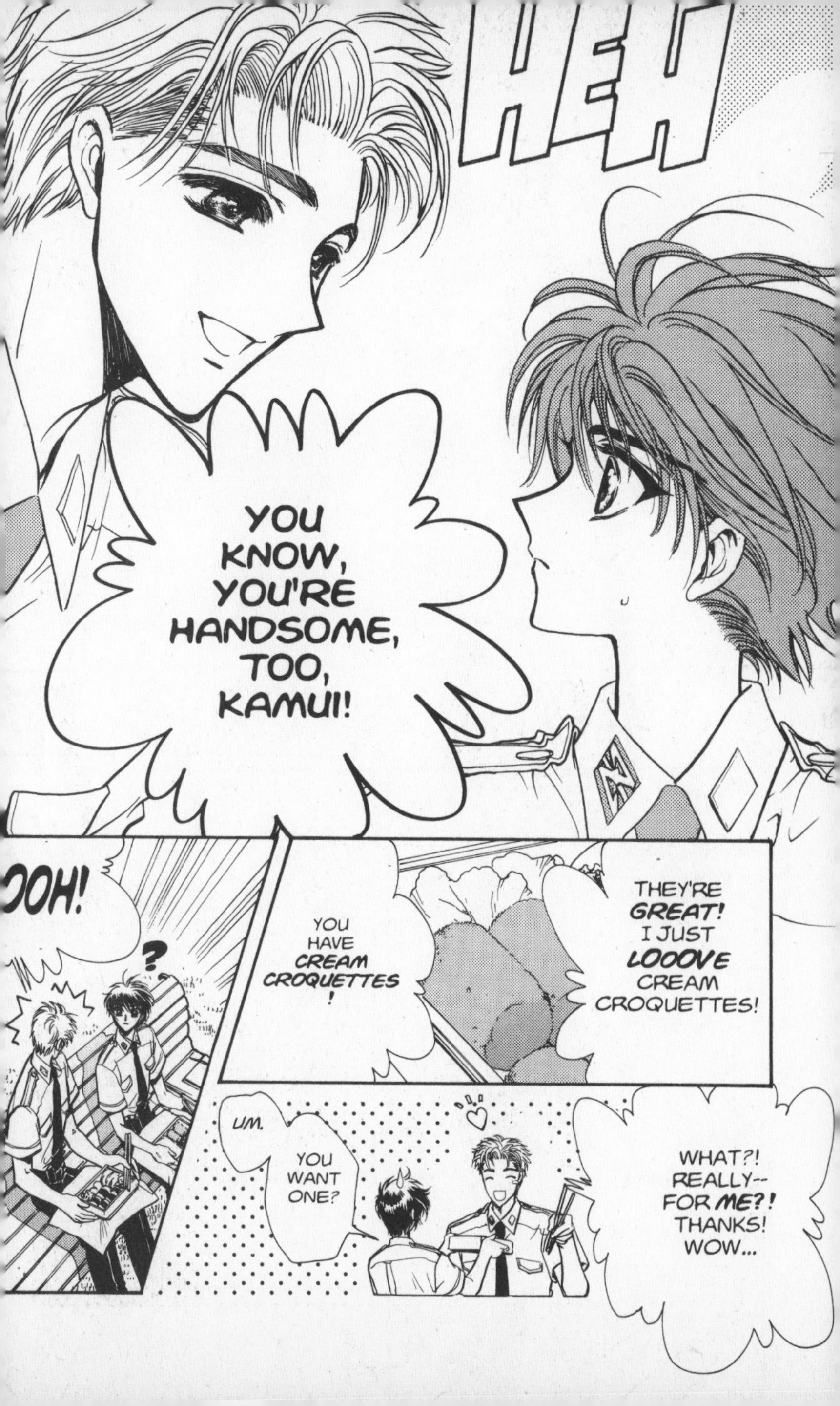
HEH
YOU KNOW, YOU'RE HANDSOME, TOO, KAMUI!
OOH!
?
YOU HAVE CREAM CROQUETTES!
THEY'RE GREAT! I JUST LOOOVE CREAM CROQUETTES!
UM.
YOU WANT ONE?
WHAT?! REALLY-- FOR ME?! THANKS! WOW...

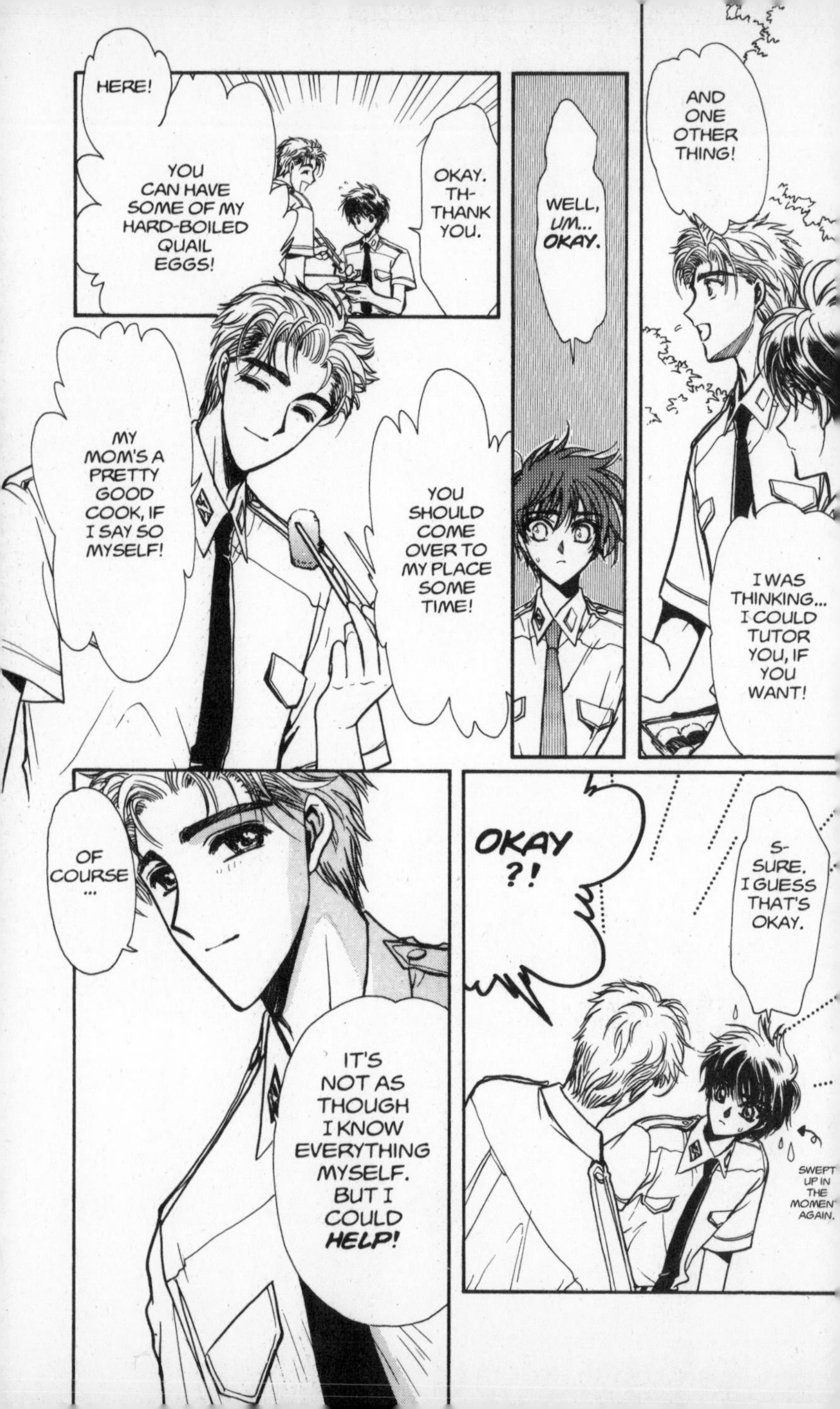
HERE!
YOU CAN HAVE SOME OF MY HARD-BOILED QUAIL EGGS!
OKAY. TH-THANK YOU.
MY MOM'S A PRETTY GOOD COOK, IF I SAY SO MYSELF!
YOU SHOULD COME OVER TO MY PLACE SOME TIME!
WELL, UM... *OKAY.*
AND ONE OTHER THING!
I WAS THINKING... I COULD TUTOR YOU, IF YOU WANT!
OF COURSE...
IT'S NOT AS THOUGH I KNOW EVERYTHING MYSELF. BUT I COULD *HELP!*
OKAY ?!
S-SURE. I GUESS THAT'S OKAY.
...
SWEPT UP IN THE MOMEN AGAIN.

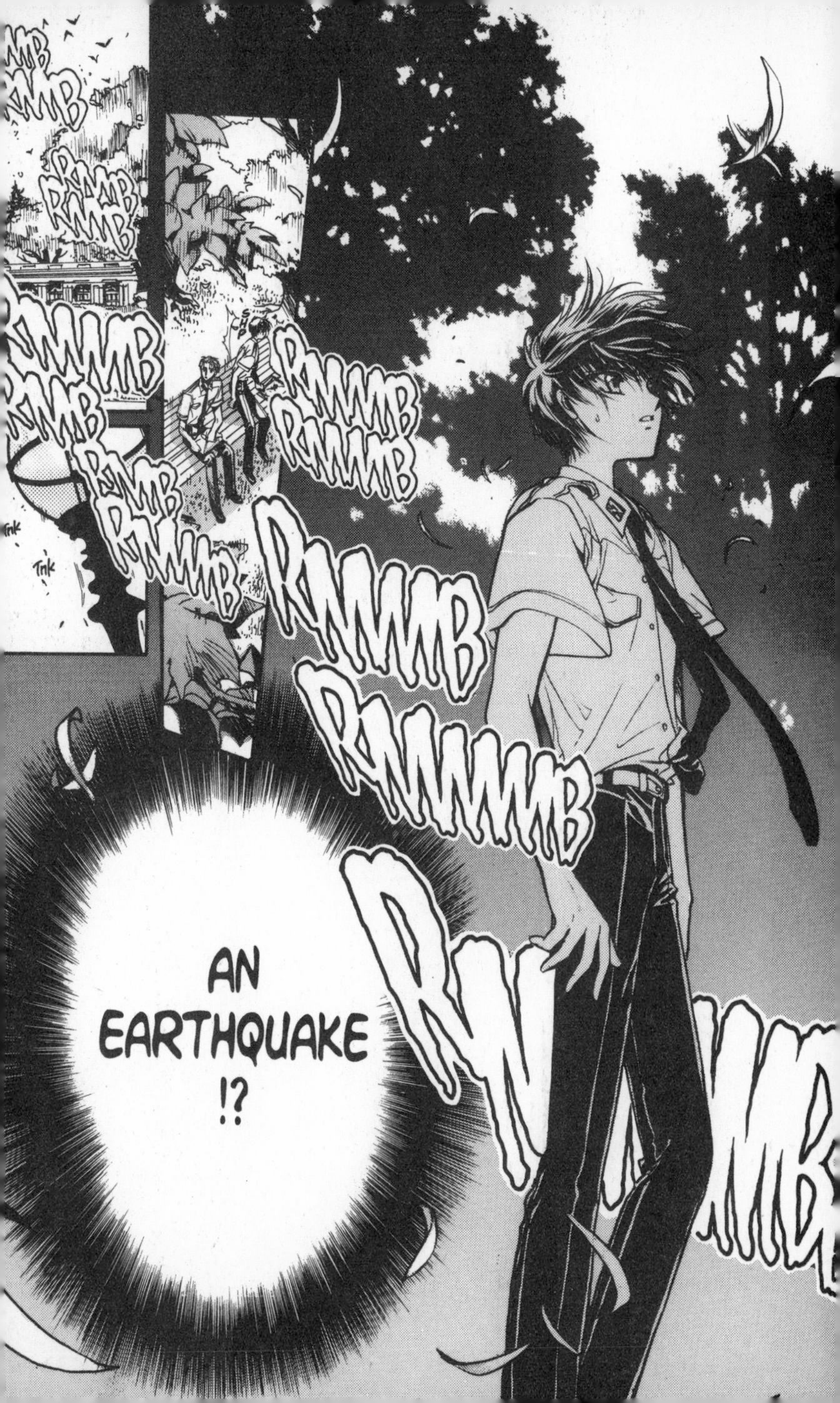
RMMB RMMB
Tnk
Tnk
SHP
RMMMB RMMMB
RMMMB
RMMMMMB
AN EARTHQUAKE !?

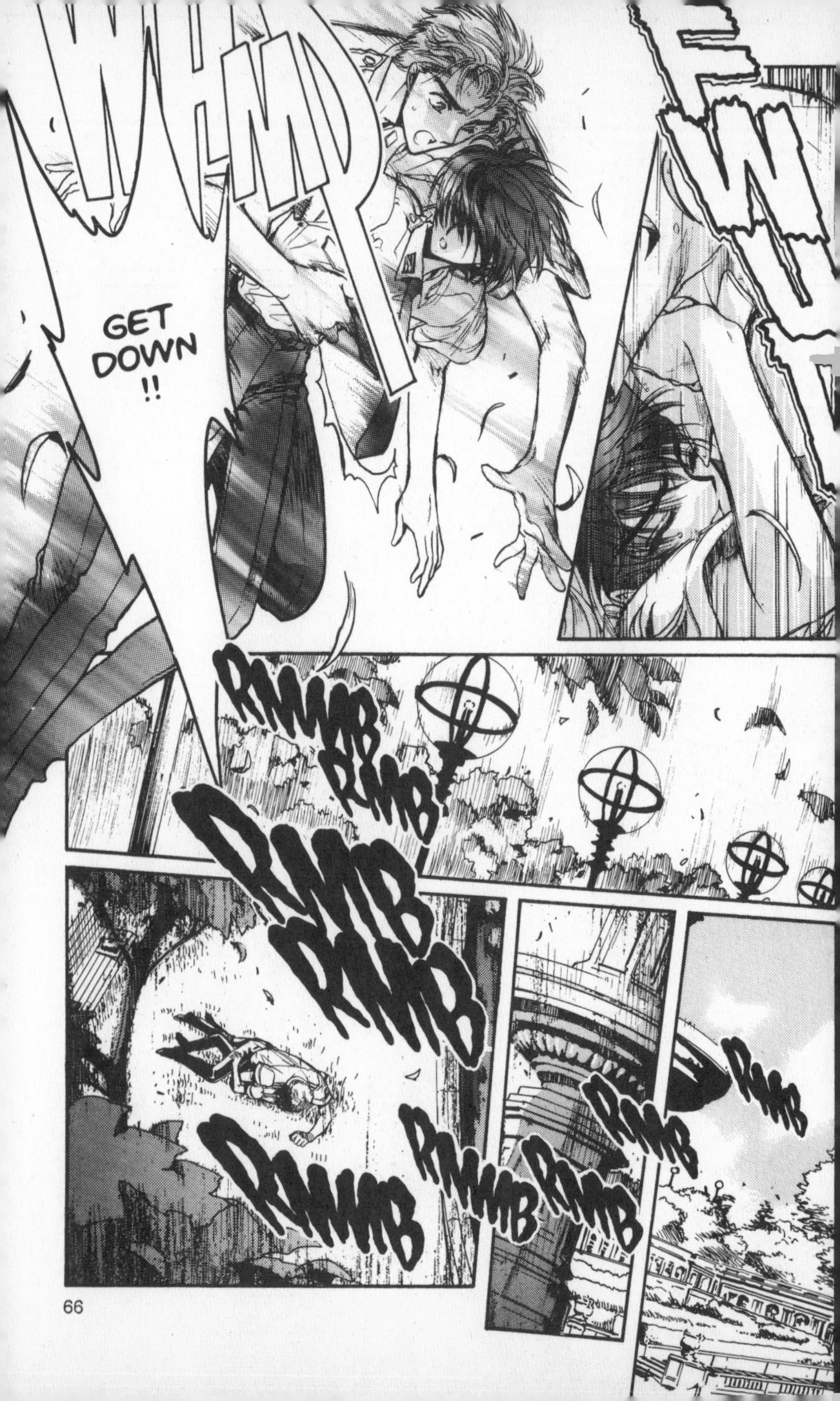
WHMP
GET DOWN !!
RMMB
RMB
RMB
RMMB
RMMMB
RMMB
RMMB
RMB
RMMB

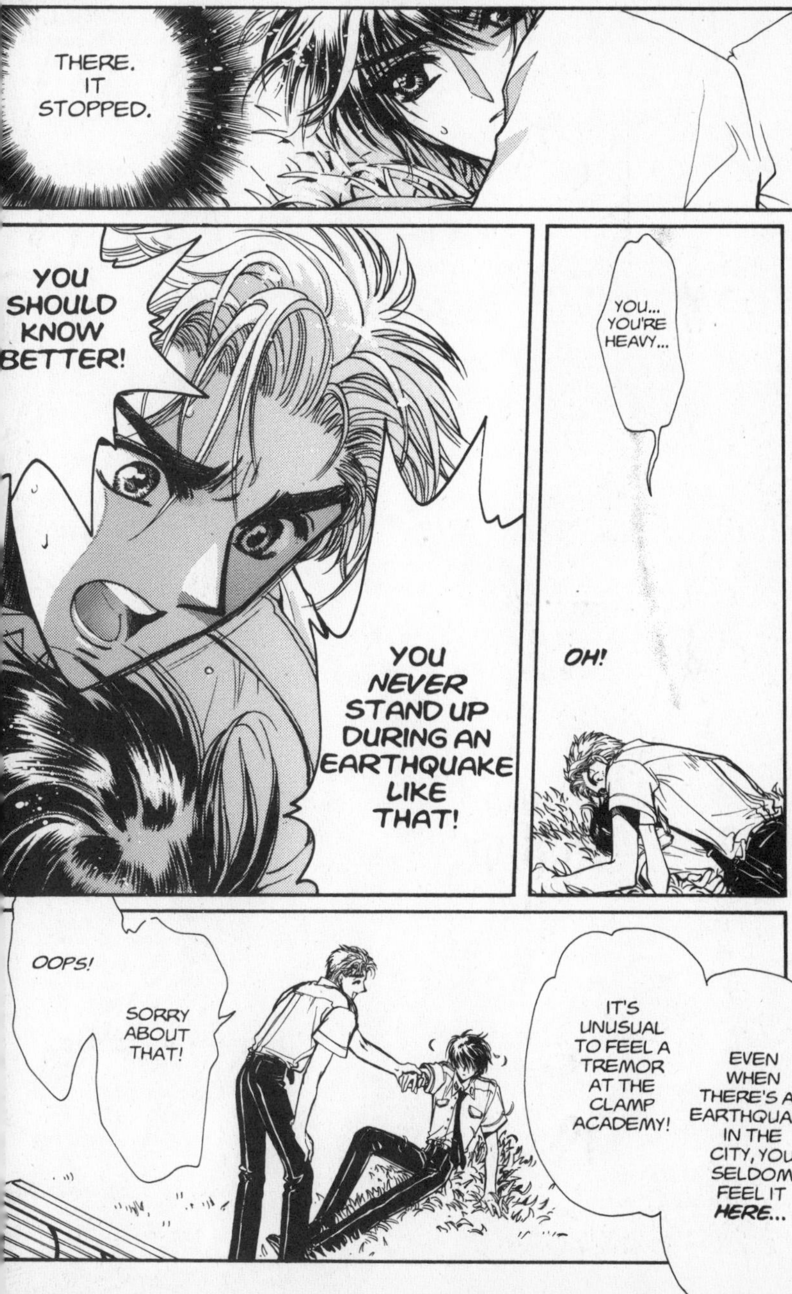
THERE. IT STOPPED.
YOU SHOULD KNOW BETTER!
YOU *NEVER* STAND UP DURING AN EARTHQUAKE LIKE THAT!
YOU... YOU'RE HEAVY...
OH!
OOPS!
SORRY ABOUT THAT!
IT'S UNUSUAL TO FEEL A TREMOR AT THE CLAMP ACADEMY!
EVEN WHEN THERE'S AN EARTHQUAKE IN THE CITY, YOU SELDOM FEEL IT ***HERE...***

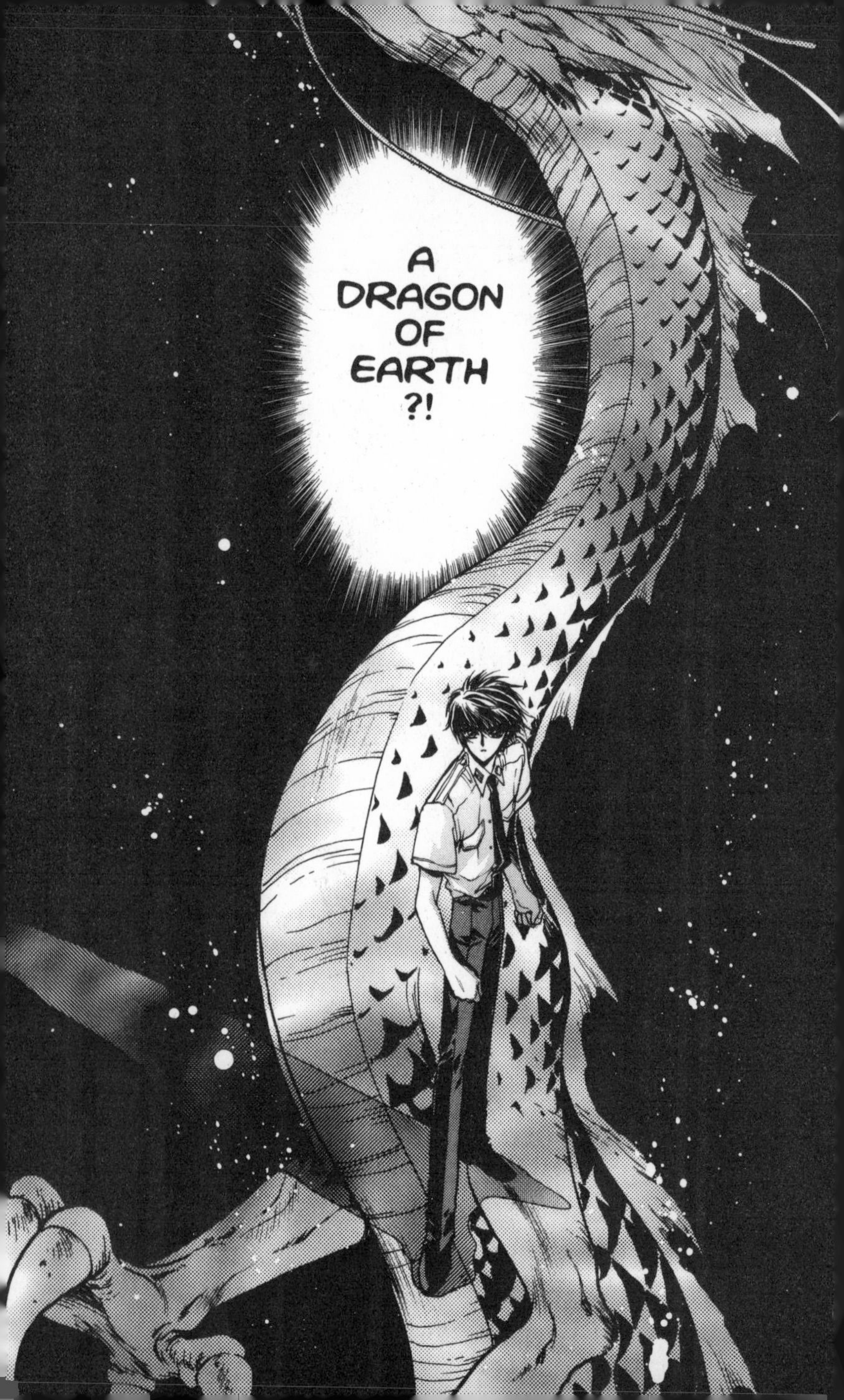
A DRAGON OF EARTH ?!

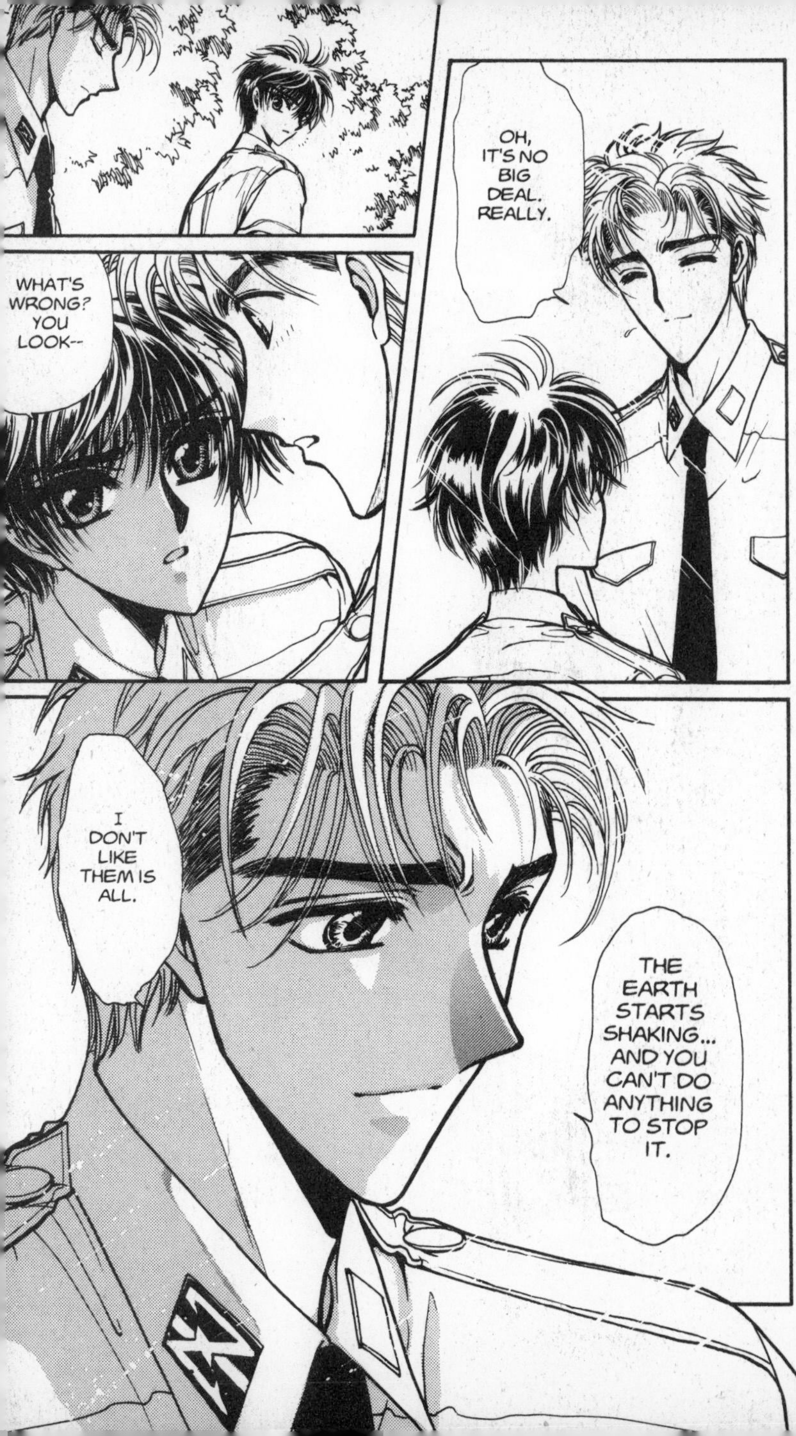
WHAT'S WRONG? YOU LOOK--
OH, IT'S NO BIG DEAL. REALLY.
I DON'T LIKE THEM IS ALL.
THE EARTH STARTS SHAKING... AND YOU CAN'T DO ANYTHING TO STOP IT.

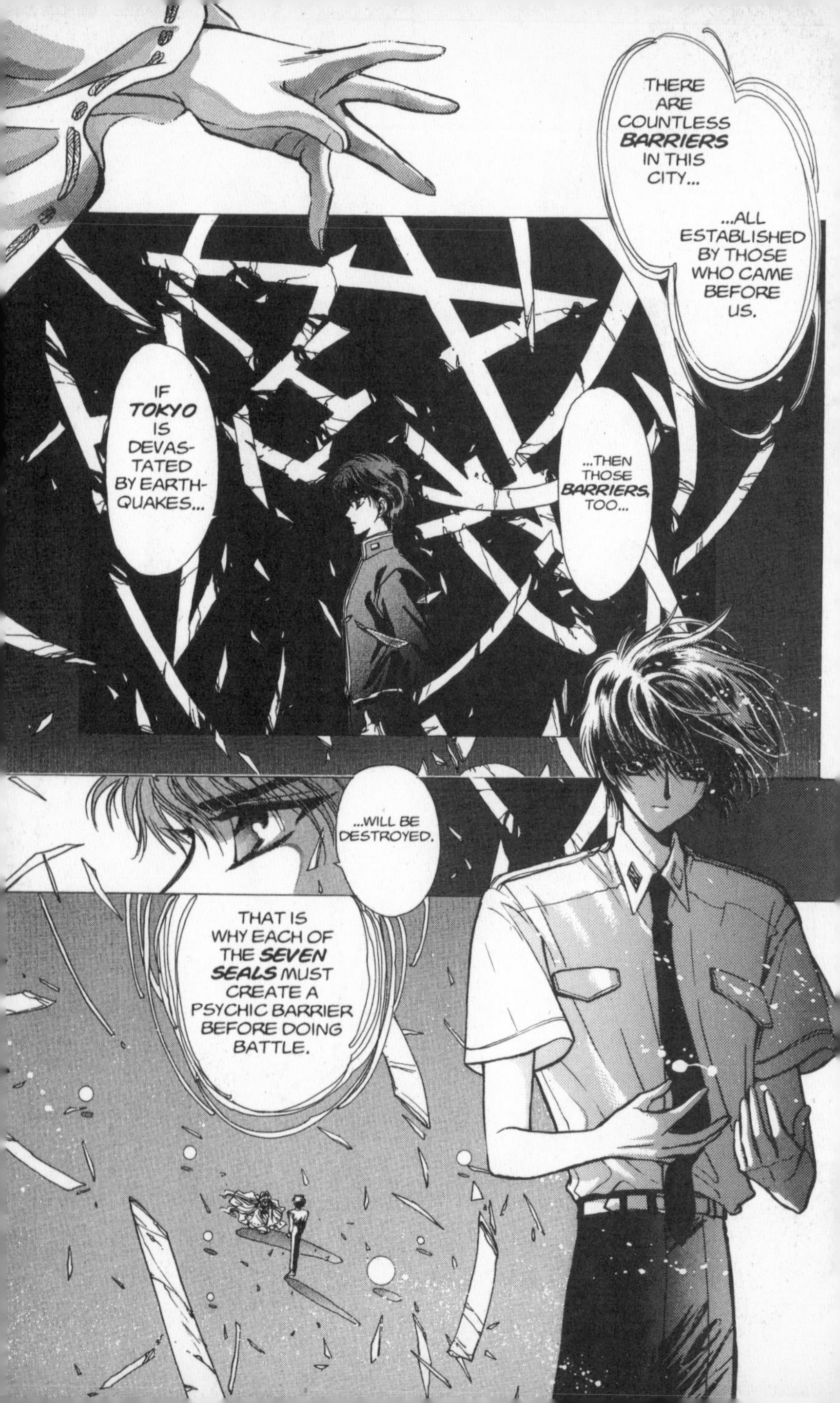
THERE ARE COUNTLESS BARRIERS IN THIS CITY...
...ALL ESTABLISHED BY THOSE WHO CAME BEFORE US.
IF TOKYO IS DEVAS-TATED BY EARTH-QUAKES...
...THEN THOSE BARRIERS, TOO...
...WILL BE DESTROYED.
THAT IS WHY EACH OF THE SEVEN SEALS MUST CREATE A PSYCHIC BARRIER BEFORE DOING BATTLE.

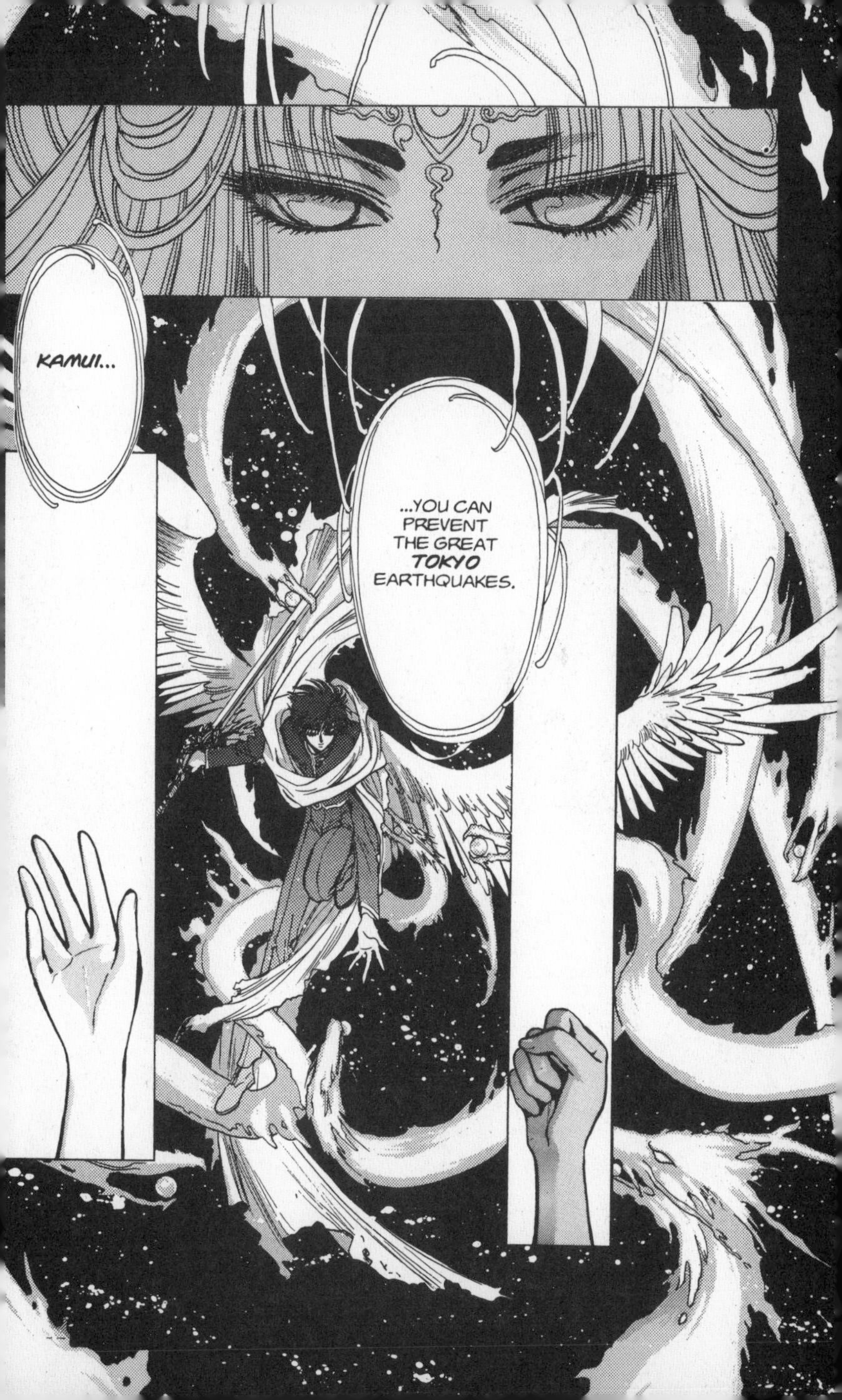
KAMUI...
...YOU CAN PREVENT THE GREAT TOKYO EARTHQUAKES.

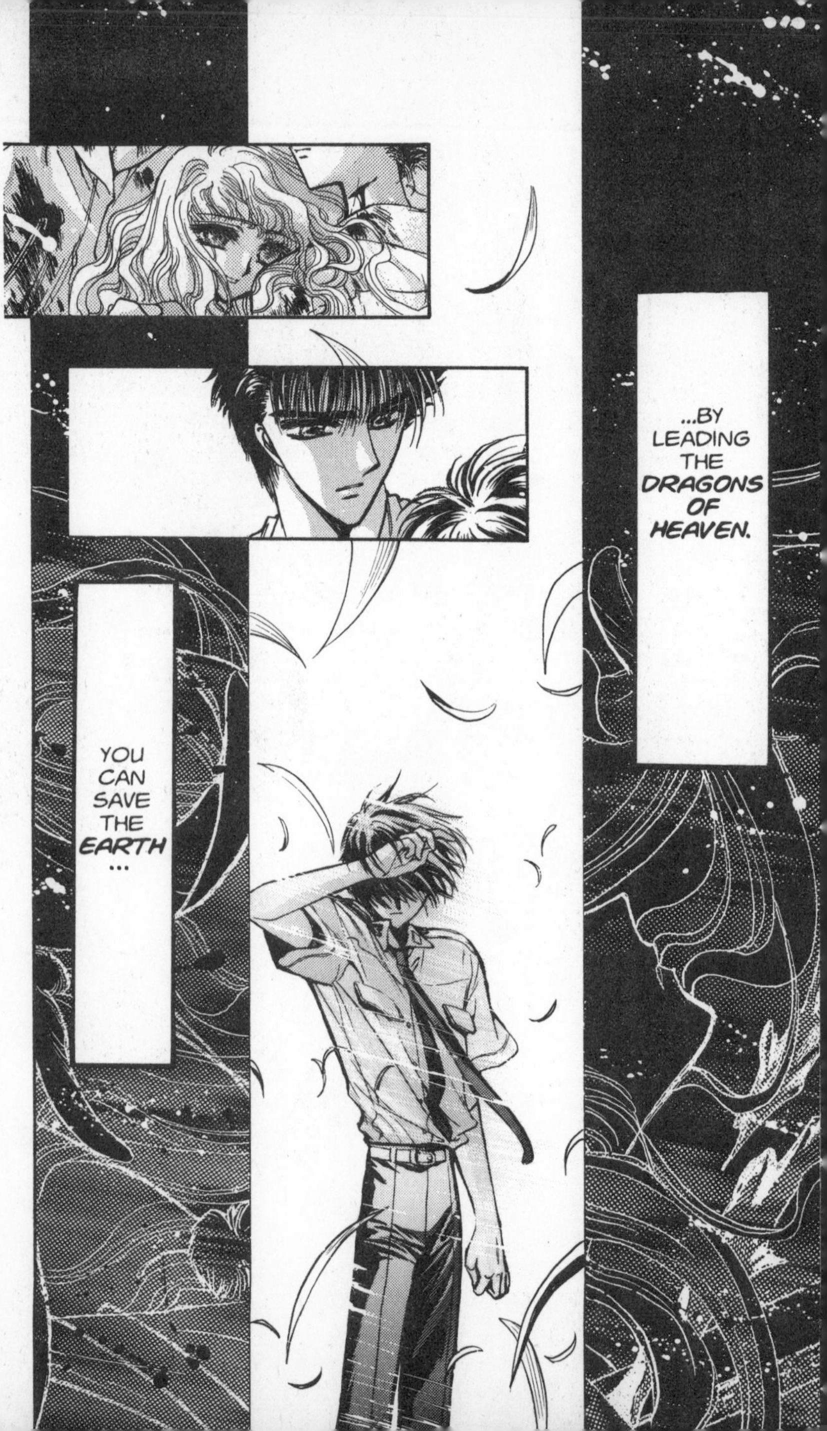
YOU CAN SAVE THE EARTH ...
...BY LEADING THE DRAGONS OF HEAVEN.

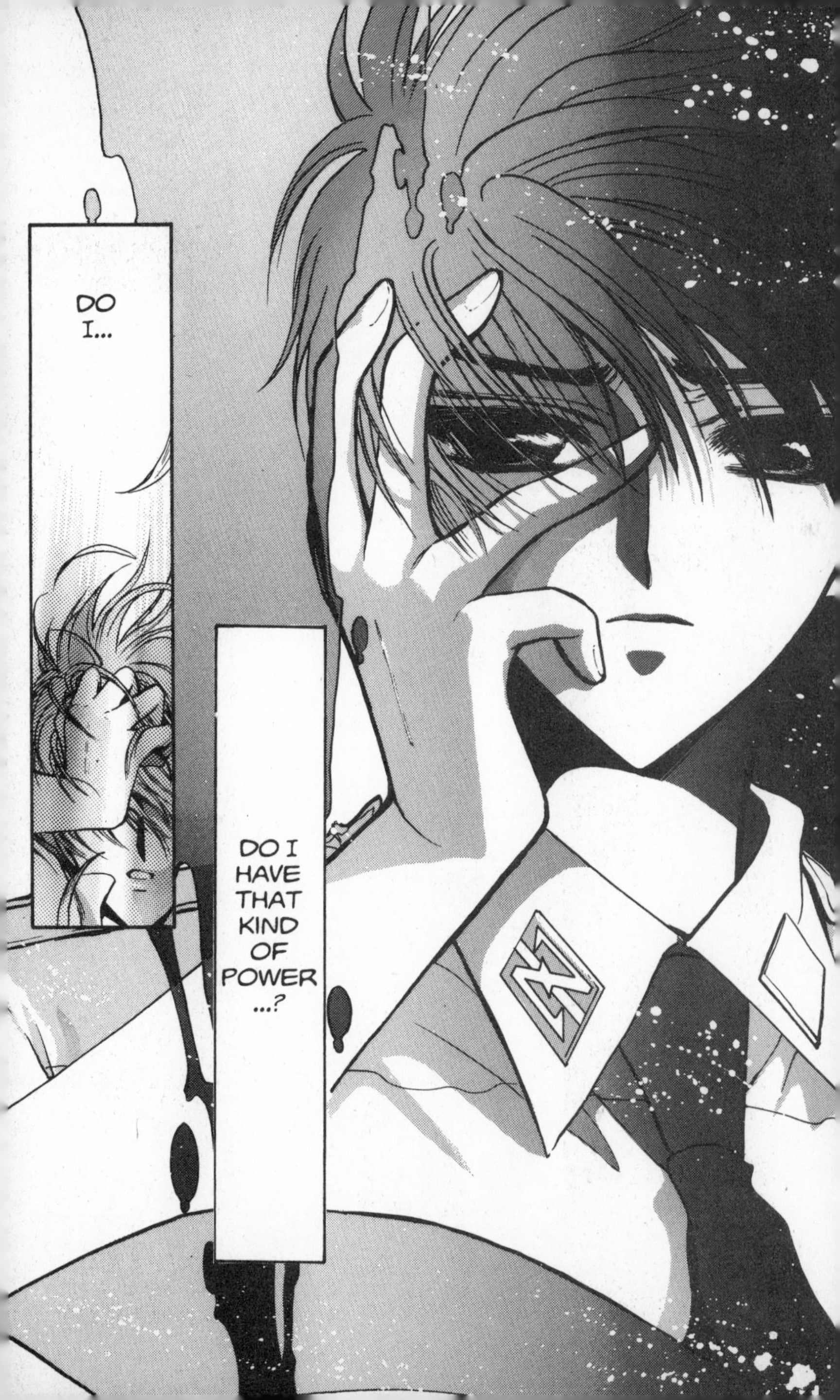
DO I...
DO I HAVE THAT KIND OF POWER ...?

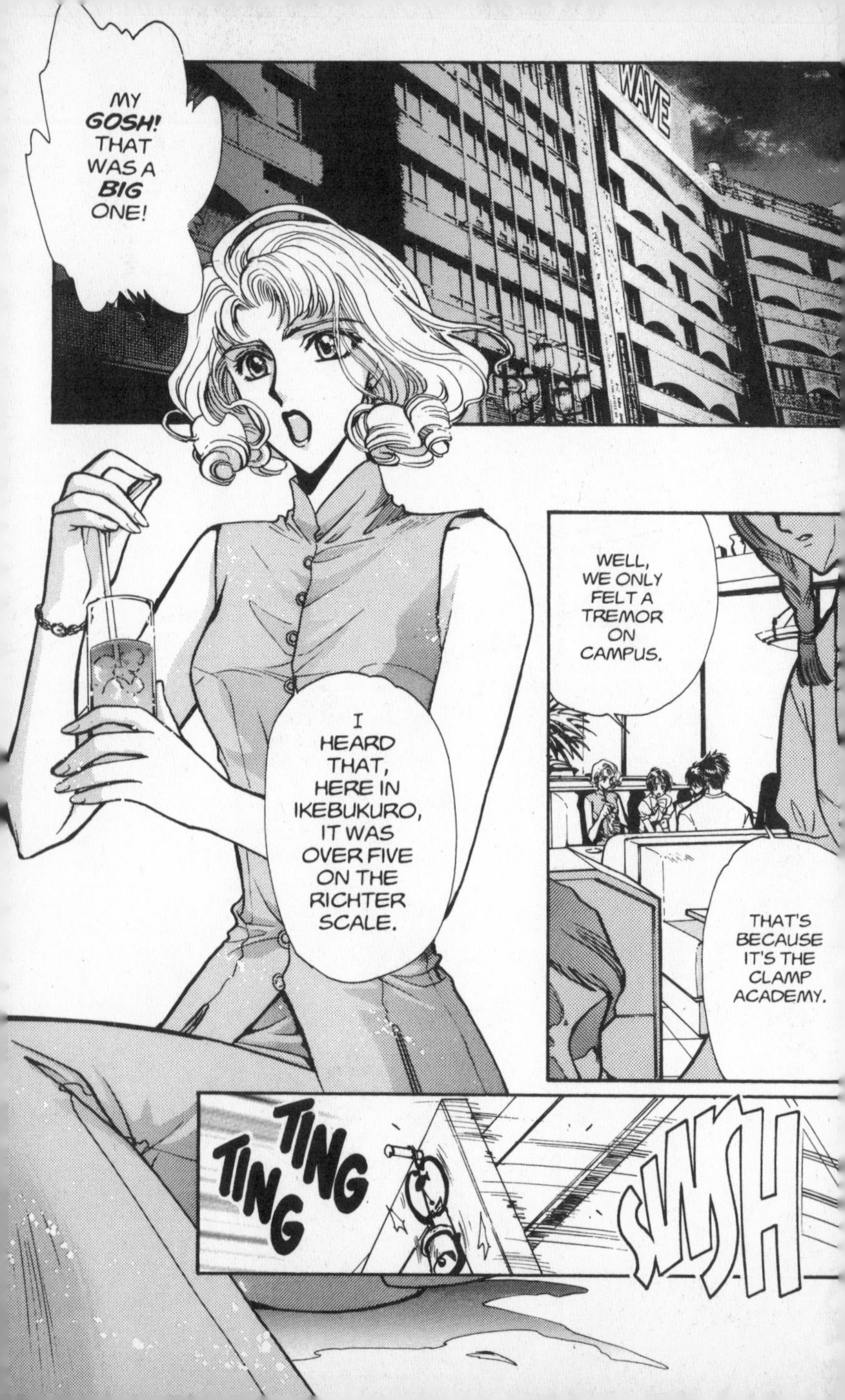
MY GOSH! THAT WAS A BIG ONE!
WAVE
I HEARD THAT, HERE IN IKEBUKURO, IT WAS OVER FIVE ON THE RICHTER SCALE.
WELL, WE ONLY FELT A TREMOR ON CAMPUS.
THAT'S BECAUSE IT'S THE CLAMP ACADEMY.
TING TING
SWISH

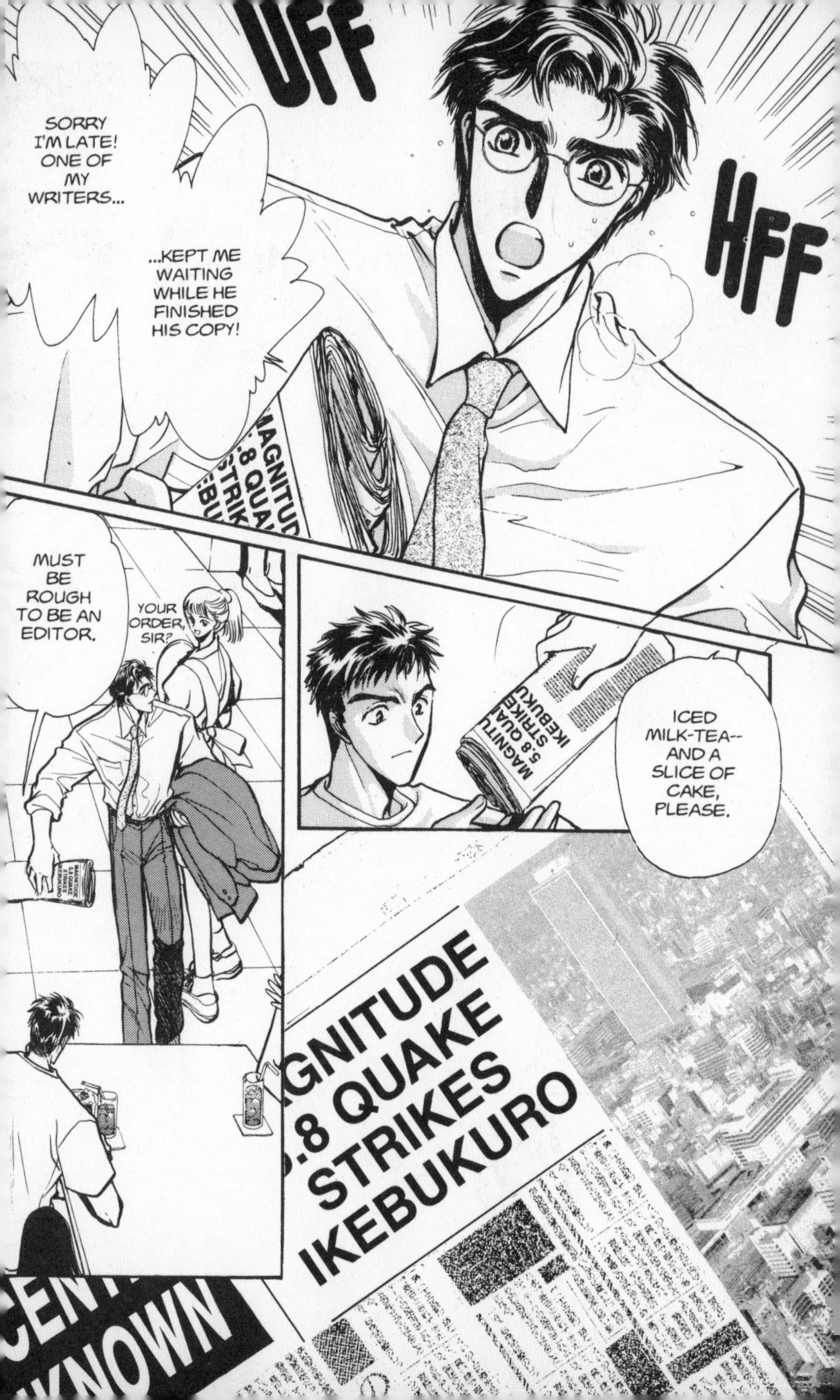
UFF
SORRY I'M LATE! ONE OF MY WRITERS...
...KEPT ME WAITING WHILE HE FINISHED HIS COPY!
HFF
MUST BE ROUGH TO BE AN EDITOR.
YOUR ORDER, SIR?
ICED MILK-TEA-- AND A SLICE OF CAKE, PLEASE.
MAGNITUDE 5.8 QUAKE STRIKES IKEBUKURO
GNITUDE
.8 QUAKE
STRIKES
IKEBUKURO
KNOWN

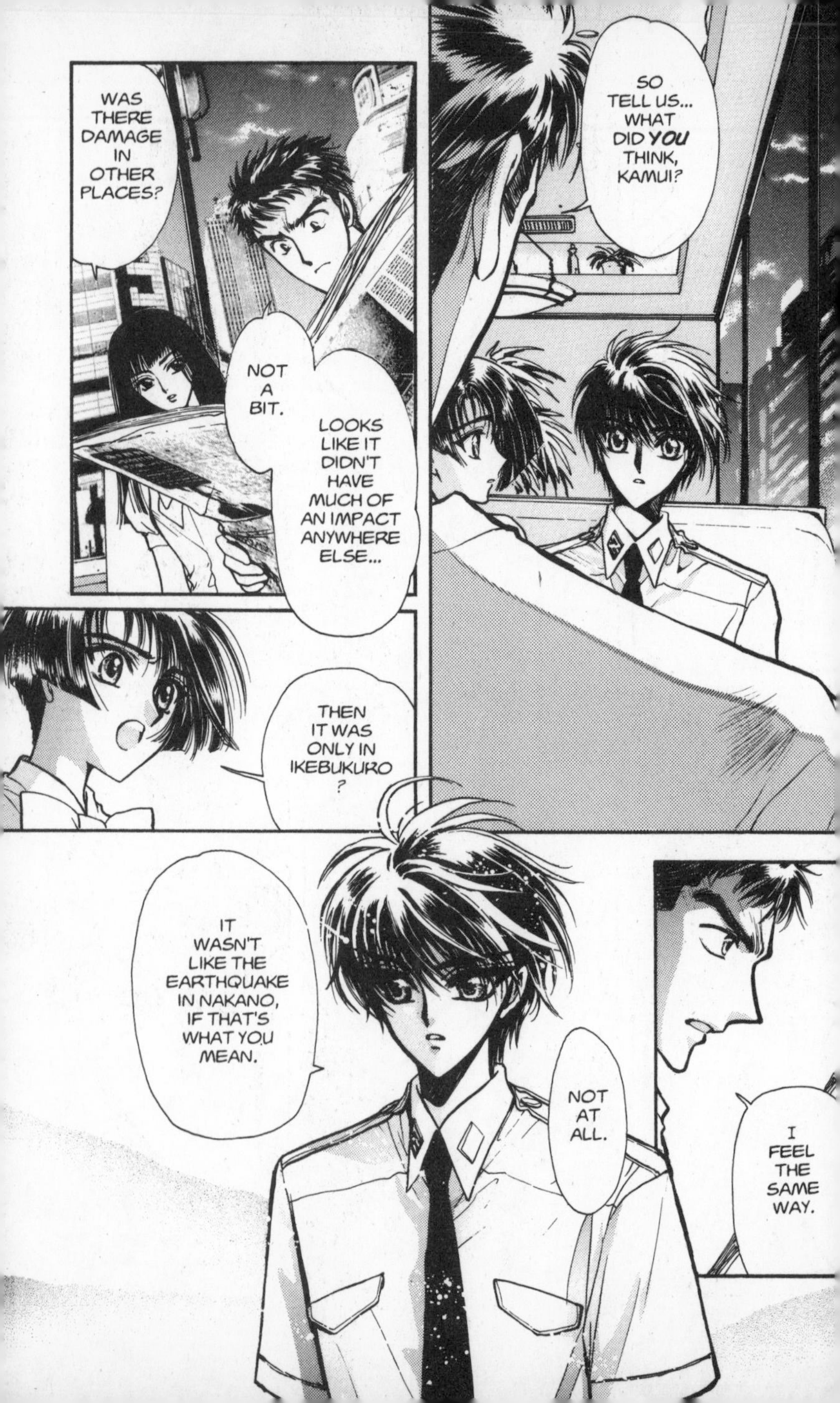
WAS THERE DAMAGE IN OTHER PLACES?
NOT A BIT.
LOOKS LIKE IT DIDN'T HAVE MUCH OF AN IMPACT ANYWHERE ELSE...
THEN IT WAS ONLY IN IKEBUKURO?
SO TELL US... WHAT DID YOU THINK, KAMUI?
IT WASN'T LIKE THE EARTHQUAKE IN NAKANO, IF THAT'S WHAT YOU MEAN.
NOT AT ALL.
I FEEL THE SAME WAY.

AND YET...

...I CAN'T HELP BUT FEEL LIKE *IT* WAS HERE.

WHAT DO YOU MEAN?

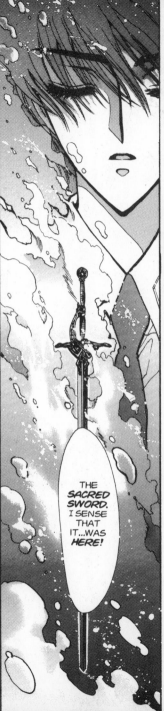

THE *SACRED SWORD*. I SENSE THAT IT...WAS *HERE!*

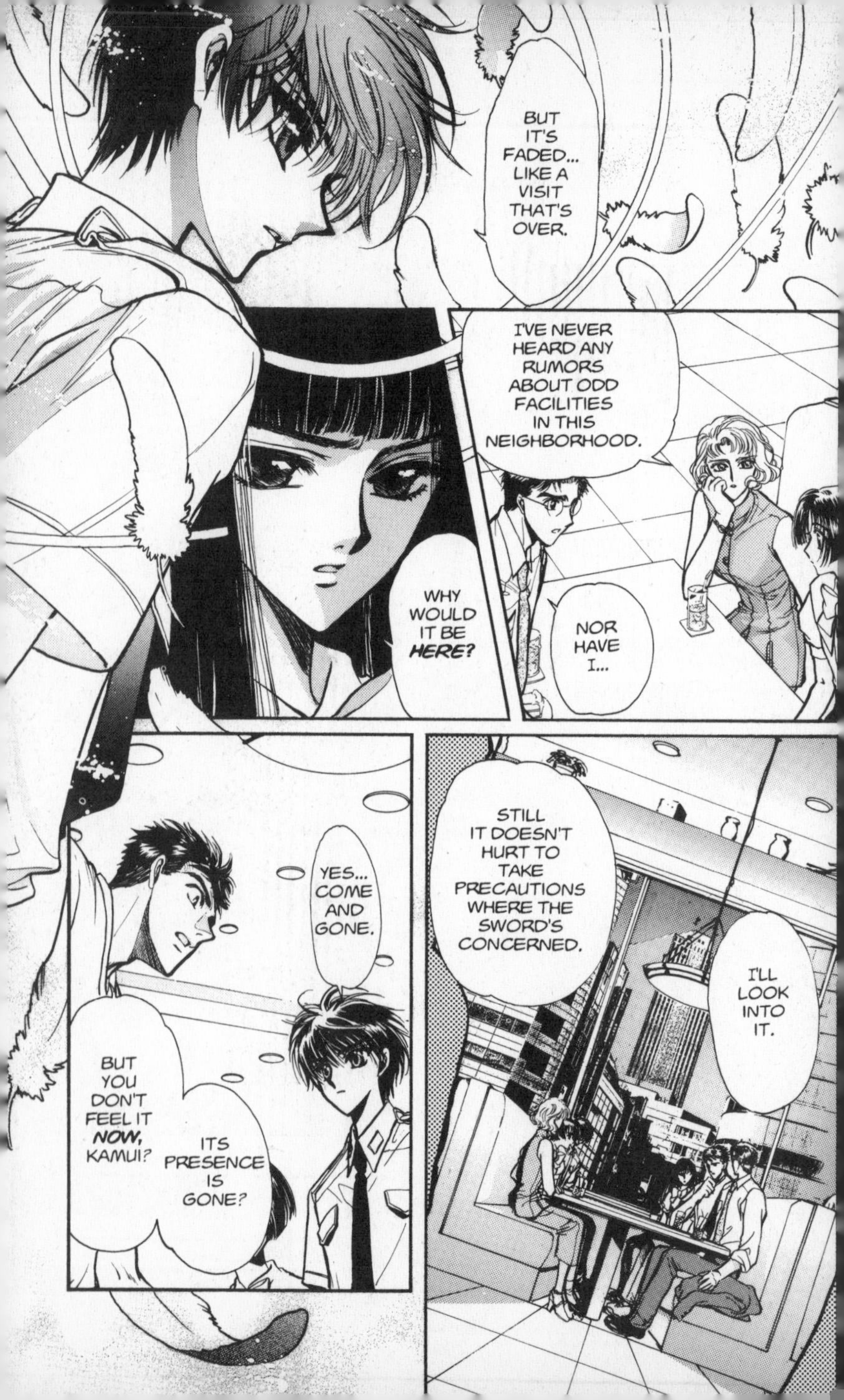
BUT IT'S FADED... LIKE A VISIT THAT'S OVER.
WHY WOULD IT BE *HERE?*
I'VE NEVER HEARD ANY RUMORS ABOUT ODD FACILITIES IN THIS NEIGHBORHOOD.
NOR HAVE I...
YES... COME AND GONE.
BUT YOU DON'T FEEL IT *NOW,* KAMUI?
ITS PRESENCE IS GONE?
STILL IT DOESN'T HURT TO TAKE PRECAUTIONS WHERE THE SWORD'S CONCERNED.
I'LL LOOK INTO IT.

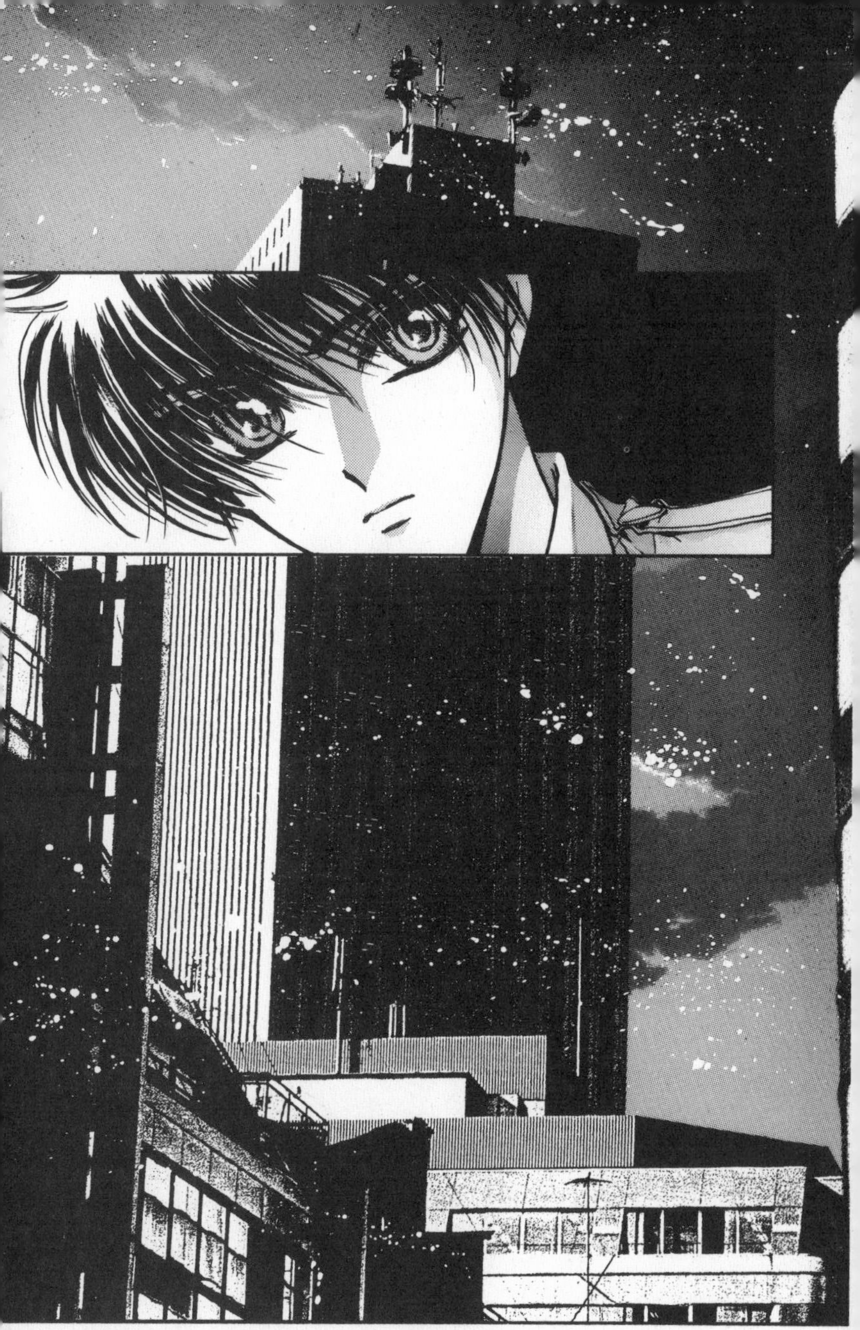

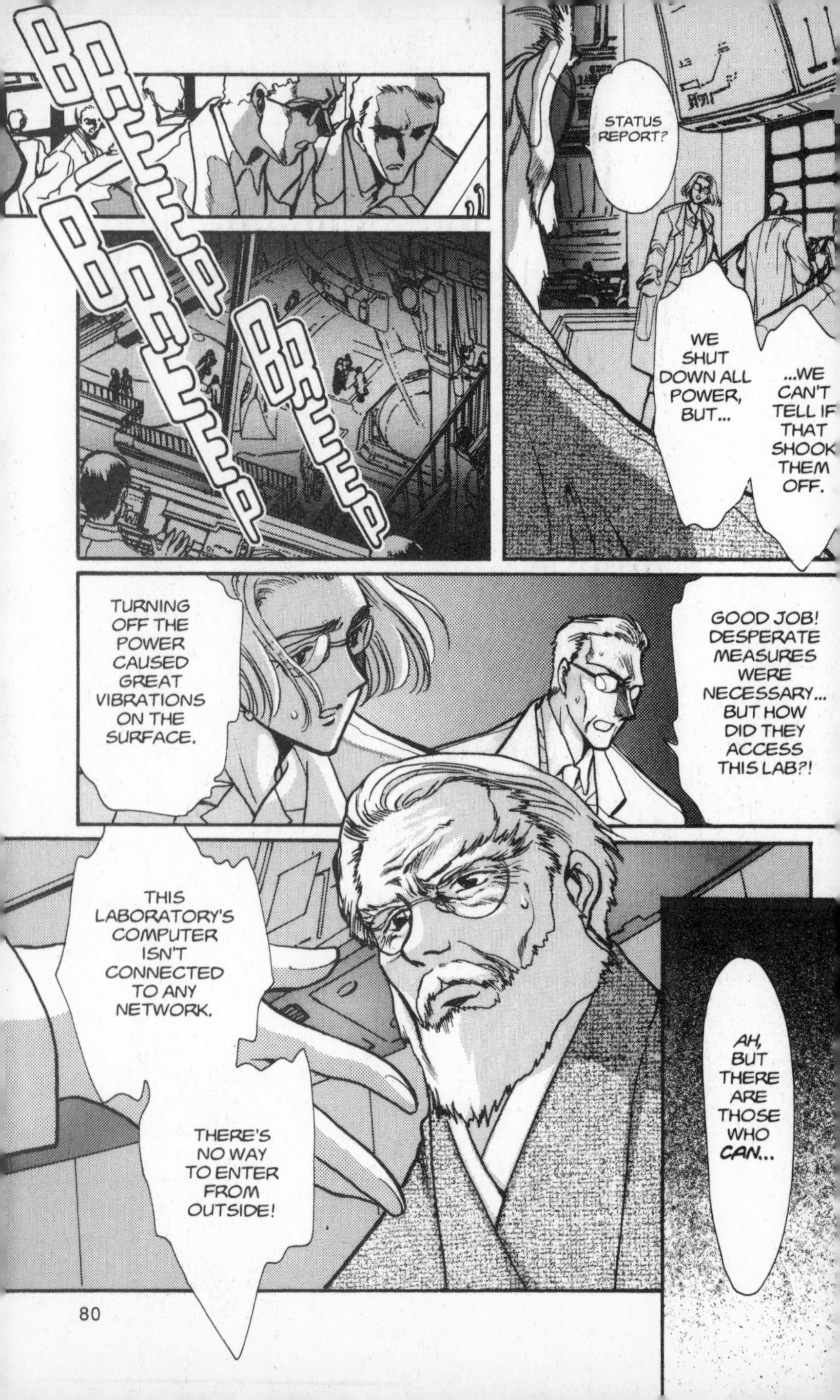
STATUS REPORT?
WE SHUT DOWN ALL POWER, BUT...
...WE CAN'T TELL IF THAT SHOOK THEM OFF.
TURNING OFF THE POWER CAUSED GREAT VIBRATIONS ON THE SURFACE.
GOOD JOB! DESPERATE MEASURES WERE NECESSARY... BUT HOW DID THEY ACCESS THIS LAB?!
THIS LABORATORY'S COMPUTER ISN'T CONNECTED TO ANY NETWORK.
THERE'S NO WAY TO ENTER FROM OUTSIDE!
AH, BUT THERE ARE THOSE WHO *CAN*...

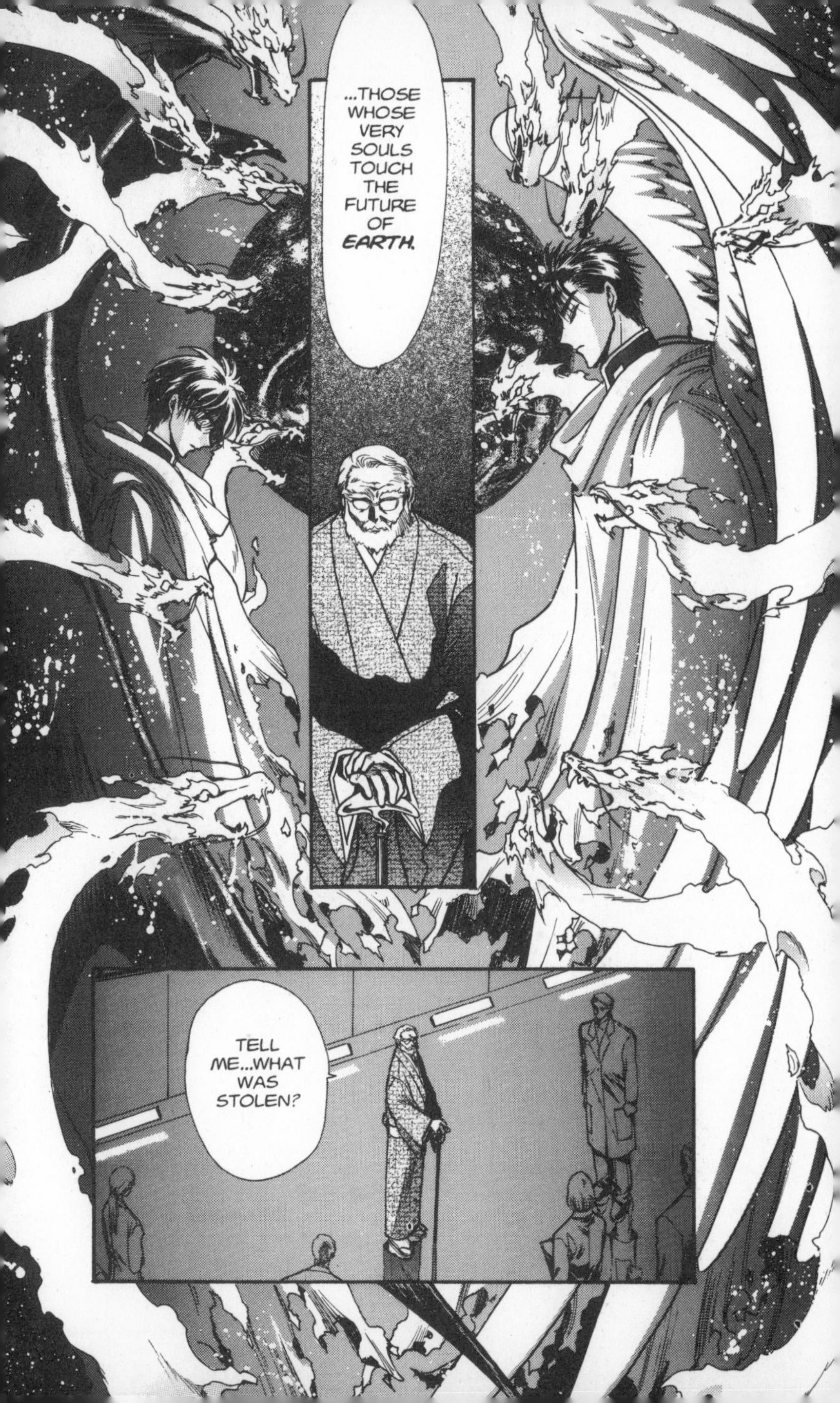
...THOSE WHOSE VERY SOULS TOUCH THE FUTURE OF EARTH.
TELL ME...WHAT WAS STOLEN?

EVERYTHING
THEY
ACCESSED...
WAS DATA
PERTAINING
TO *NATAKU!*

Bip
Bip
Bip

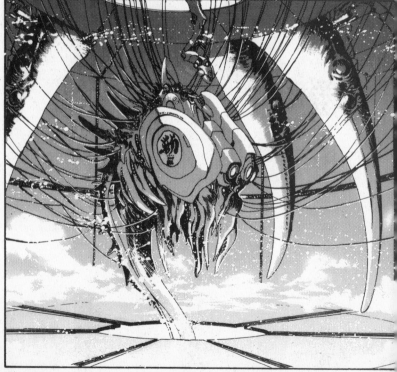

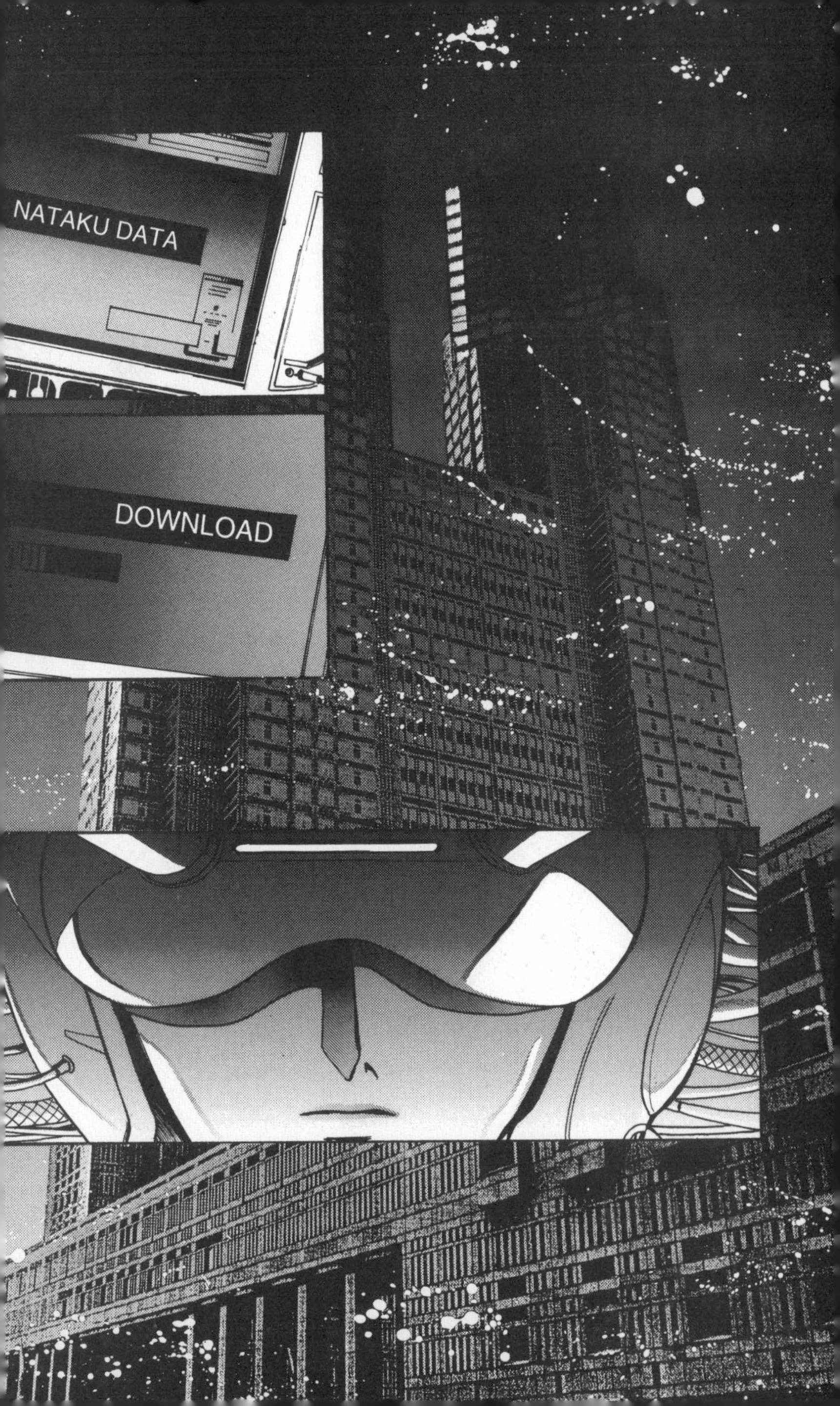
NATAKU DATA
DOWNLOAD

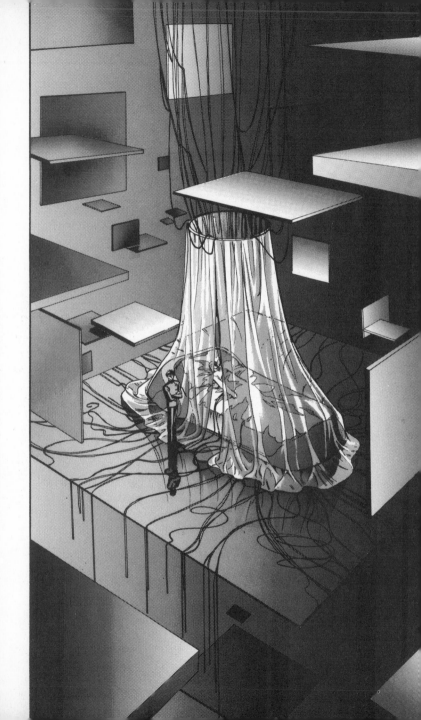

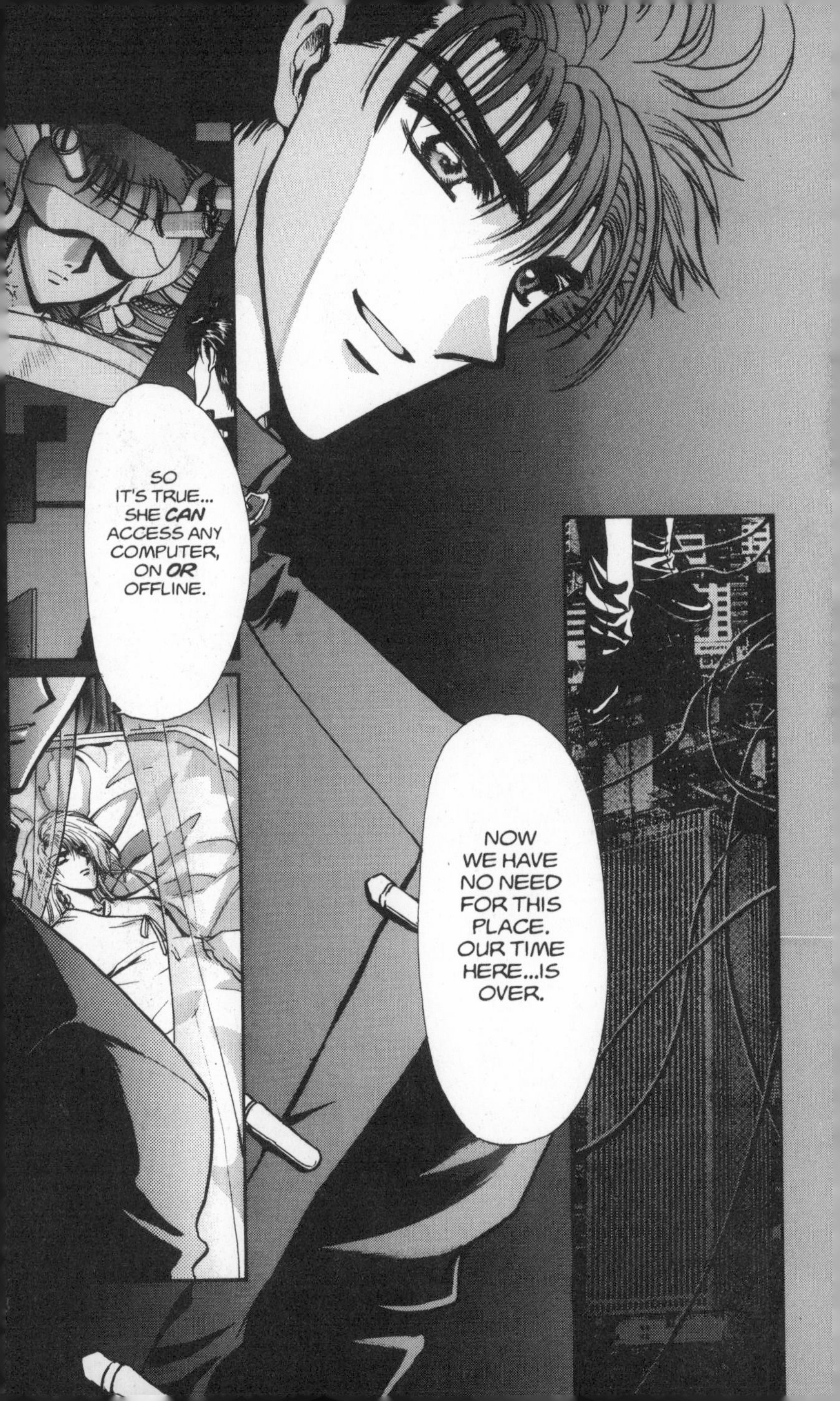
SO IT'S TRUE... SHE *CAN* ACCESS ANY COMPUTER, ON *OR* OFFLINE.
NOW WE HAVE NO NEED FOR THIS PLACE. OUR TIME HERE...IS OVER.

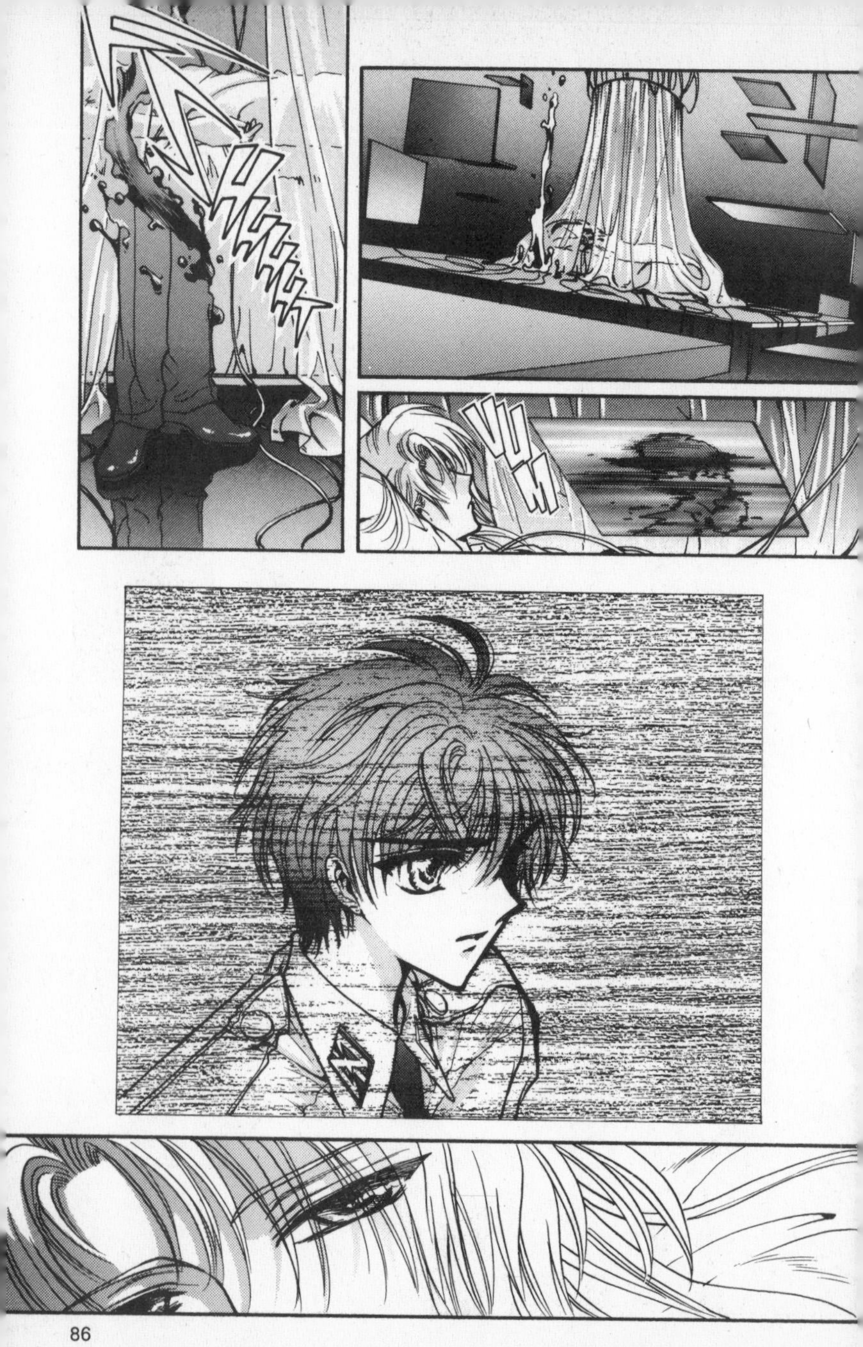
VUUM

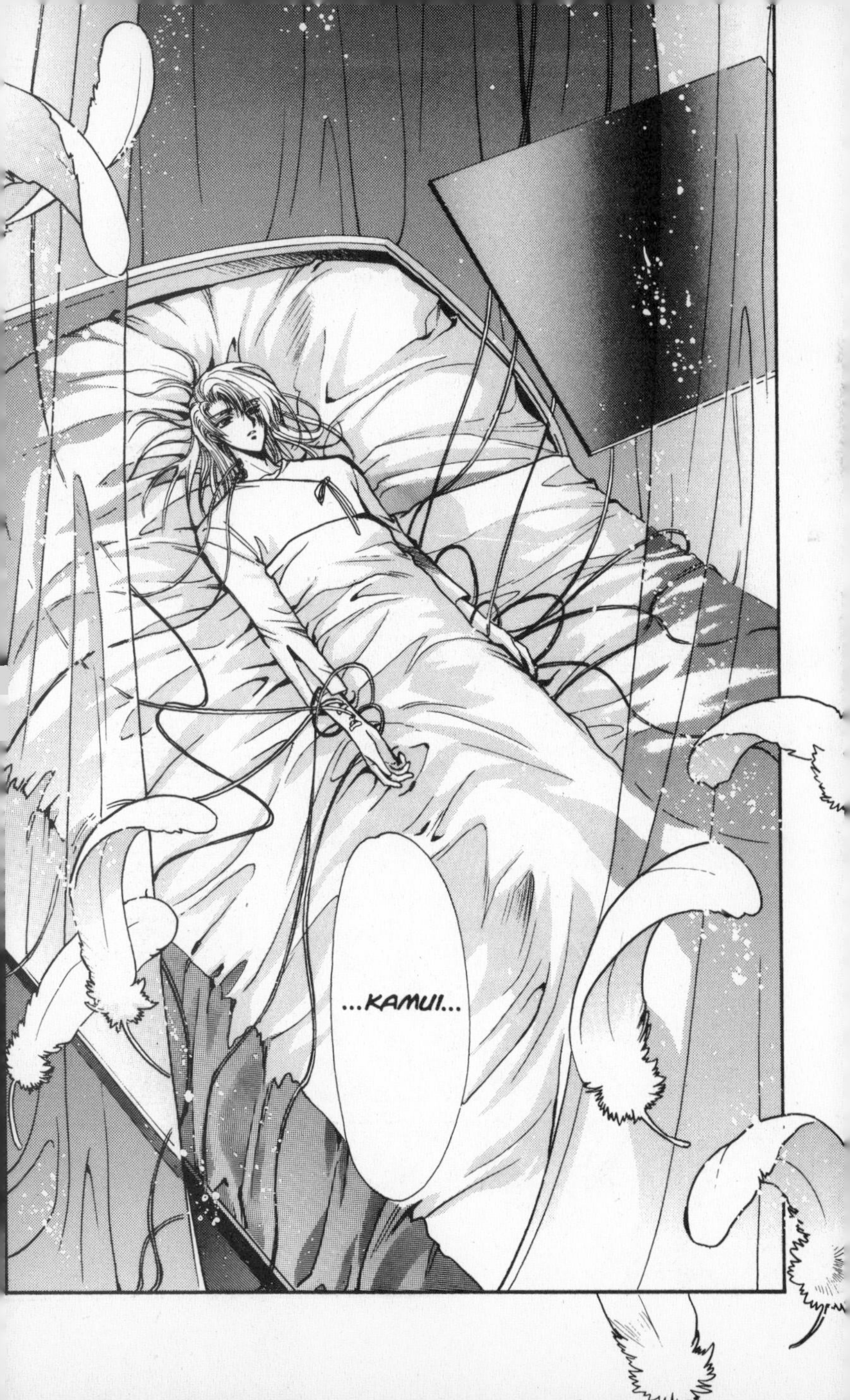
...KAMUI...

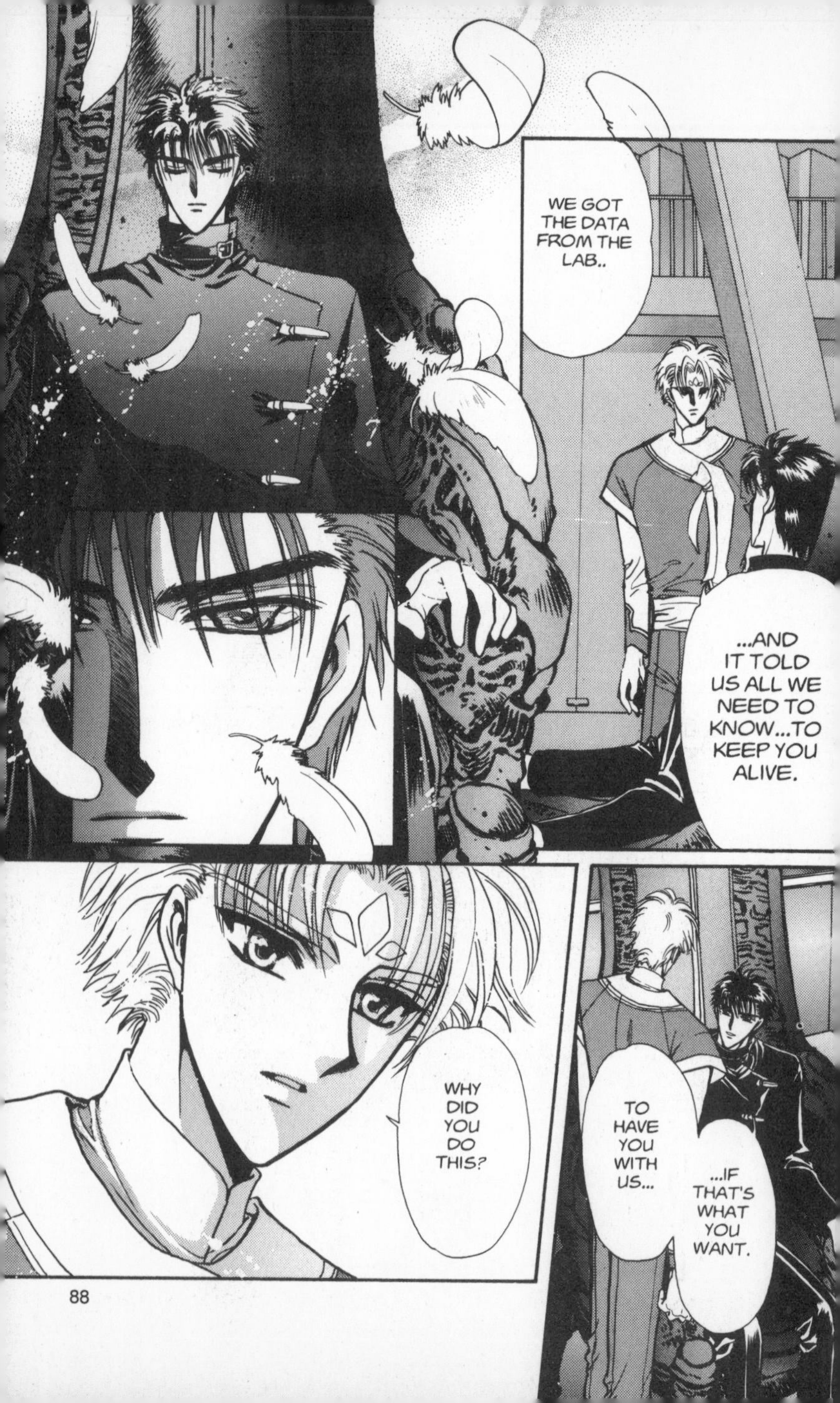
WE GOT THE DATA FROM THE LAB..
...AND IT TOLD US ALL WE NEED TO KNOW...TO KEEP YOU ALIVE.
WHY DID YOU DO THIS?
TO HAVE YOU WITH US...
...IF THAT'S WHAT YOU WANT.

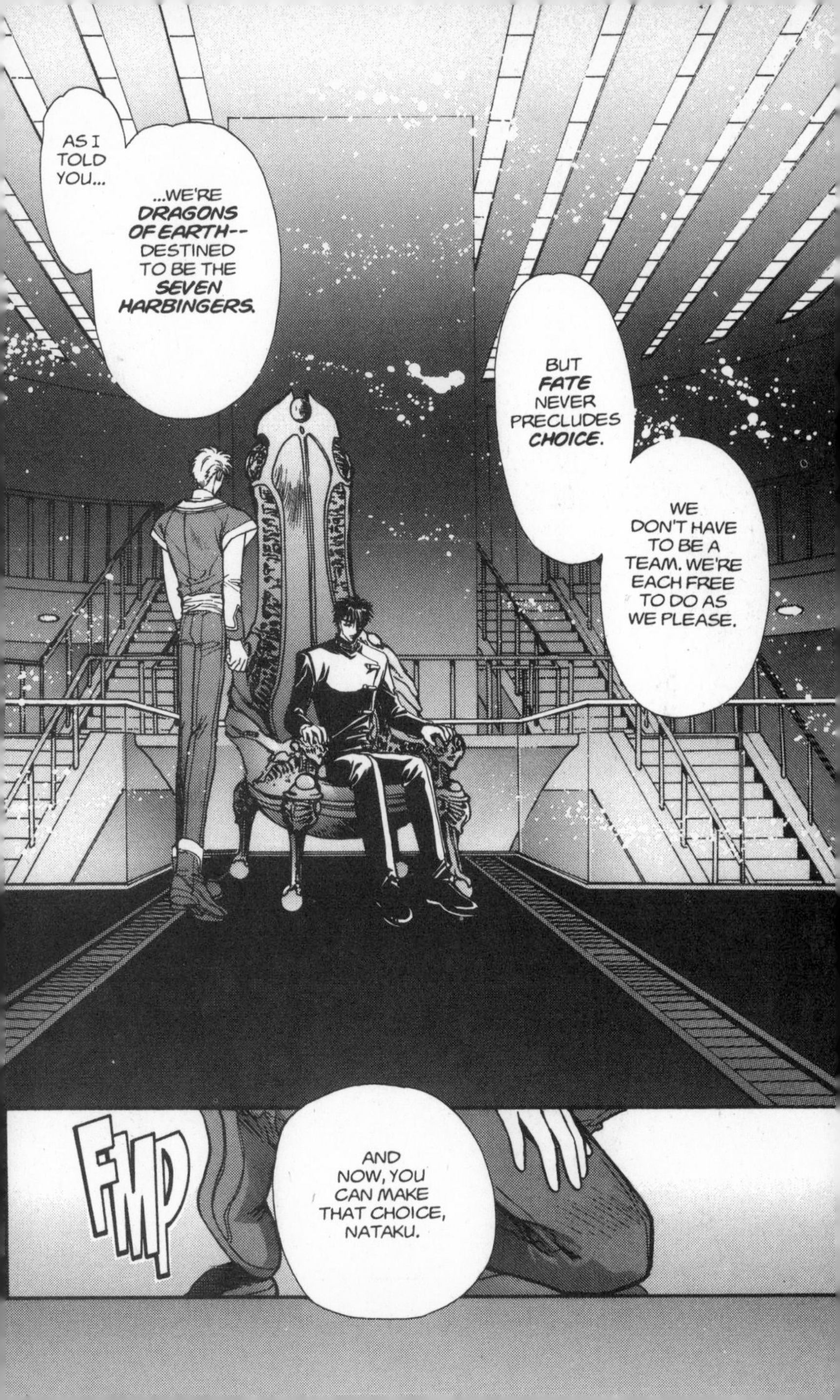
AS I TOLD YOU...
...WE'RE ***DRAGONS OF EARTH***-- DESTINED TO BE THE ***SEVEN HARBINGERS.***
BUT ***FATE*** NEVER PRECLUDES ***CHOICE.***
WE DON'T HAVE TO BE A TEAM. WE'RE EACH FREE TO DO AS WE PLEASE.
FMP
AND NOW, YOU CAN MAKE THAT CHOICE, NATAKU.

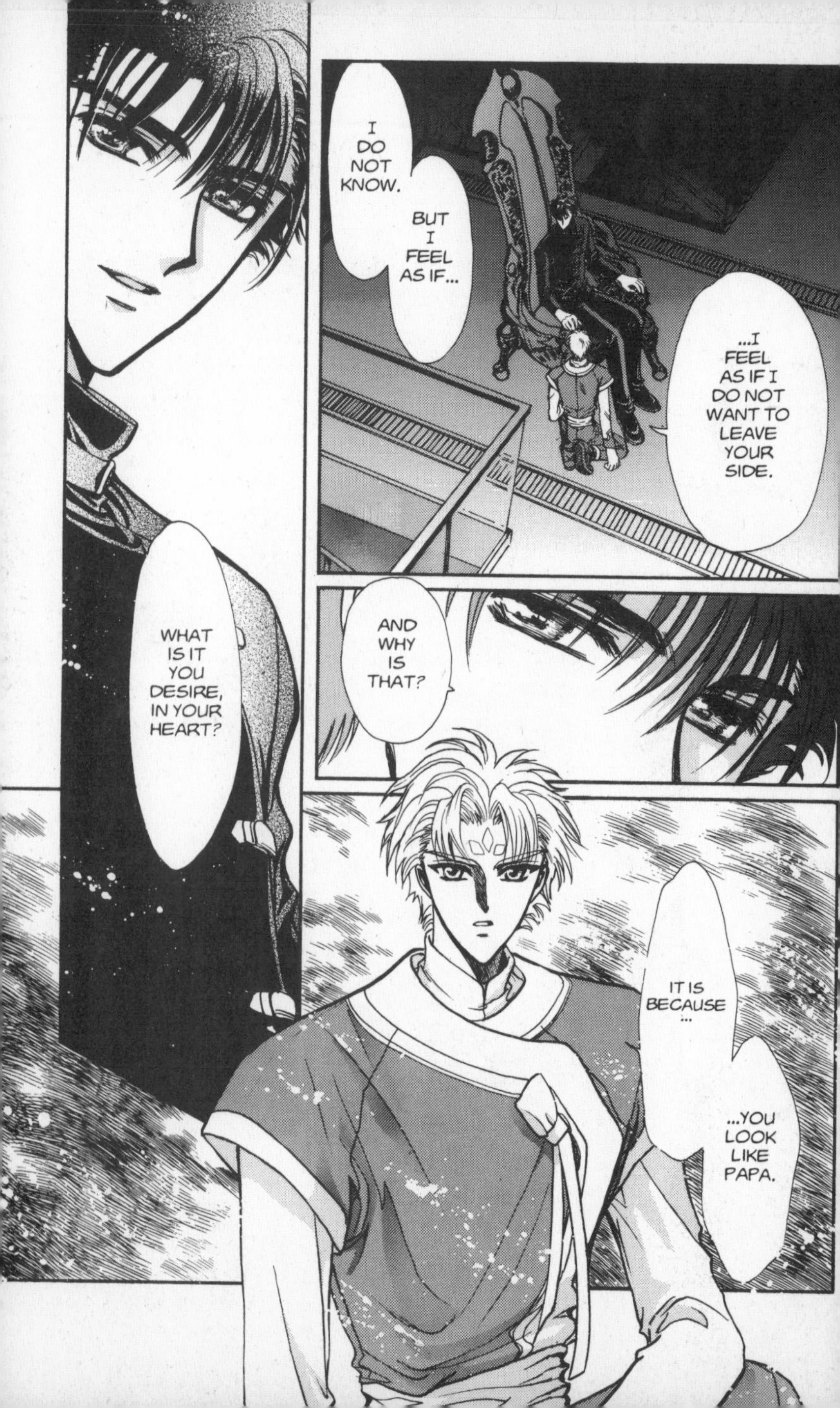
WHAT IS IT YOU DESIRE, IN YOUR HEART?
I DO NOT KNOW.
BUT I FEEL AS IF...
...I FEEL AS IF I DO NOT WANT TO LEAVE YOUR SIDE.
AND WHY IS THAT?
IT IS BECAUSE...
...YOU LOOK LIKE PAPA.

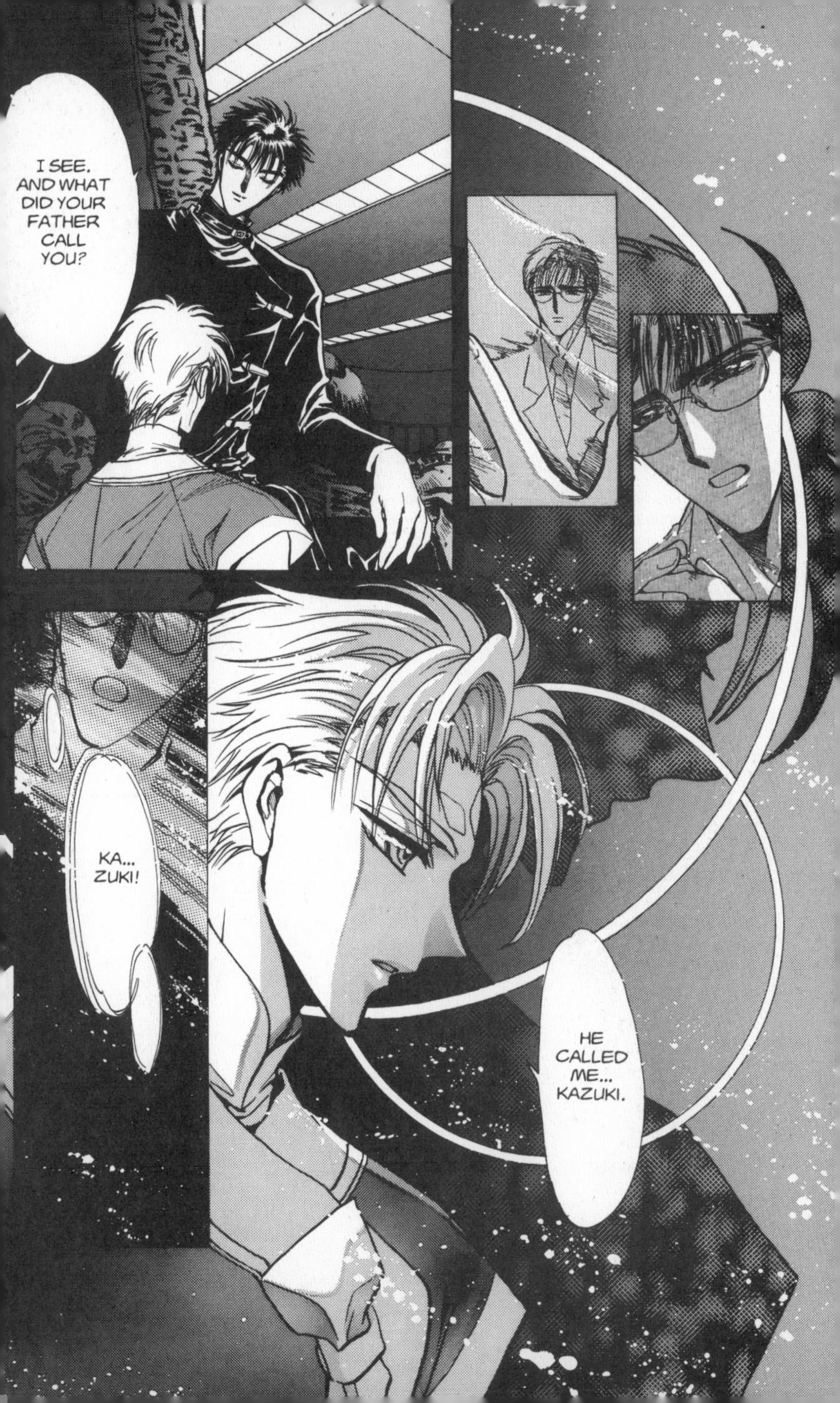
I SEE. AND WHAT DID YOUR FATHER CALL YOU?
KA... ZUKI!
HE CALLED ME... KAZUKI.

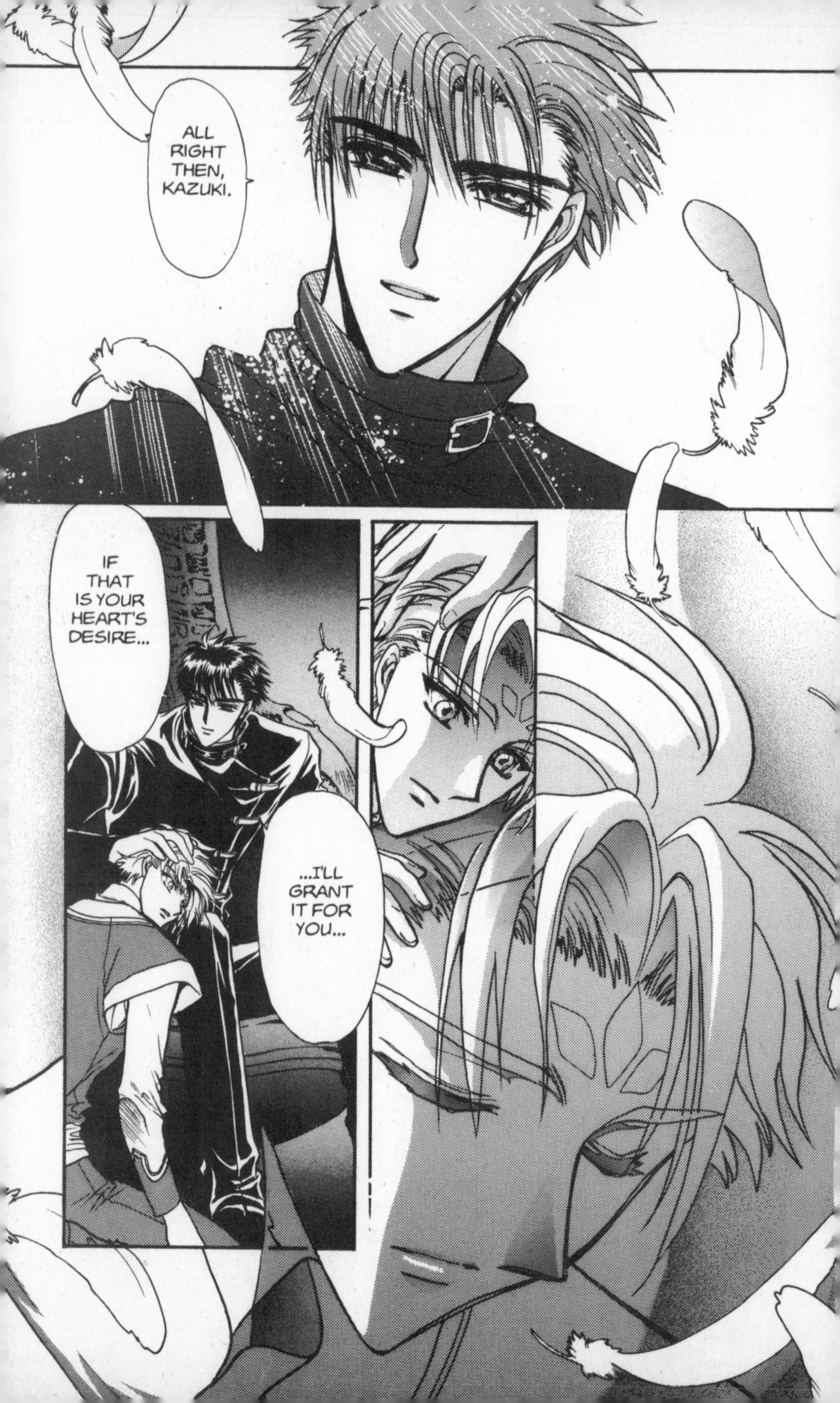
ALL RIGHT THEN, KAZUKI.
IF THAT IS YOUR HEART'S DESIRE...
...I'LL GRANT IT FOR YOU...

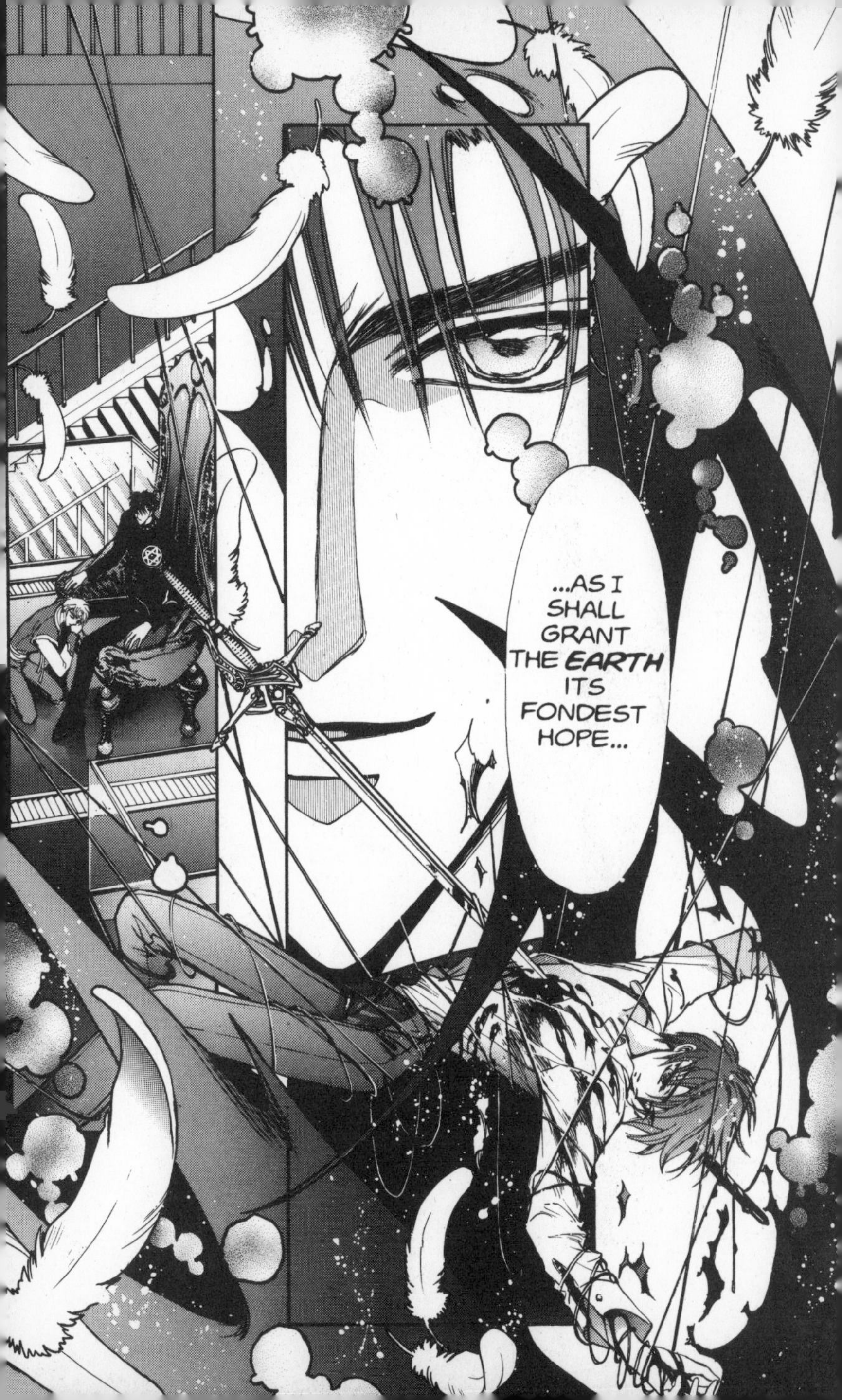
...AS I SHALL GRANT THE EARTH ITS FONDEST HOPE...

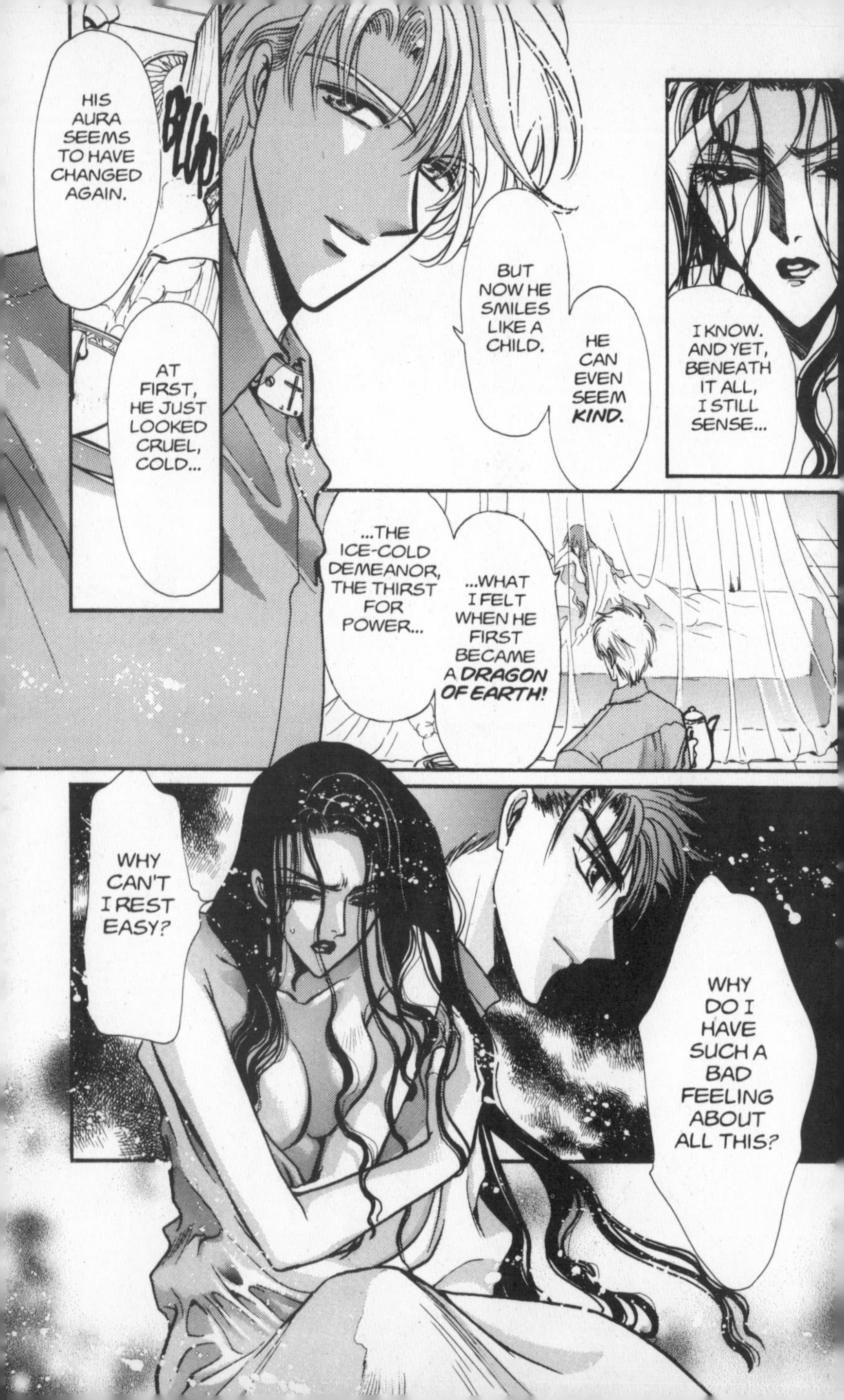
HIS AURA SEEMS TO HAVE CHANGED AGAIN.
BLUP
AT FIRST, HE JUST LOOKED CRUEL, COLD...
BUT NOW HE SMILES LIKE A CHILD.
HE CAN EVEN SEEM KIND.
I KNOW. AND YET, BENEATH IT ALL, I STILL SENSE...
...THE ICE-COLD DEMEANOR, THE THIRST FOR POWER...
...WHAT I FELT WHEN HE FIRST BECAME A DRAGON OF EARTH!
WHY CAN'T I REST EASY?
WHY DO I HAVE SUCH A BAD FEELING ABOUT ALL THIS?

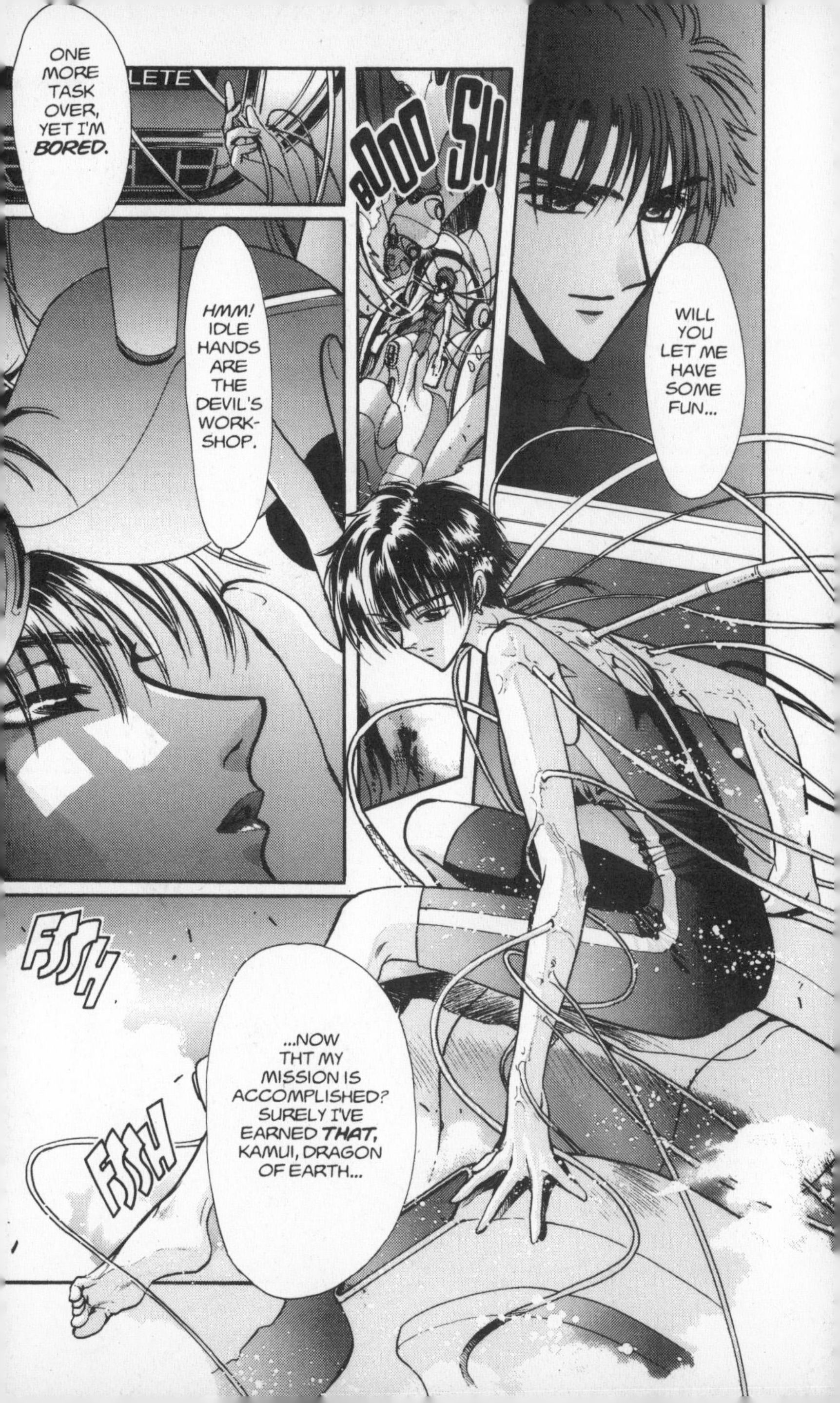

LETE
ONE MORE TASK OVER, YET I'M ***BORED***.
HMM! IDLE HANDS ARE THE DEVIL'S WORK-SHOP.
BOOOSH
WILL YOU LET ME HAVE SOME FUN...
FSSH
...NOW THT MY MISSION IS ACCOMPLISHED? SURELY I'VE EARNED ***THAT***, KAMUI, DRAGON OF EARTH...
FSSH

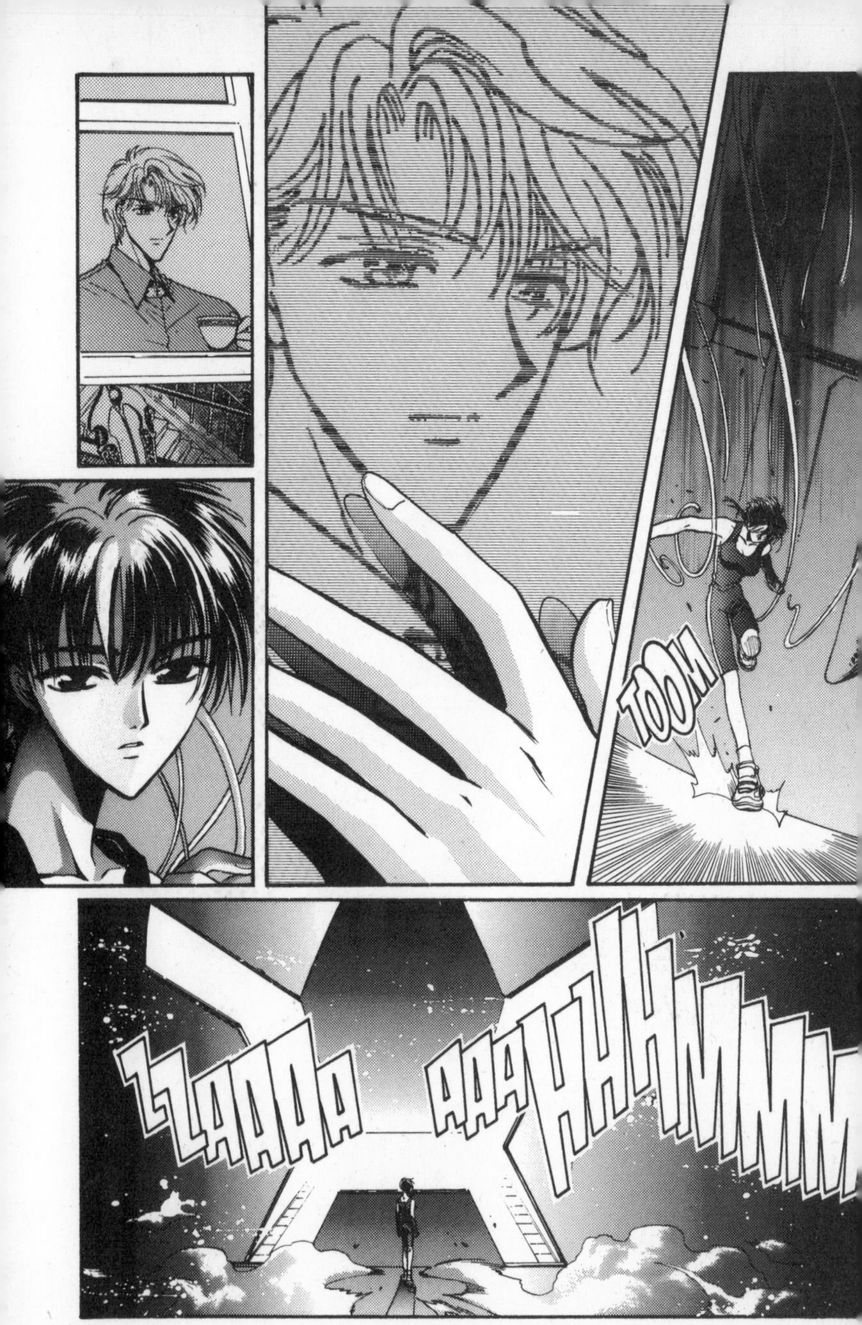
TOOM
ZZAAAA AAAHHHMMMM

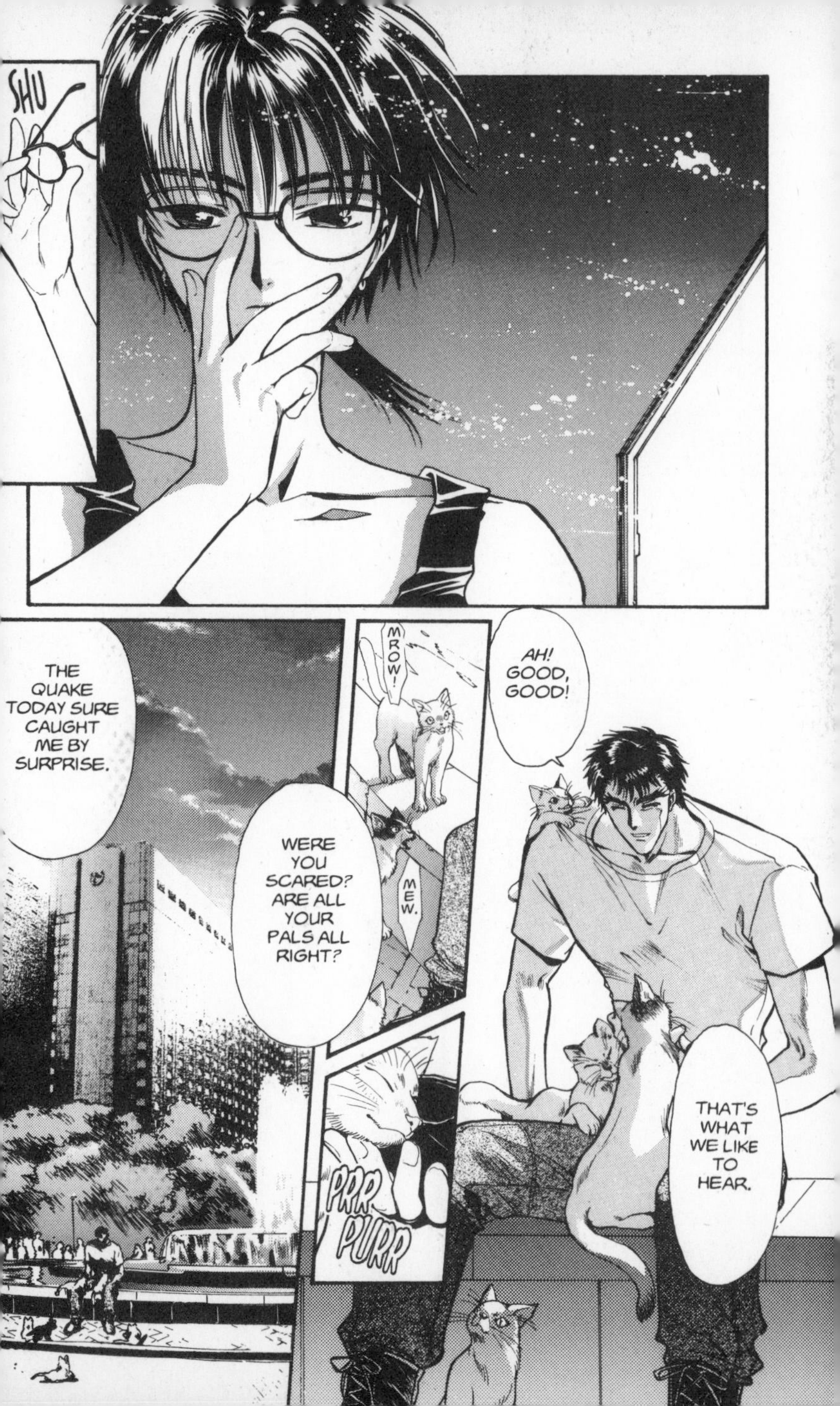
SHU
THE QUAKE TODAY SURE CAUGHT ME BY SURPRISE.
MROW!
WERE YOU SCARED? ARE ALL YOUR PALS ALL RIGHT?
MEW.
PRR PURR
AH! GOOD, GOOD!
THAT'S WHAT WE LIKE TO HEAR.

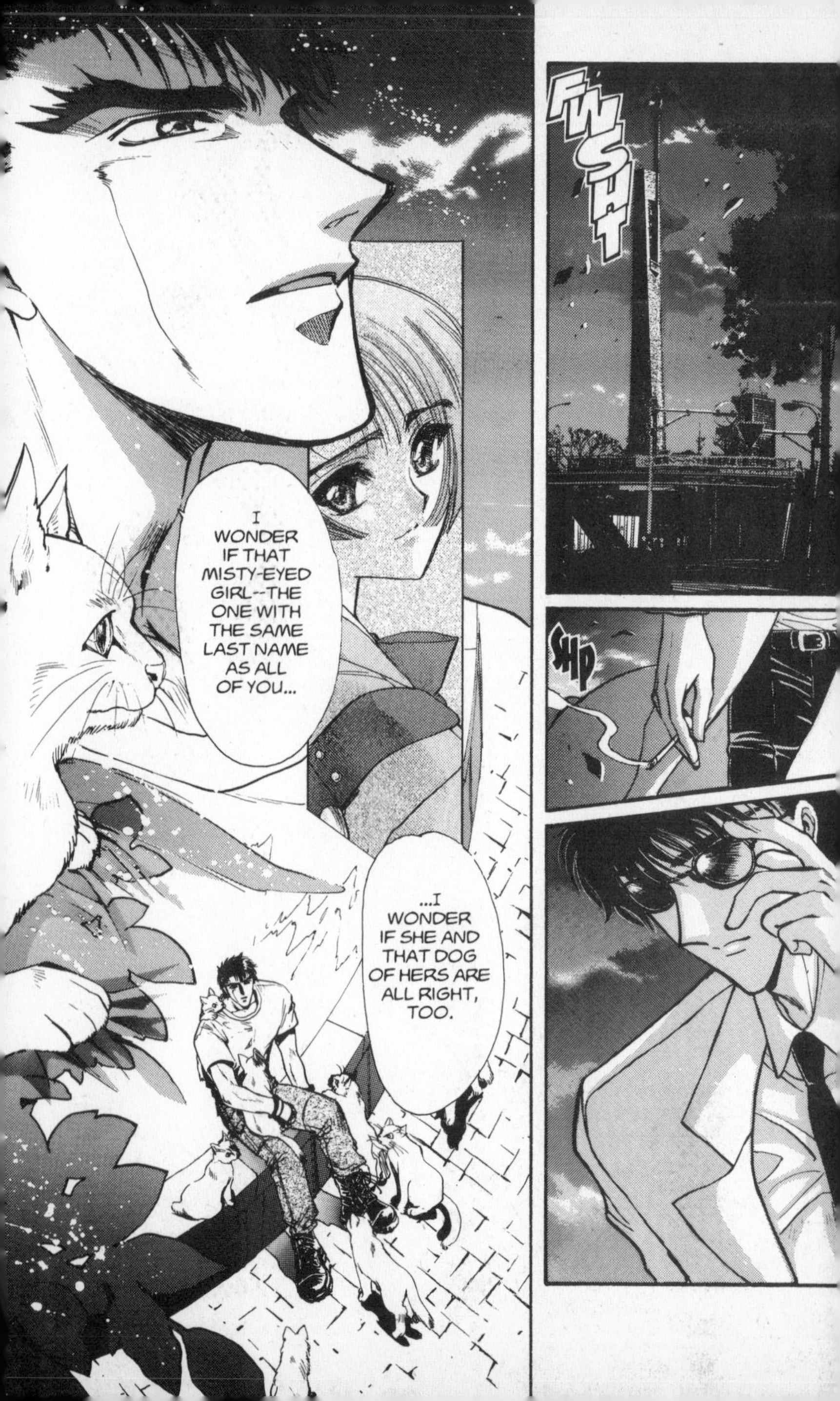
I WONDER IF THAT MISTY-EYED GIRL--THE ONE WITH THE SAME LAST NAME AS ALL OF YOU...
...I WONDER IF SHE AND THAT DOG OF HERS ARE ALL RIGHT, TOO.
FWSHAT
SHP

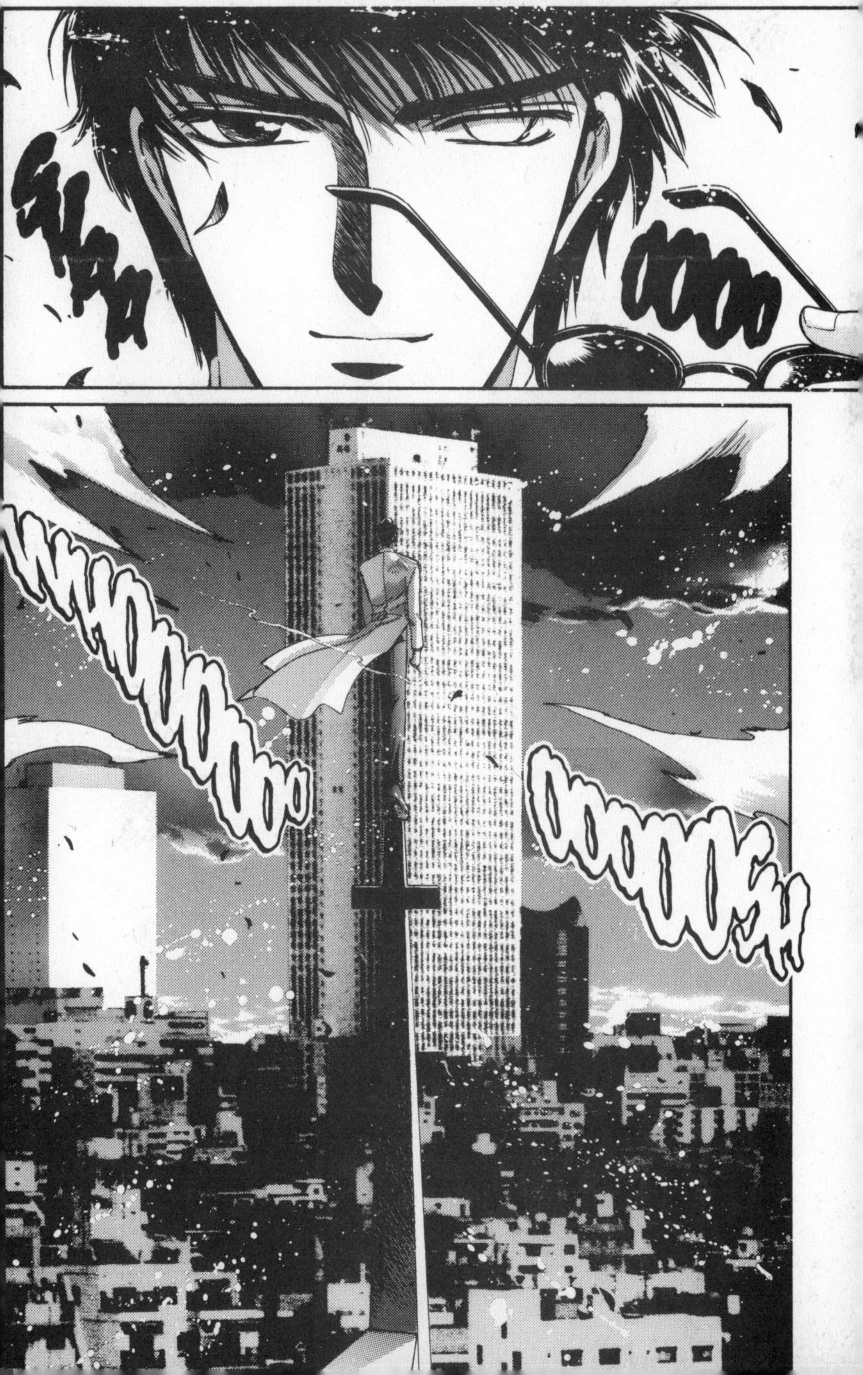
SHAA
AAAA
WHOOOOOOOO
OOOOOSH

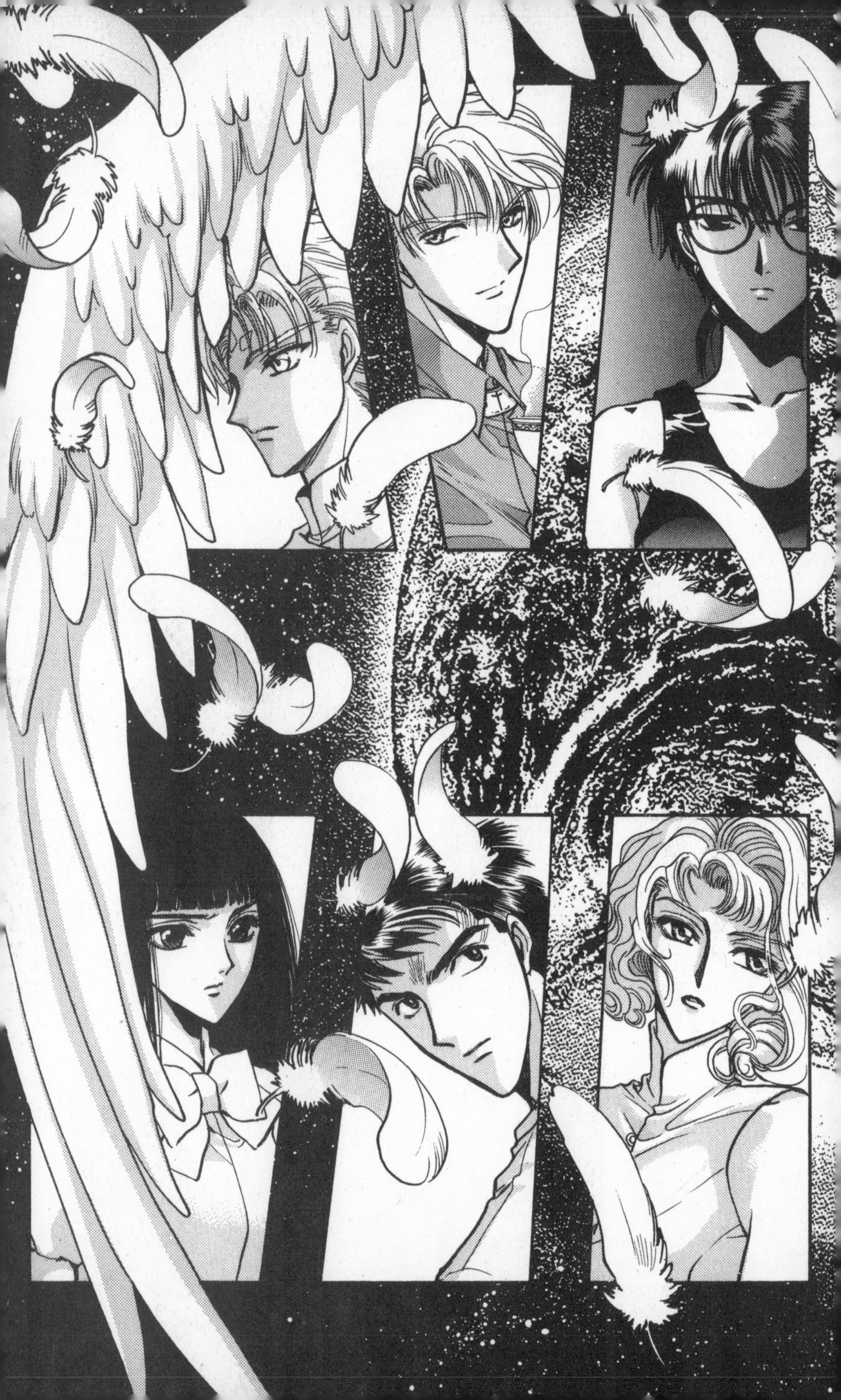

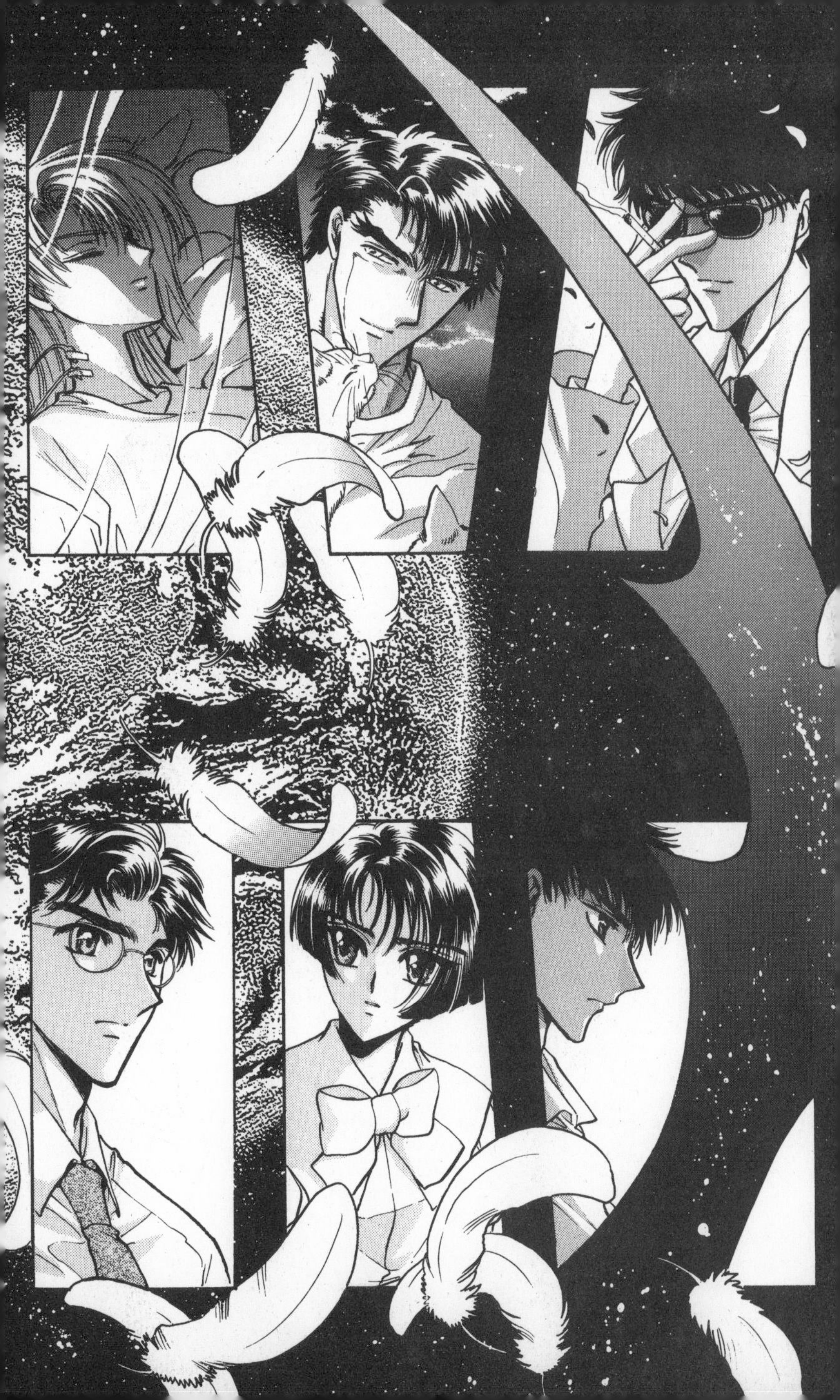

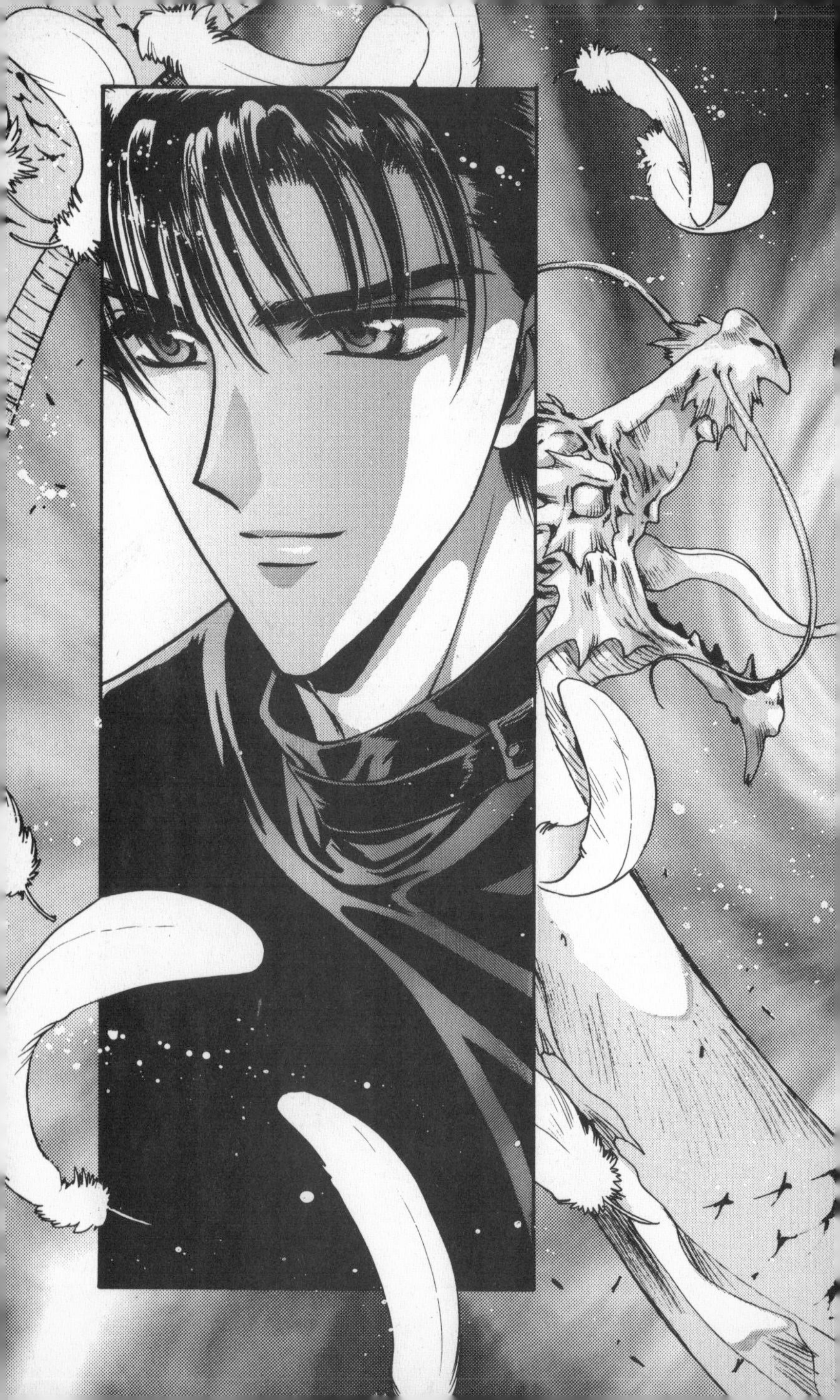

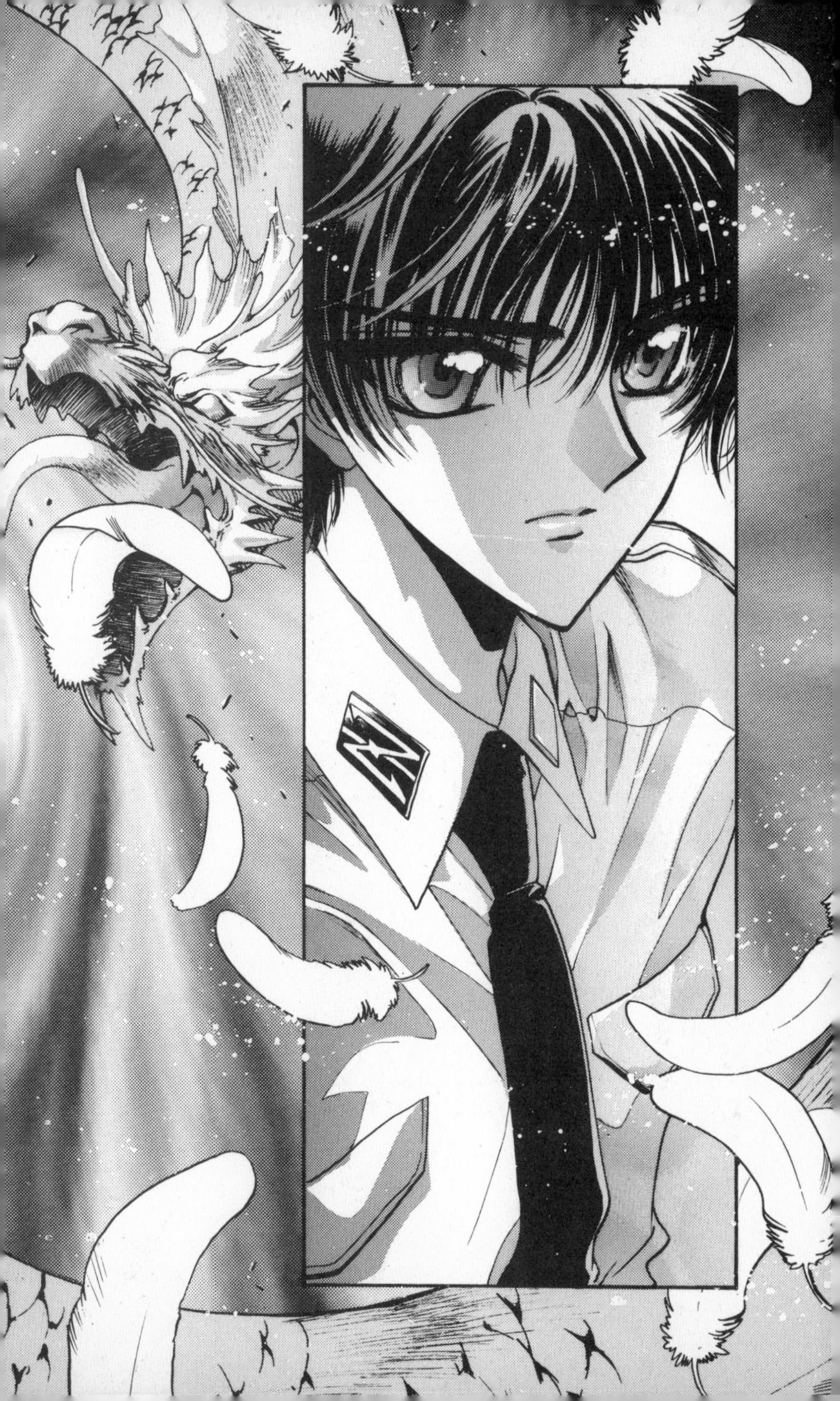

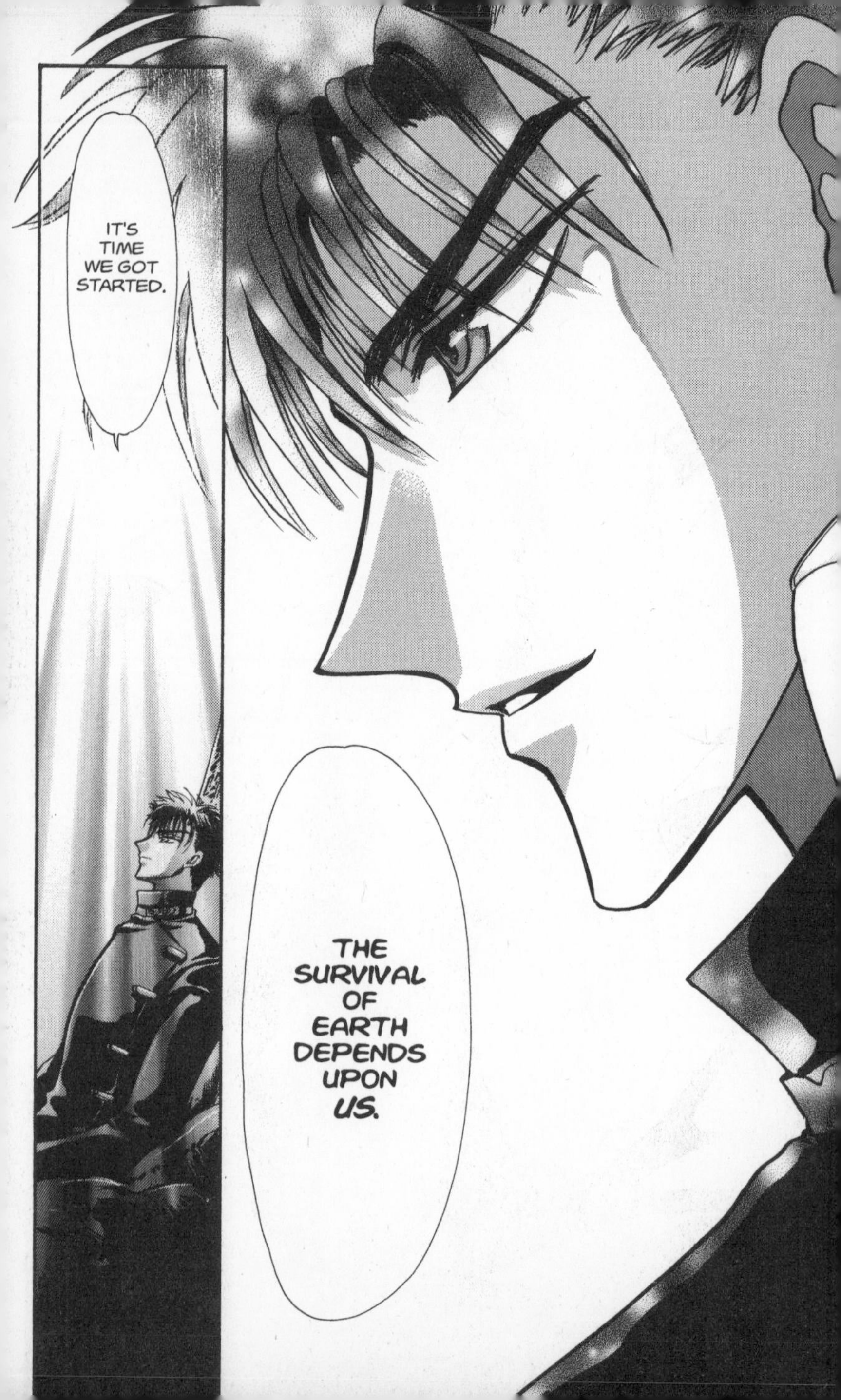
IT'S TIME WE GOT STARTED.
THE SURVIVAL OF EARTH DEPENDS UPON US.

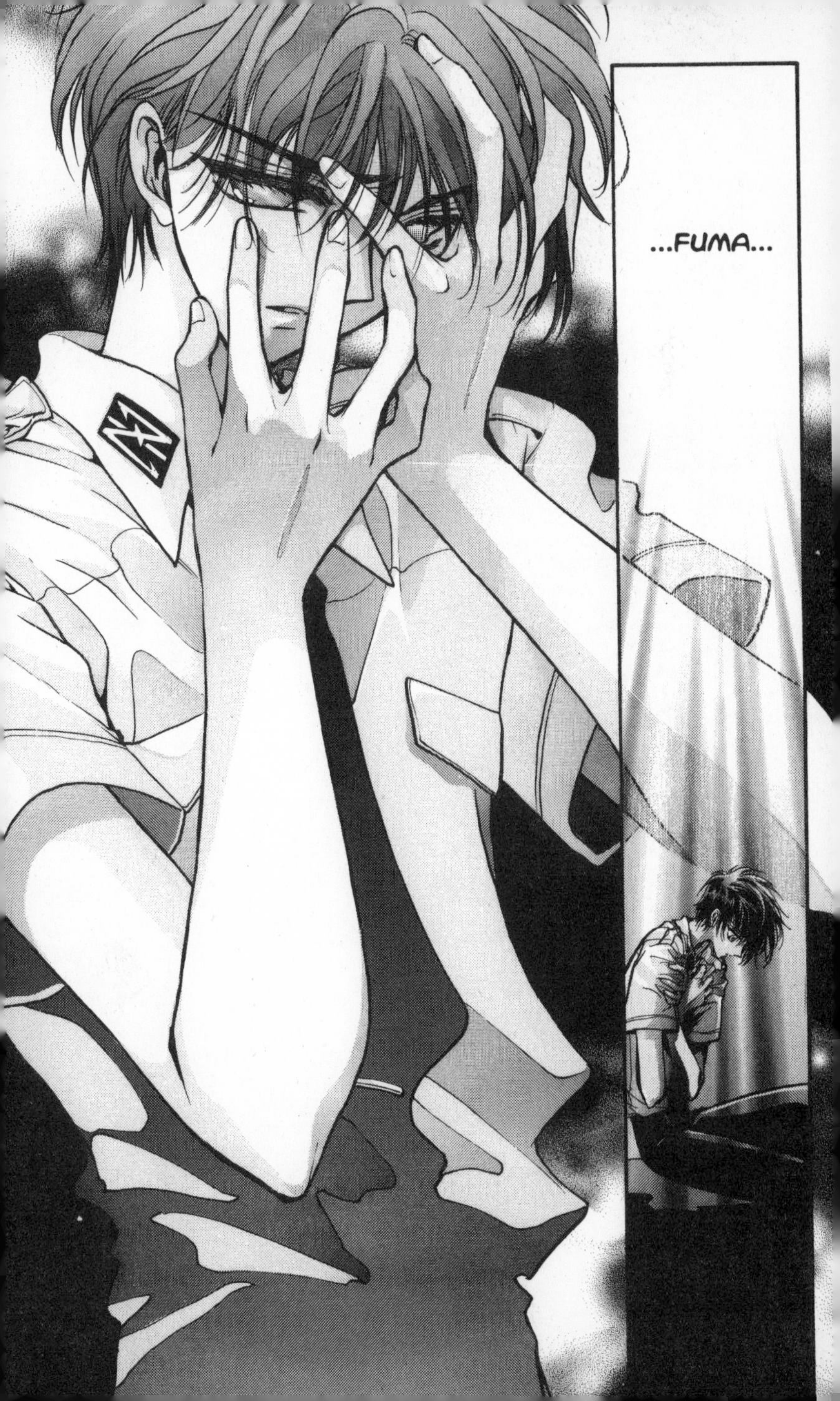
...FUMA...

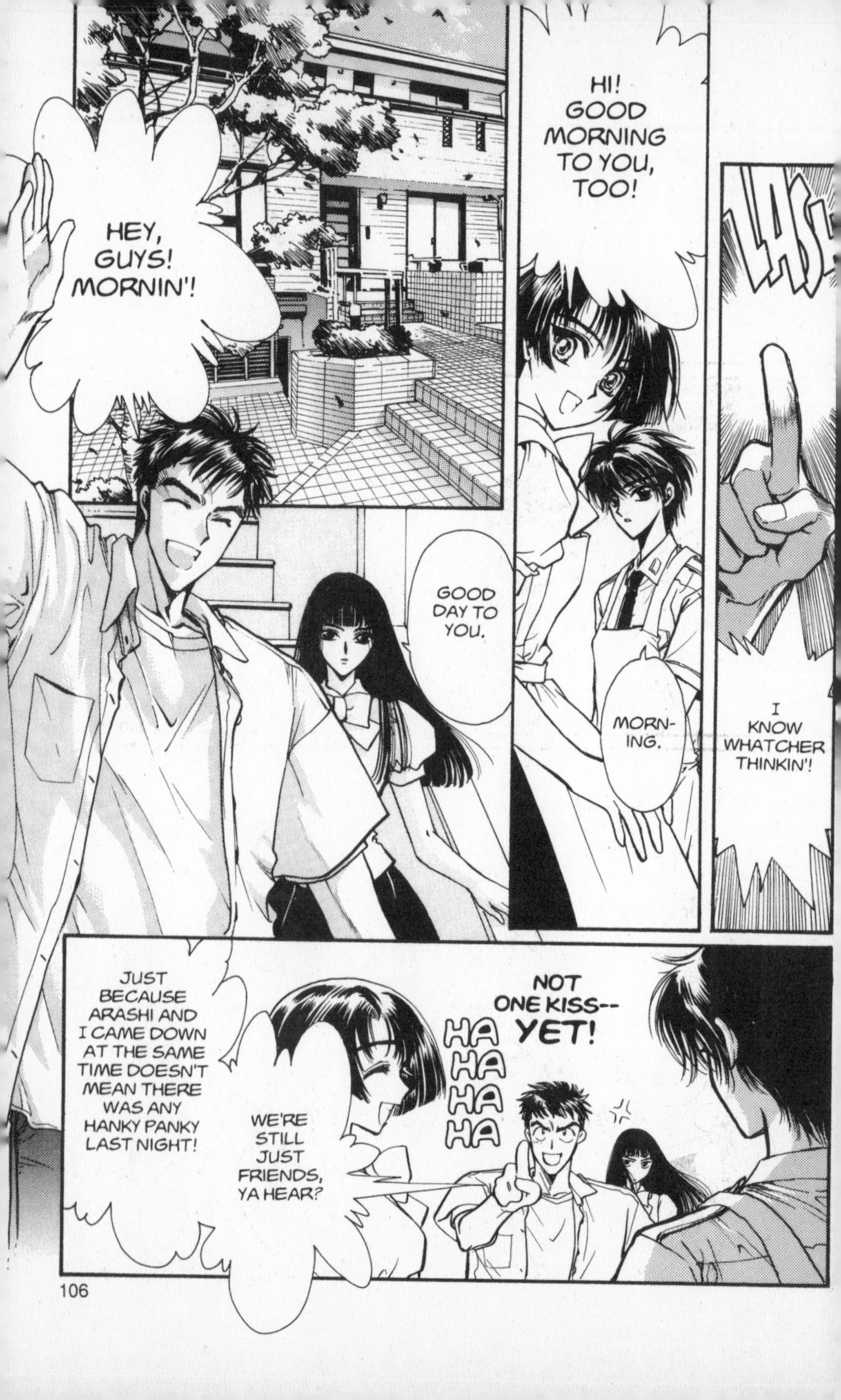
HEY, GUYS! MORNIN'!
GOOD DAY TO YOU.
HI! GOOD MORNING TO YOU, TOO!
MORN-ING.
I KNOW WHATCHER THINKIN'!
JUST BECAUSE ARASHI AND I CAME DOWN AT THE SAME TIME DOESN'T MEAN THERE WAS ANY HANKY PANKY LAST NIGHT!
WE'RE STILL JUST FRIENDS, YA HEAR?
HA HA HA HA HA
NOT ONE KISS-- YET!

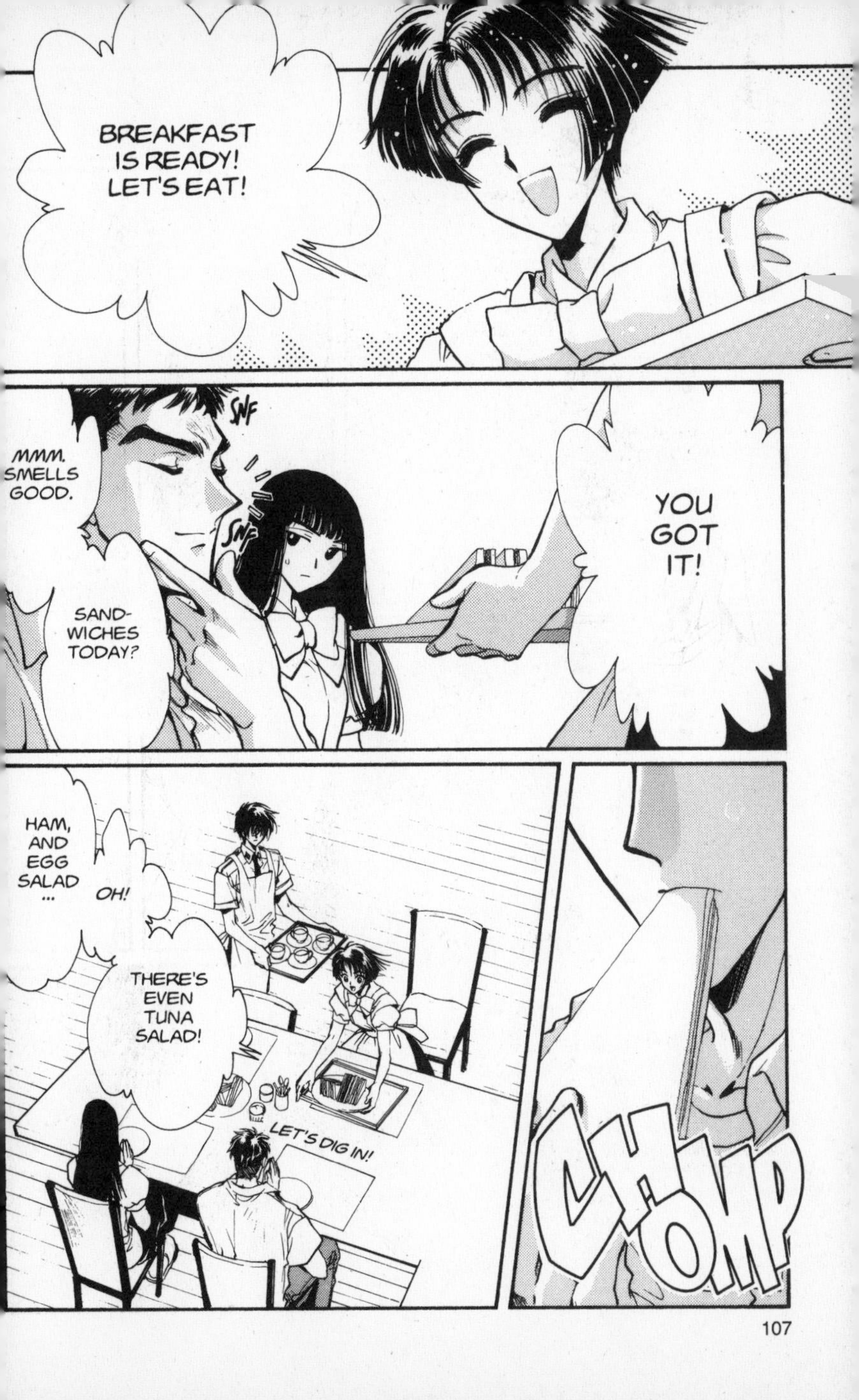
BREAKFAST IS READY! LET'S EAT!
MMM. SMELLS GOOD.
SNF
SNF
SAND-WICHES TODAY?
YOU GOT IT!
HAM, AND EGG SALAD ...
OH!
THERE'S EVEN TUNA SALAD!
LET'S DIG IN!
CHOMP

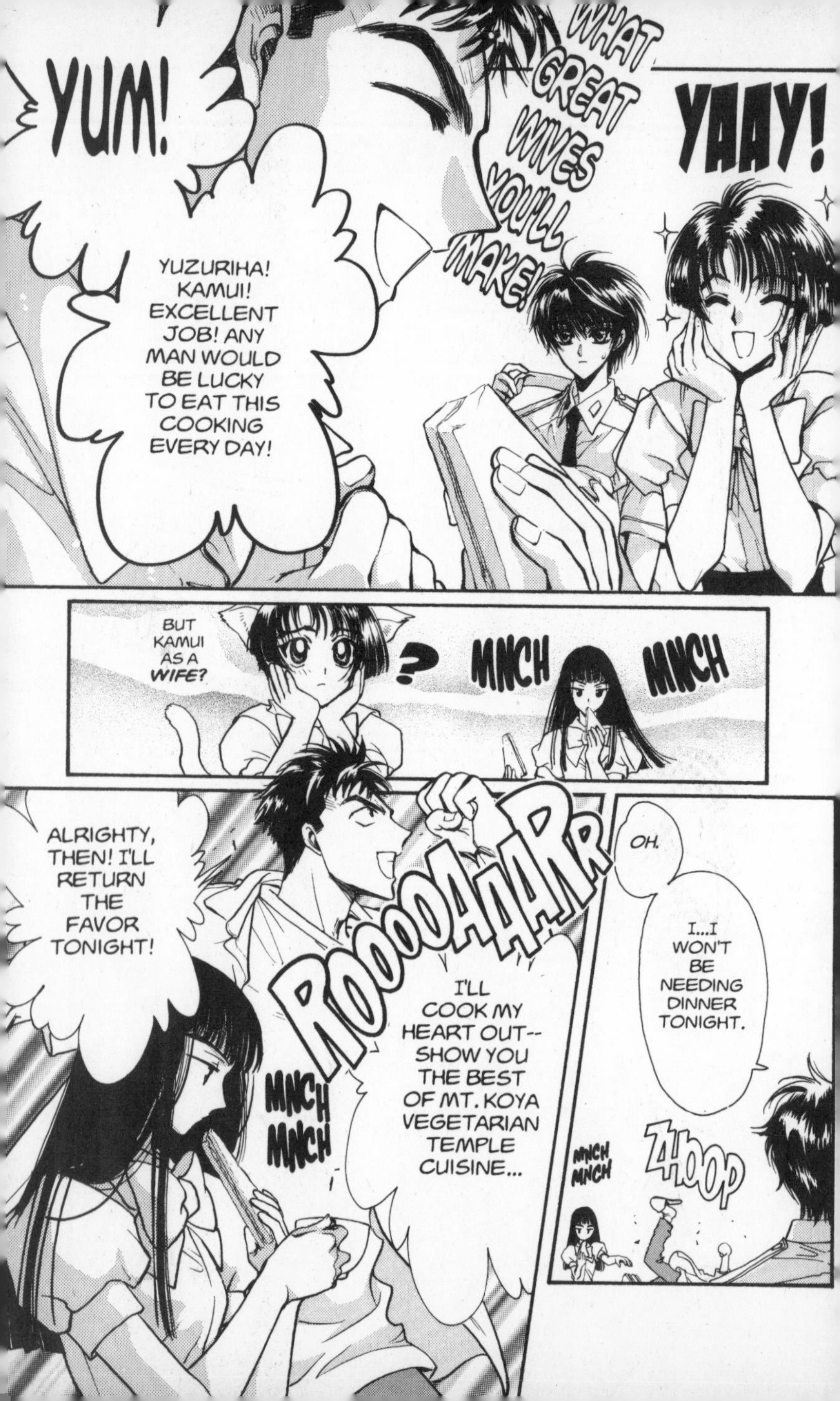
YUM!
YUZURIHA! KAMUI! EXCELLENT JOB! ANY MAN WOULD BE LUCKY TO EAT THIS COOKING EVERY DAY!
WHAT GREAT WIVES YOU'LL MAKE!
YAAY!
BUT KAMUI AS A WIFE?
?
MNCH
MNCH
ALRIGHTY, THEN! I'LL RETURN THE FAVOR TONIGHT!
ROOOOAAARR
I'LL COOK MY HEART OUT-- SHOW YOU THE BEST OF MT. KOYA VEGETARIAN TEMPLE CUISINE...
MNCH MNCH
OH.
I...I WON'T BE NEEDING DINNER TONIGHT.
MNCH MNCH
ZHOOP

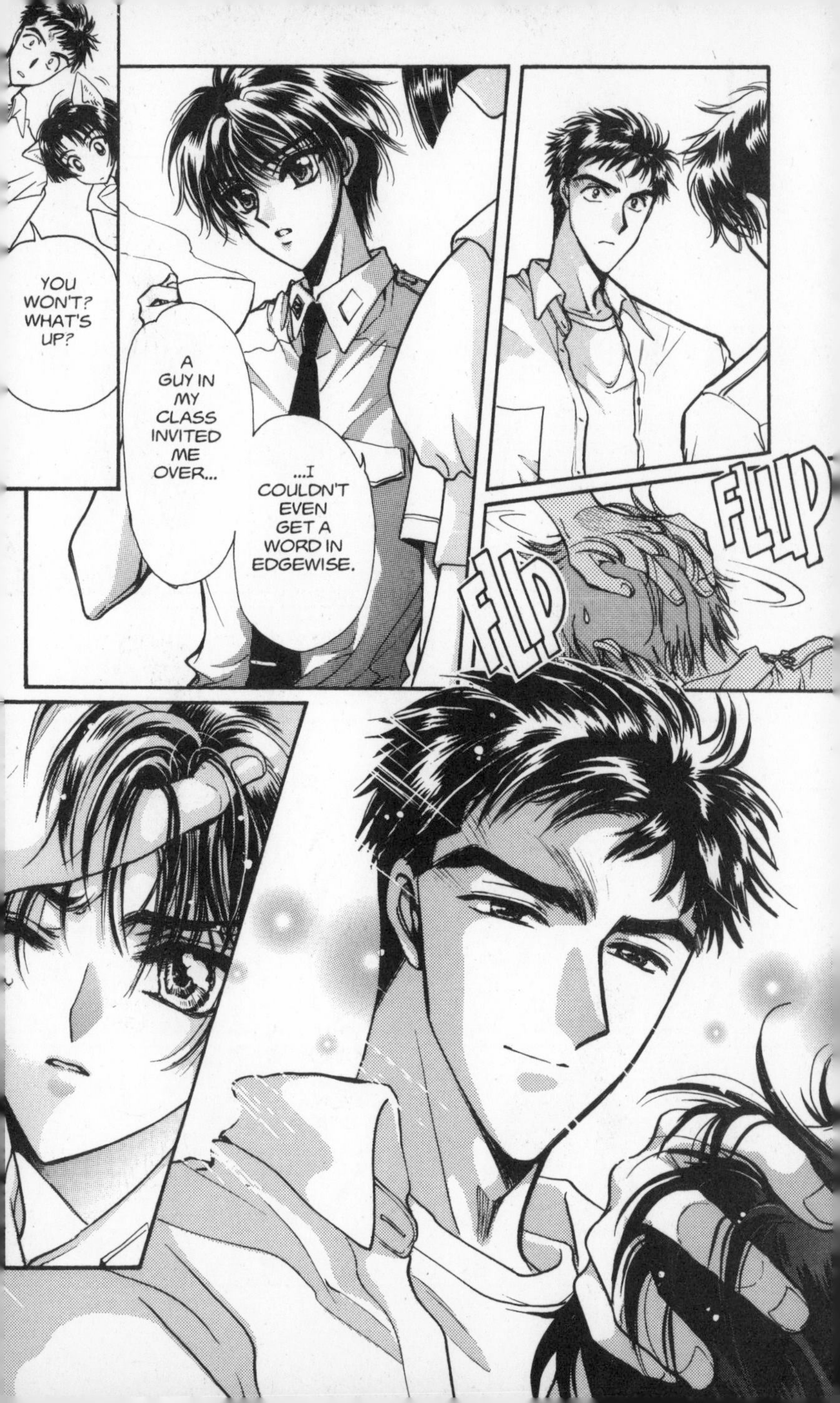
YOU WON'T? WHAT'S UP?
A GUY IN MY CLASS INVITED ME OVER...
...I COULDN'T EVEN GET A WORD IN EDGEWISE.
FLIP
FLIP

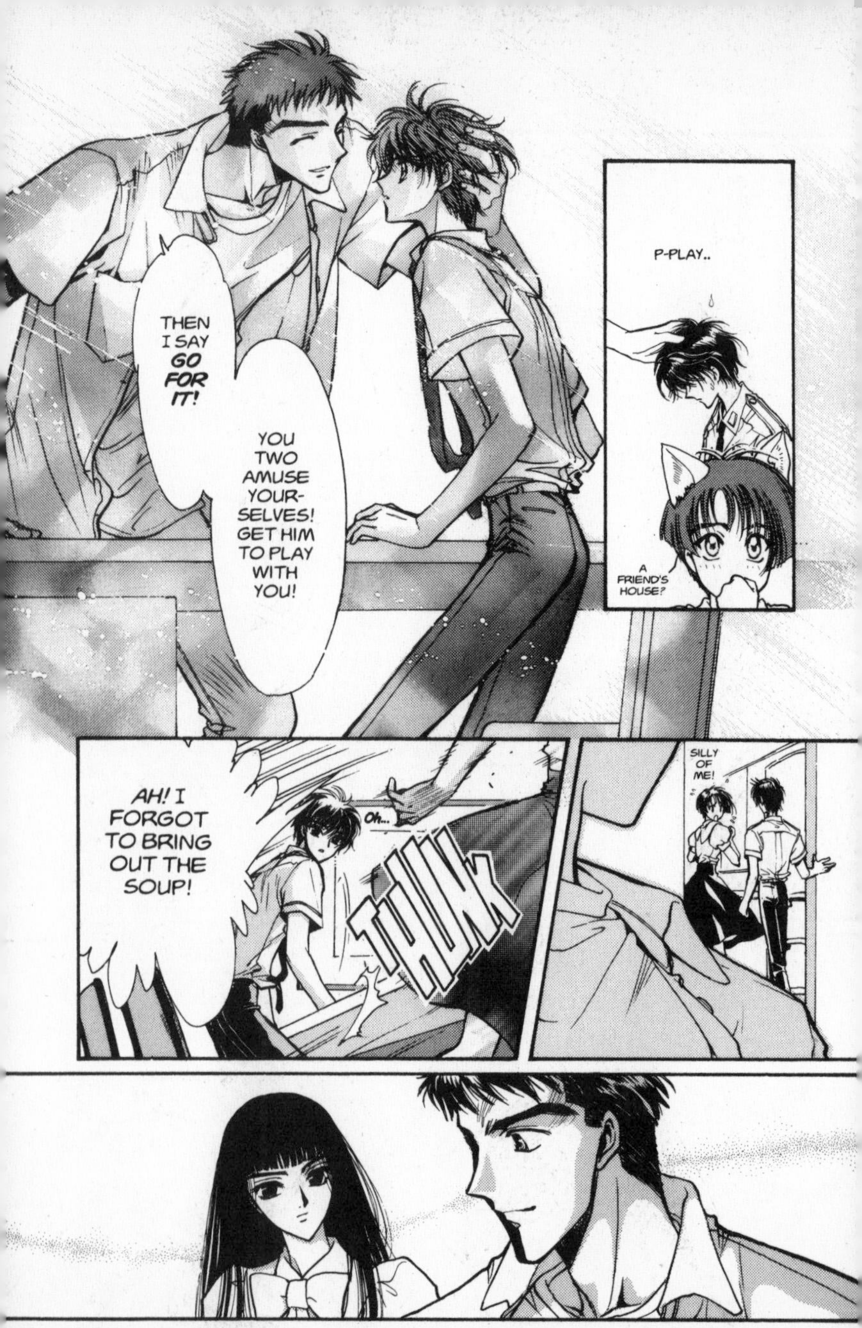
THEN I SAY GO FOR IT!
YOU TWO AMUSE YOURSELVES! GET HIM TO PLAY WITH YOU!
P-PLAY..
A FRIEND'S HOUSE?
AH! I FORGOT TO BRING OUT THE SOUP!
Oh...
THUNK
SILLY OF ME!

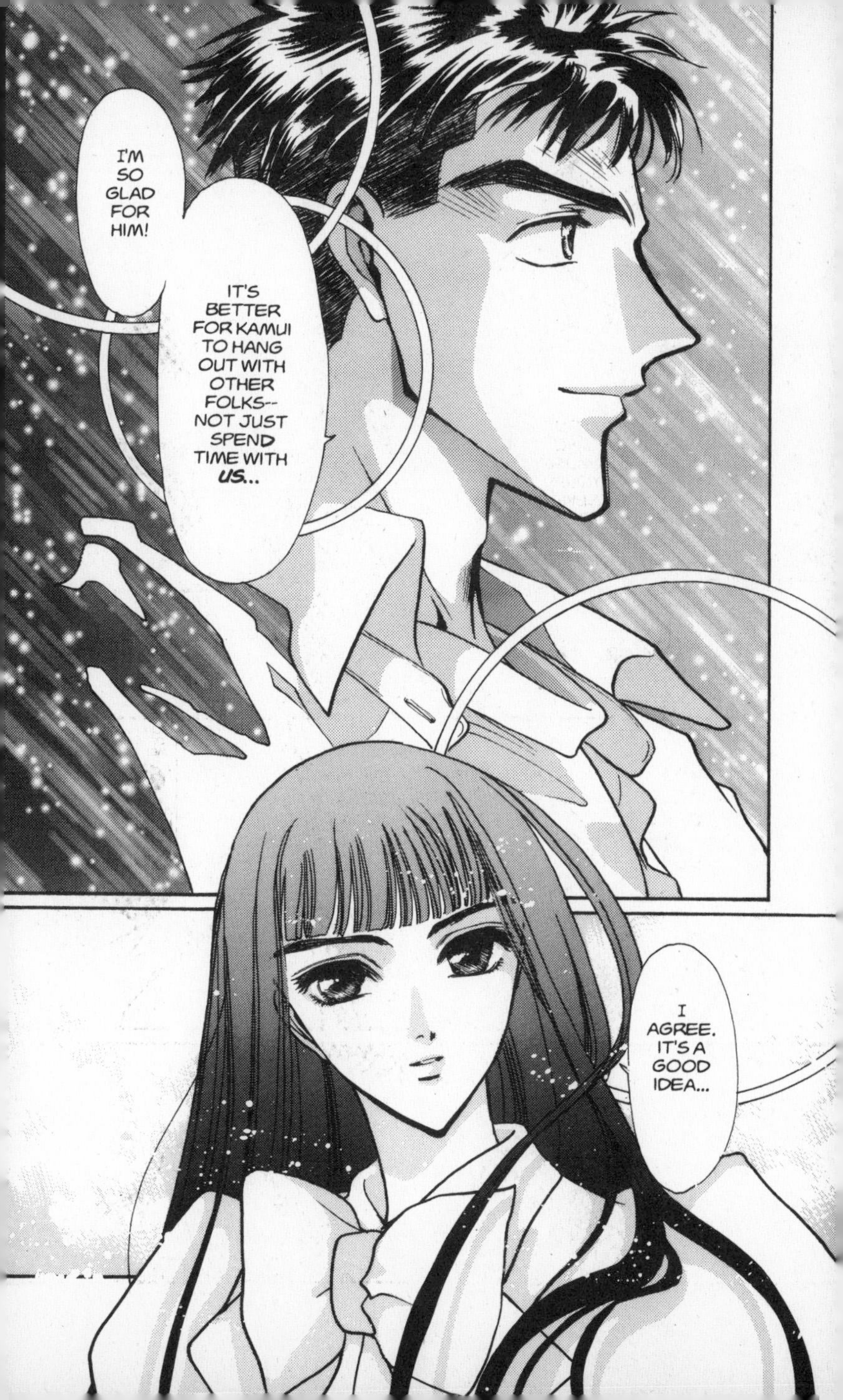
I'M SO GLAD FOR HIM!
IT'S BETTER FOR KAMUI TO HANG OUT WITH OTHER FOLKS-- NOT JUST SPEND TIME WITH US...
I AGREE. IT'S A GOOD IDEA...

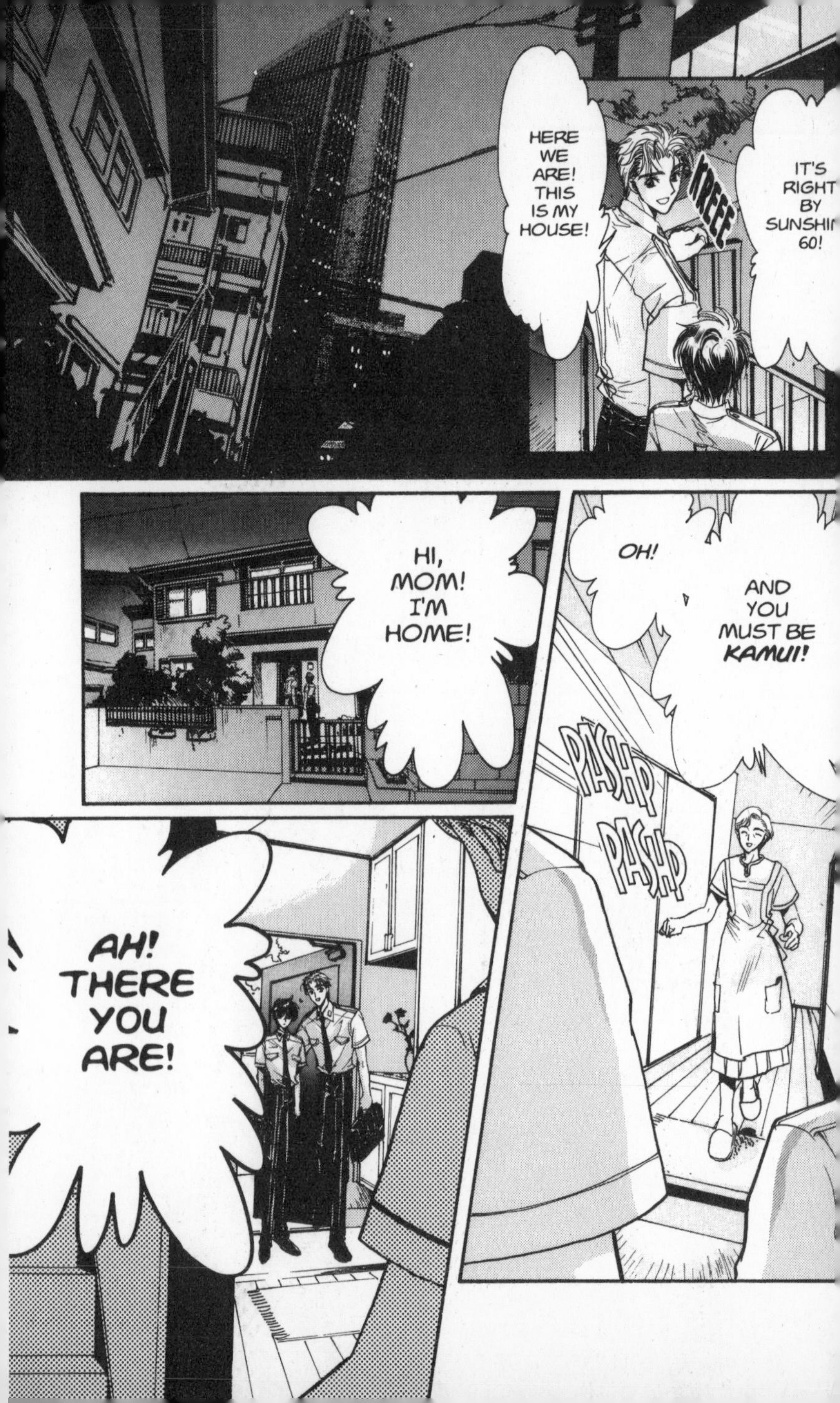
HERE WE ARE! THIS IS MY HOUSE!
KREEE
IT'S RIGHT BY SUNSHI 60!
HI, MOM! I'M HOME!
AH! THERE YOU ARE!
OH!
AND YOU MUST BE KAMUI!
PASHP
PASHP

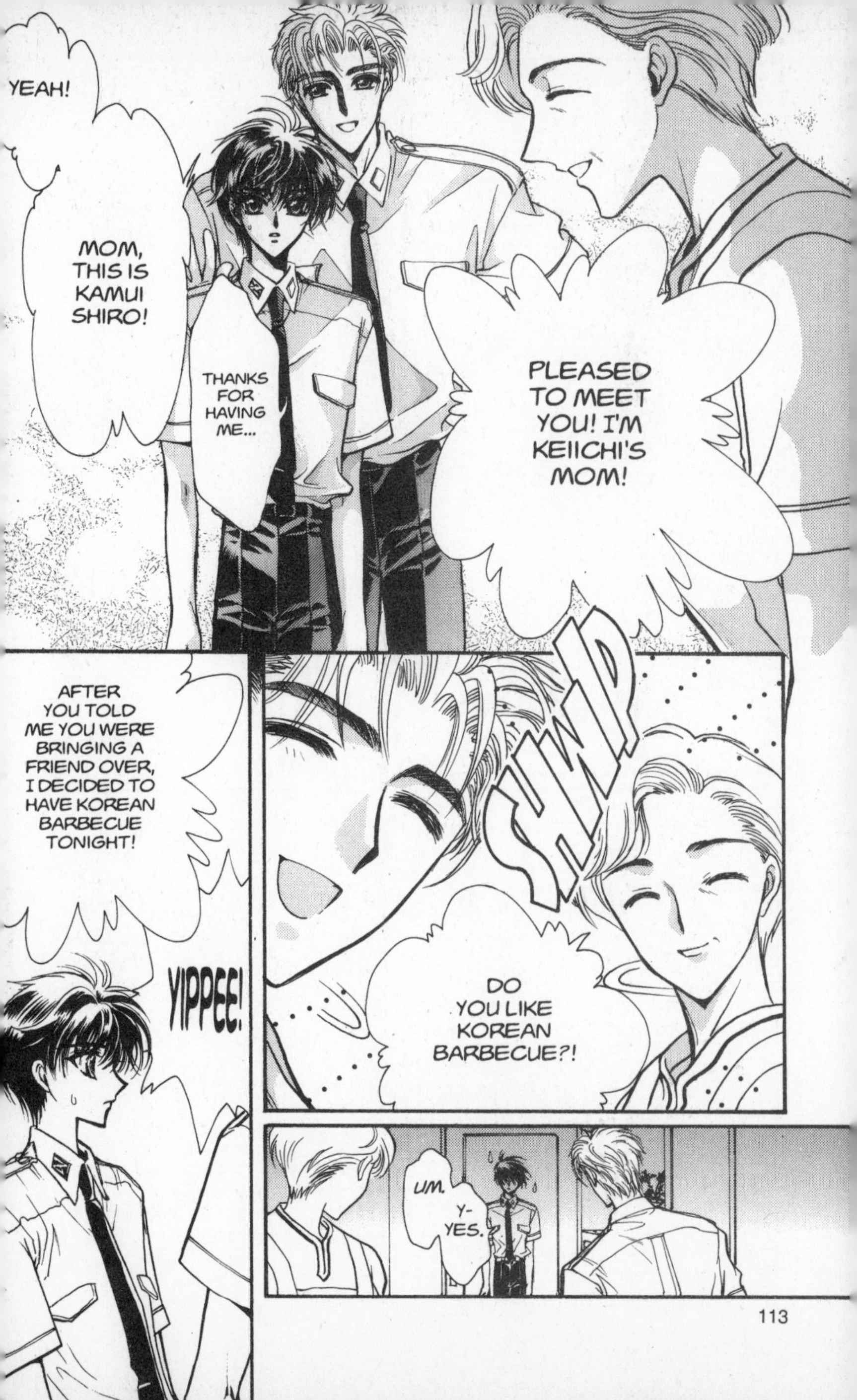

YEAH!
MOM, THIS IS KAMUI SHIRO!
THANKS FOR HAVING ME...
PLEASED TO MEET YOU! I'M KEIICHI'S MOM!
AFTER YOU TOLD ME YOU WERE BRINGING A FRIEND OVER, I DECIDED TO HAVE KOREAN BARBECUE TONIGHT!
YIPPEE!
SHMP
DO YOU LIKE KOREAN BARBECUE?!
UM.
Y-YES.

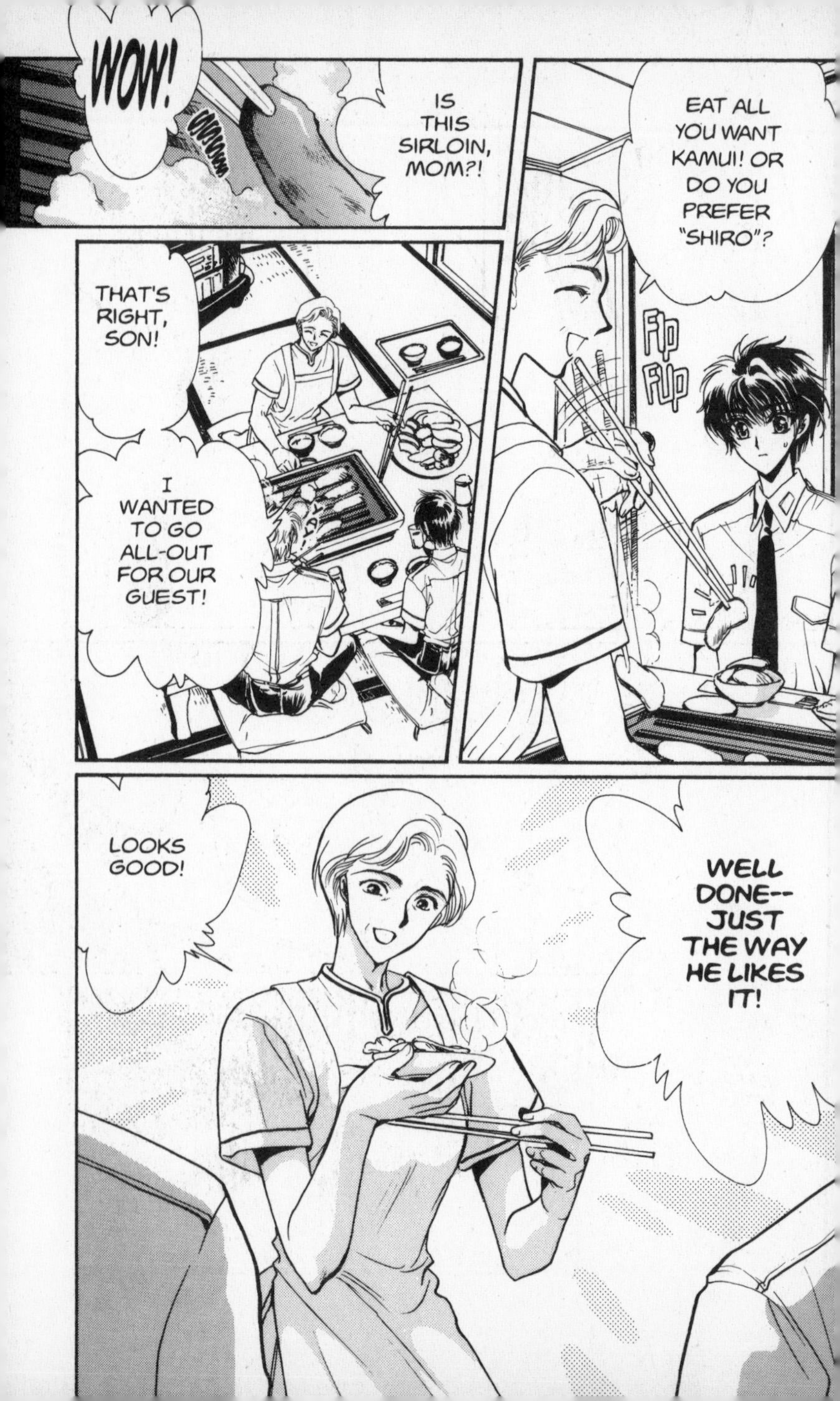
WOW!
IS THIS SIRLOIN, MOM?!
THAT'S RIGHT, SON!
I WANTED TO GO ALL-OUT FOR OUR GUEST!
EAT ALL YOU WANT KAMUI! OR DO YOU PREFER "SHIRO"?
FLP FLIP
LOOKS GOOD!
WELL DONE--JUST THE WAY HE LIKES IT!

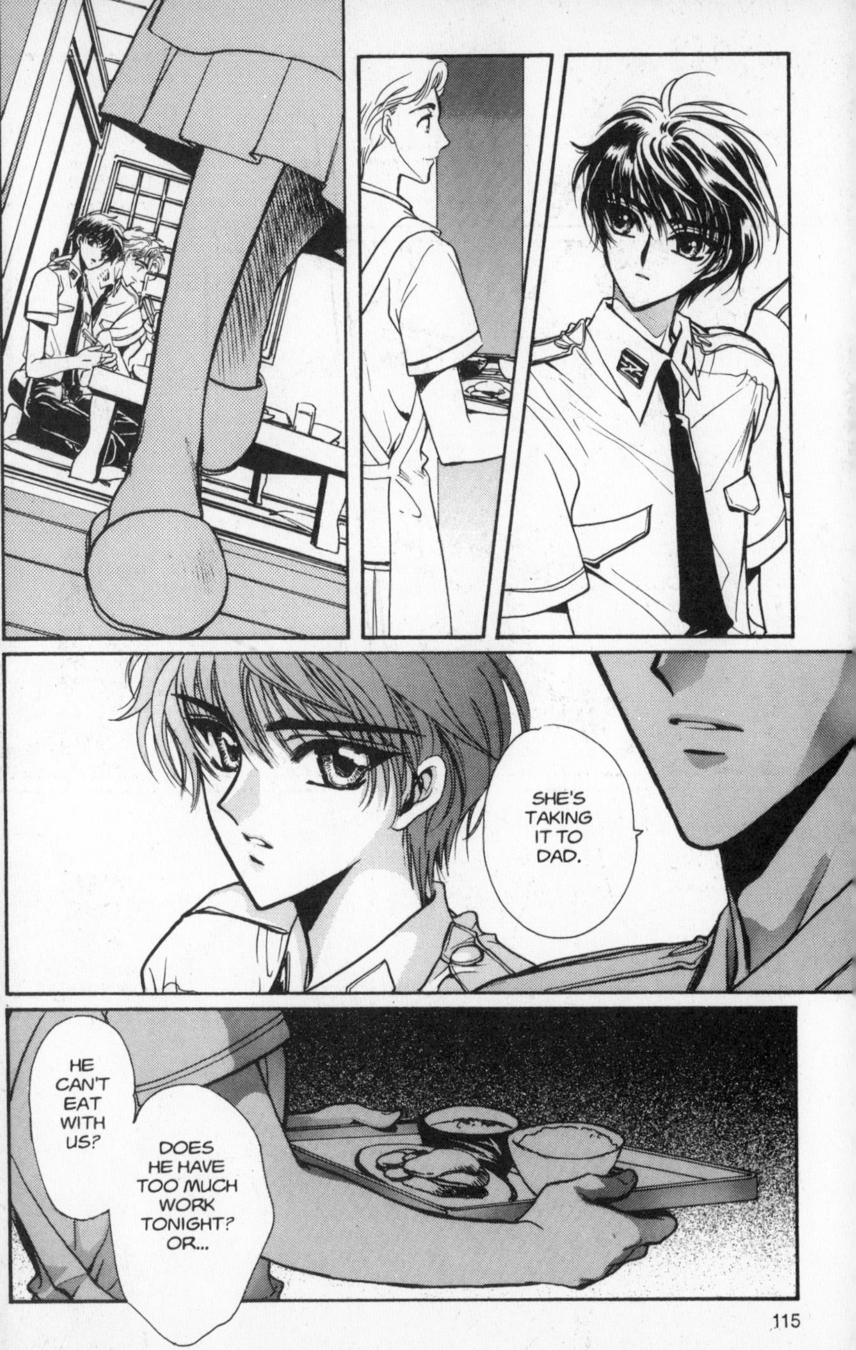
SHE'S TAKING IT TO DAD.
HE CAN'T EAT WITH US?
DOES HE HAVE TOO MUCH WORK TONIGHT? OR...

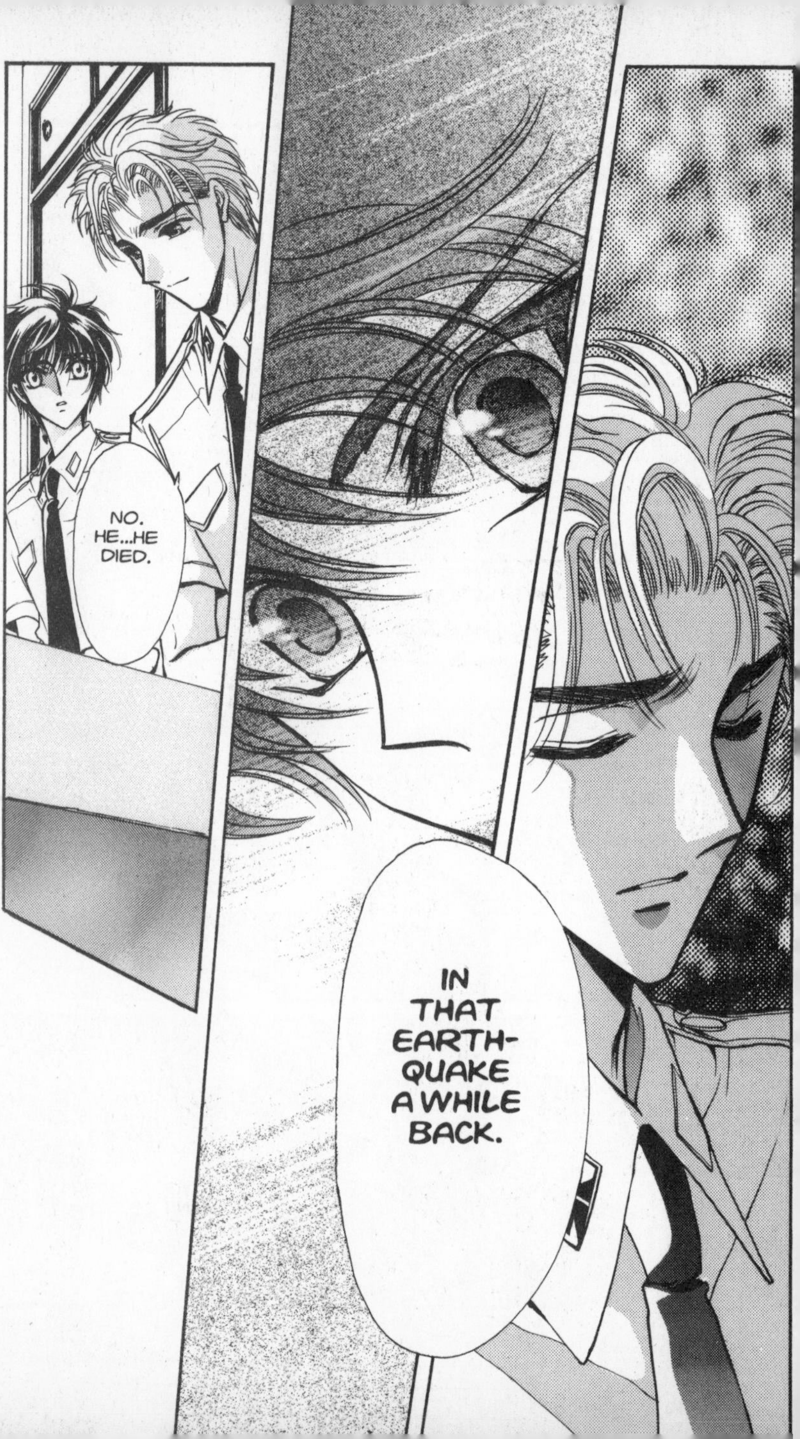
NO. HE...HE DIED.
IN THAT EARTH-QUAKE A WHILE BACK.

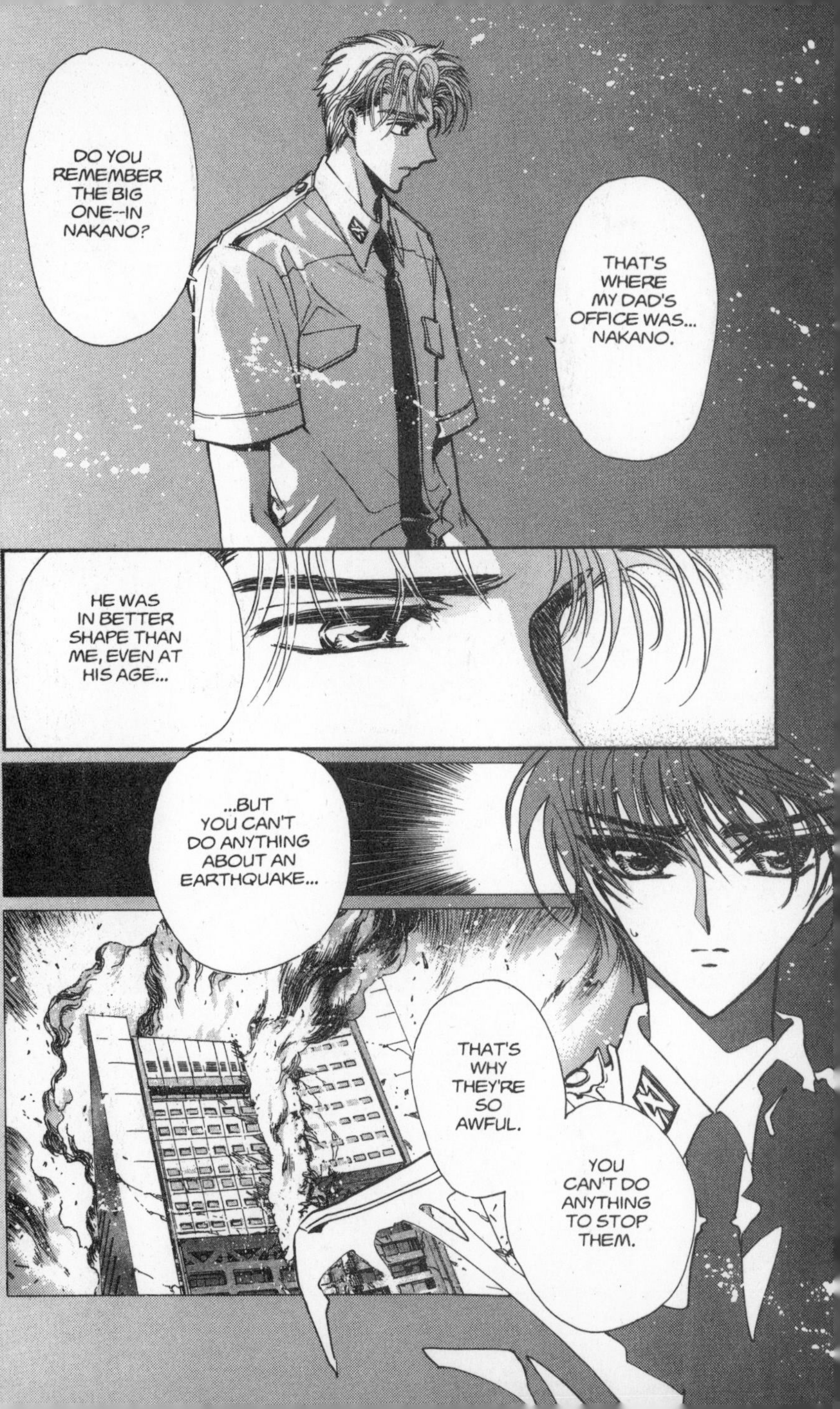
DO YOU REMEMBER THE BIG ONE--IN NAKANO?
THAT'S WHERE MY DAD'S OFFICE WAS... NAKANO.
HE WAS IN BETTER SHAPE THAN ME, EVEN AT HIS AGE...
...BUT YOU CAN'T DO ANYTHING ABOUT AN EARTHQUAKE...
THAT'S WHY THEY'RE SO AWFUL.
YOU CAN'T DO ANYTHING TO STOP THEM.

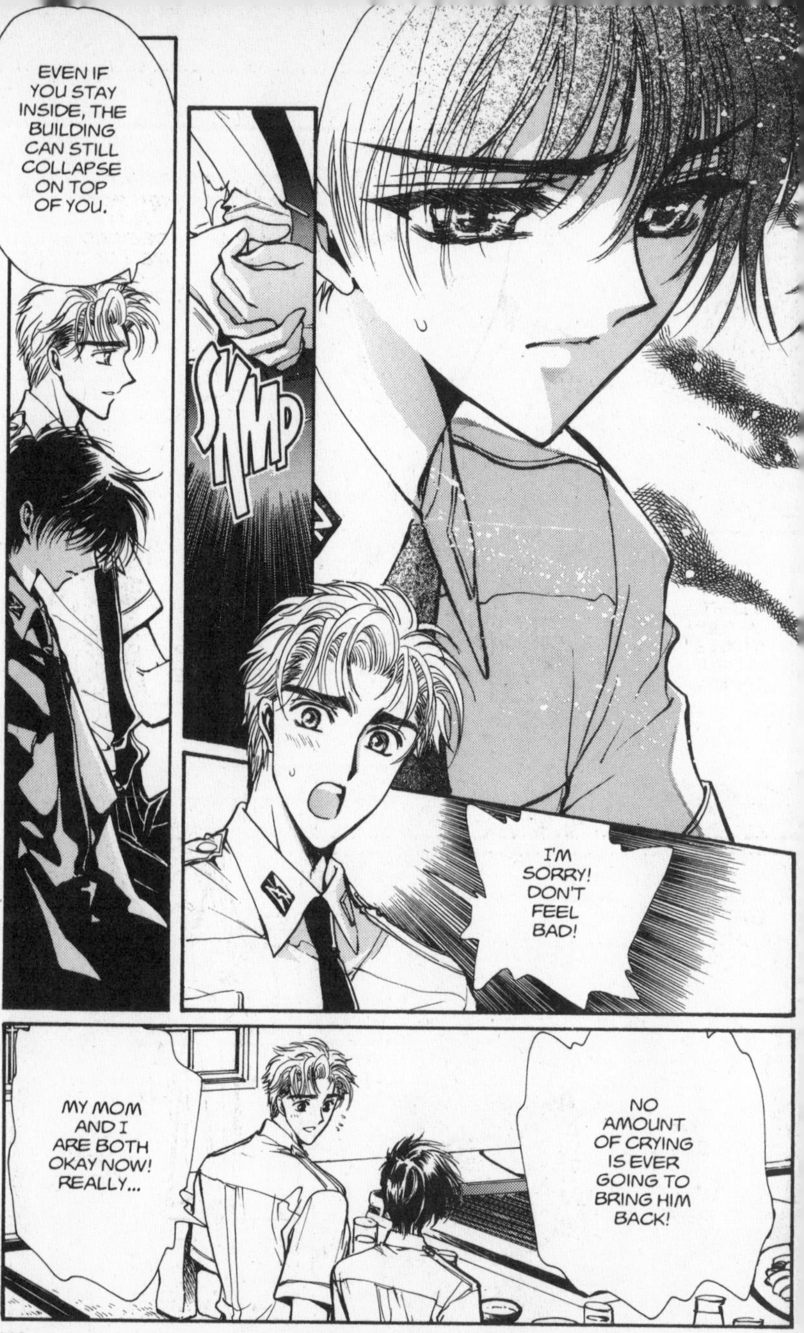
EVEN IF YOU STAY INSIDE, THE BUILDING CAN STILL COLLAPSE ON TOP OF YOU.
SKMP
I'M SORRY! DON'T FEEL BAD!
MY MOM AND I ARE BOTH OKAY NOW! REALLY...
NO AMOUNT OF CRYING IS EVER GOING TO BRING HIM BACK!

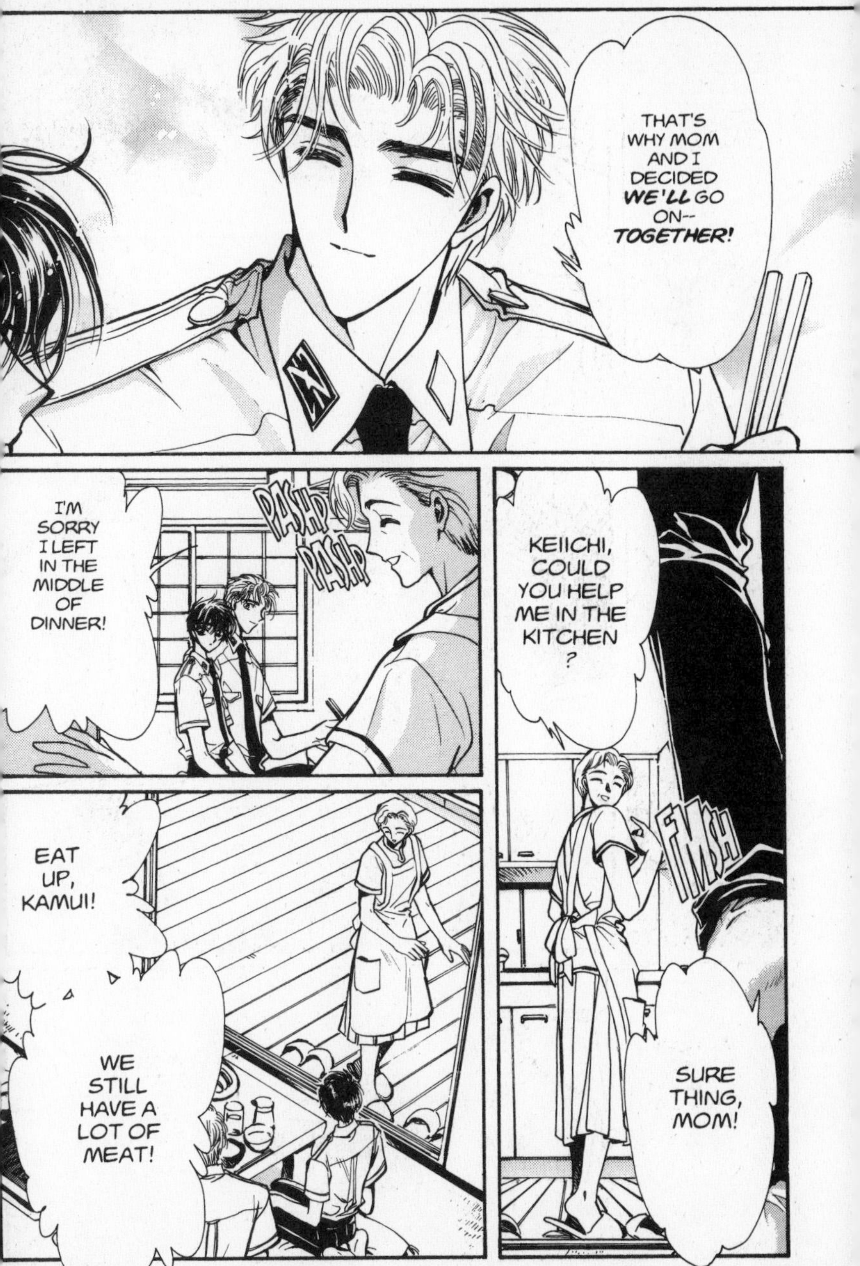

THAT'S WHY MOM AND I DECIDED **WE'LL** GO ON-- ***TOGETHER!***
I'M SORRY I LEFT IN THE MIDDLE OF DINNER!
PASHP
PASHP
EAT UP, KAMUI!
WE STILL HAVE A LOT OF MEAT!
KEIICHI, COULD YOU HELP ME IN THE KITCHEN ?
FMSH
SURE THING, MOM!

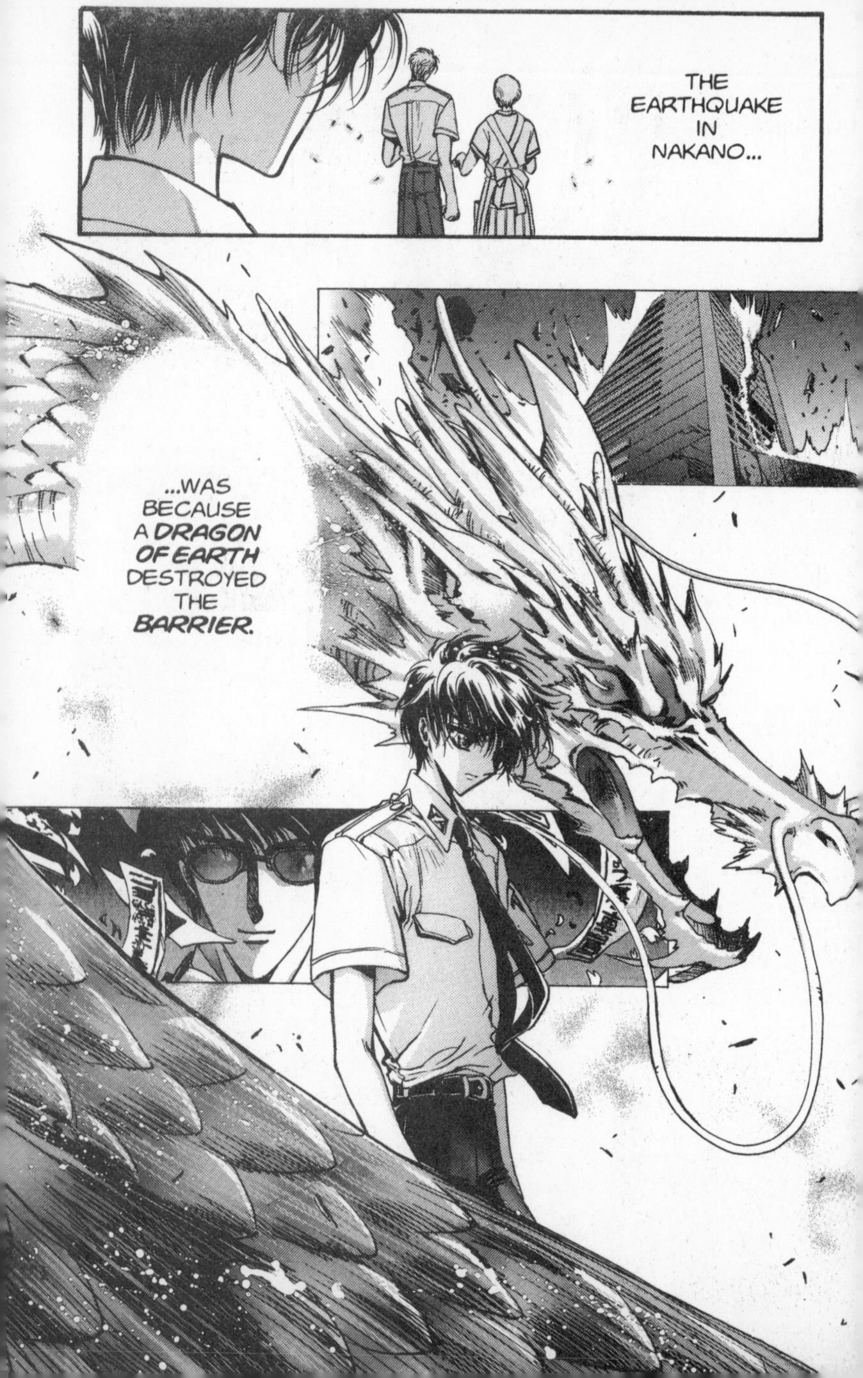
THE EARTHQUAKE IN NAKANO...
...WAS BECAUSE A DRAGON OF EARTH DESTROYED THE BARRIER.

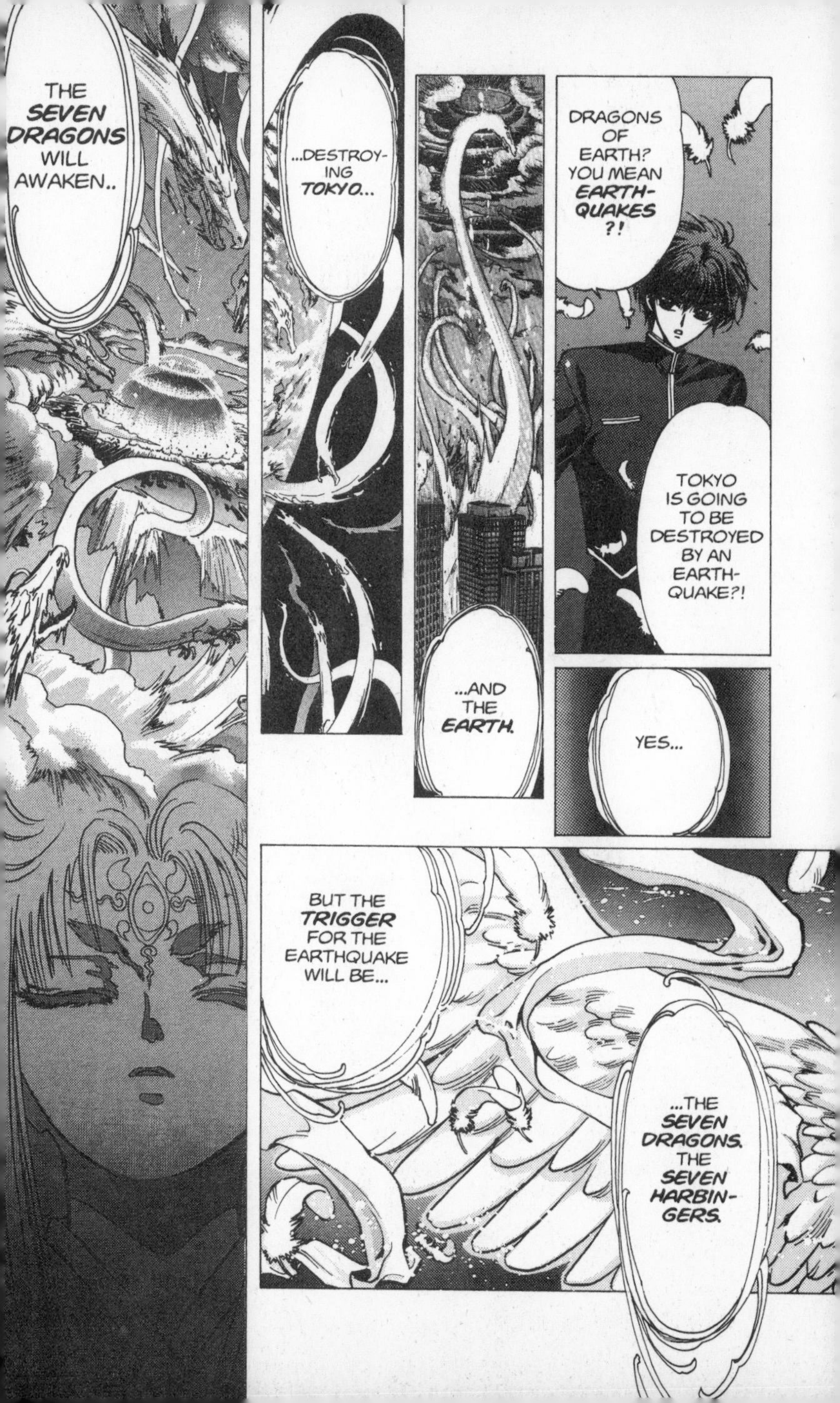
THE SEVEN DRAGONS WILL AWAKEN..
...DESTROYING TOKYO...
...AND THE EARTH.
DRAGONS OF EARTH? YOU MEAN EARTHQUAKES?!
TOKYO IS GOING TO BE DESTROYED BY AN EARTHQUAKE?!
YES...
BUT THE TRIGGER FOR THE EARTHQUAKE WILL BE...
...THE SEVEN DRAGONS. THE SEVEN HARBINGERS.

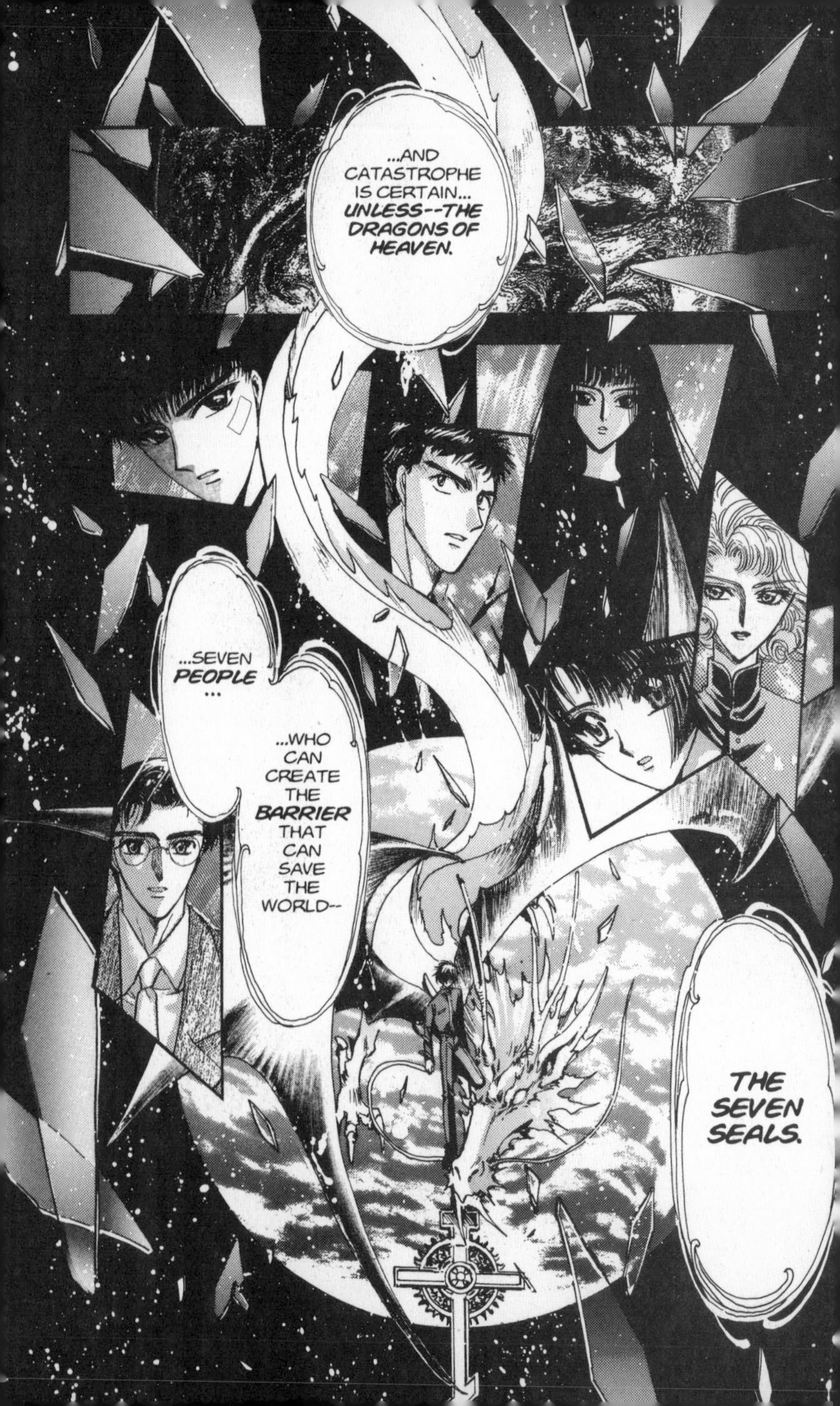
...AND CATASTROPHE IS CERTAIN... UNLESS--THE DRAGONS OF HEAVEN.
...SEVEN PEOPLE ...
...WHO CAN CREATE THE BARRIER THAT CAN SAVE THE WORLD--
THE SEVEN SEALS.

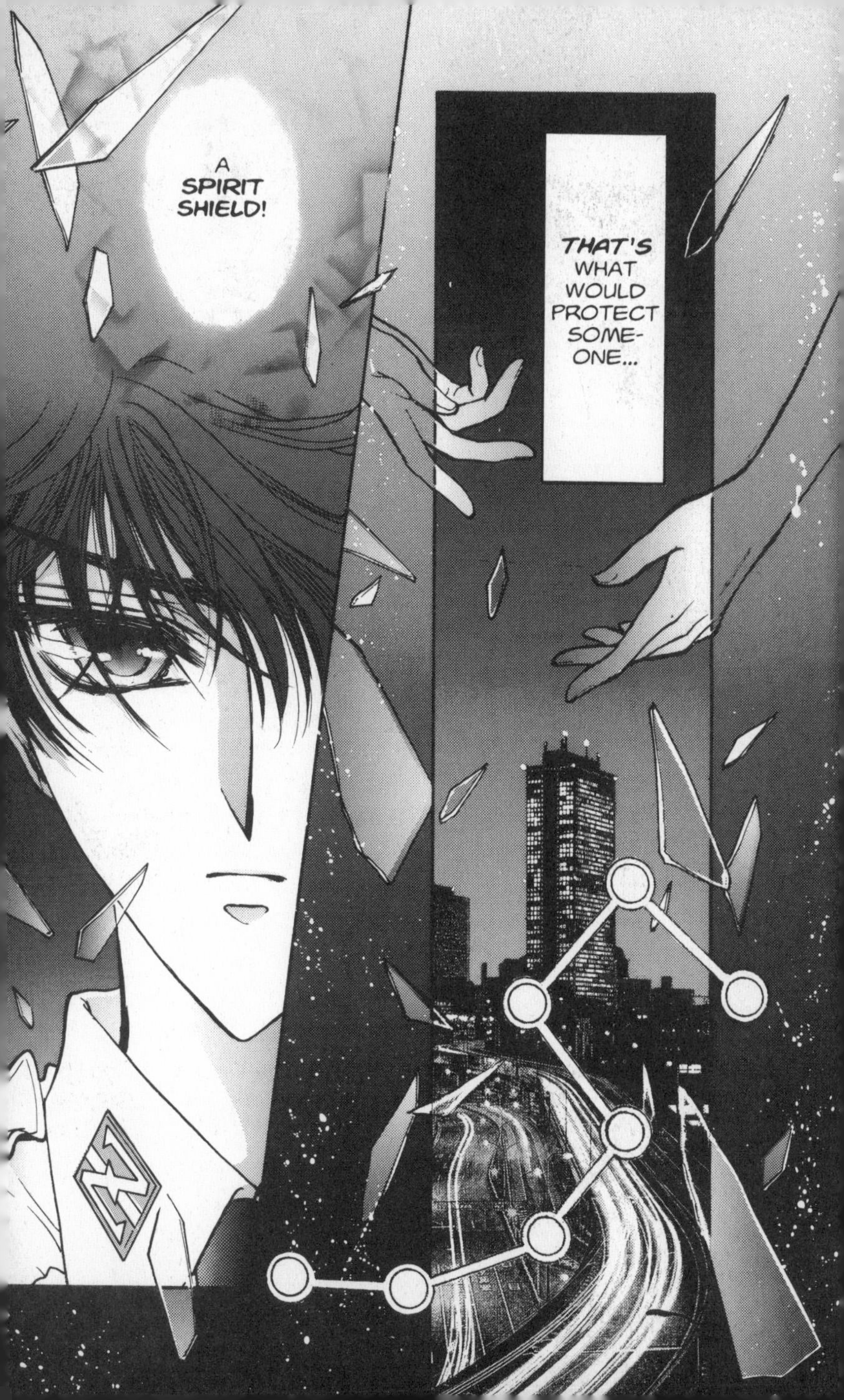
A SPIRIT SHIELD!
THAT'S WHAT WOULD PROTECT SOME-ONE...

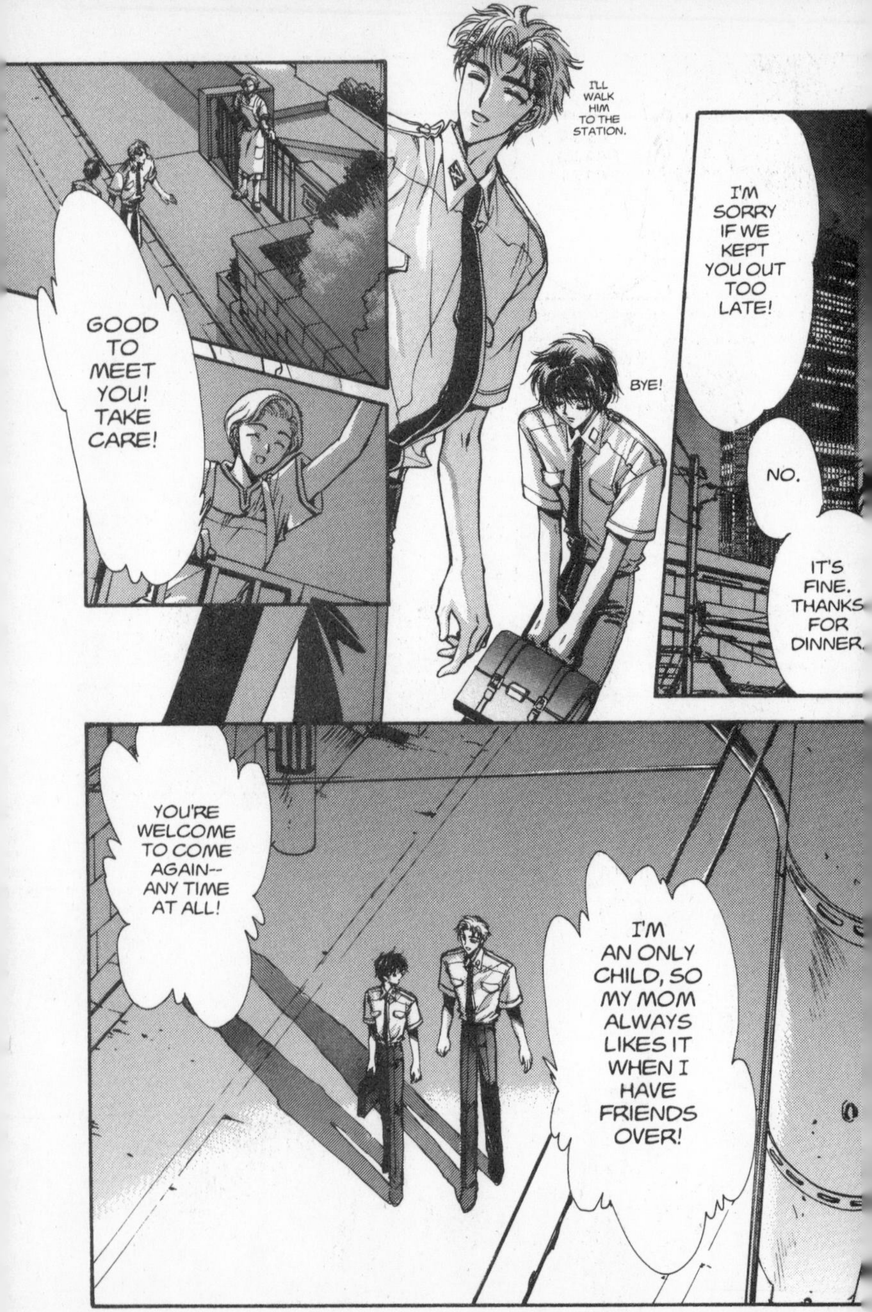
GOOD TO MEET YOU! TAKE CARE!
I'LL WALK HIM TO THE STATION.
BYE!
I'M SORRY IF WE KEPT YOU OUT TOO LATE!
NO.
IT'S FINE. THANKS FOR DINNER.
YOU'RE WELCOME TO COME AGAIN-- ANY TIME AT ALL!
I'M AN ONLY CHILD, SO MY MOM ALWAYS LIKES IT WHEN I HAVE FRIENDS OVER!

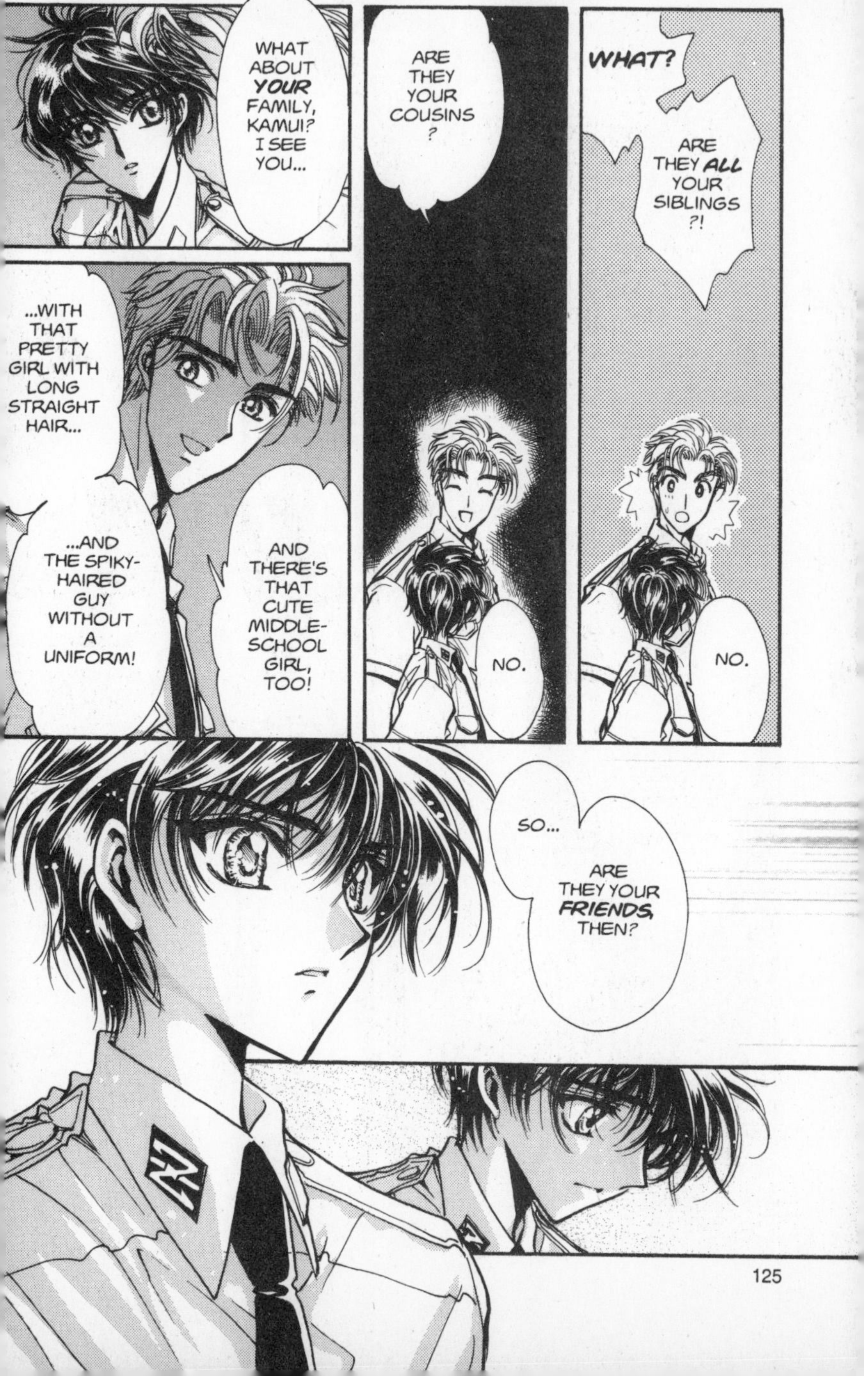
WHAT ABOUT YOUR FAMILY, KAMUI? I SEE YOU...
...WITH THAT PRETTY GIRL WITH LONG STRAIGHT HAIR...
...AND THE SPIKY-HAIRED GUY WITHOUT A UNIFORM!
AND THERE'S THAT CUTE MIDDLE-SCHOOL GIRL, TOO!
ARE THEY YOUR COUSINS?
NO.
WHAT?
ARE THEY ALL YOUR SIBLINGS?!
NO.
SO...
ARE THEY YOUR FRIENDS, THEN?

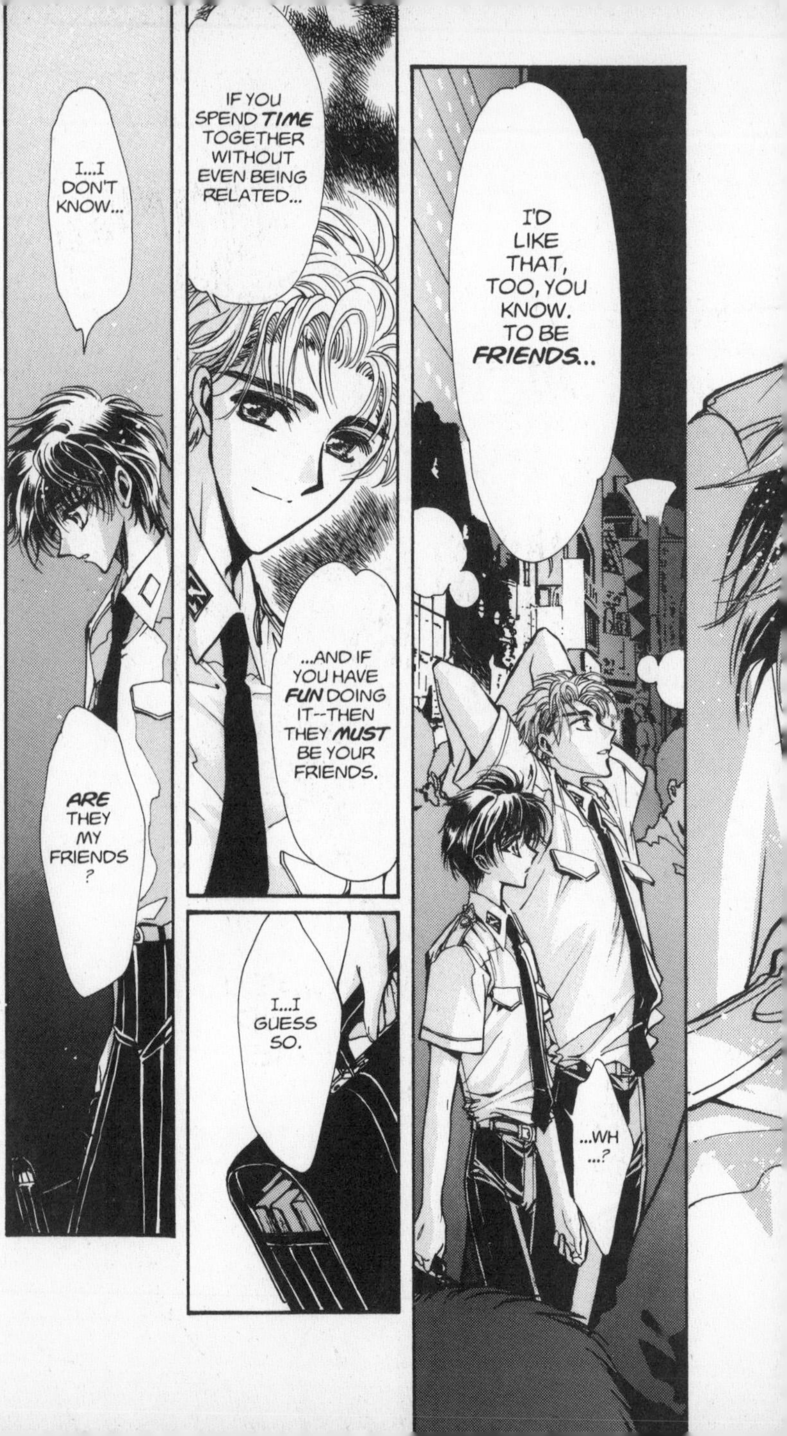
I...I DON'T KNOW...
ARE THEY MY FRIENDS?
IF YOU SPEND TIME TOGETHER WITHOUT EVEN BEING RELATED...
...AND IF YOU HAVE FUN DOING IT--THEN THEY MUST BE YOUR FRIENDS.
I...I GUESS SO.
I'D LIKE THAT, TOO, YOU KNOW. TO BE FRIENDS...
...WH...?

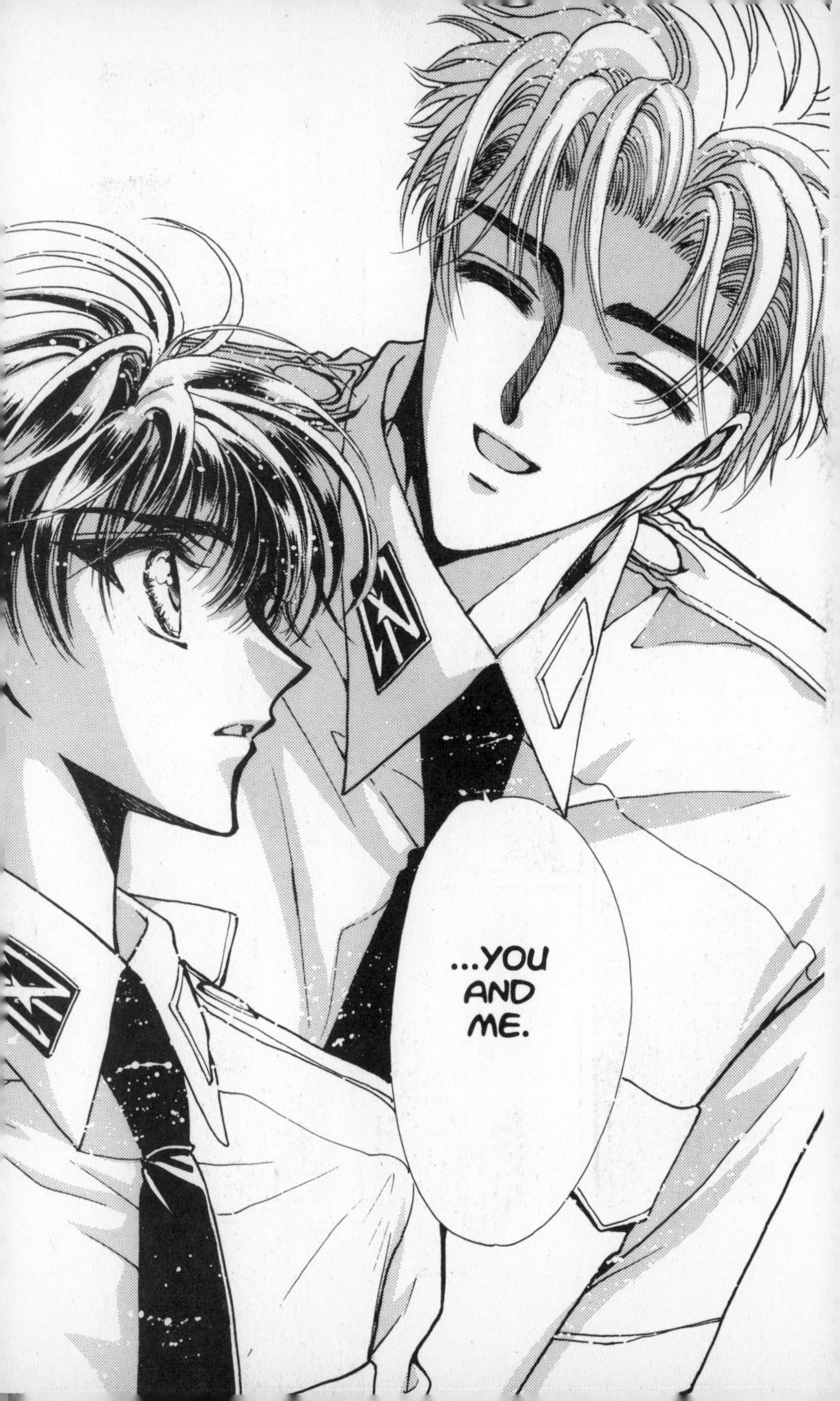
...YOU AND ME.

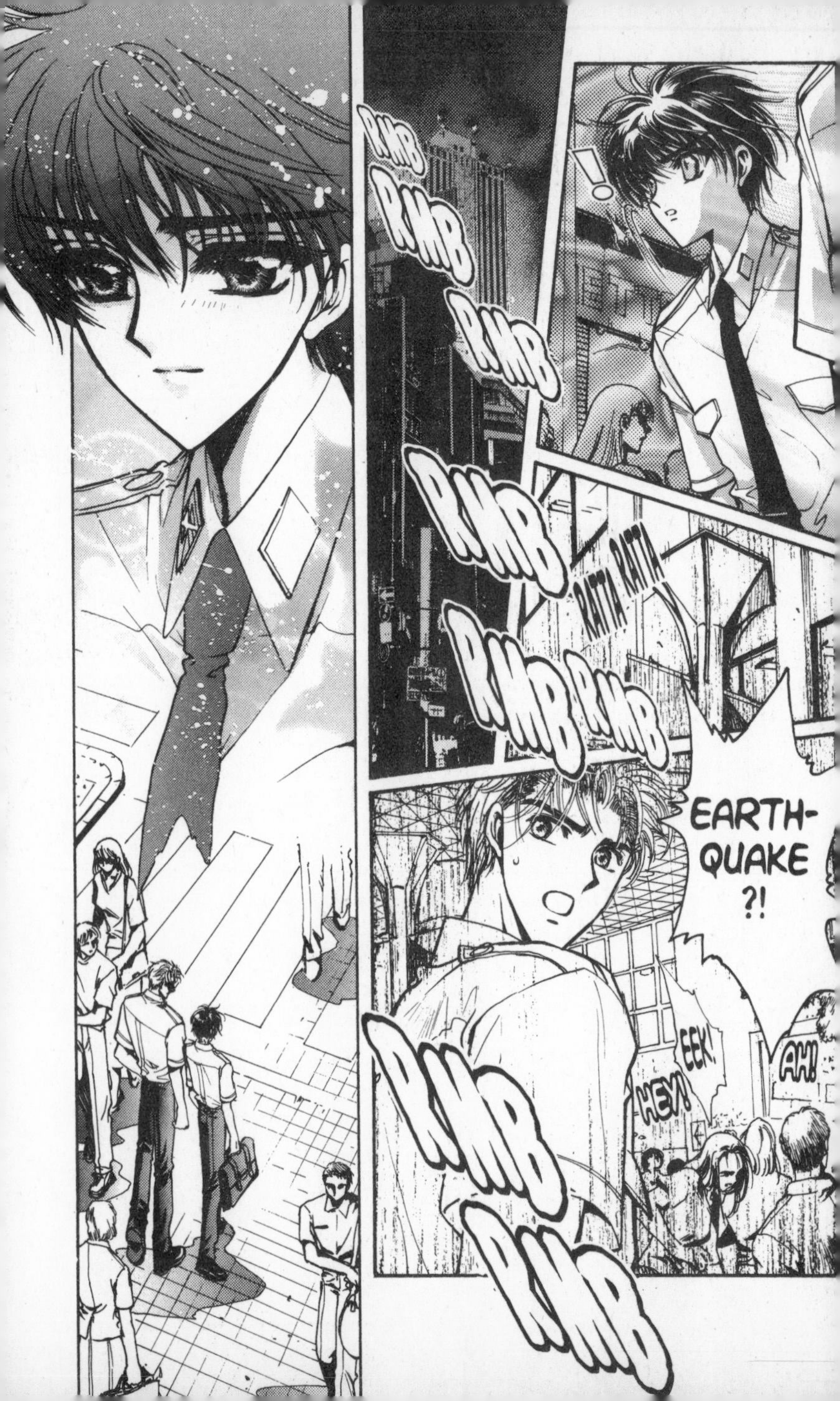

RMB
RMB
RMB
!
RMB
RATTA RATTA
RMB RMB
EARTH-
QUAKE
?!
EEK!
HEY!
AH!
RMB
RMB

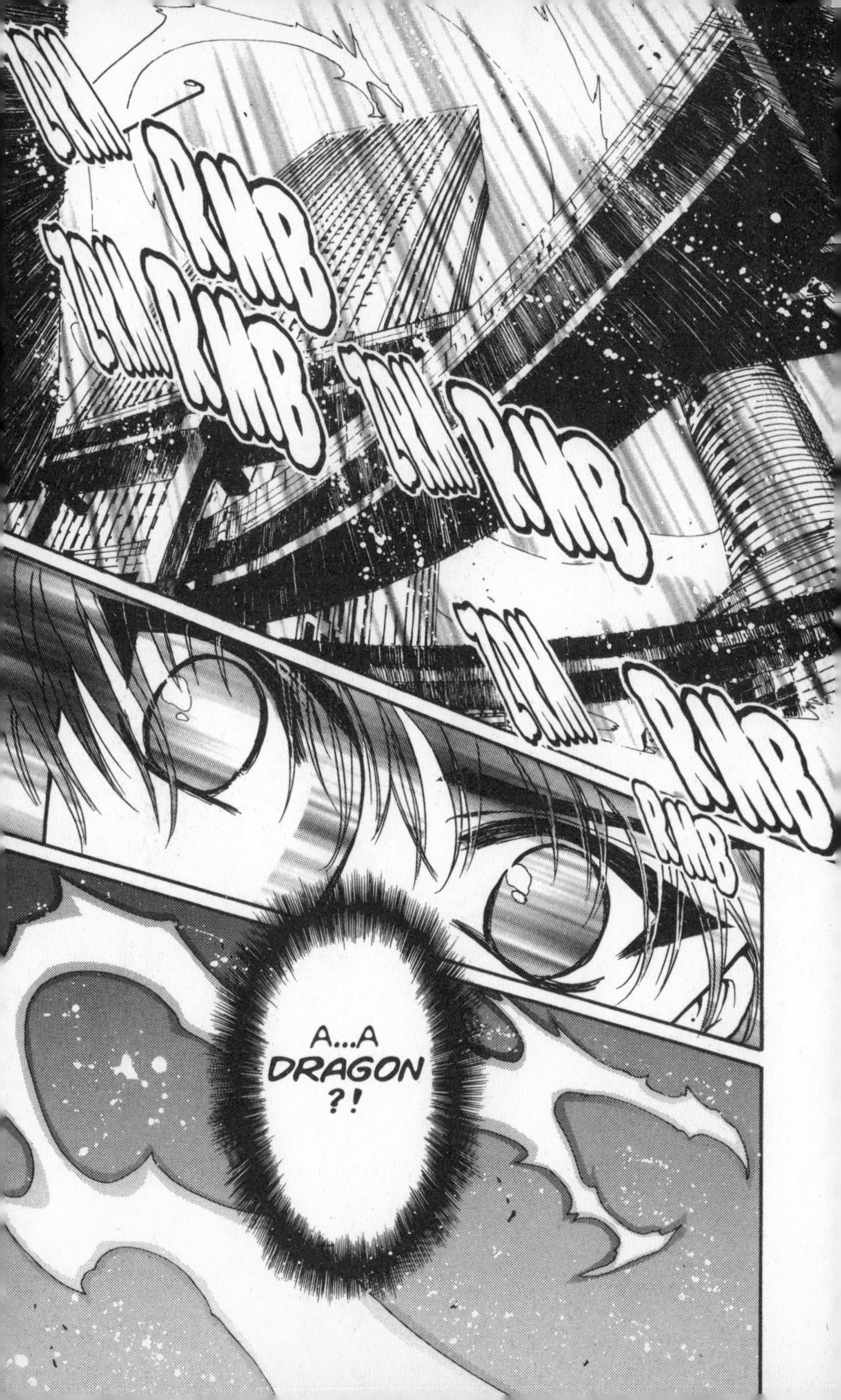
A...A DRAGON ?!

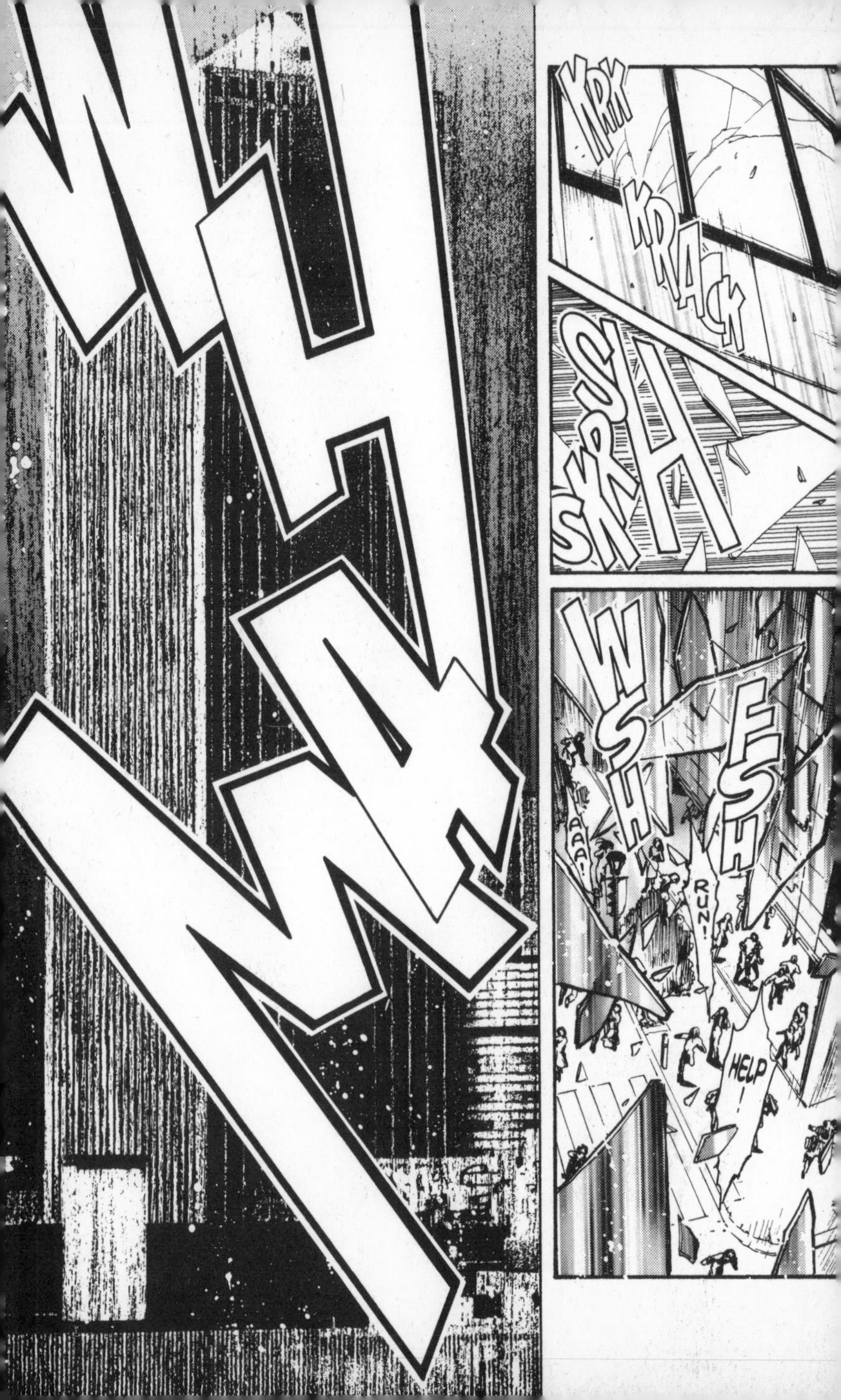
KRK
KRACK
WSH
FSH
AAA!
RUN!
HELP!

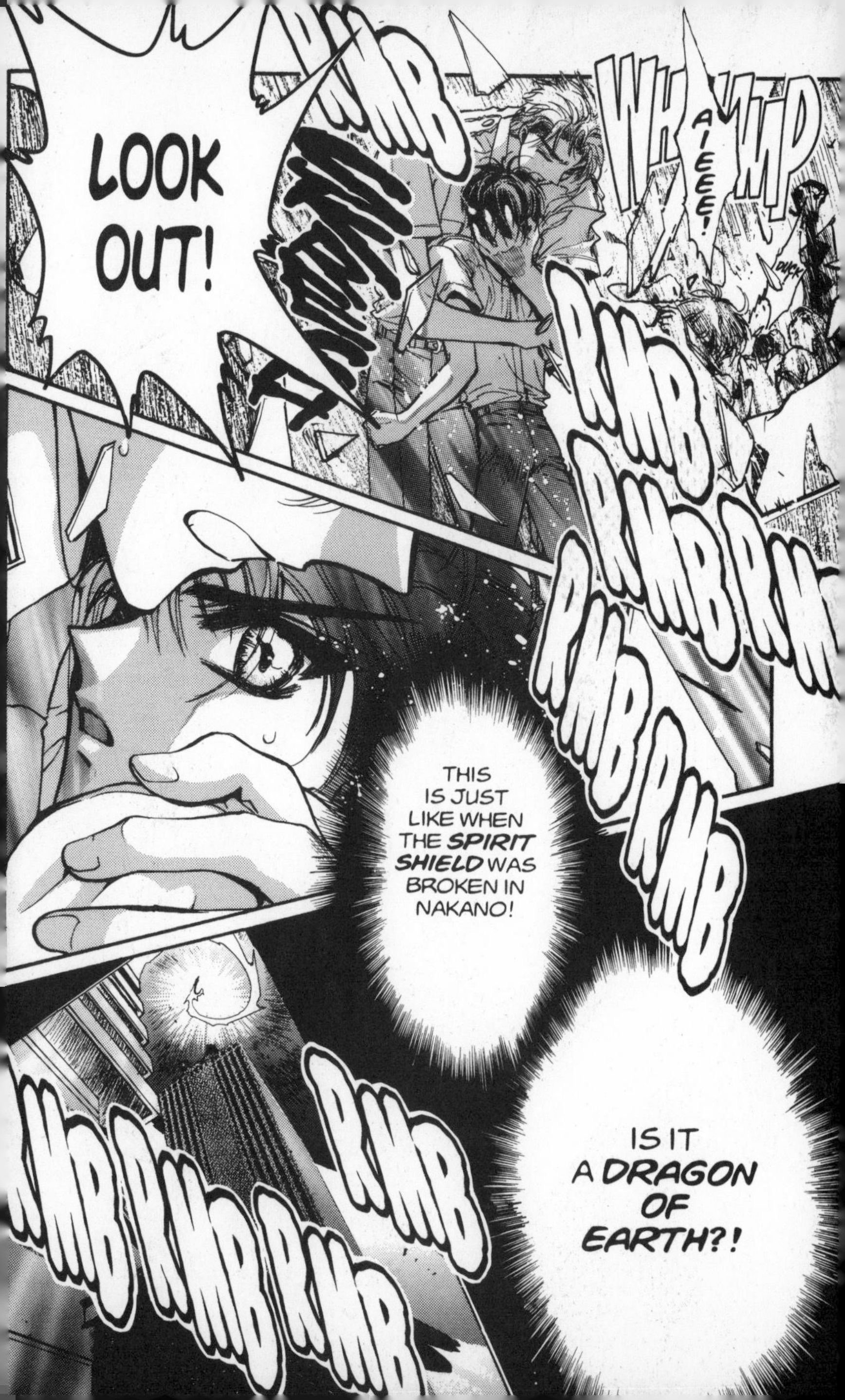
LOOK OUT!
AIEEE!
DUCK
RMB RMB RMB RMB
THIS IS JUST LIKE WHEN THE *SPIRIT SHIELD* WAS BROKEN IN NAKANO!
RMB RMB RMB
IS IT A *DRAGON OF EARTH*?!

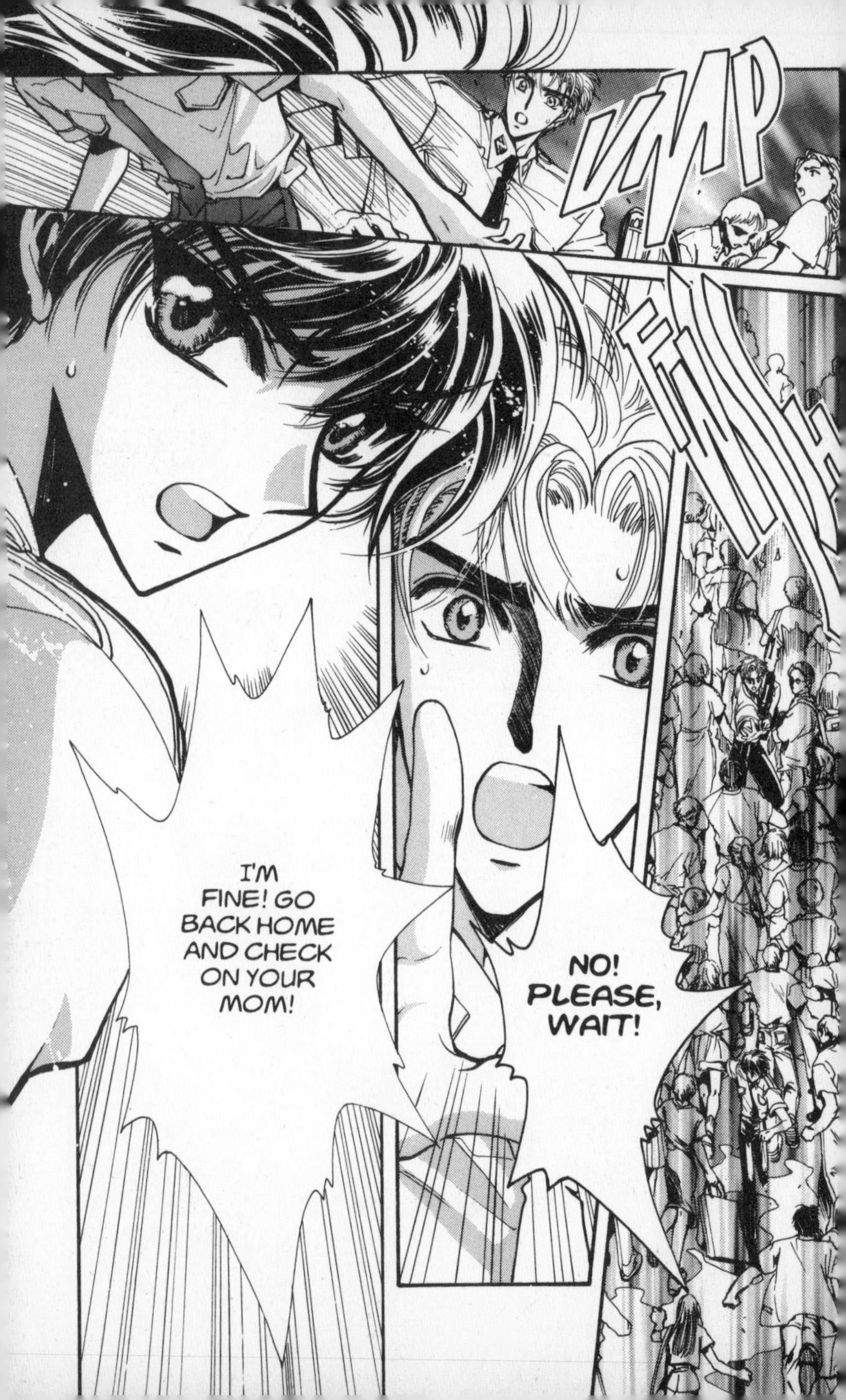
I'M FINE! GO BACK HOME AND CHECK ON YOUR MOM!
NO! PLEASE, WAIT!

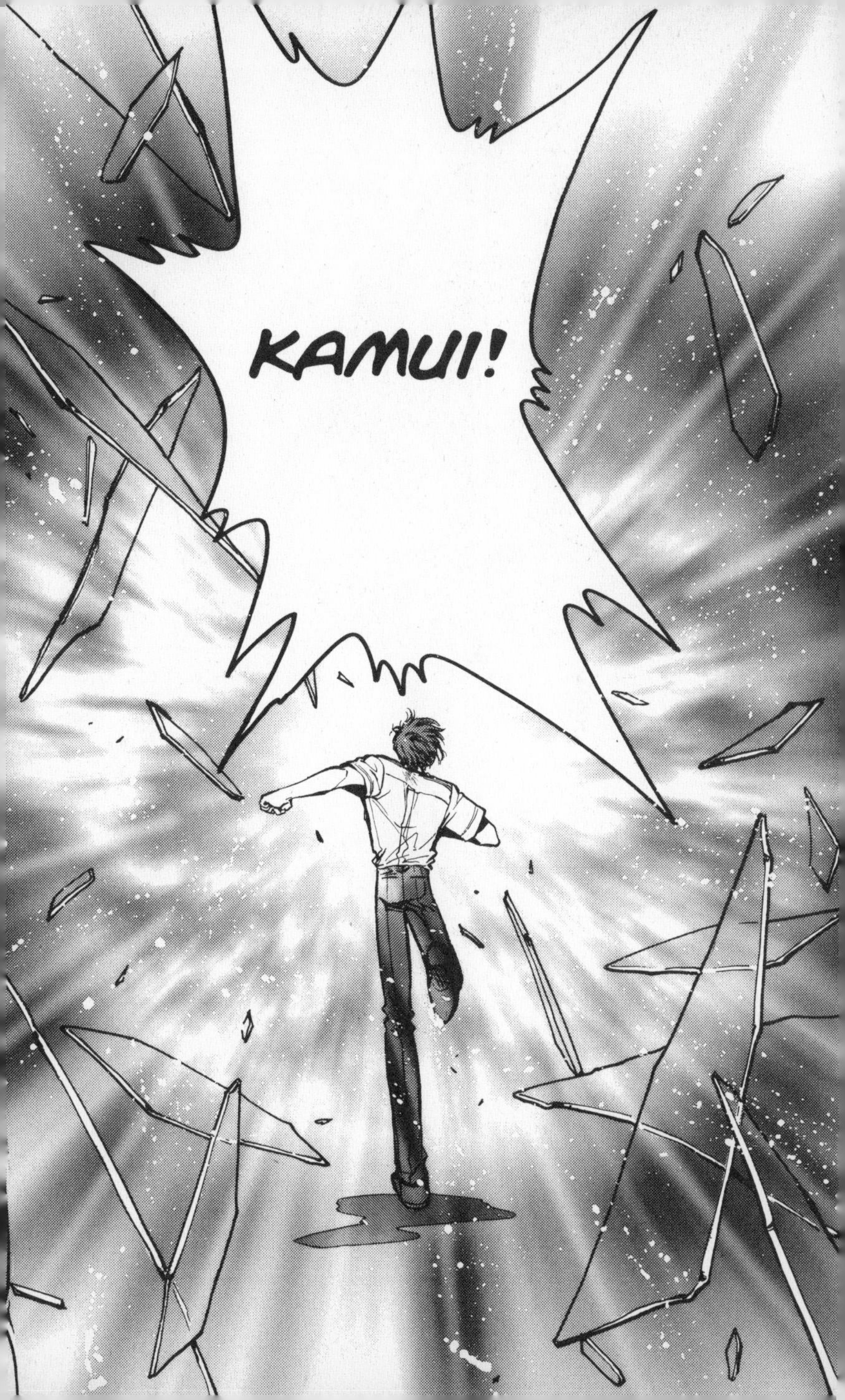
KAMUI!

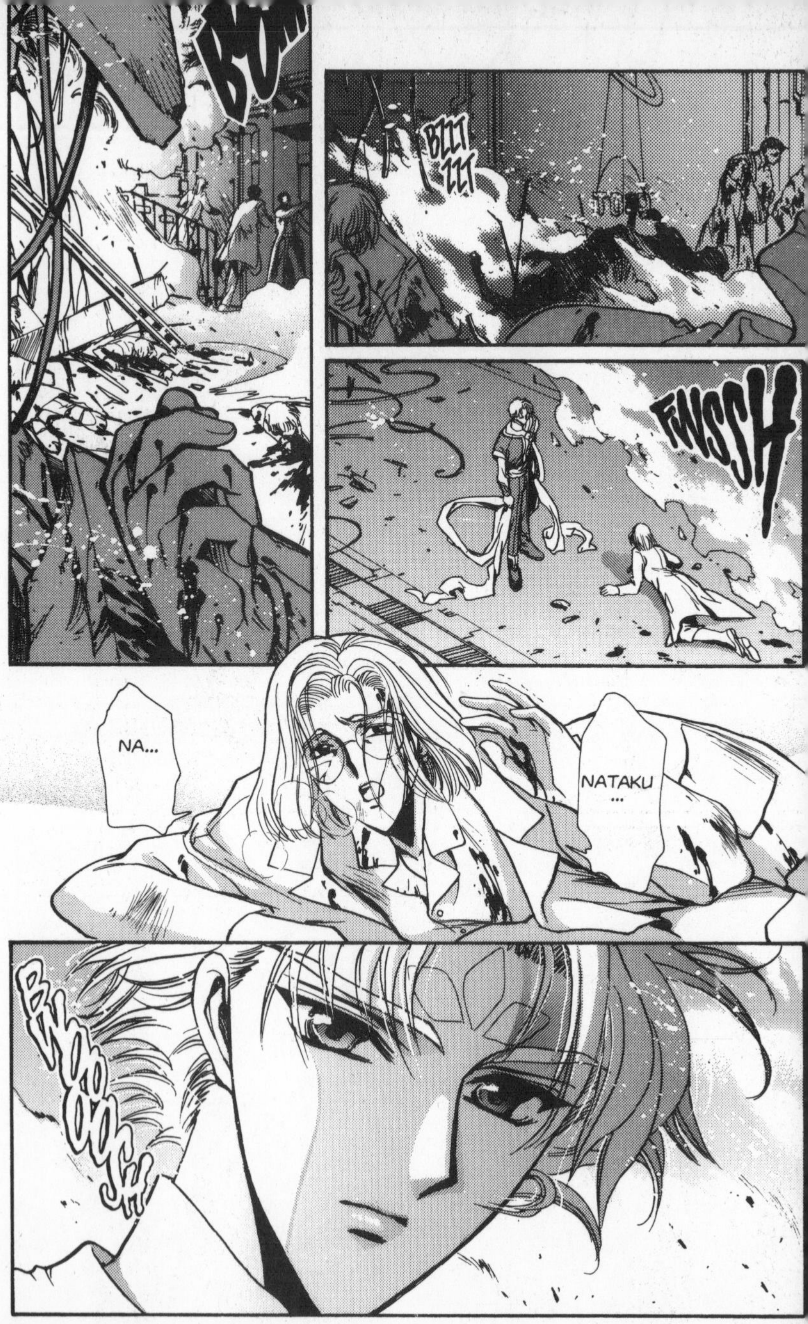
BZZZ ZZT
FWSSH
NA...
NATAKU ...
BWOOOOSH

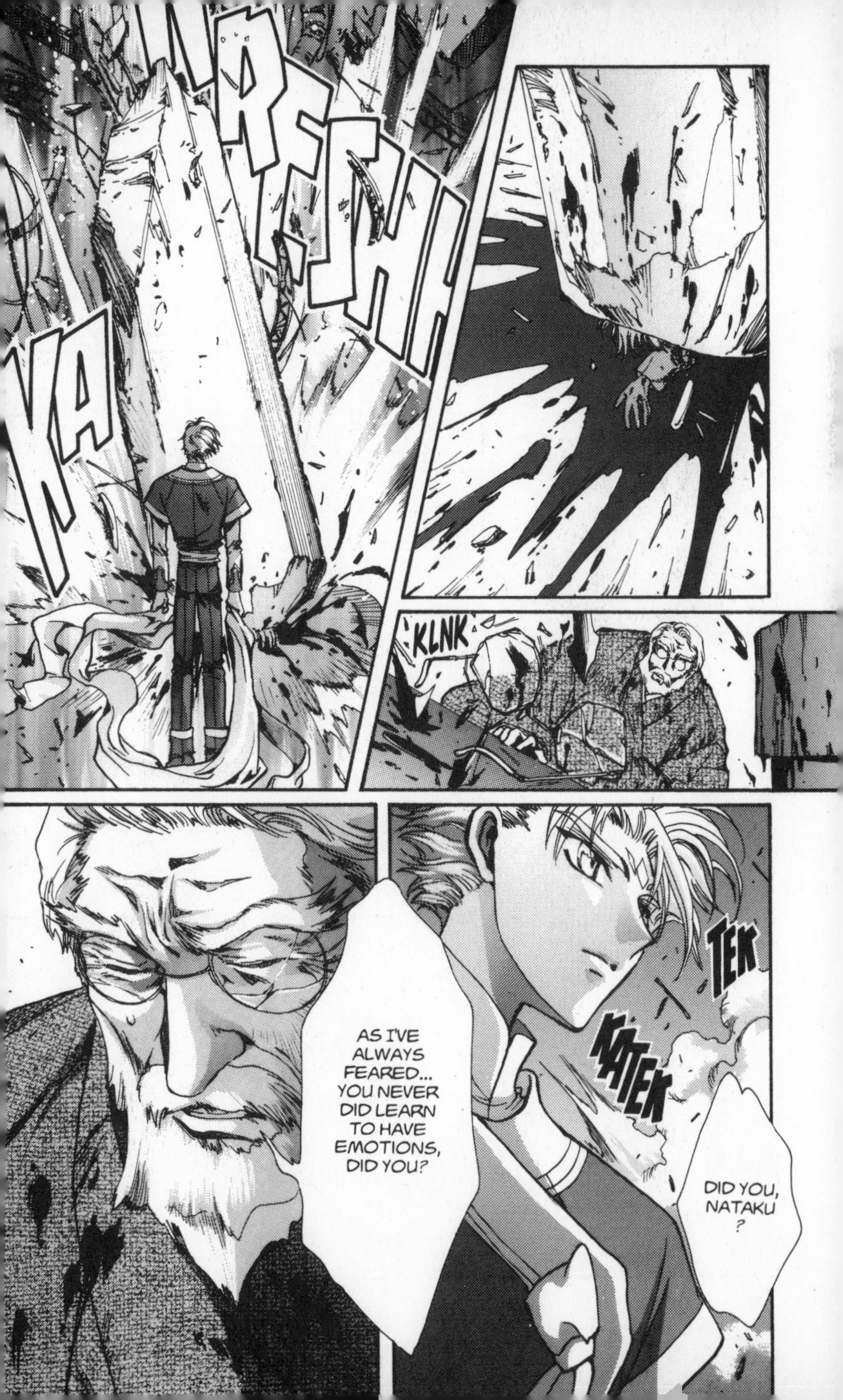
KA
KLNK
TEK
KATEK
AS I'VE ALWAYS FEARED... YOU NEVER DID LEARN TO HAVE EMOTIONS, DID YOU?
DID YOU, NATAKU?

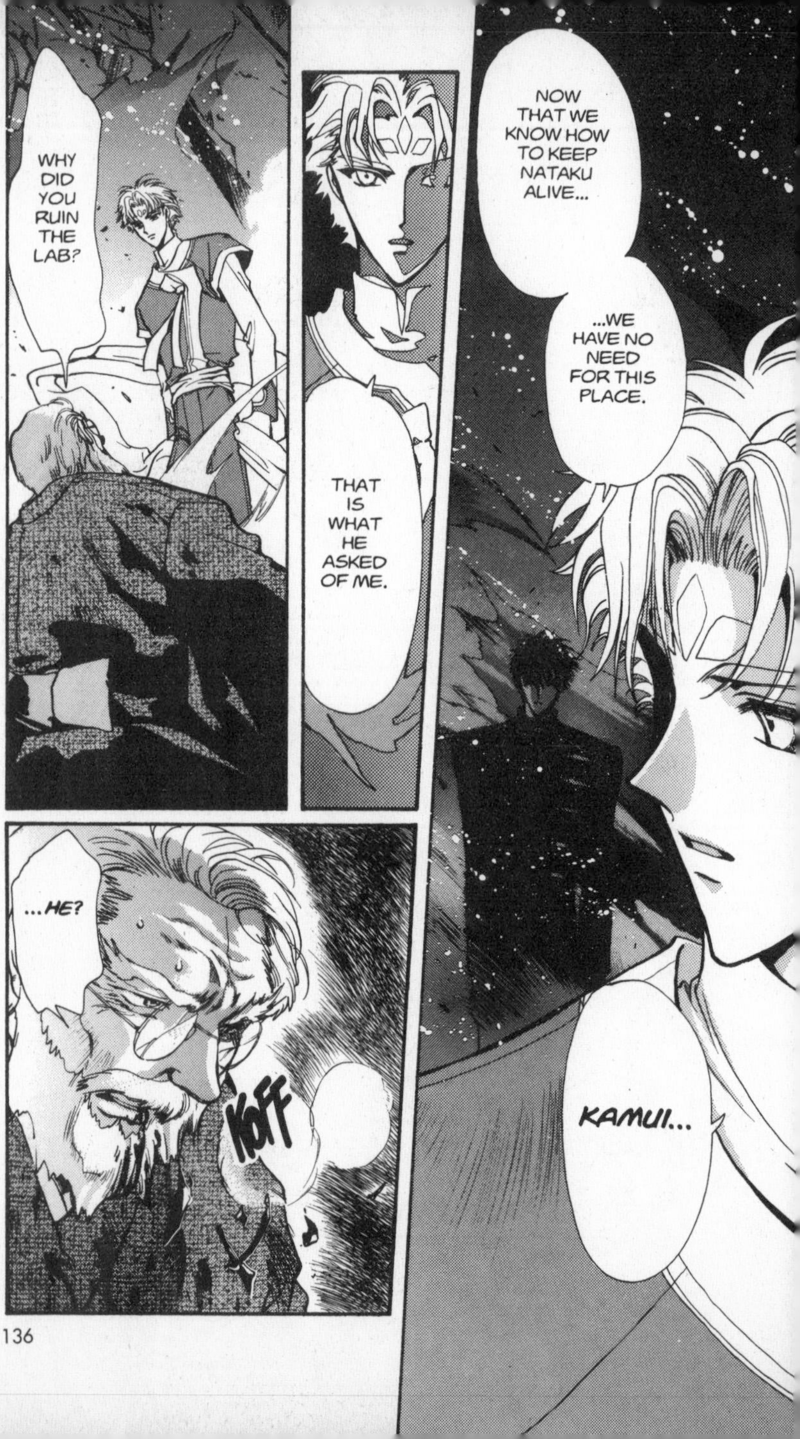
WHY DID YOU RUIN THE LAB?
THAT IS WHAT HE ASKED OF ME.
...HE?
KOFF
NOW THAT WE KNOW HOW TO KEEP NATAKU ALIVE...
...WE HAVE NO NEED FOR THIS PLACE.
KAMUI...

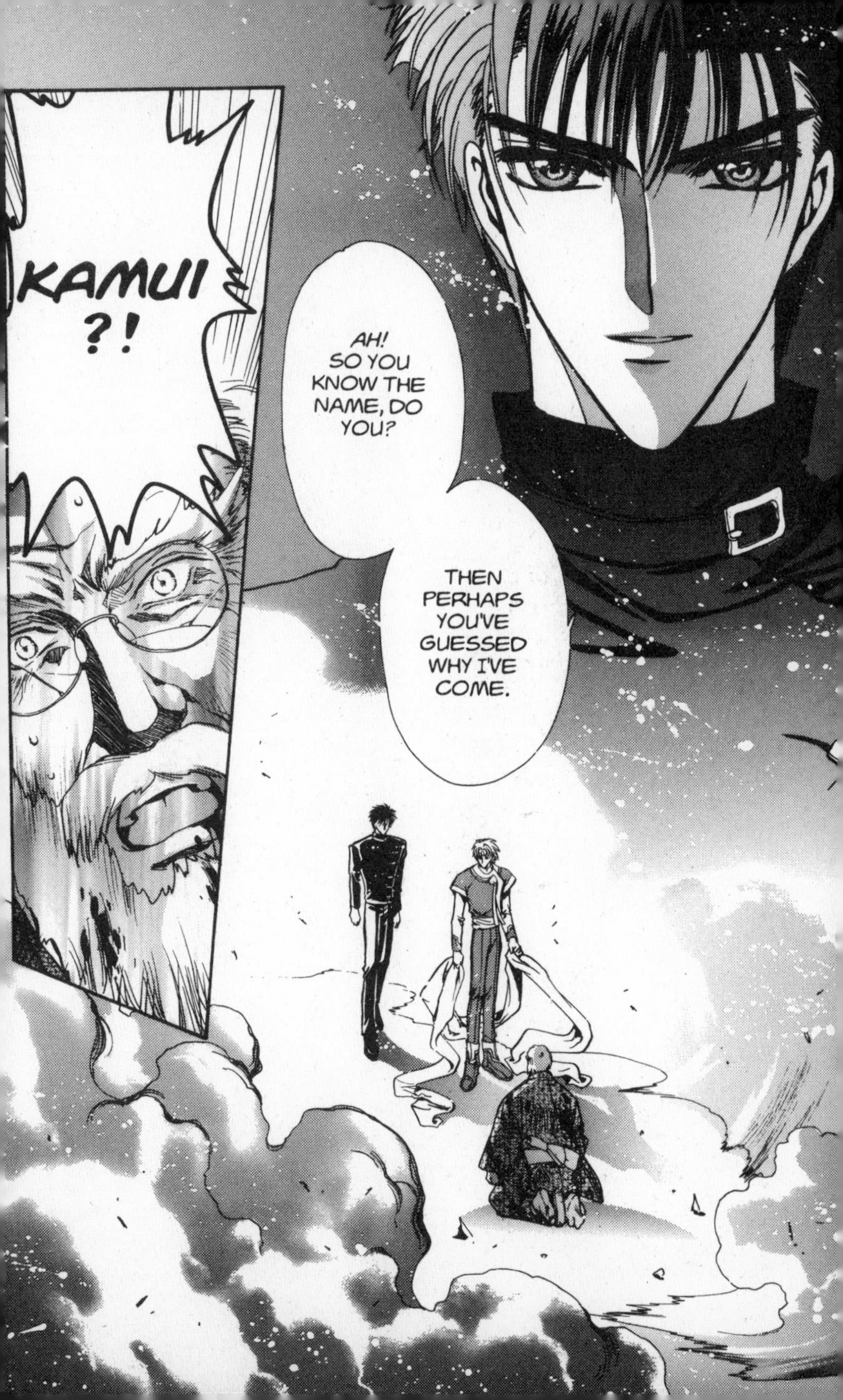
KAMUI ?!
AH! SO YOU KNOW THE NAME, DO YOU?
THEN PERHAPS YOU'VE GUESSED WHY I'VE COME.

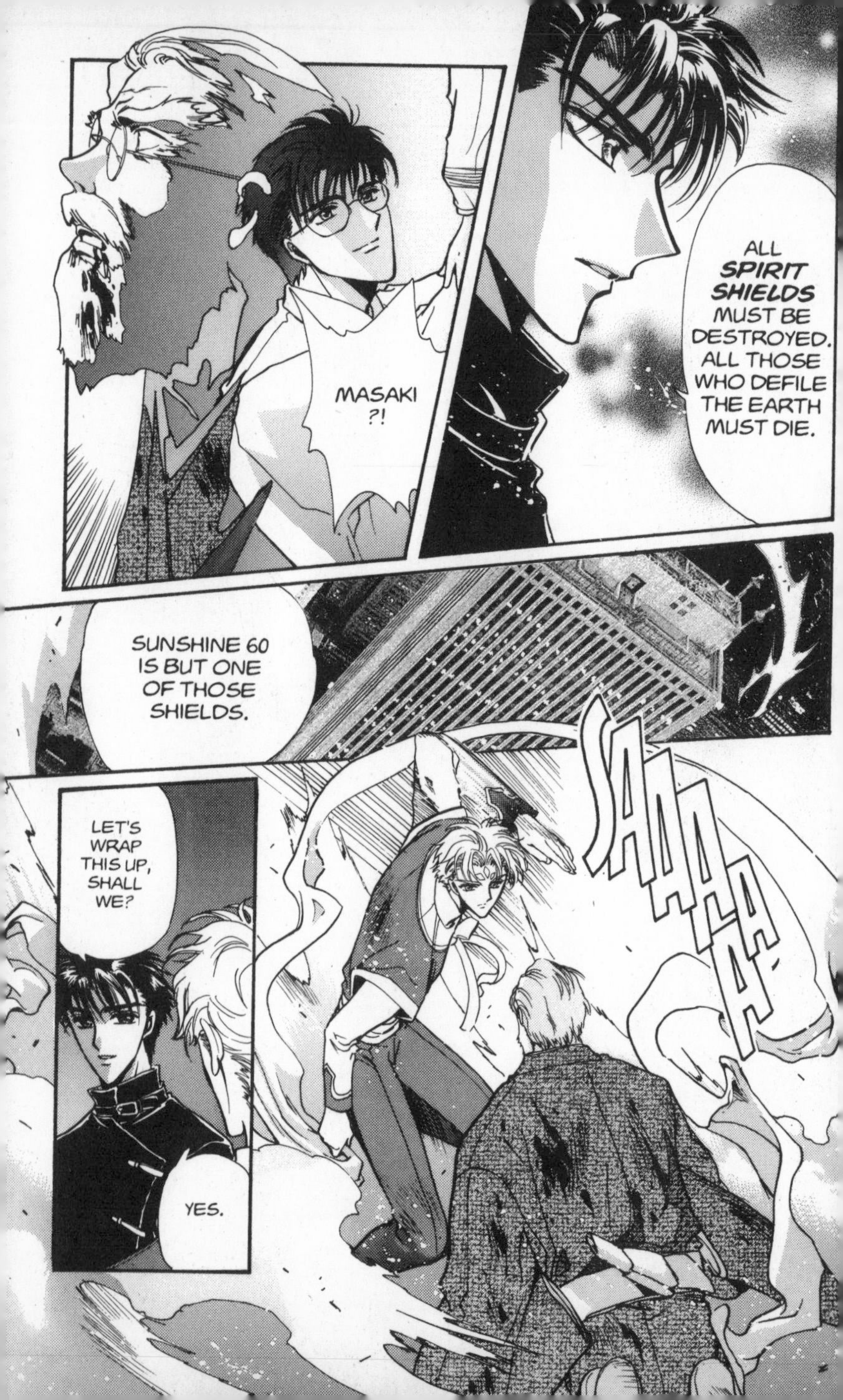
MASAKI ?!
ALL **SPIRIT SHIELDS** MUST BE DESTROYED. ALL THOSE WHO DEFILE THE EARTH MUST DIE.
SUNSHINE 60 IS BUT ONE OF THOSE SHIELDS.
SAAAAA
LET'S WRAP THIS UP, SHALL WE?
YES.

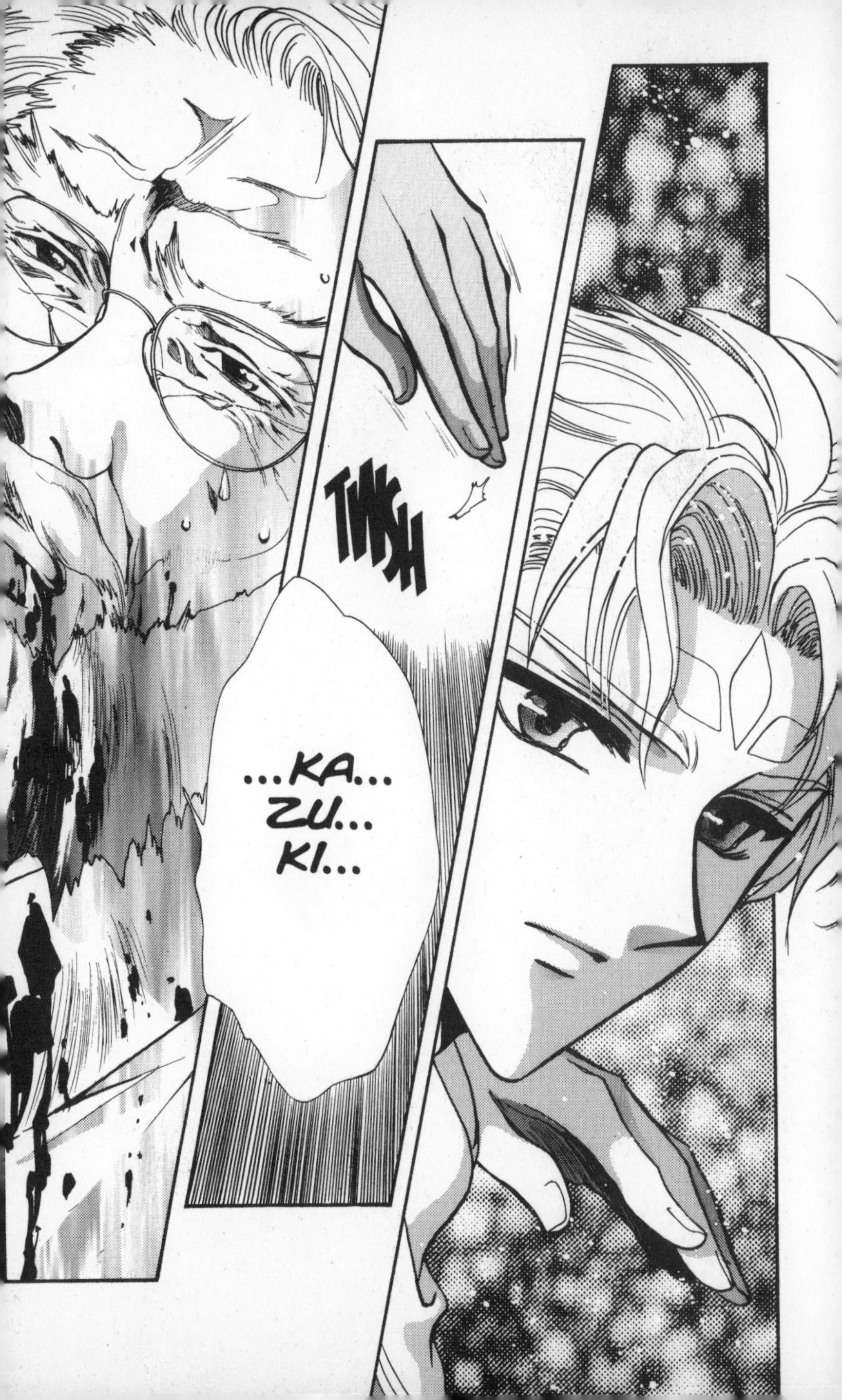
TWSH
...KA...
ZU...
KI...

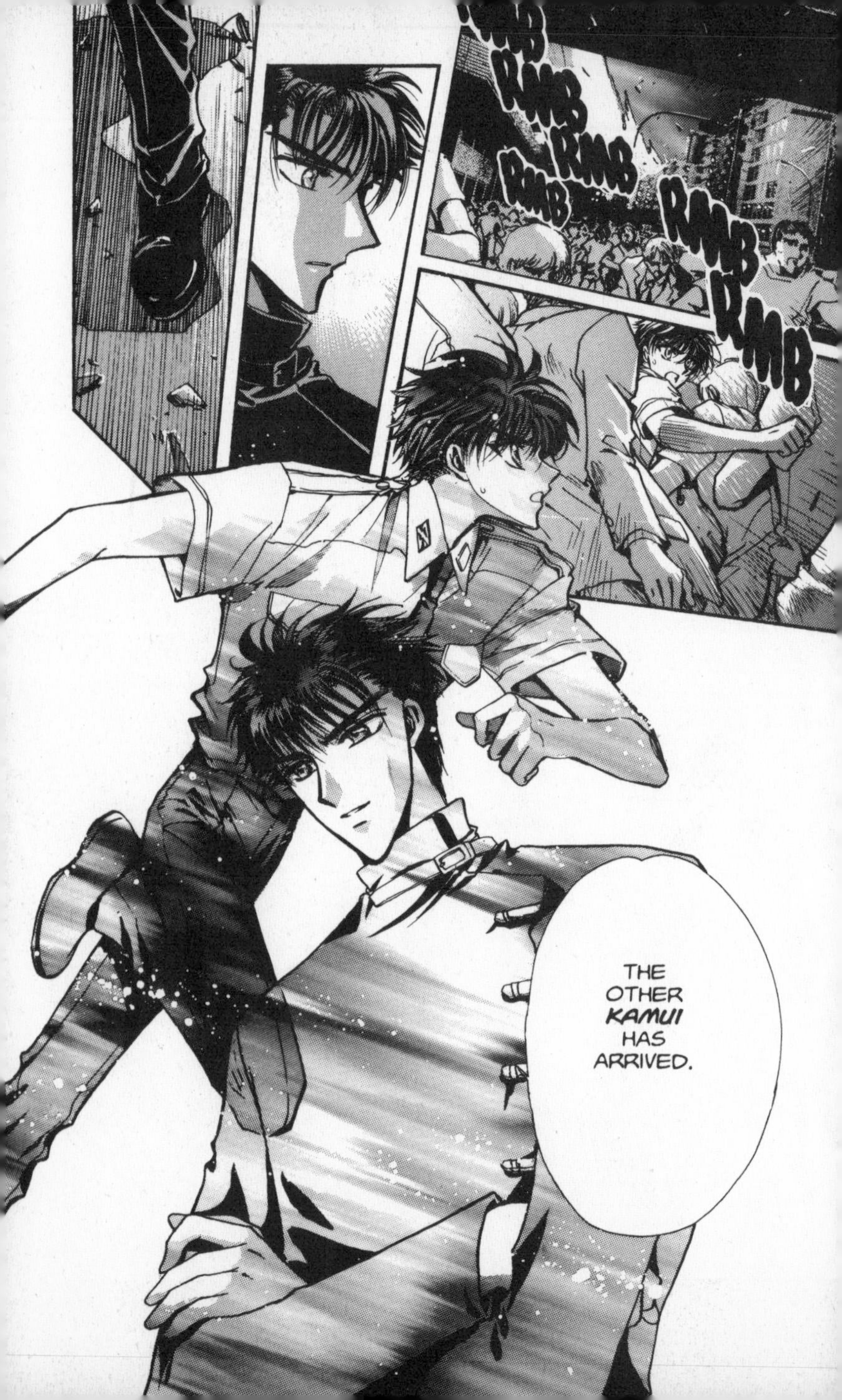
RMB RMB
RMB RMB
RMB
RMB RMB
THE OTHER KAMUI HAS ARRIVED.

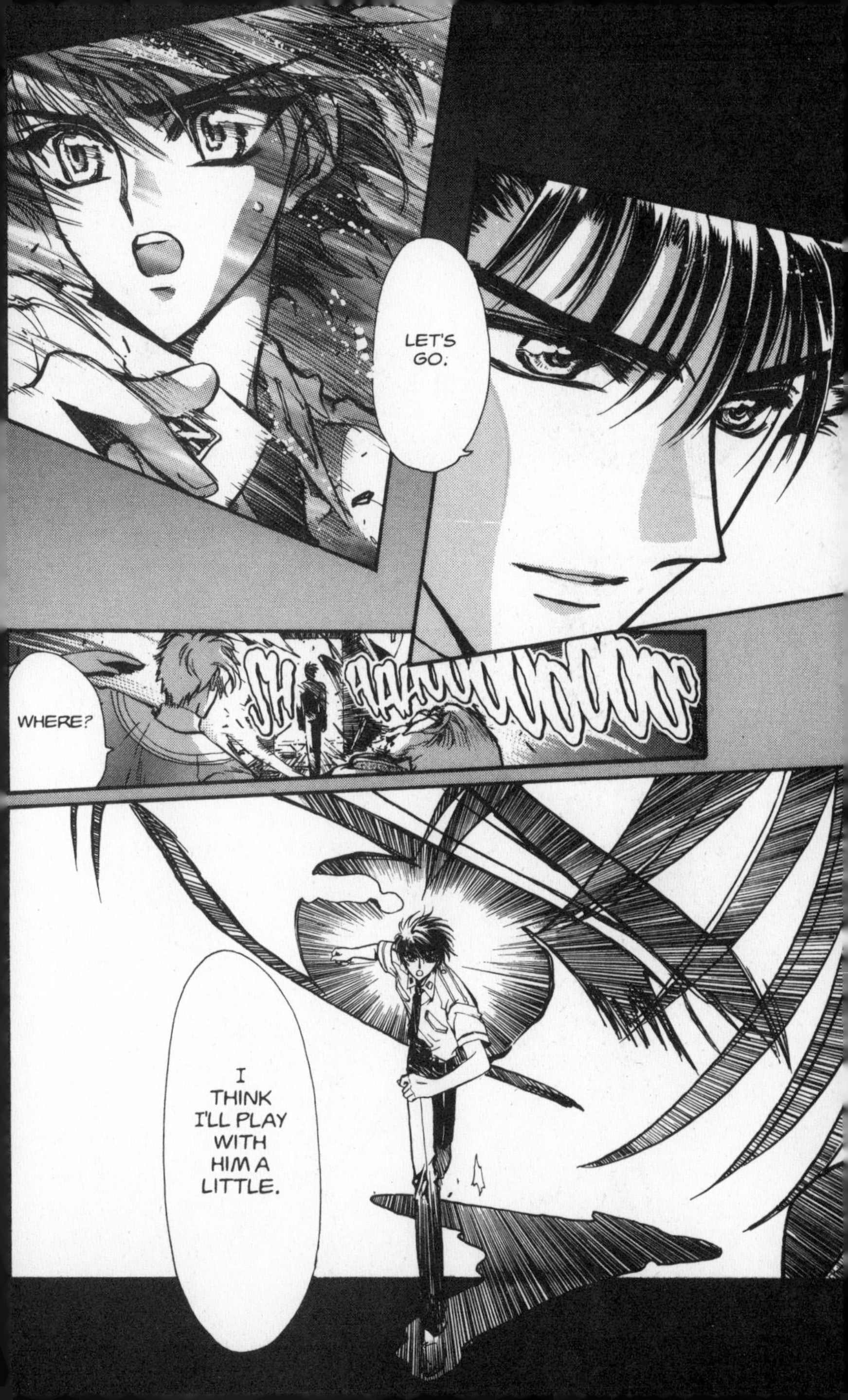
LET'S GO.
WHERE?
I THINK I'LL PLAY WITH HIM A LITTLE.

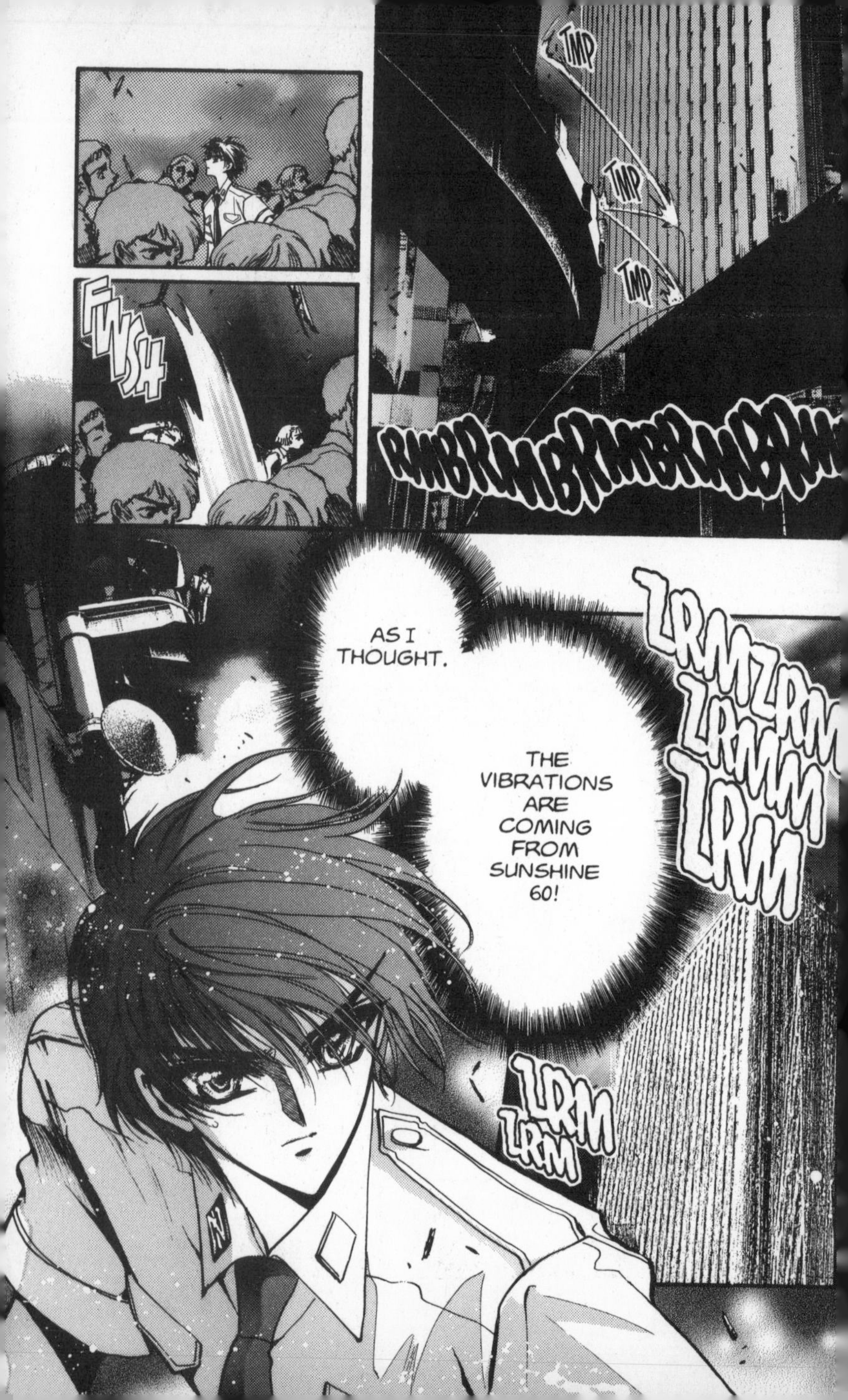
FWNSH
TMP
TMP
TMP
RMBRMBRMBRMBRM
AS I THOUGHT.
THE VIBRATIONS ARE COMING FROM SUNSHINE 60!
ZRMZRM
ZRMM
ZRM
ZRM
ZRM

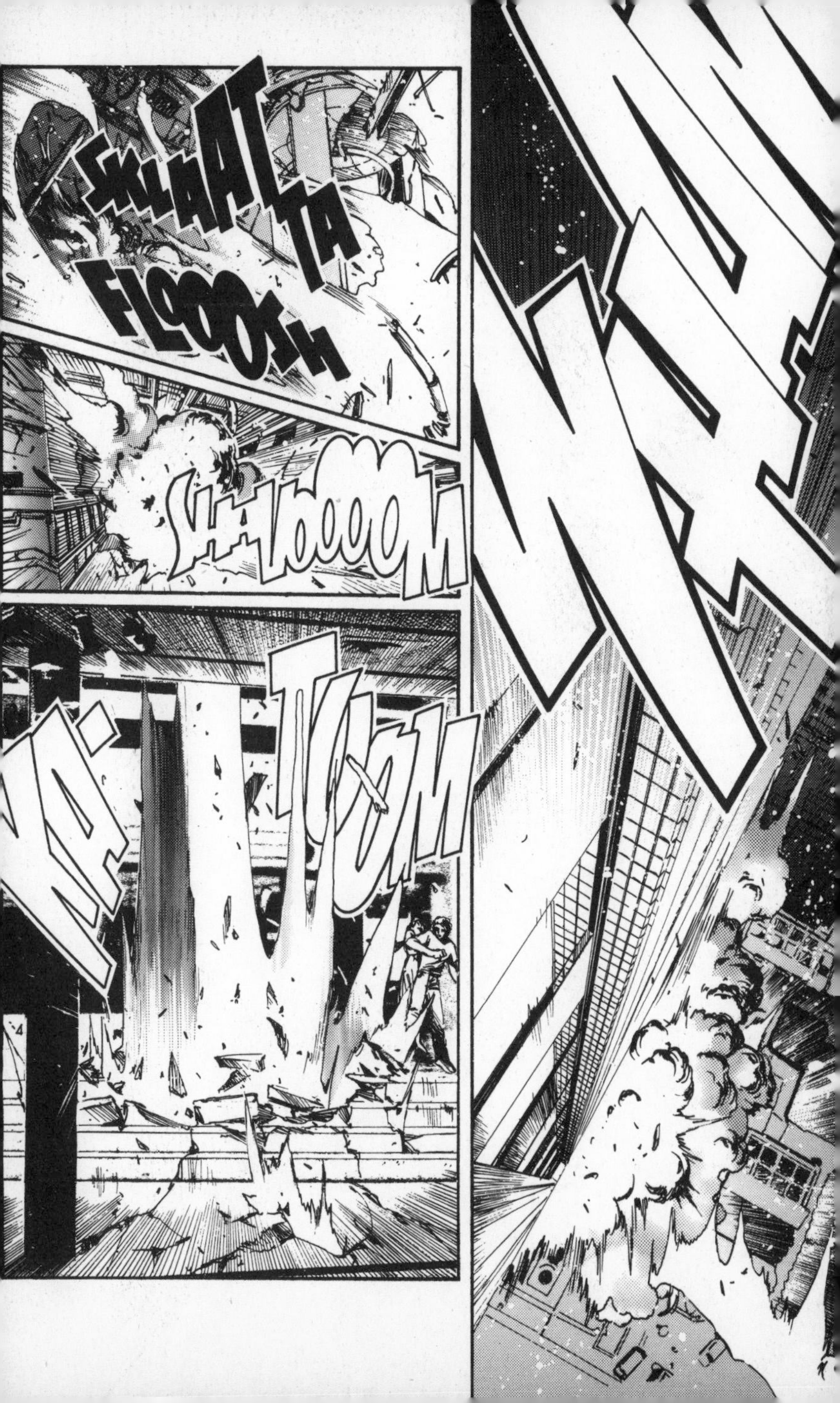
FLOOOSH
SHALOOOOM

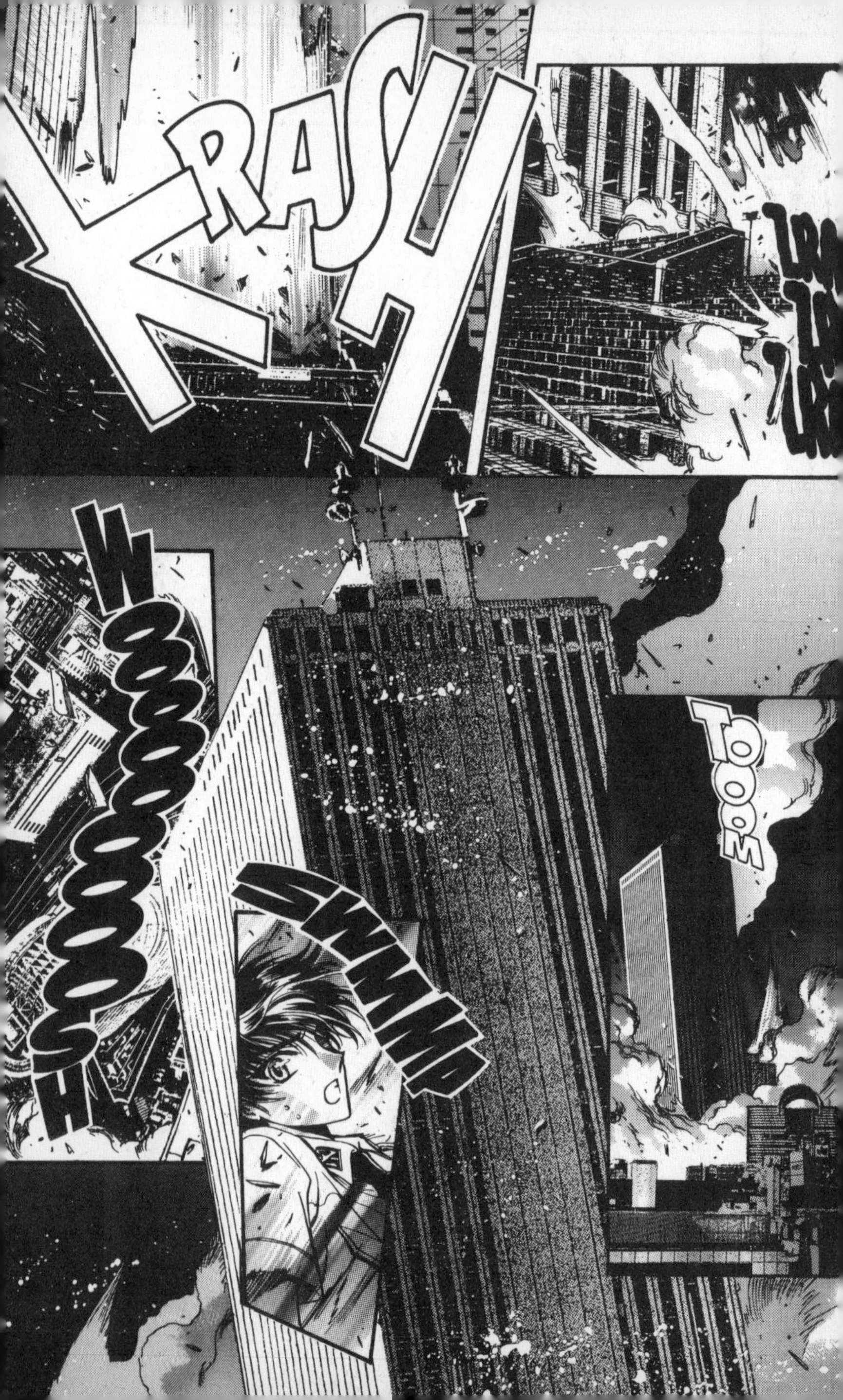
KRASH
WHOOOOOOOOSH
SWMMP
TOOOM

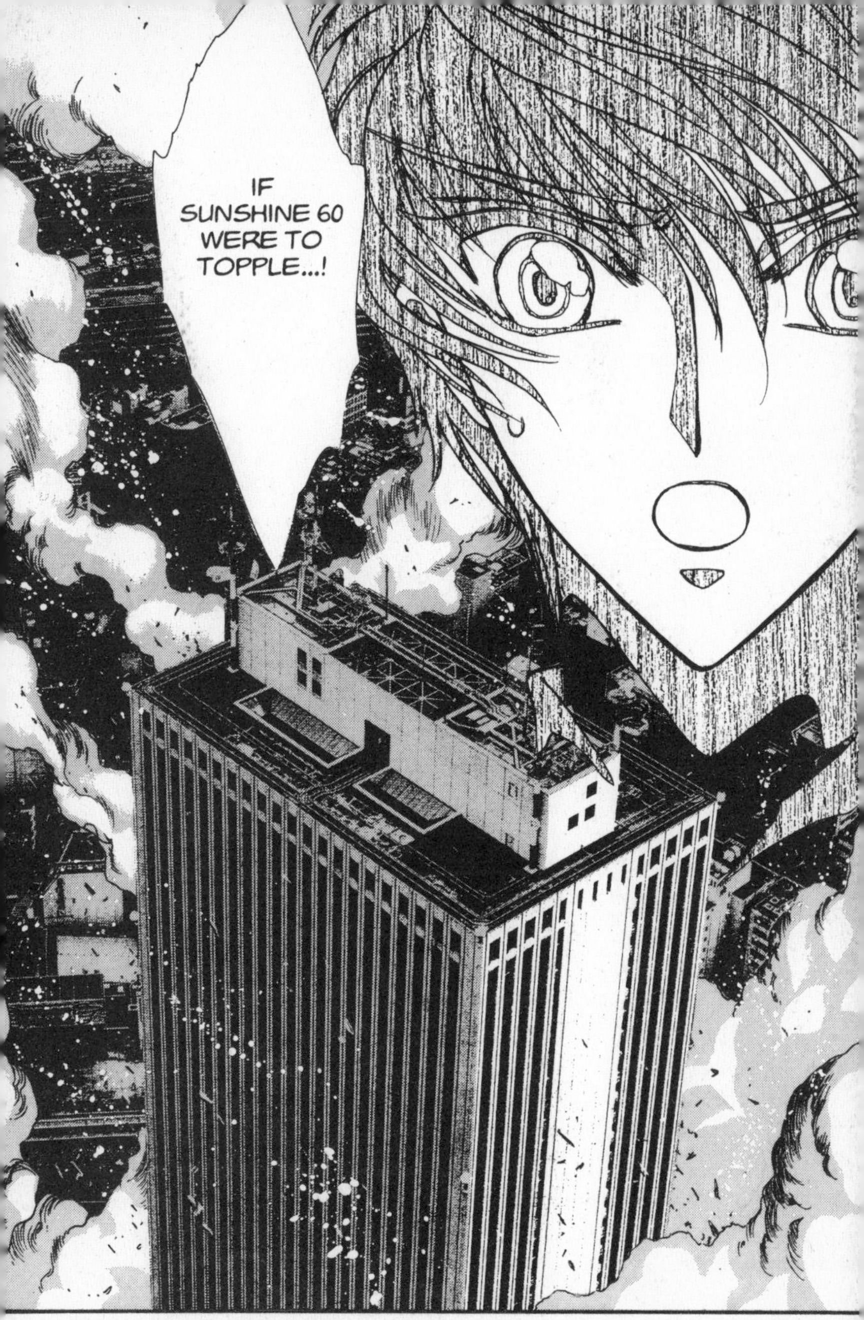
IF SUNSHINE 60 WERE TO TOPPLE...!

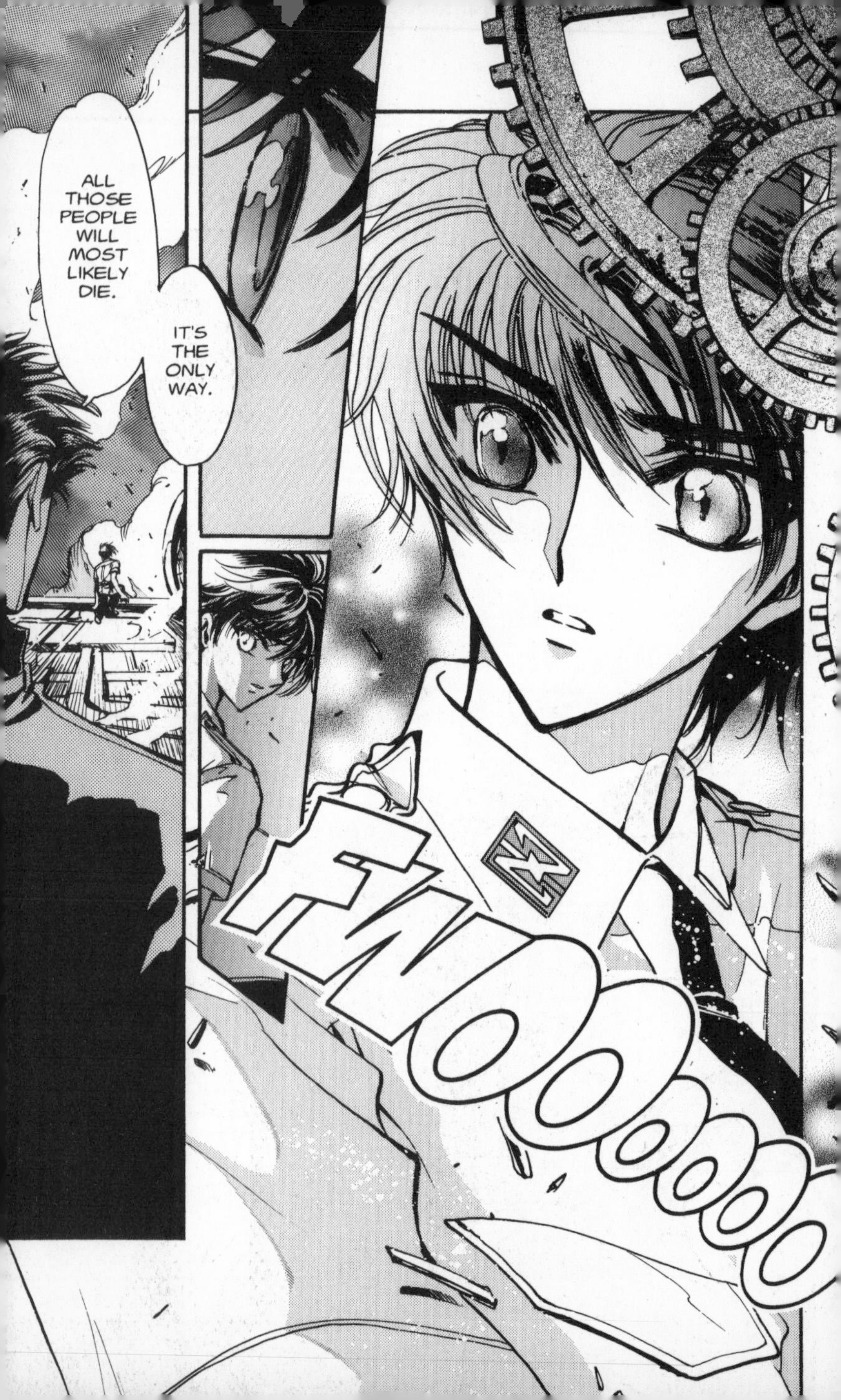
ALL THOSE PEOPLE WILL MOST LIKELY DIE.
IT'S THE ONLY WAY.
FWOOOOOOO

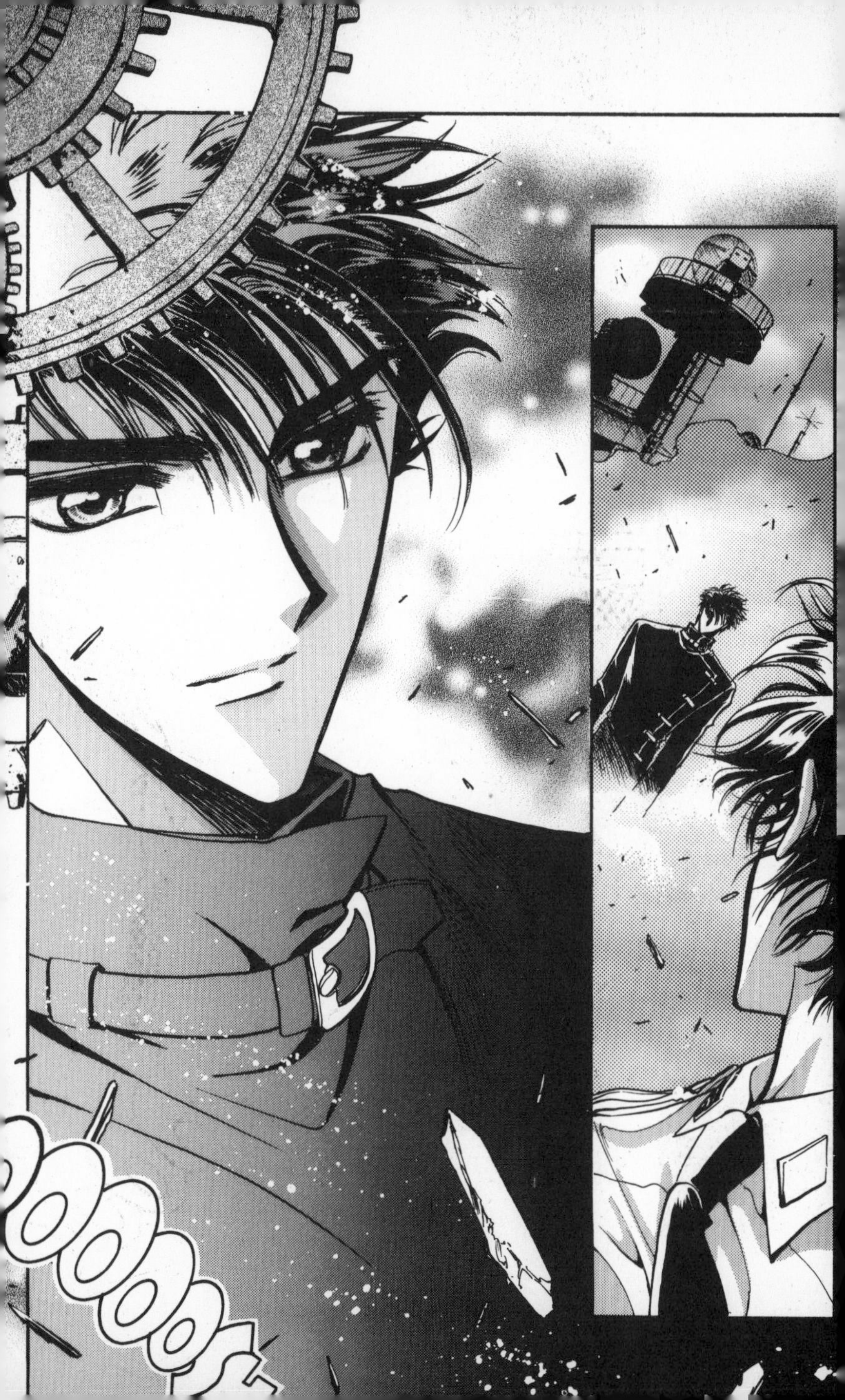
OOOOOS

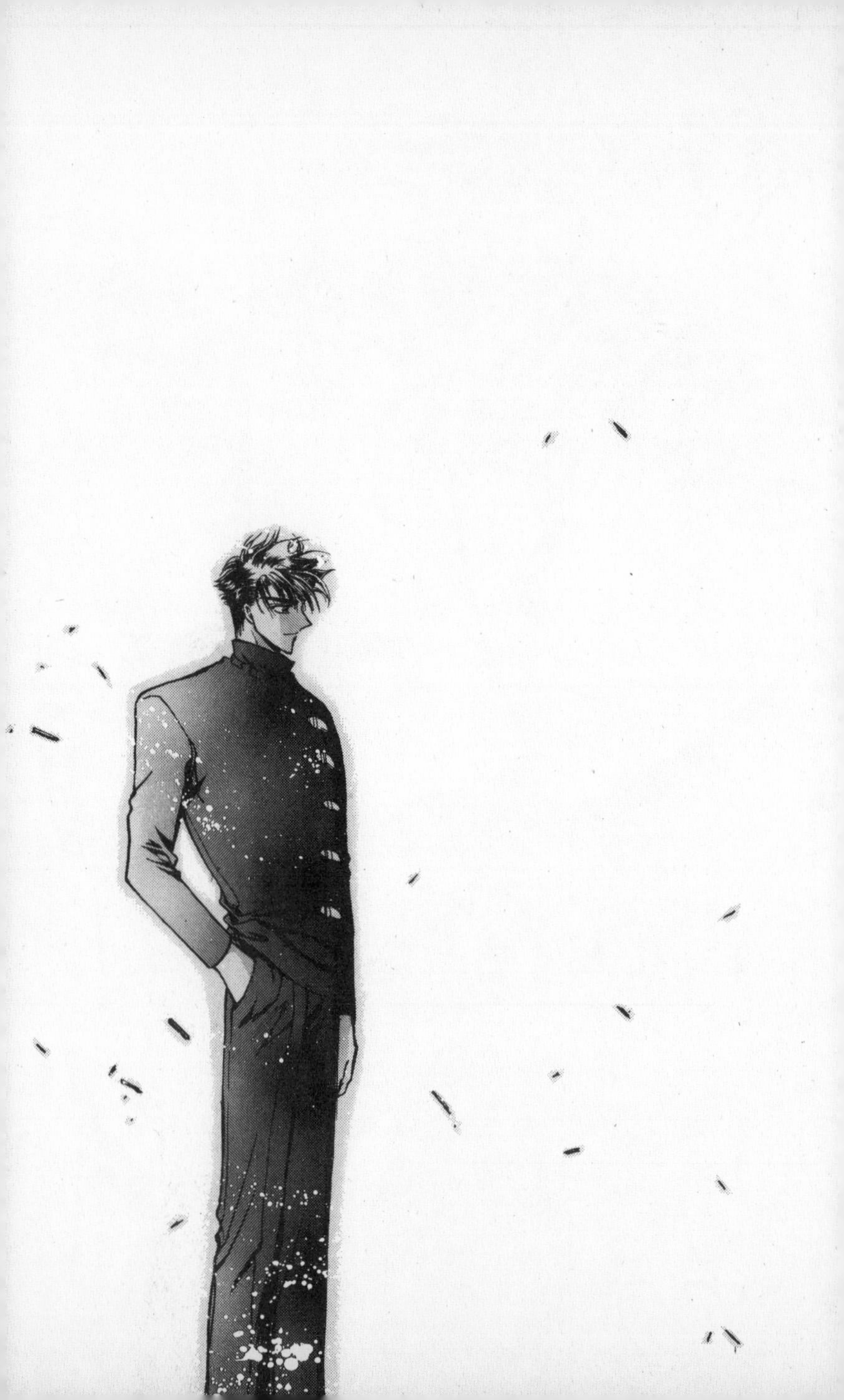

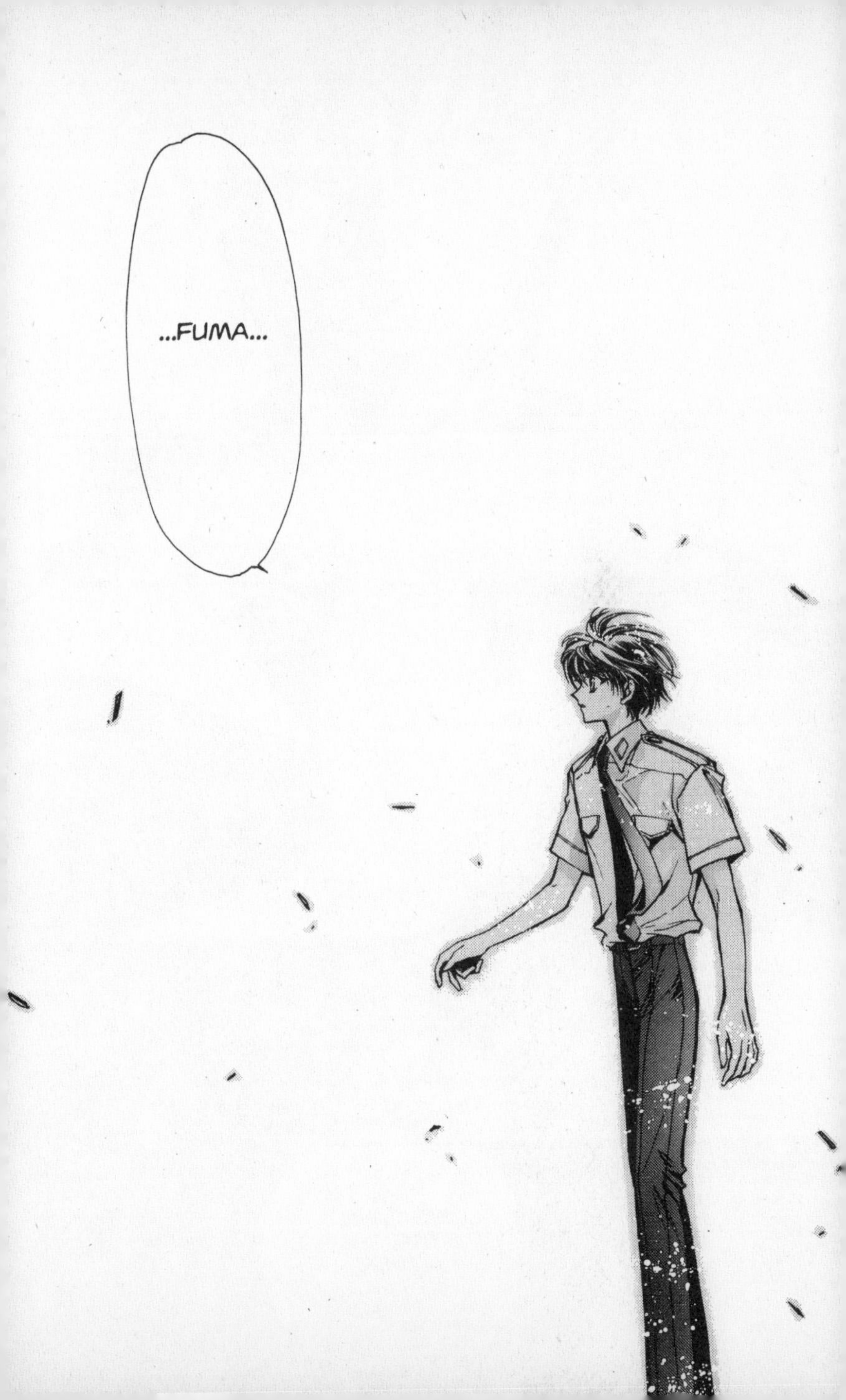
...FUMA...

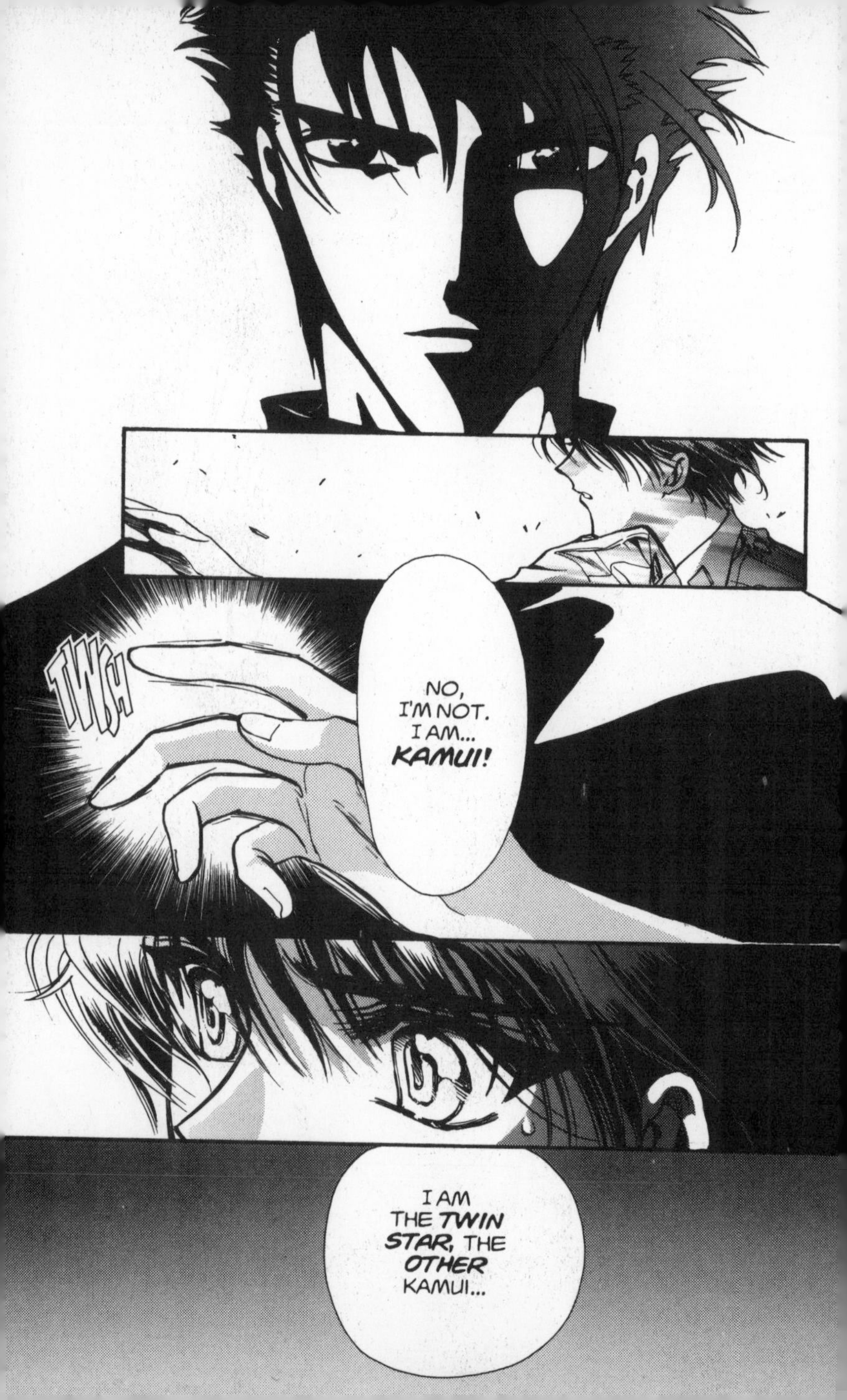
TWCH
NO, I'M NOT. I AM... KAMUI!
I AM THE TWIN STAR, THE OTHER KAMUI...

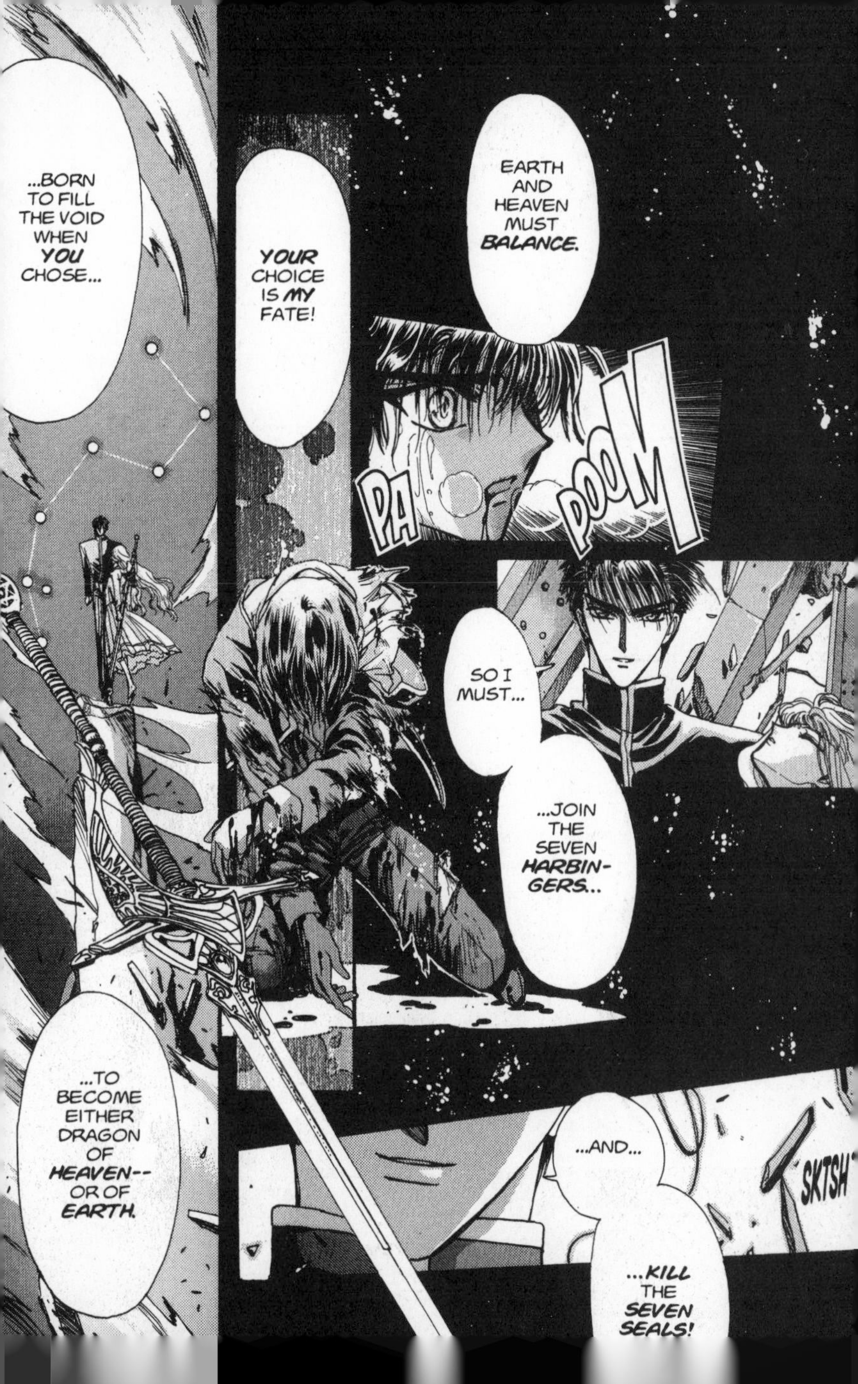
...BORN TO FILL THE VOID WHEN YOU CHOSE...
...TO BECOME EITHER DRAGON OF HEAVEN-- OR OF EARTH.
YOUR CHOICE IS MY FATE!
EARTH AND HEAVEN MUST BALANCE.
PA POOM
SO I MUST...
...JOIN THE SEVEN HARBIN-GERS...
...AND...
SKTSH
...KILL THE SEVEN SEALS!

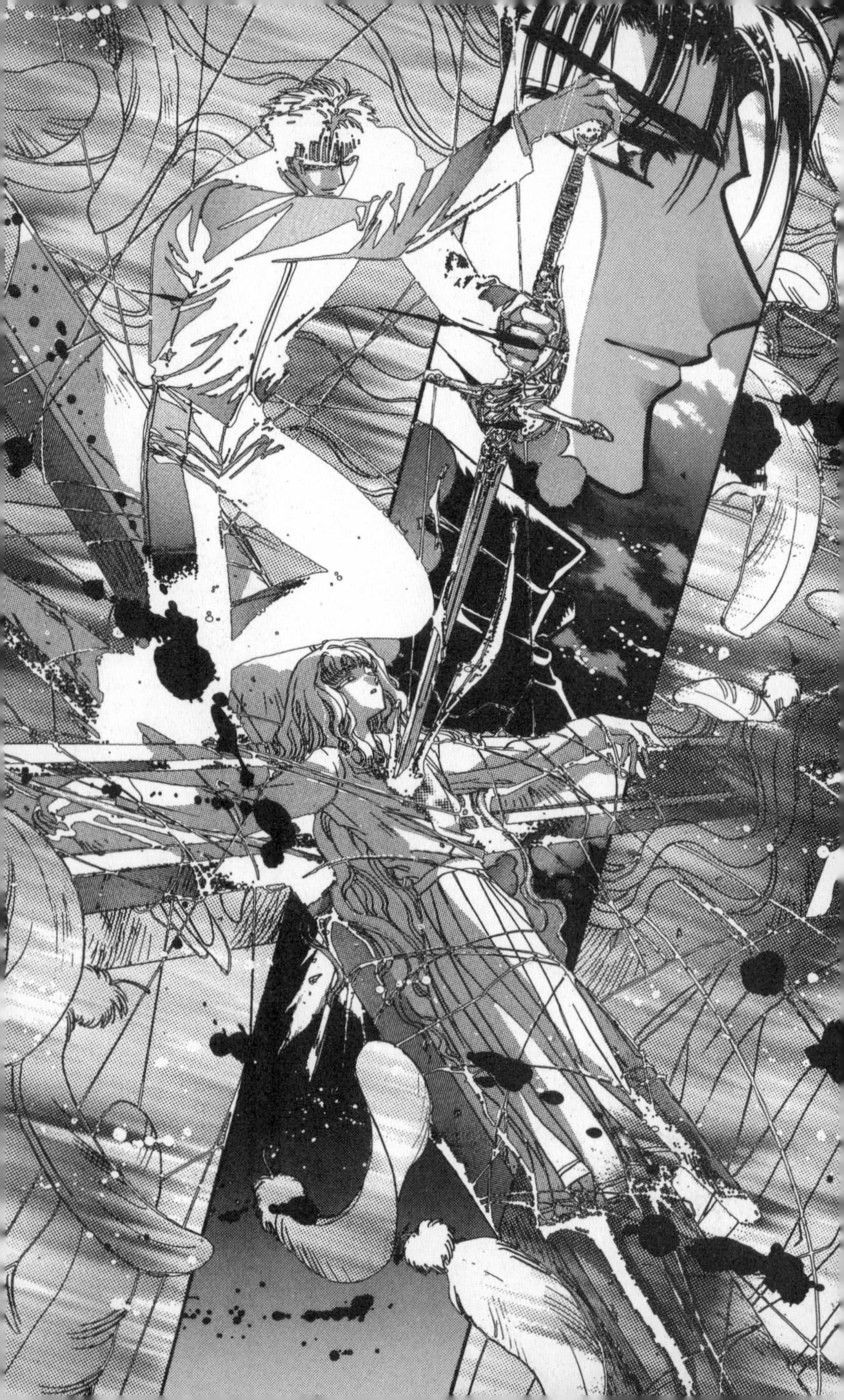

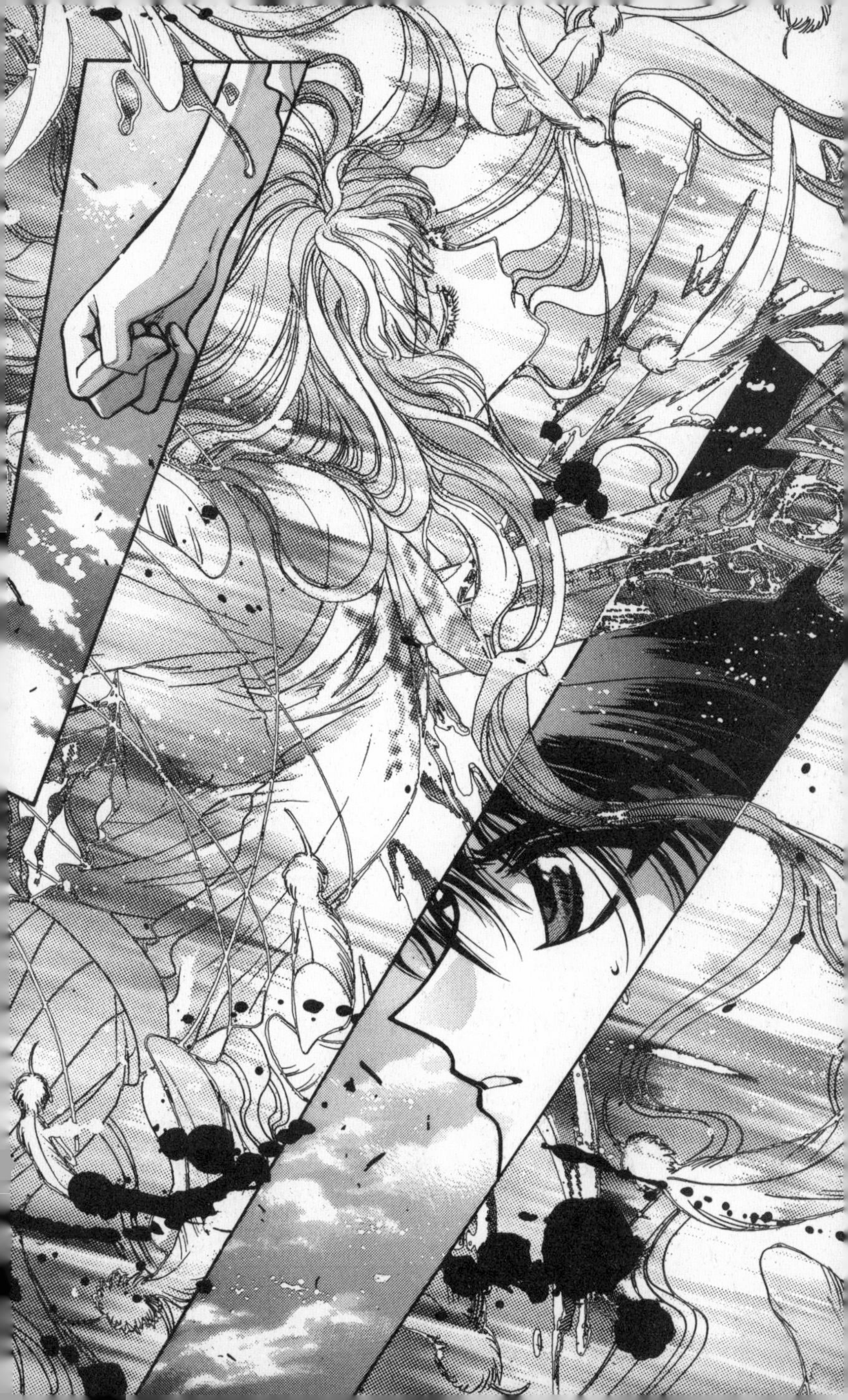

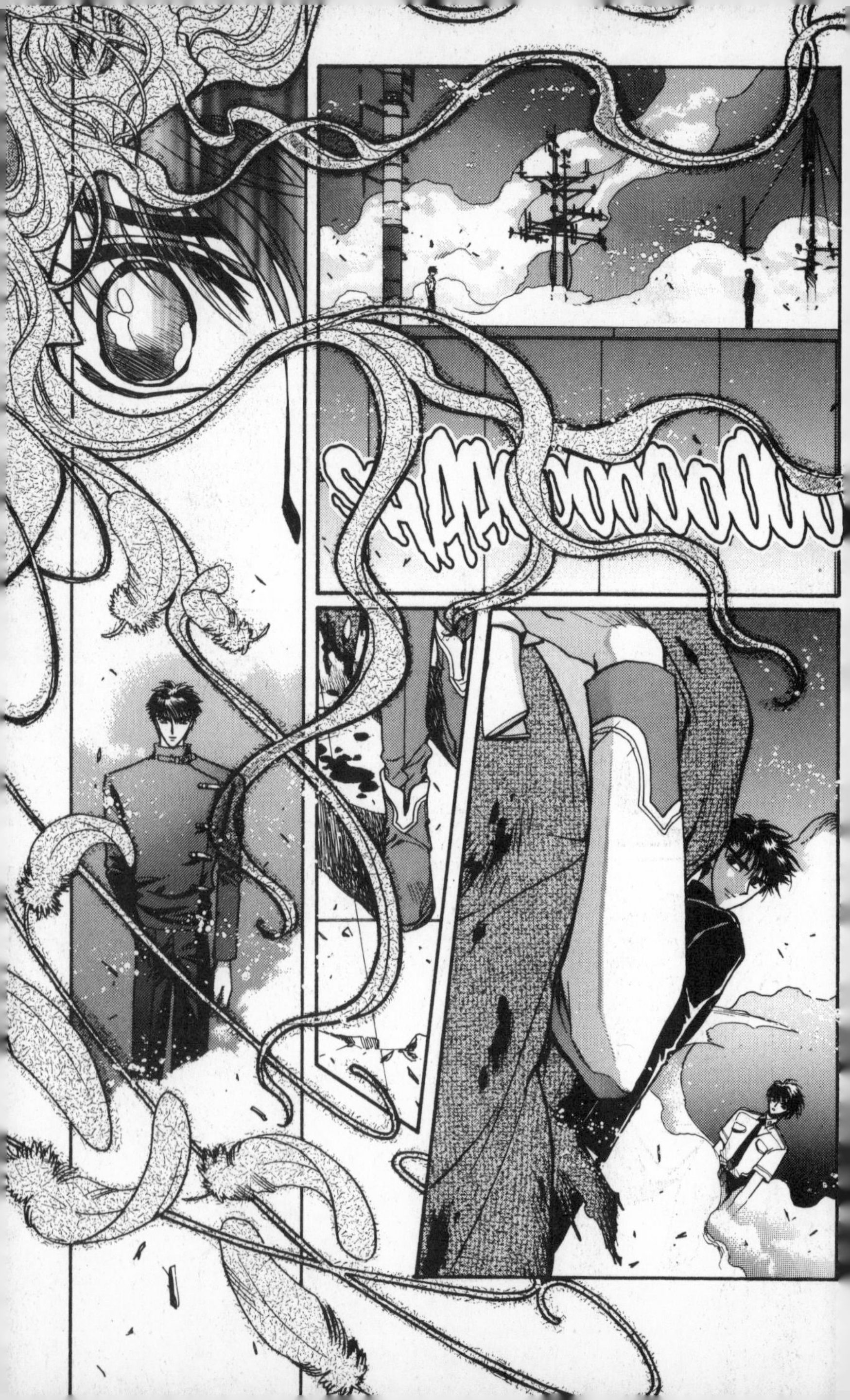
SHAAOOOOOOOO

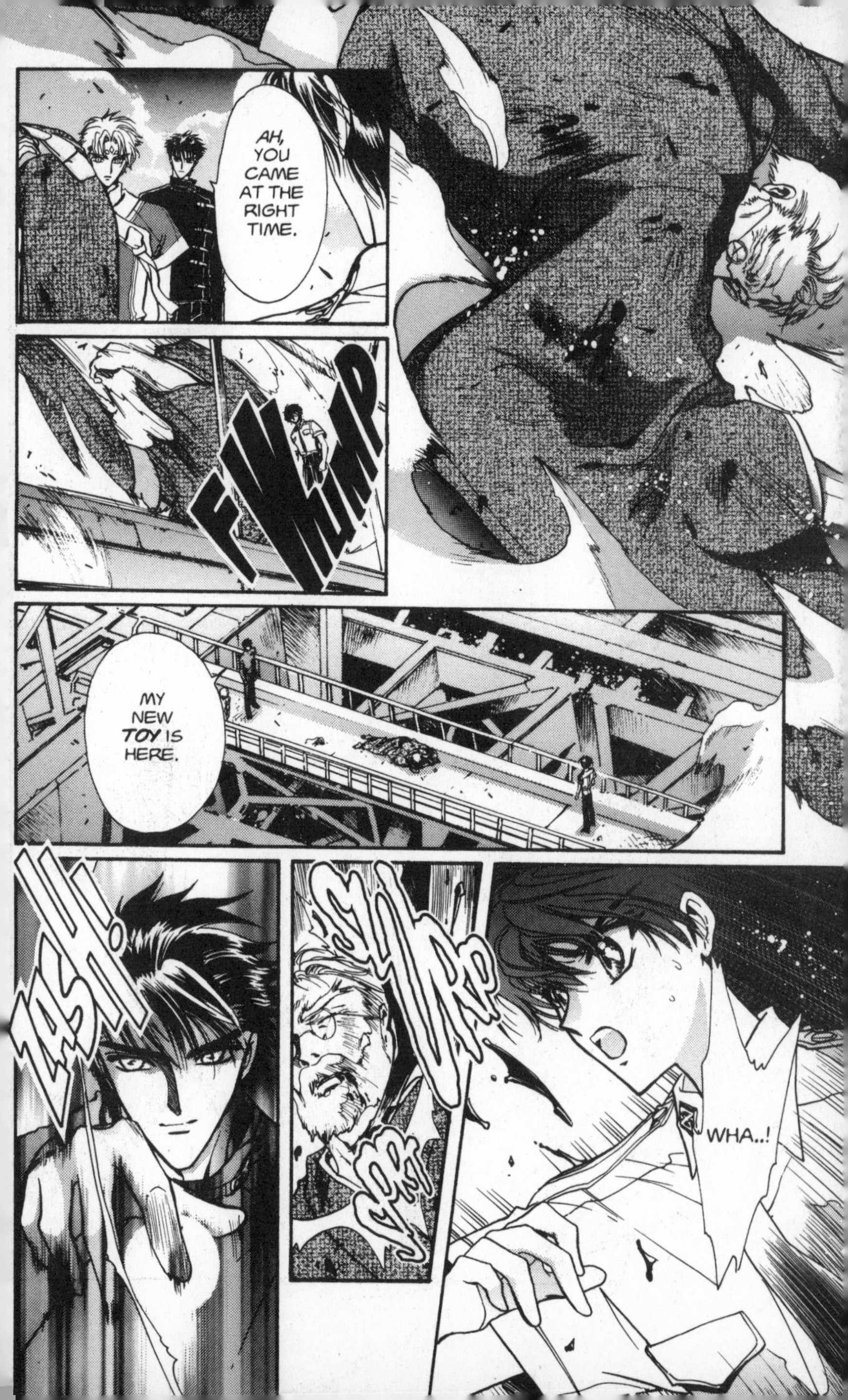
AH, YOU CAME AT THE RIGHT TIME.
FWUMP
MY NEW TOY IS HERE.
ZASH!!
WHA..!

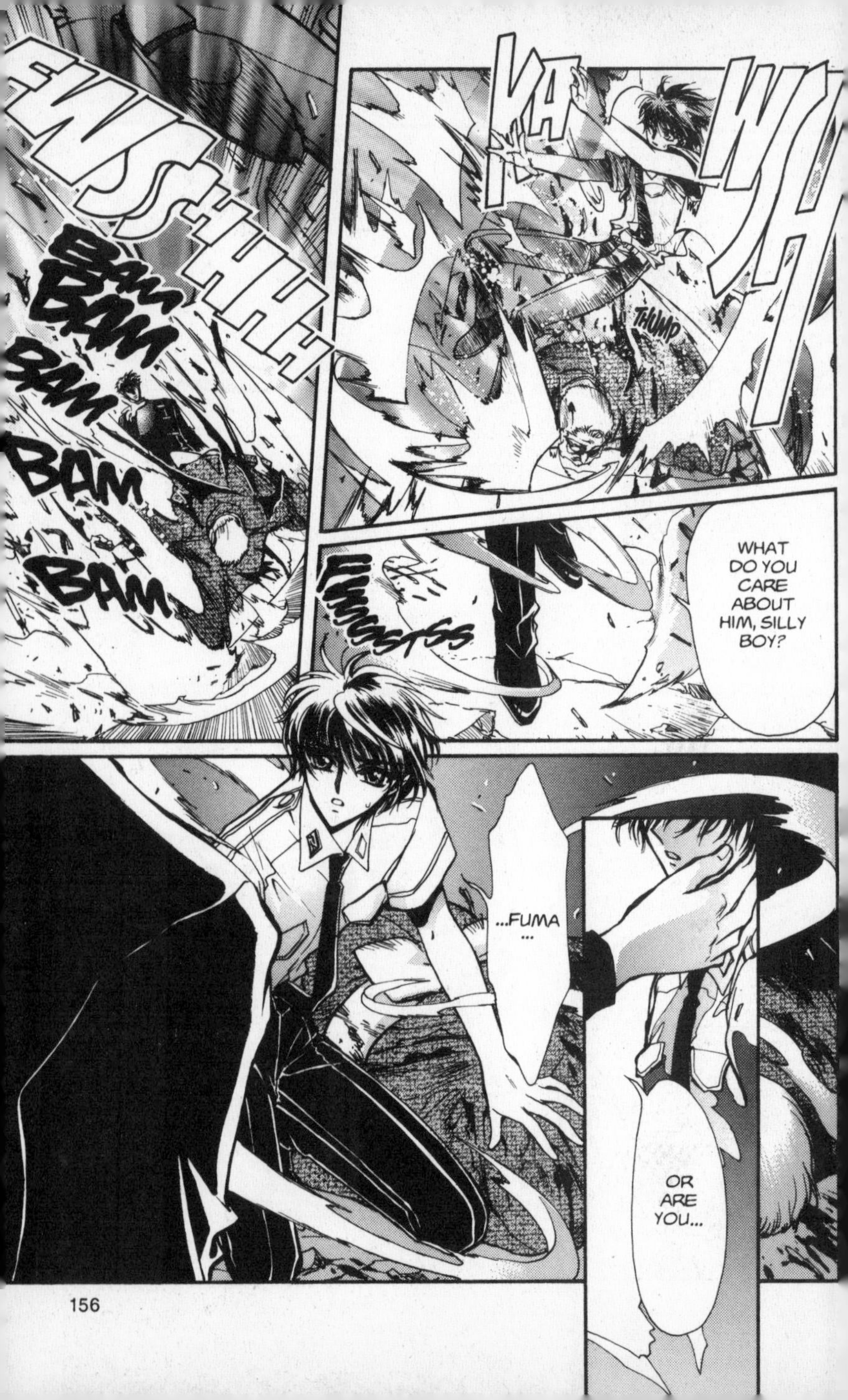

BAM
BAM
BAM
BAM
BAM
KA
THUMP
WHAT DO YOU CARE ABOUT HIM, SILLY BOY?
...FUMA ...
OR ARE YOU...

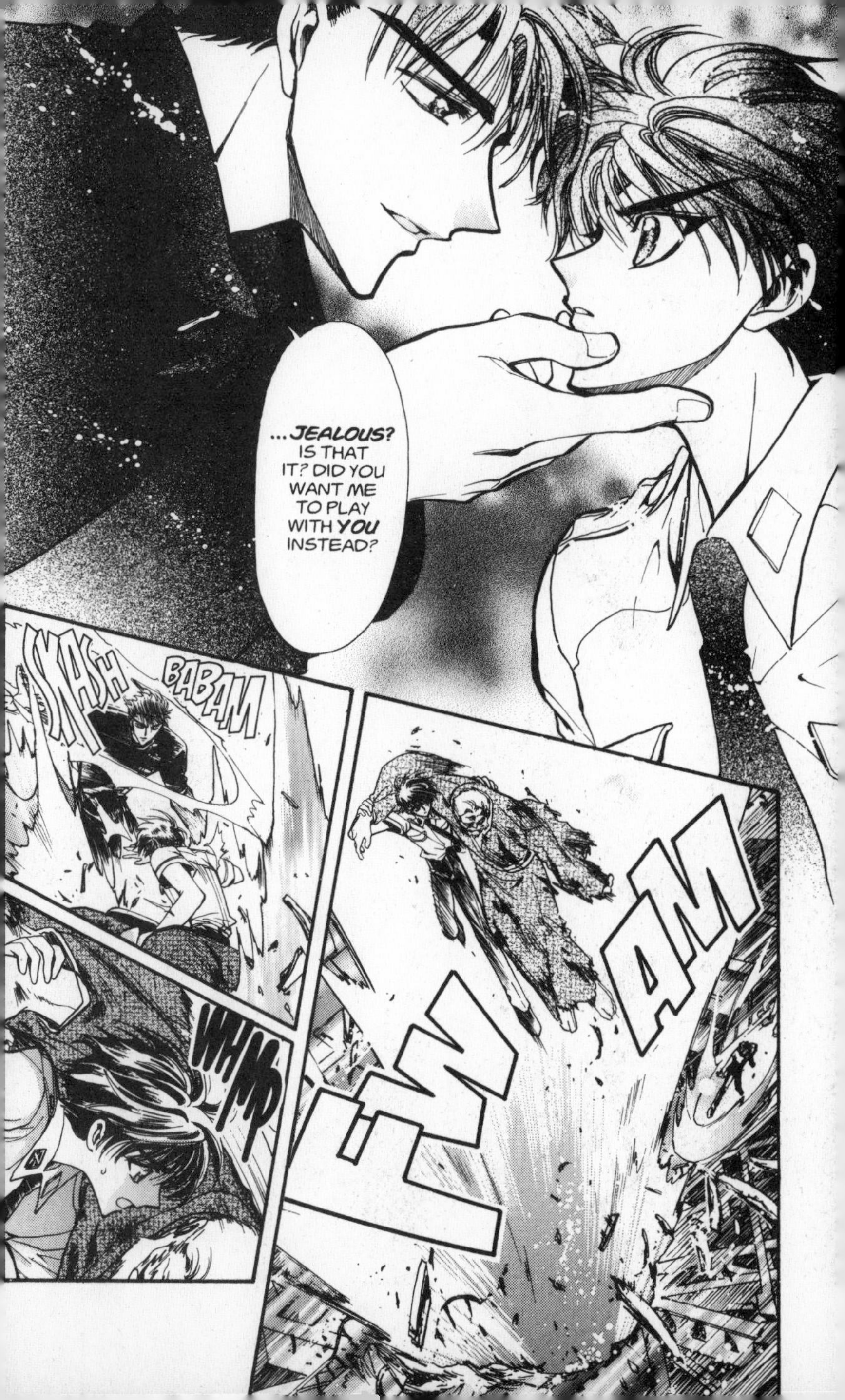
...JEALOUS? IS THAT IT? DID YOU WANT ME TO PLAY WITH YOU INSTEAD?
SLASH
BABAM
WHMP
BLAM

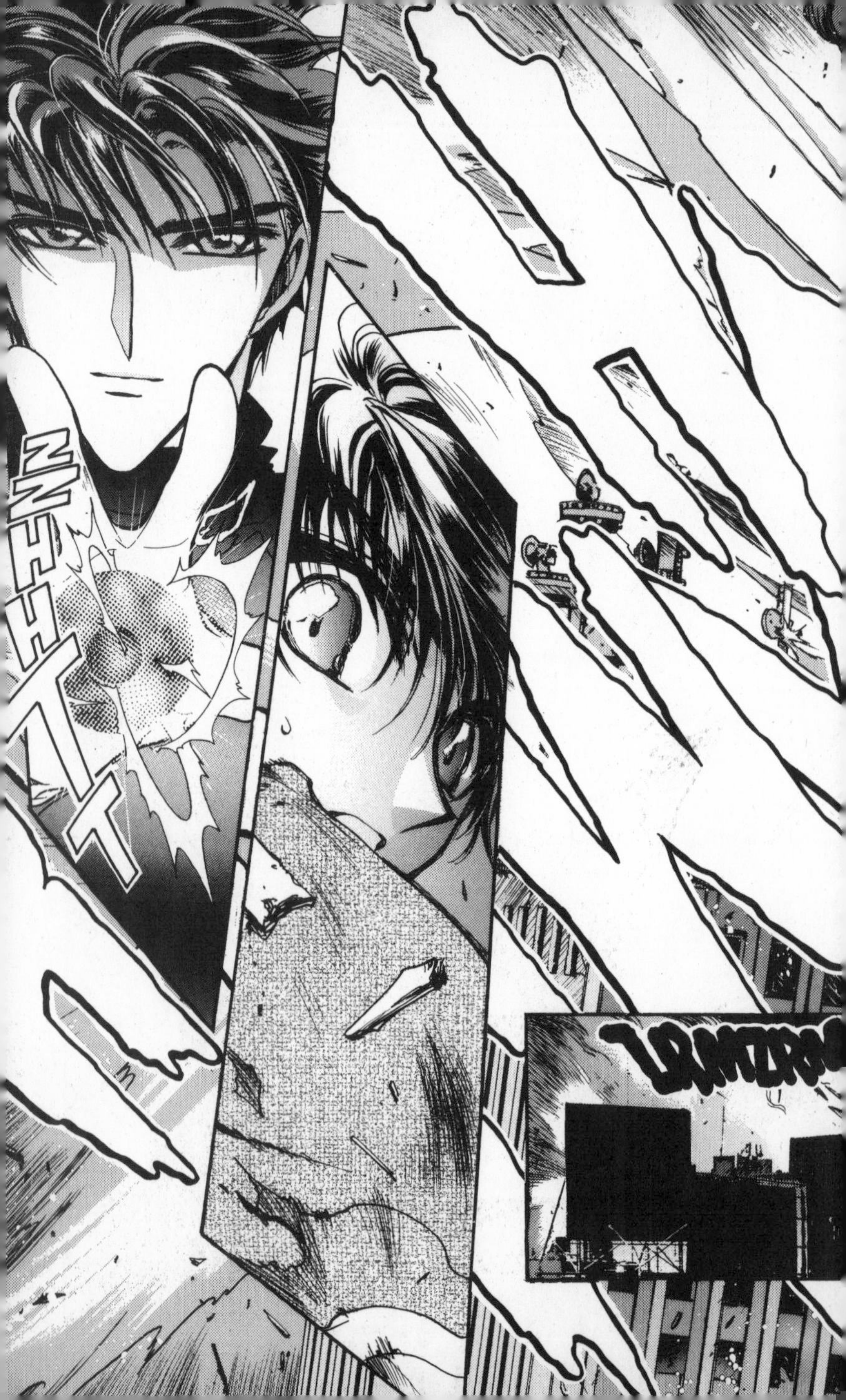

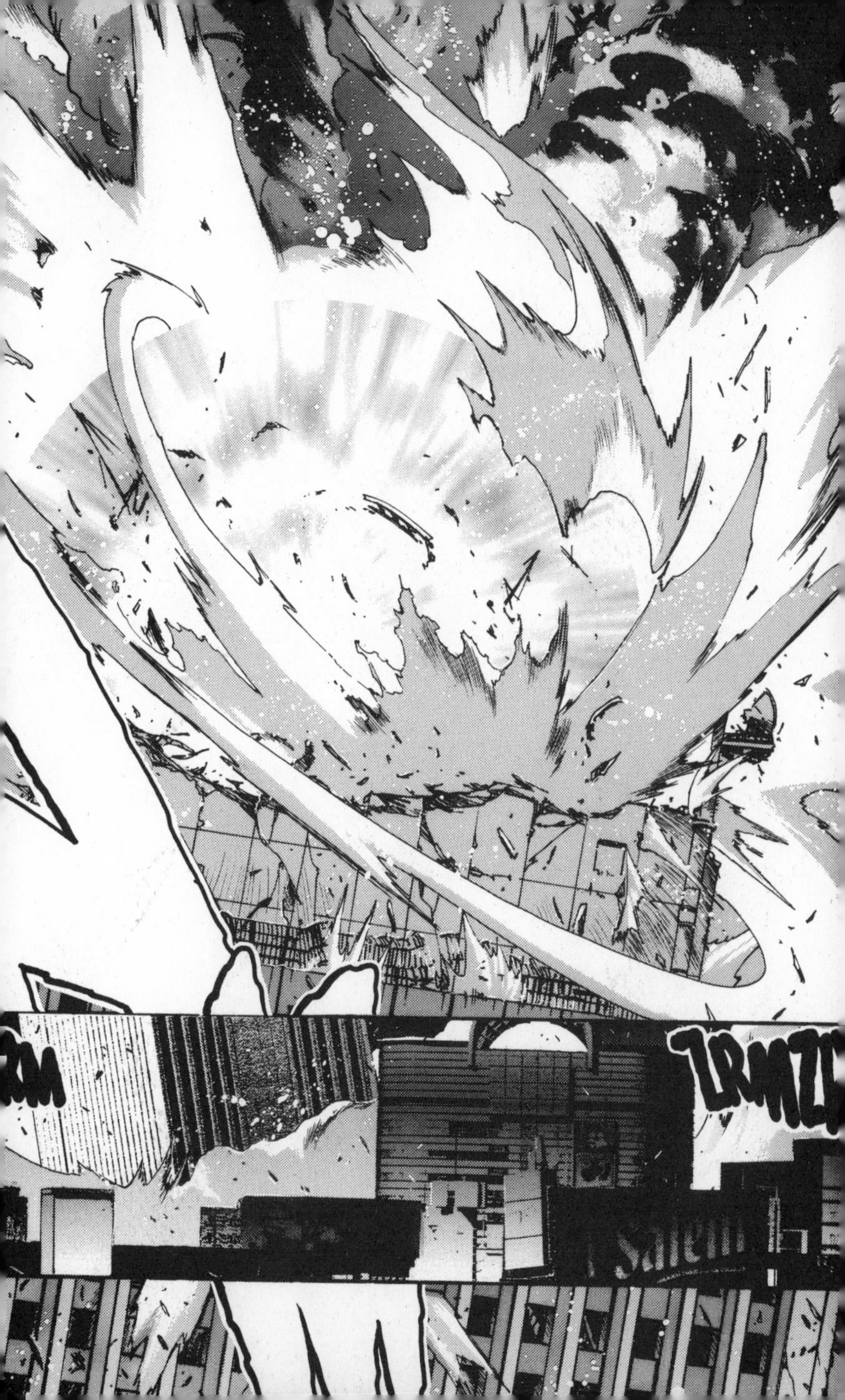

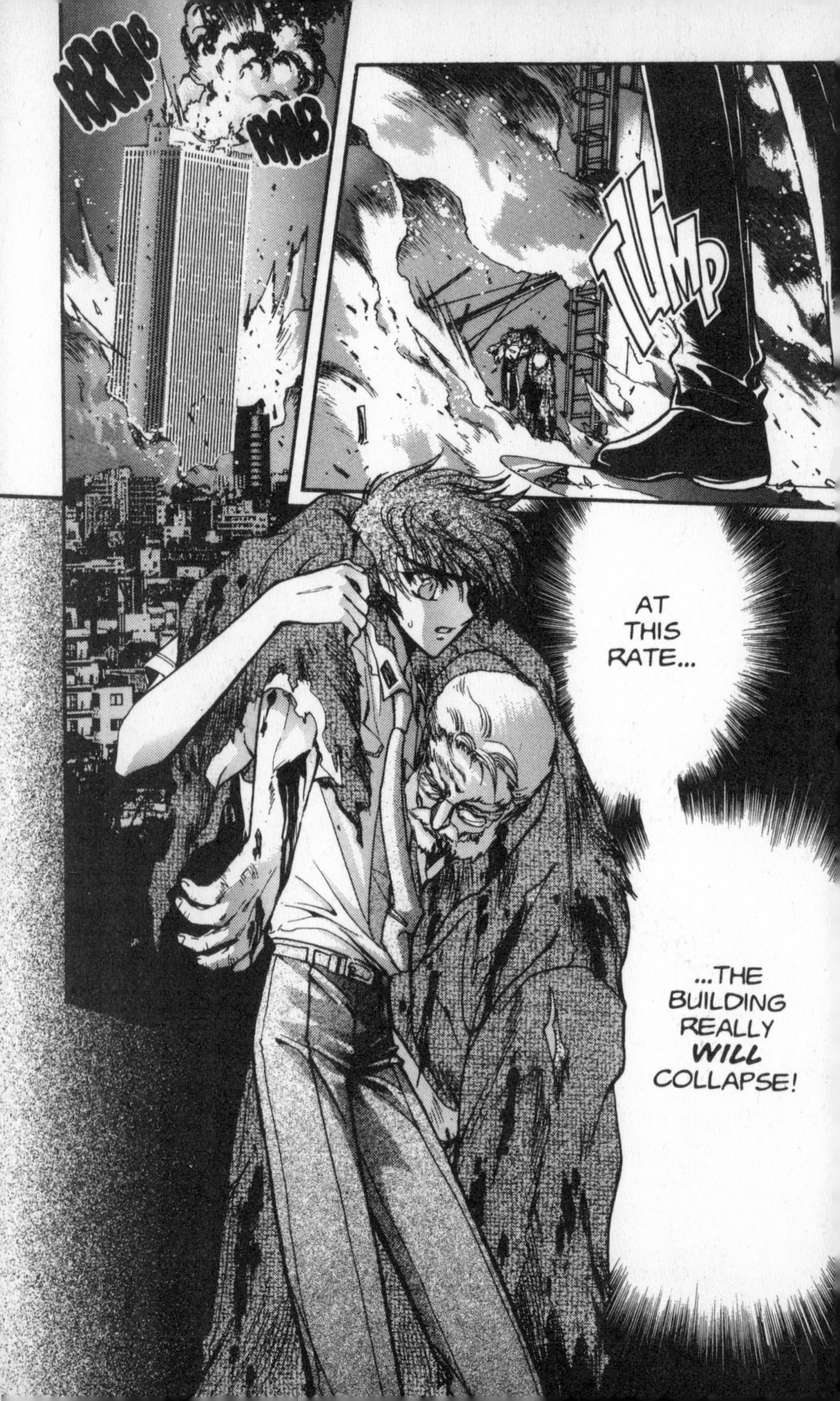
RRMMB
RMMB
THUMP
AT THIS RATE...
...THE BUILDING REALLY *WILL* COLLAPSE!

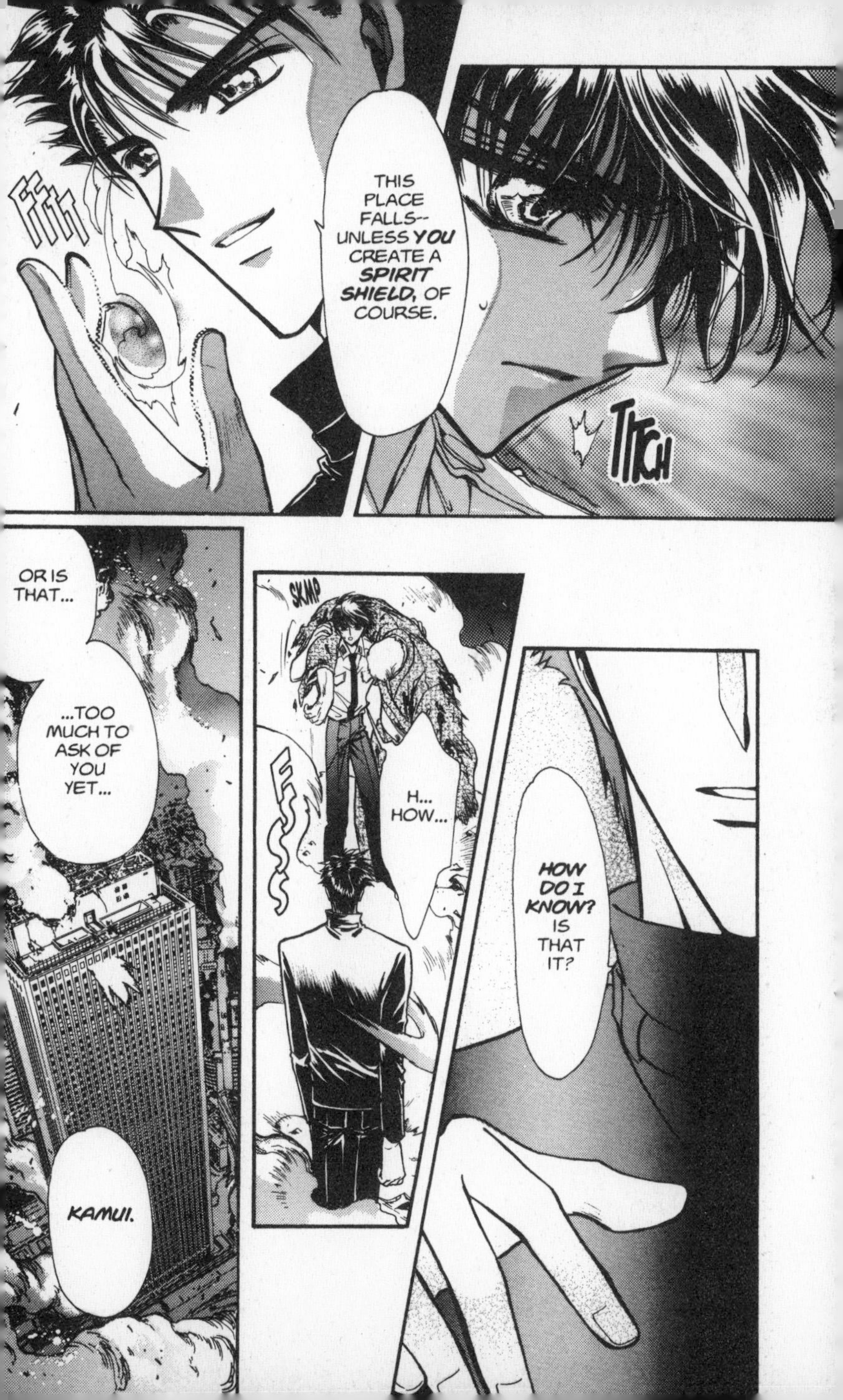

THIS PLACE FALLS-- UNLESS ***YOU*** CREATE A ***SPIRIT SHIELD,*** OF COURSE.
TWITCH
OR IS THAT...
...TOO MUCH TO ASK OF YOU YET...
KAMUI.
SKMP
H... HOW...
HOW DO I KNOW? IS THAT IT?

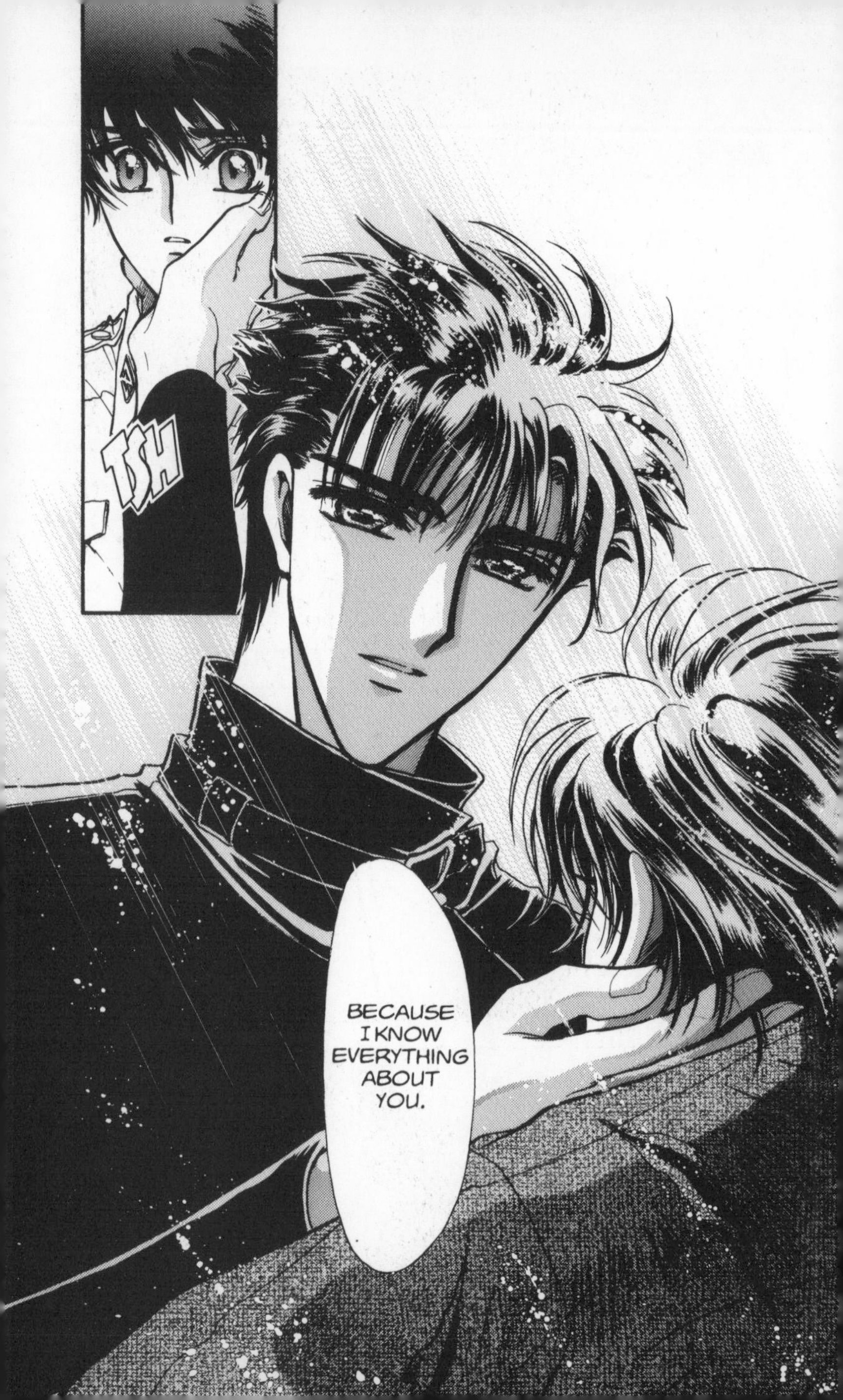
TSH
BECAUSE I KNOW EVERYTHING ABOUT YOU.

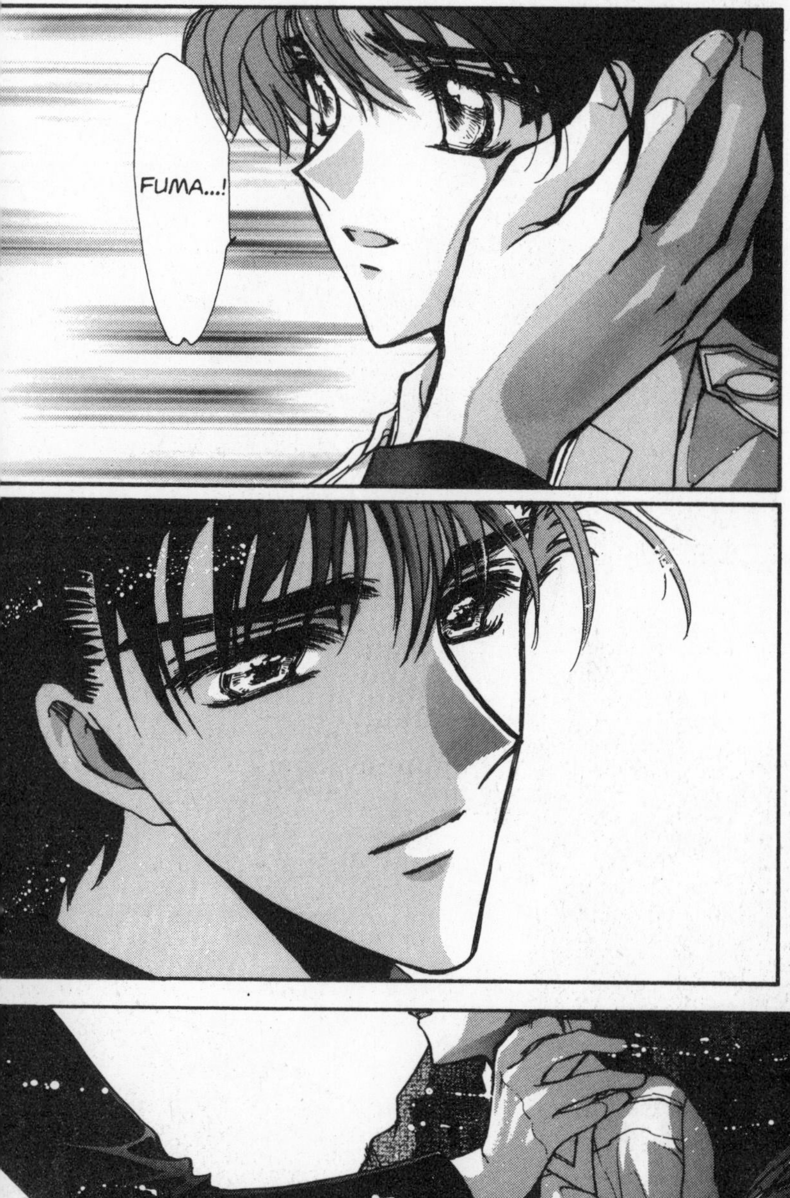
FUMA...!

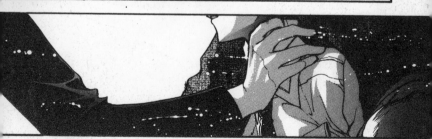

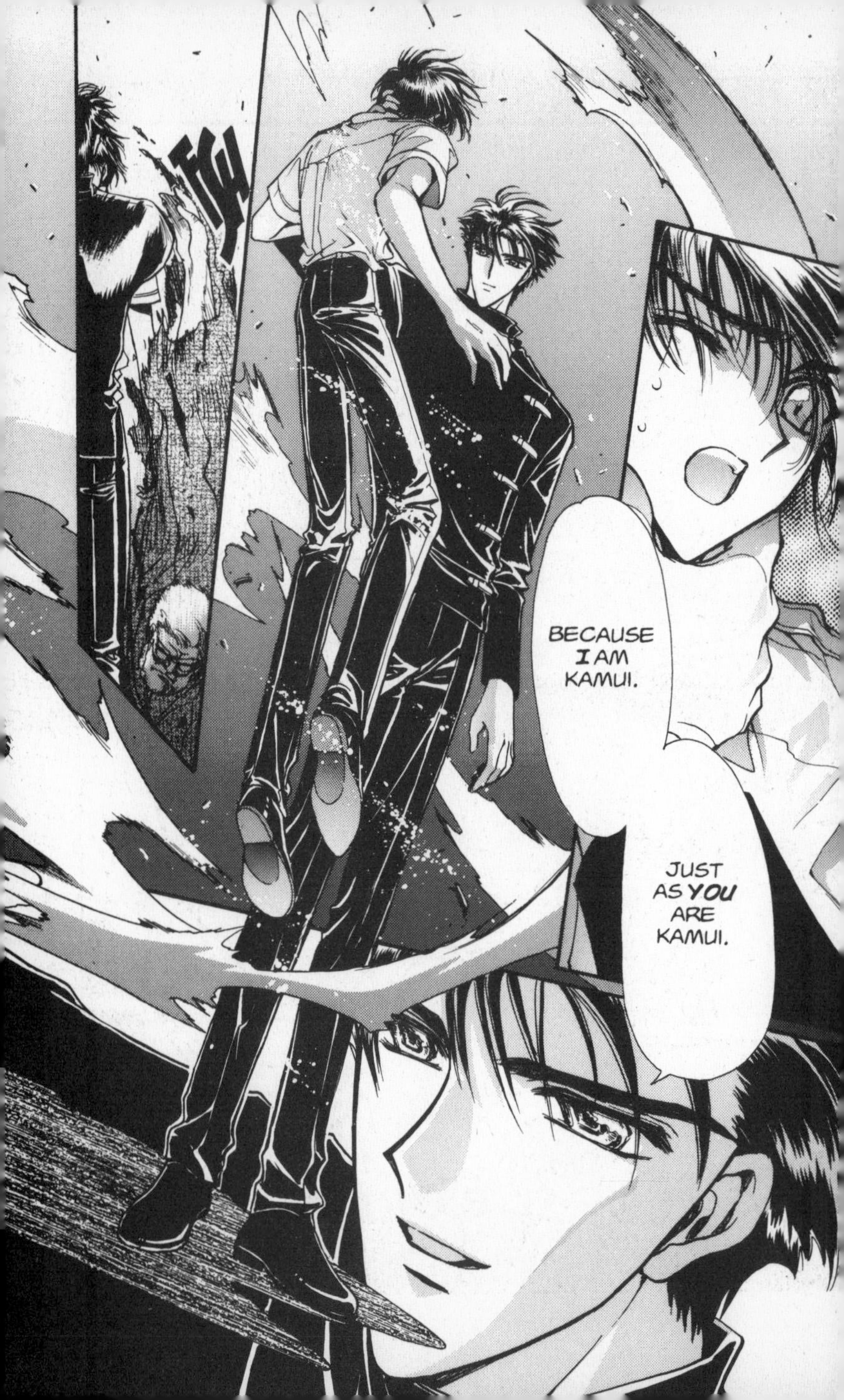
BECAUSE I AM KAMUI.
JUST AS YOU ARE KAMUI.

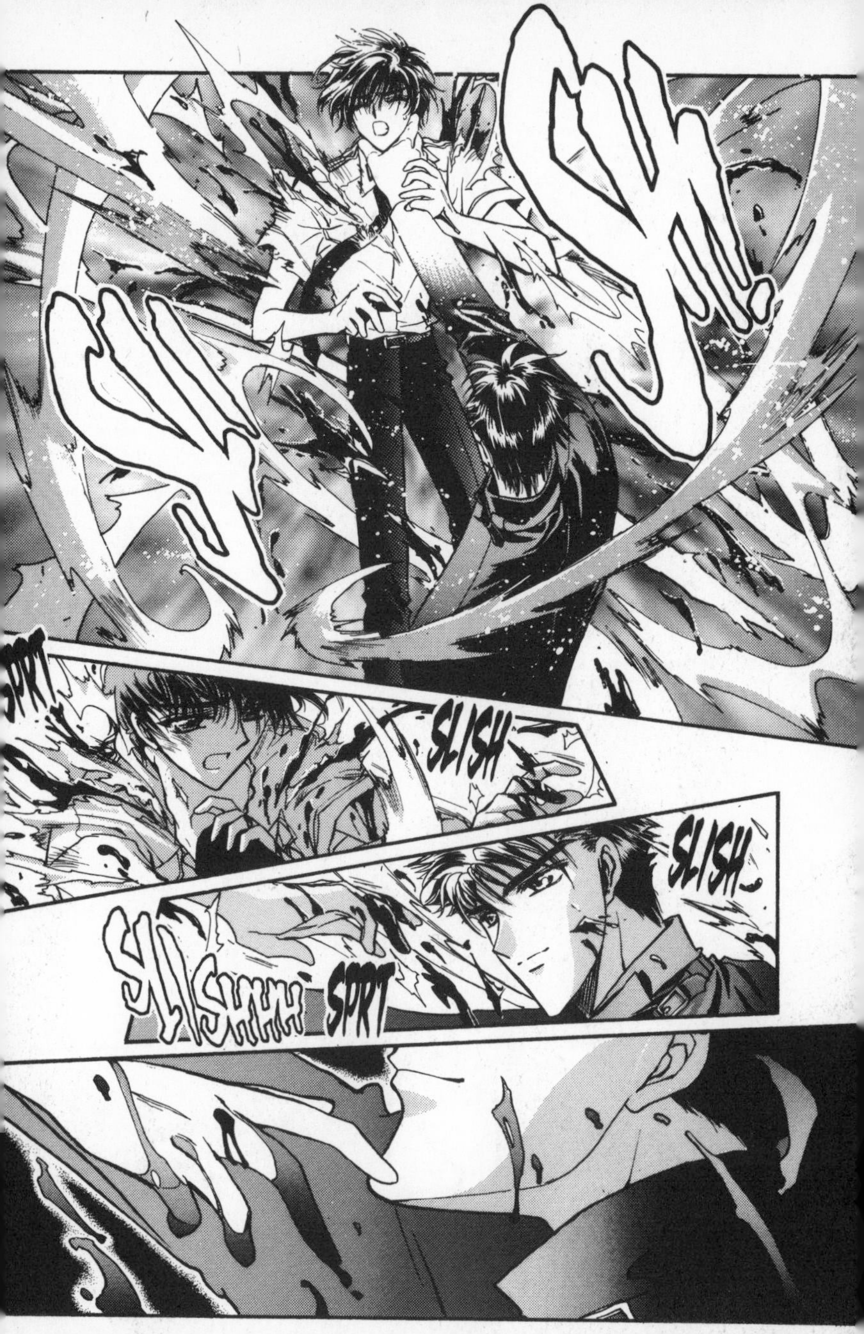
SPRT
SLISH
SLISH
SLISHHH
SPRT

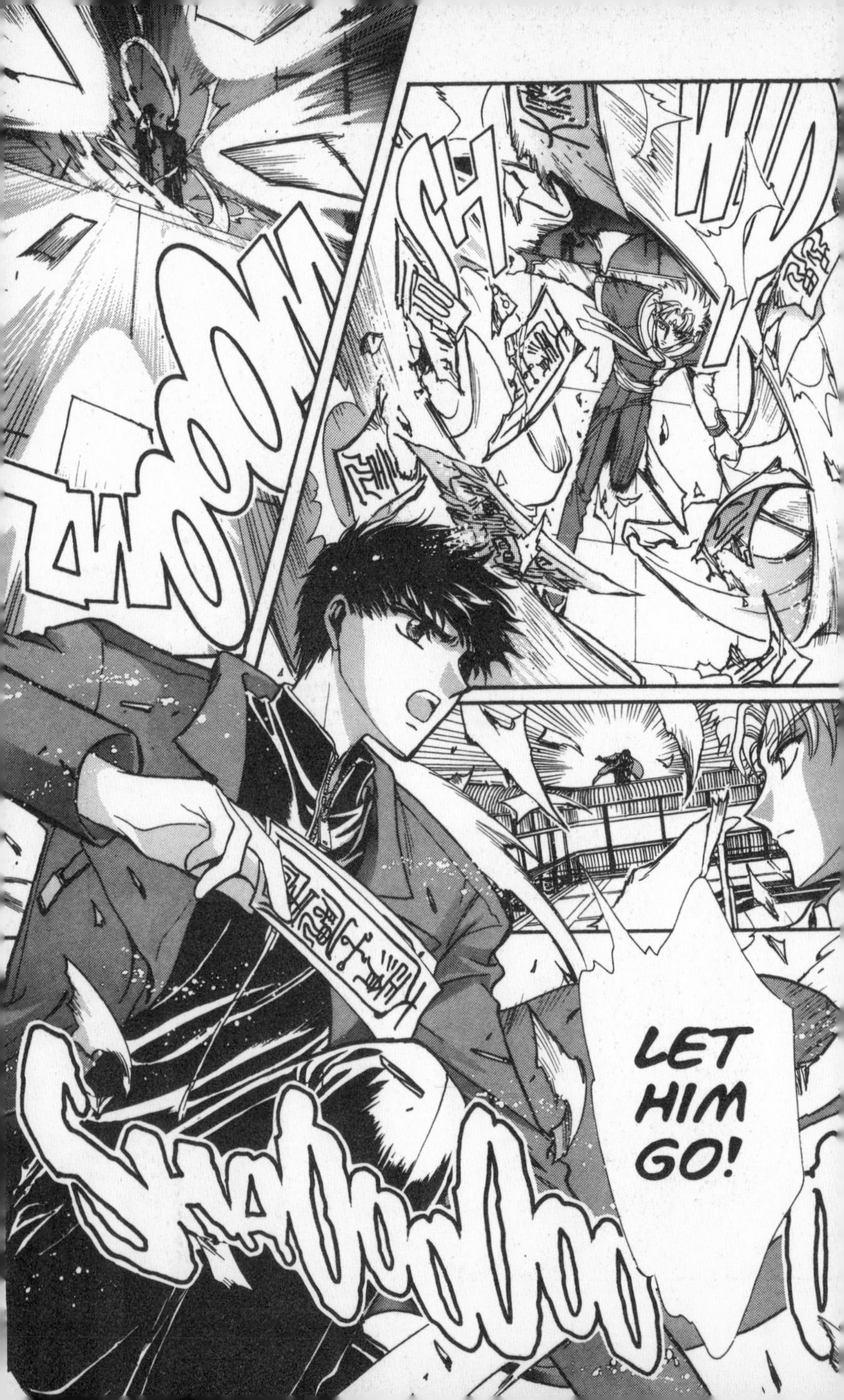
LET HIM GO!

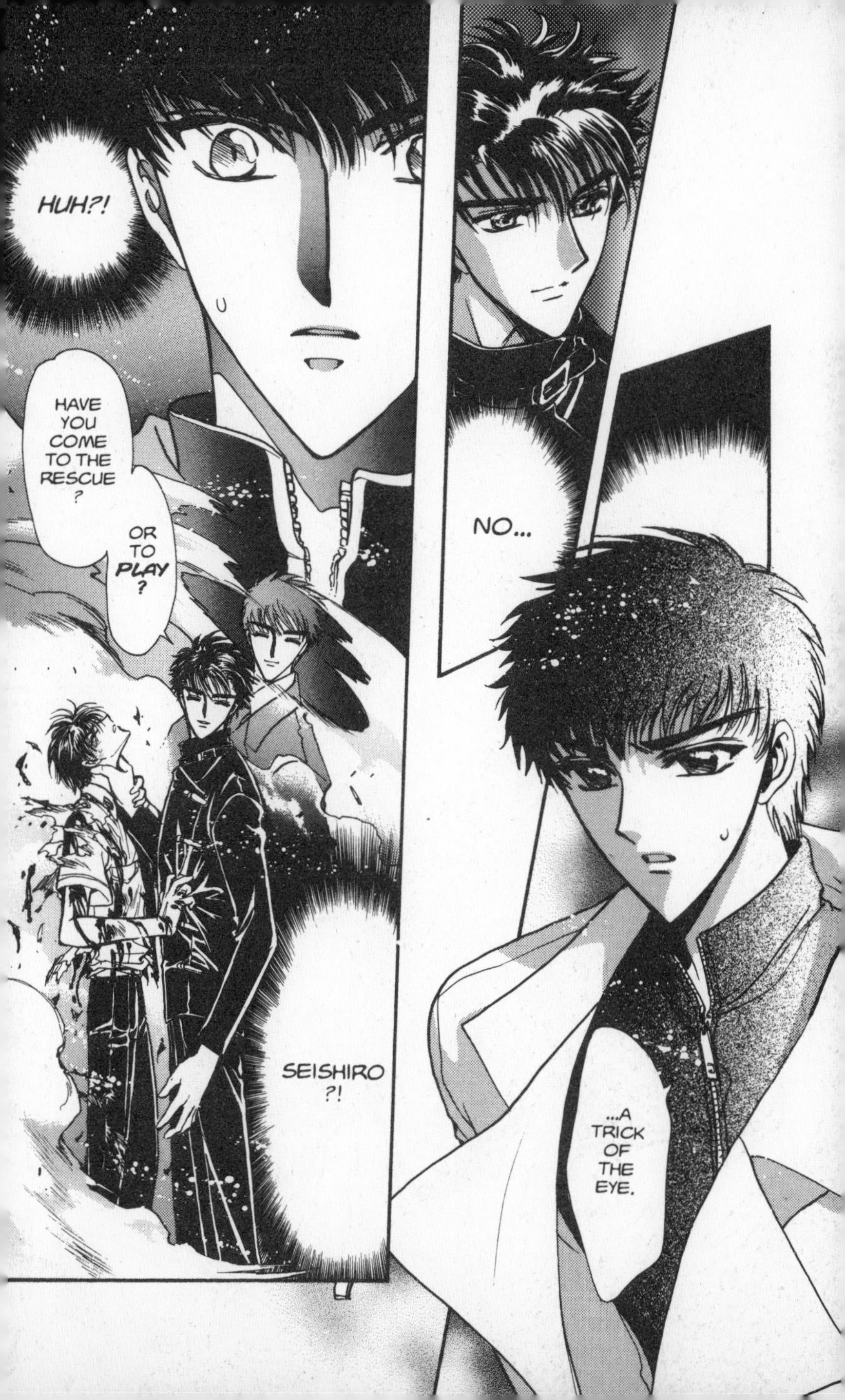
HUH?!
HAVE YOU COME TO THE RESCUE?
OR TO PLAY?
SEISHIRO?!
NO...
...A TRICK OF THE EYE.

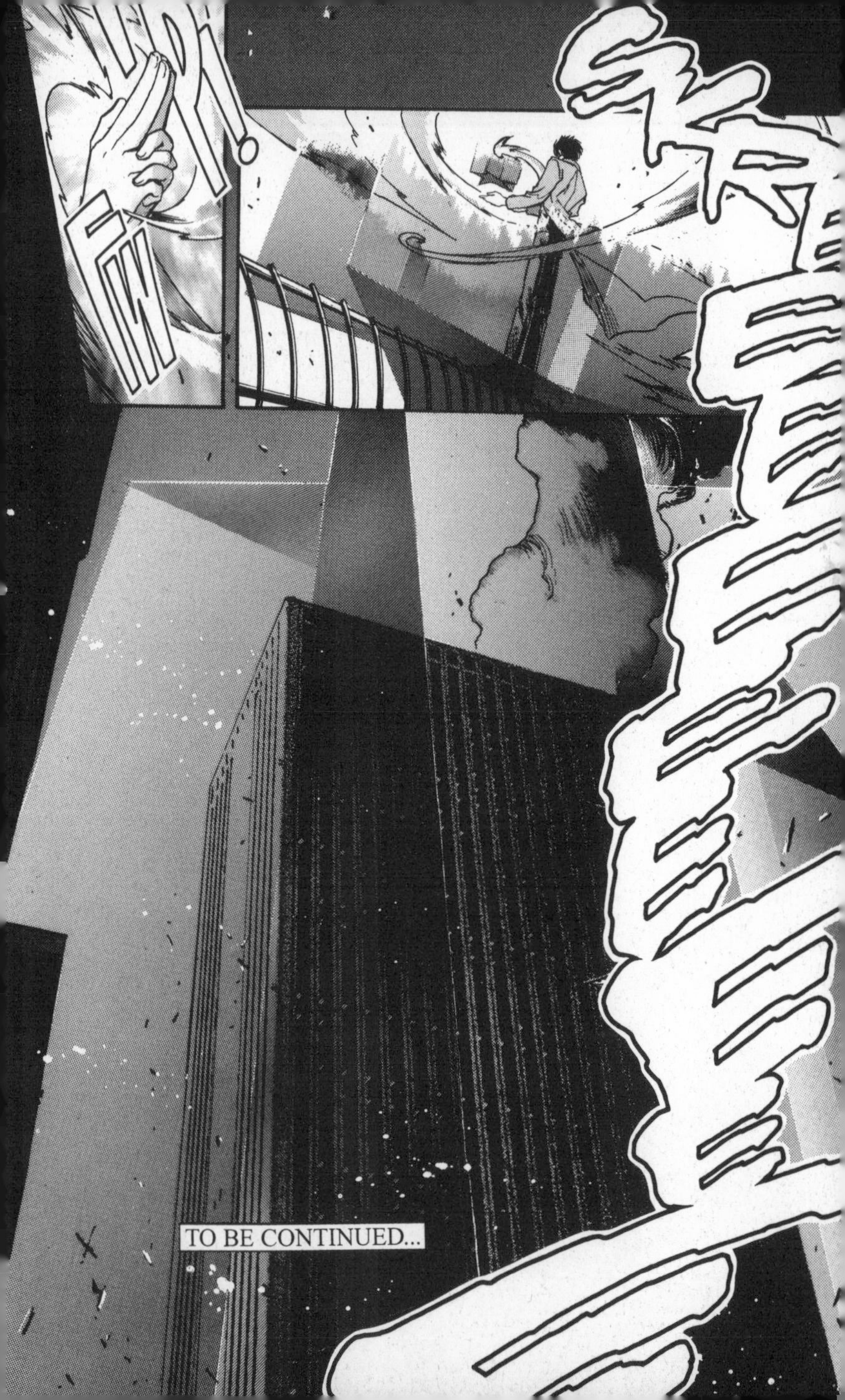
TO BE CONTINUED...

X/1999

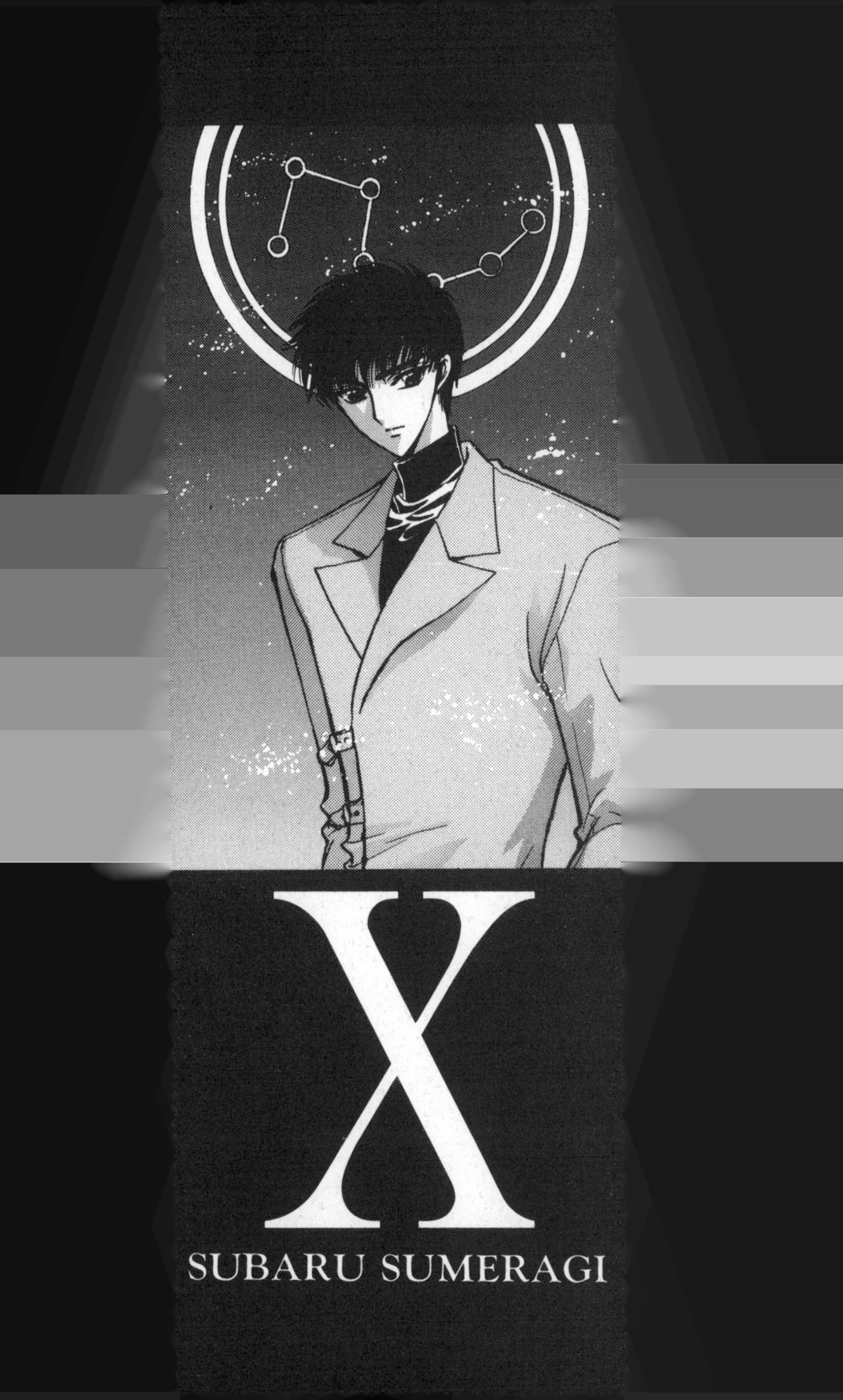
X
SUBARU SUMERAGI

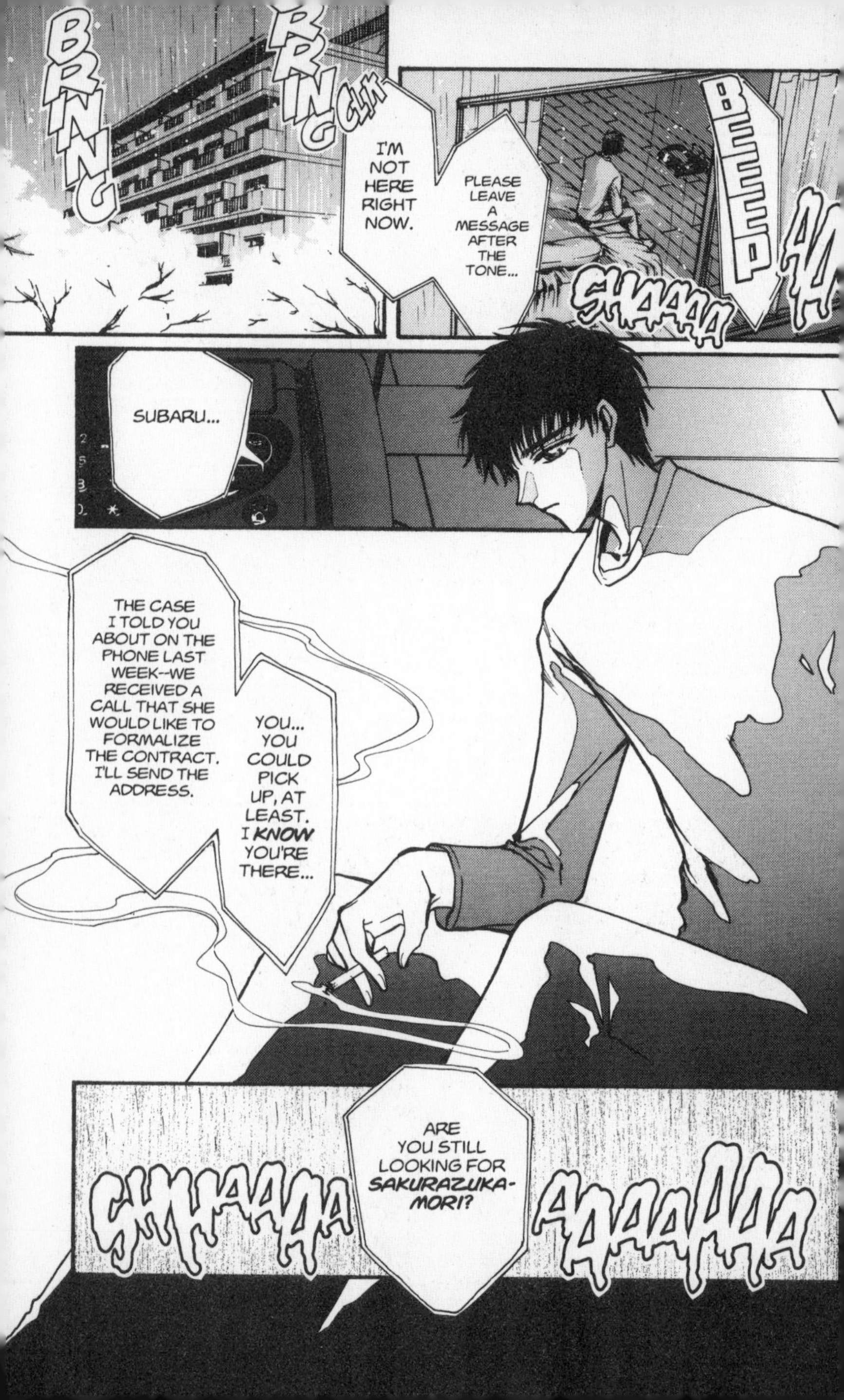
BRING BRING
CLIK
I'M NOT HERE RIGHT NOW.
PLEASE LEAVE A MESSAGE AFTER THE TONE...
BEEP
SHAAAA AA
SUBARU...
THE CASE I TOLD YOU ABOUT ON THE PHONE LAST WEEK--WE RECEIVED A CALL THAT SHE WOULD LIKE TO FORMALIZE THE CONTRACT. I'LL SEND THE ADDRESS.
YOU... YOU COULD PICK UP, AT LEAST. I *KNOW* YOU'RE THERE...
SHAAAAA
ARE YOU STILL LOOKING FOR *SAKURAZUKA-MORI*?
AAAAAAA

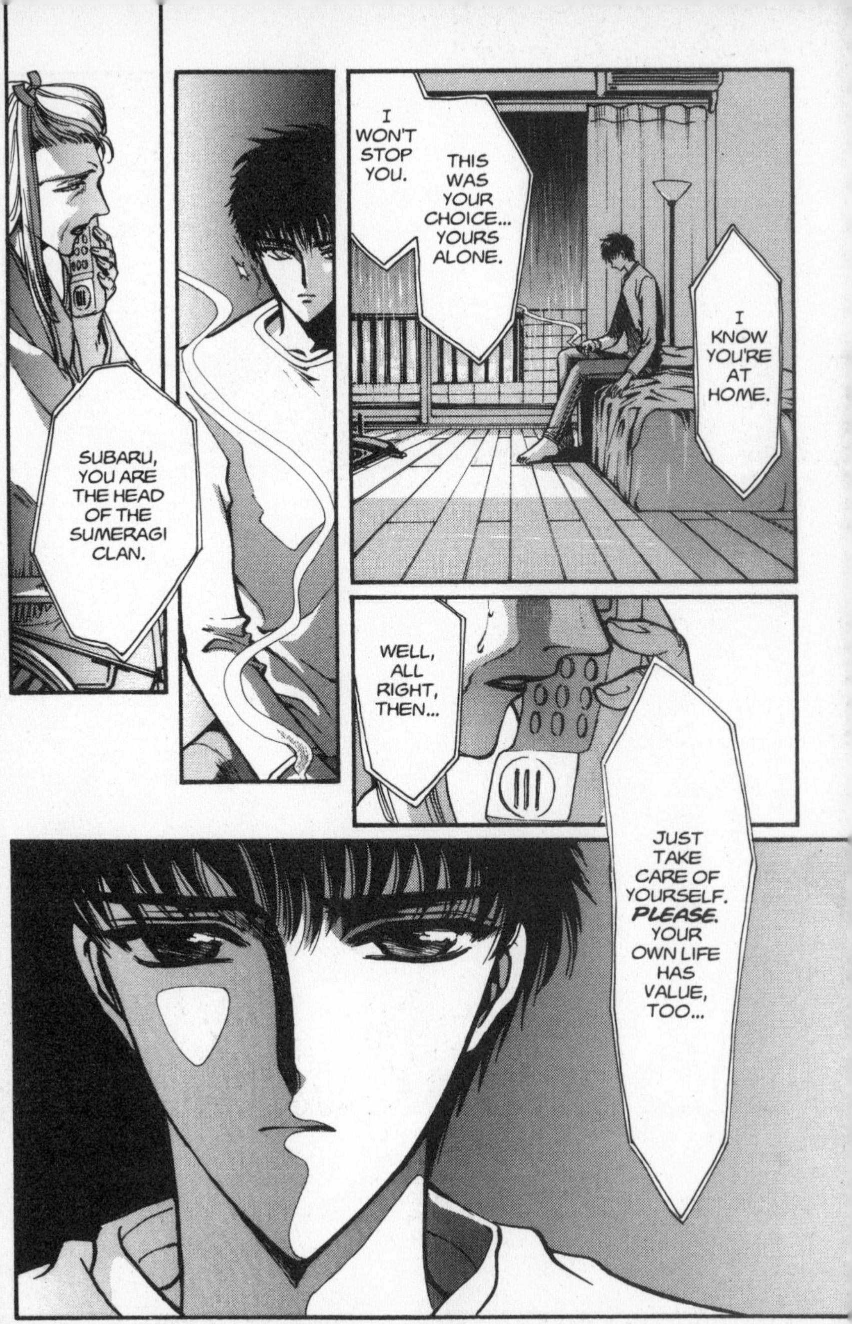

SUBARU, YOU ARE THE HEAD OF THE SUMERAGI CLAN.
I WON'T STOP YOU.
THIS WAS YOUR CHOICE... YOURS ALONE.
I KNOW YOU'RE AT HOME.
WELL, ALL RIGHT, THEN...
JUST TAKE CARE OF YOURSELF. ***PLEASE.*** YOUR OWN LIFE HAS VALUE, TOO...

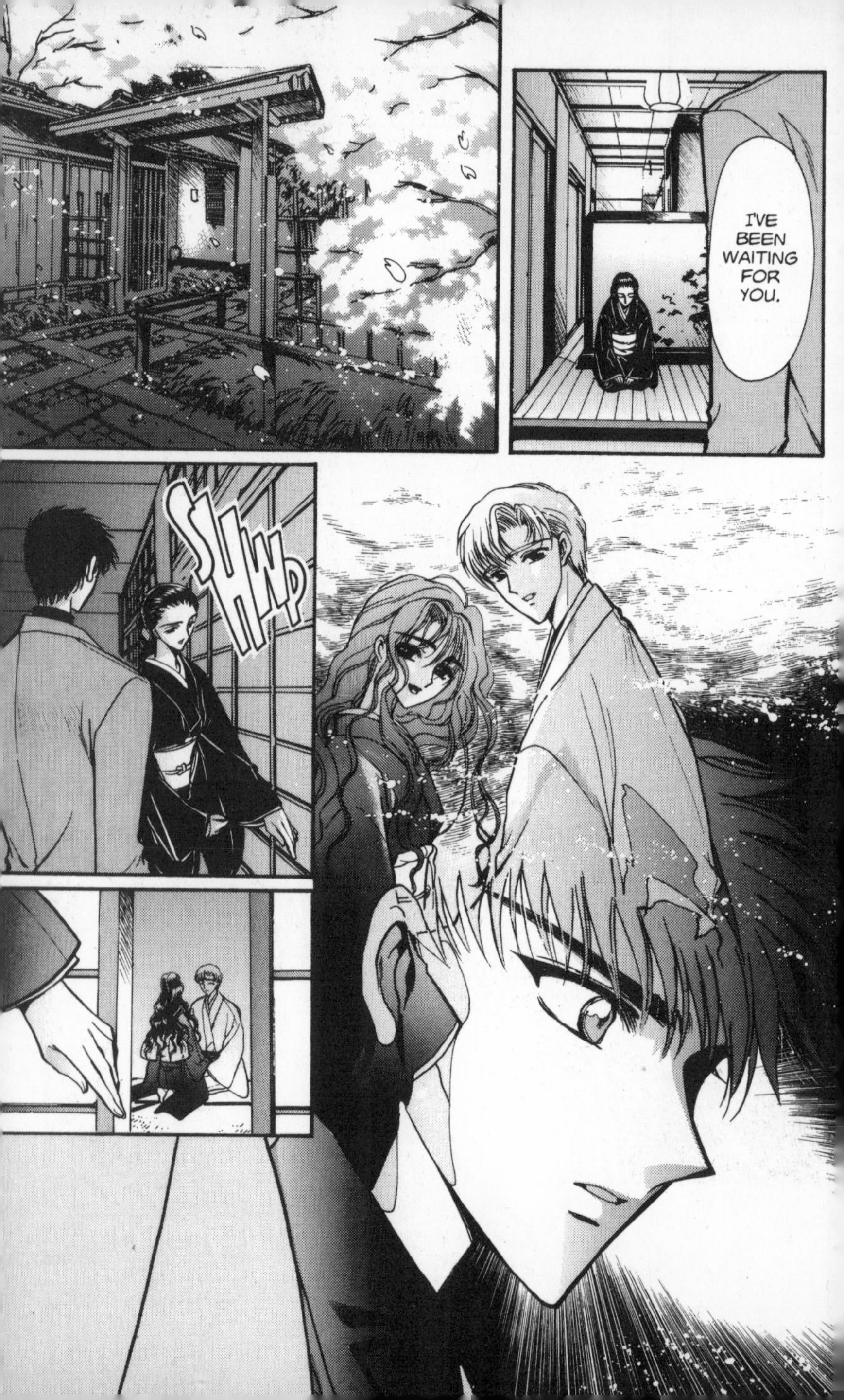
I'VE BEEN WAITING FOR YOU.
SHWP

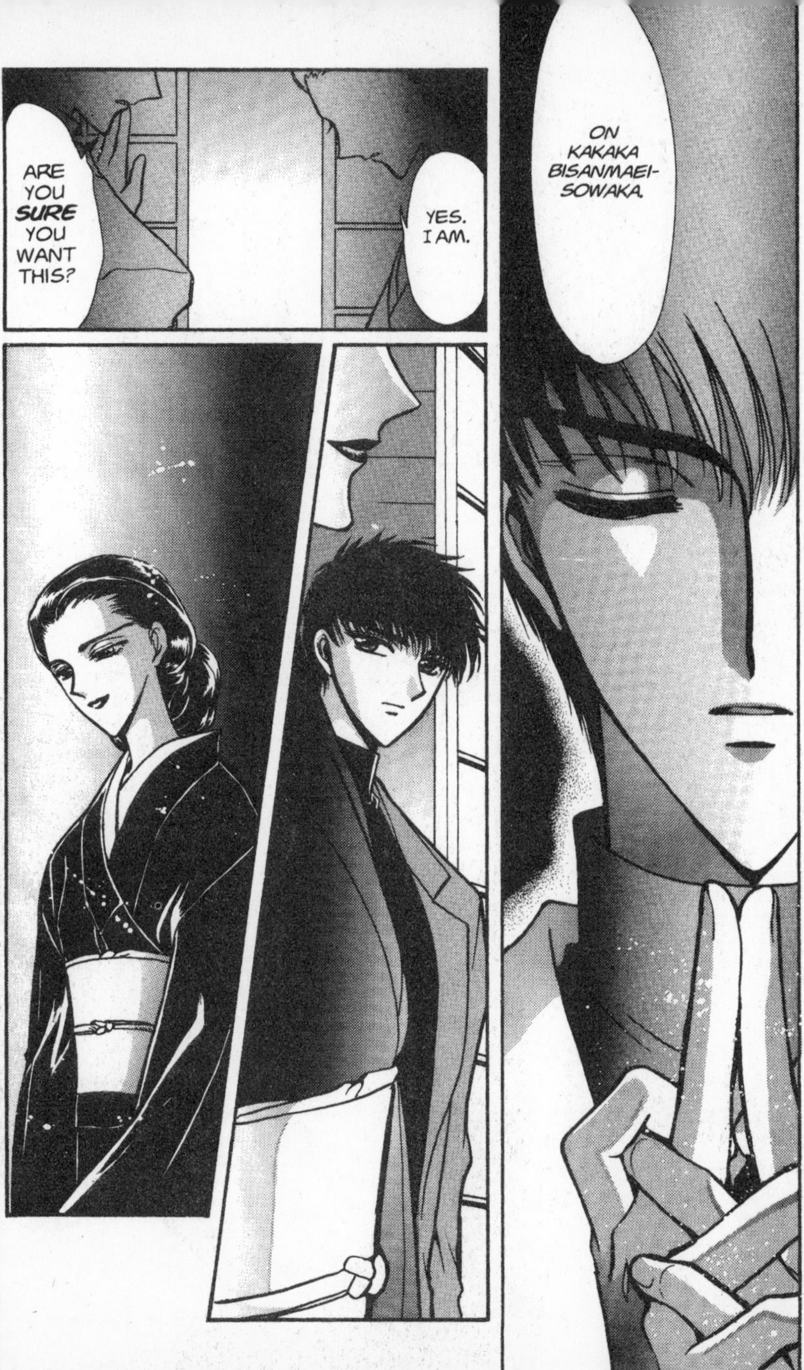
ARE YOU SURE YOU WANT THIS?
YES. I AM.
ON KAKAKA BISANMAEI-SOWAKA.

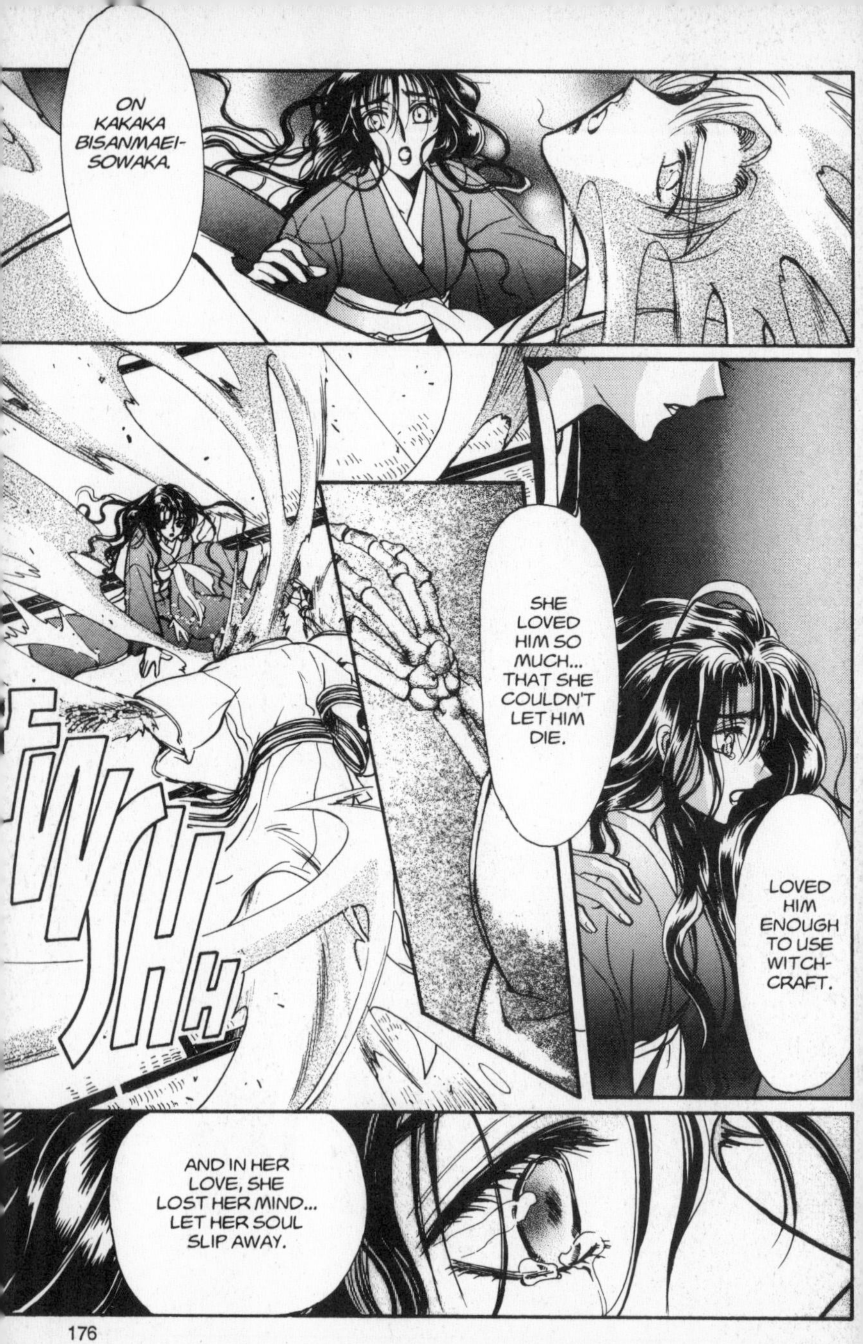
ON KAKAKA BISANMAEI-SOWAKA.
FWISHH
SHE LOVED HIM SO MUCH... THAT SHE COULDN'T LET HIM DIE.
LOVED HIM ENOUGH TO USE WITCH-CRAFT.
AND IN HER LOVE, SHE LOST HER MIND... LET HER SOUL SLIP AWAY.

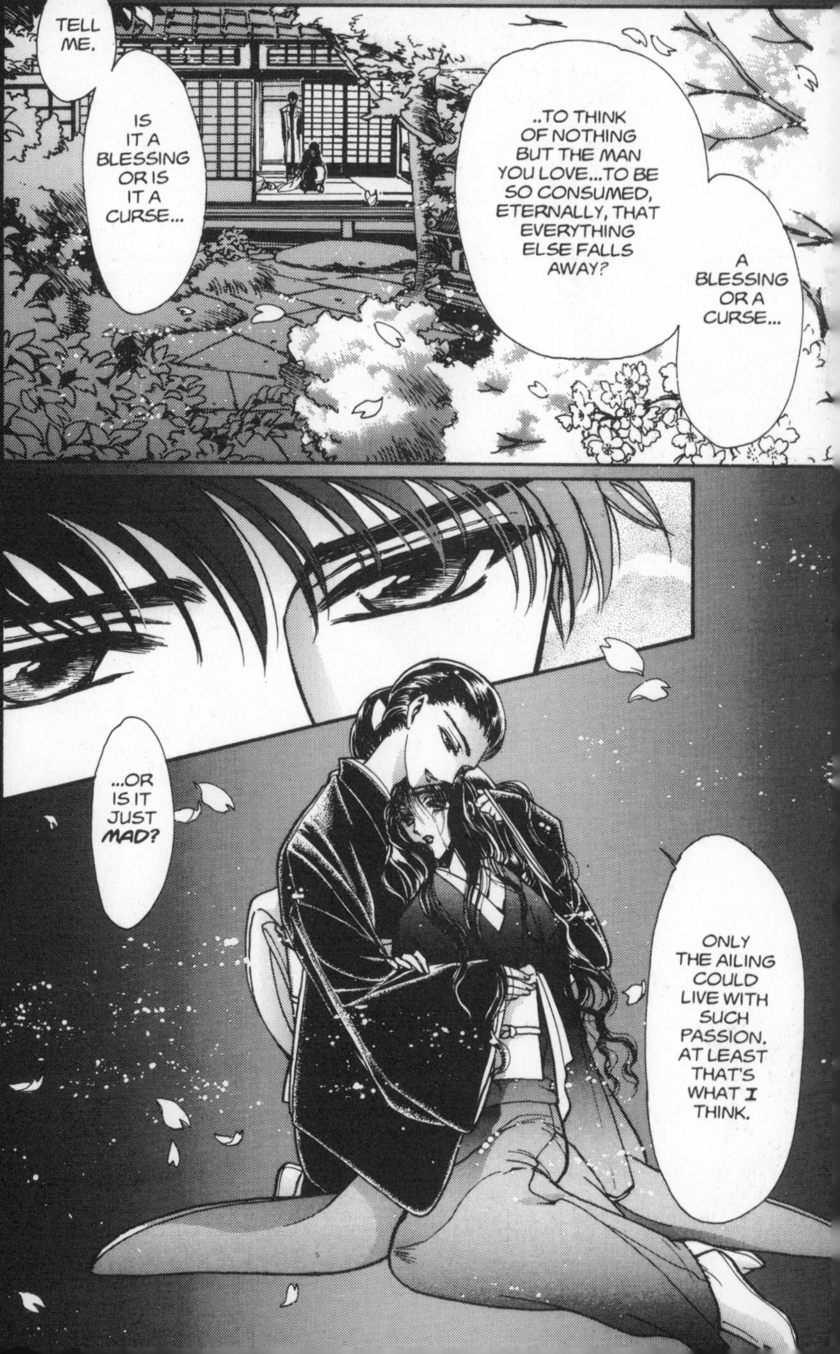
TELL ME.
IS IT A BLESSING OR IS IT A CURSE...
..TO THINK OF NOTHING BUT THE MAN YOU LOVE...TO BE SO CONSUMED, ETERNALLY, THAT EVERYTHING ELSE FALLS AWAY?
A BLESSING OR A CURSE...
...OR IS IT JUST *MAD?*
ONLY THE AILING COULD LIVE WITH SUCH PASSION. AT LEAST THAT'S WHAT *I* THINK.

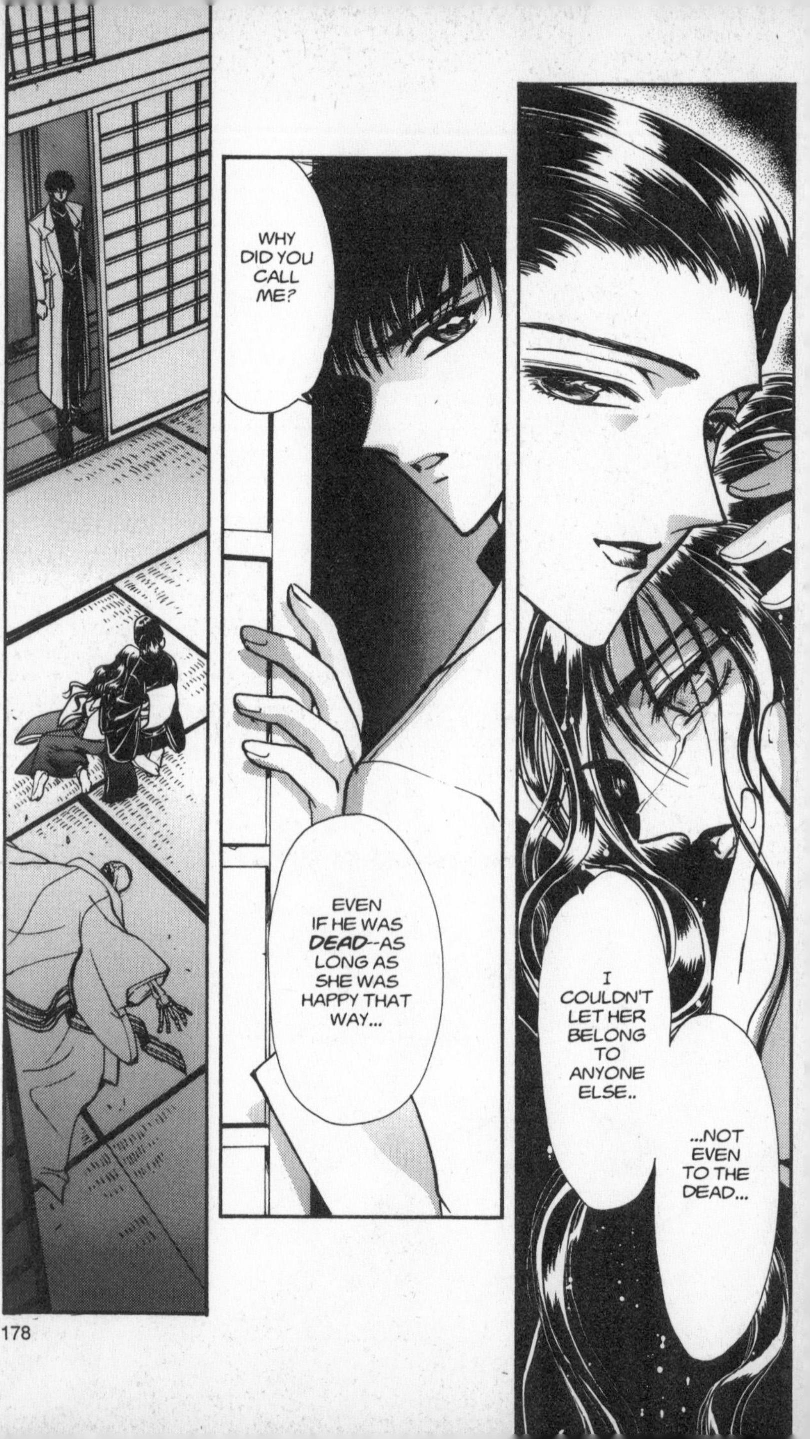
WHY DID YOU CALL ME?
EVEN IF HE WAS ***DEAD***--AS LONG AS SHE WAS HAPPY THAT WAY...
I COULDN'T LET HER BELONG TO ANYONE ELSE..
...NOT EVEN TO THE DEAD...

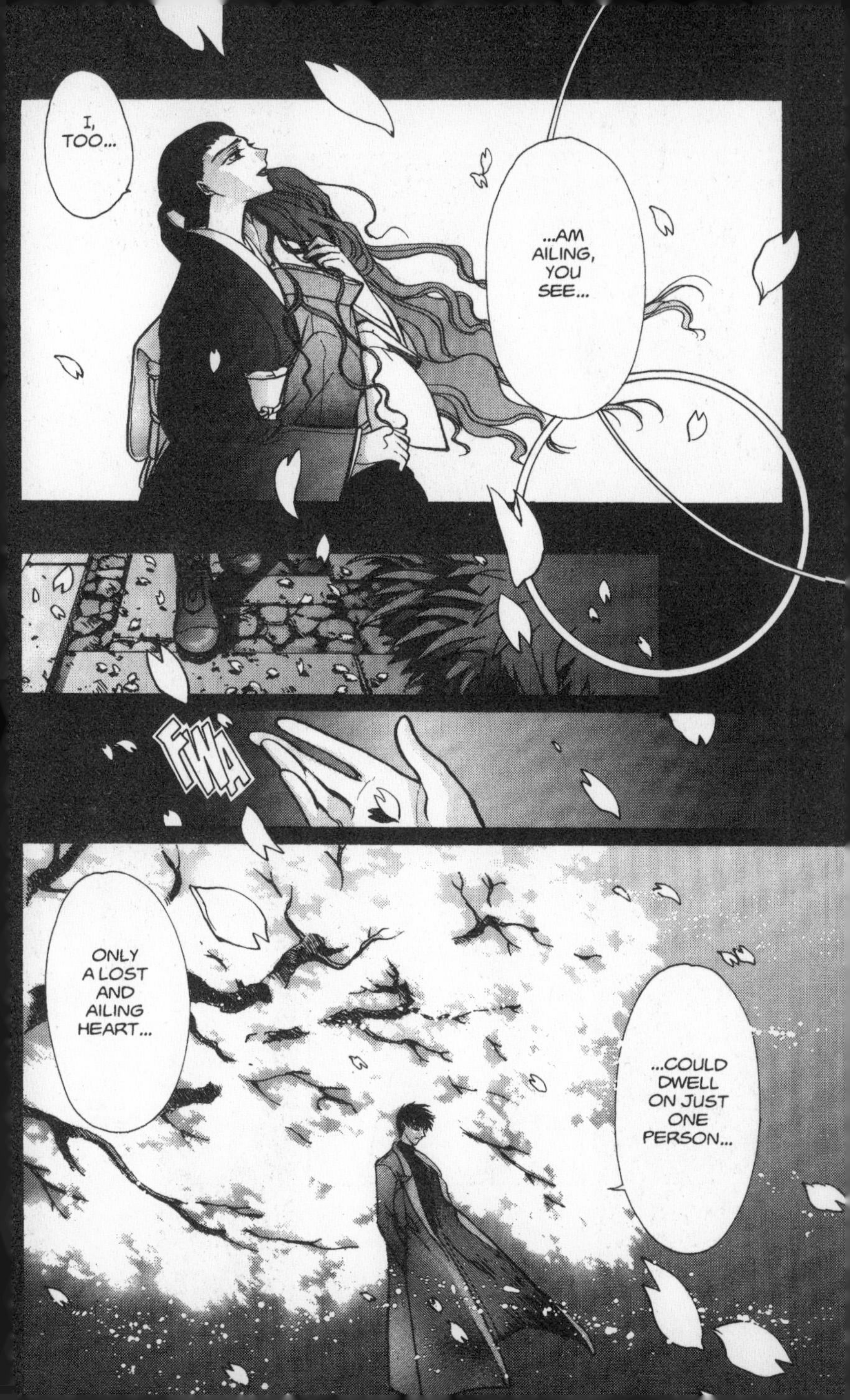
I, TOO...
...AM AILING, YOU SEE...
FWA
ONLY A LOST AND AILING HEART...
...COULD DWELL ON JUST ONE PERSON...

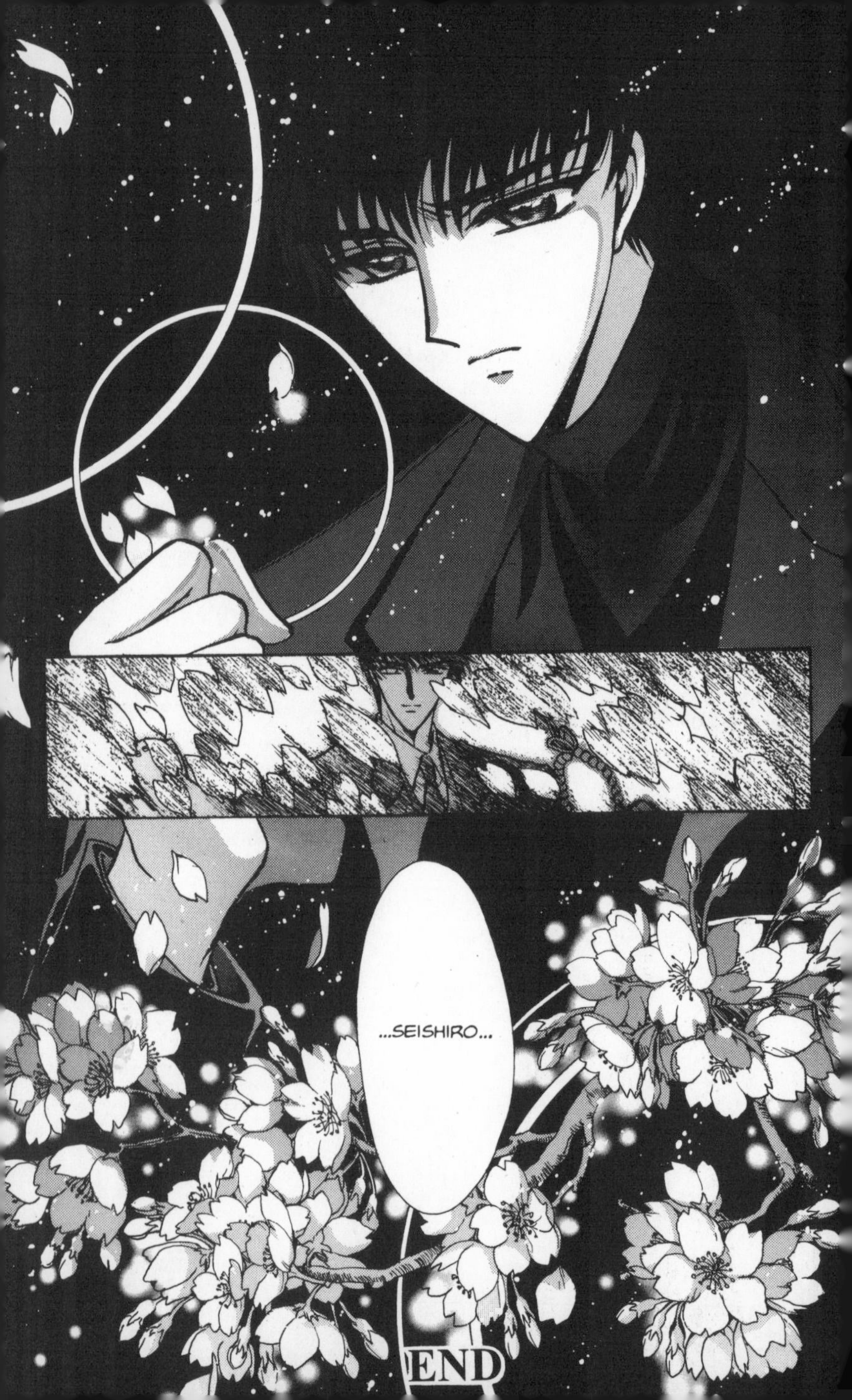
...SEISHIRO...
END

HERE'S WHAT WE RECOMMEND

YOU TRY NEX

• GYO

This horror manga by *UZUMAKI* artist Junji Ito dredges up a nightmare from the deep—monstrous, mutant fish and sea creatures that invade an Okinawa town. Ito's artwork is gorgeous and unforgettable—if you're looking for something completely different in manga, this is it.

© 2002 Junji Ito/Shogakukan

• REVOLUTIONARY GIRL UTENA

is a manga version of a popular anime series—the unique *shōjo* tale by Be-PaPas. A fiercely independent girl named Utena attends a strange school where an enigmatic student council makes the rules and mystical duels are the way to settle scores! Artist Chiho Saito took the manga in her own direction, offering new insights into this unusual tale.

© 1996 SAITO CHIHO / IKUHARA KUNIHIKO & BE-PAPAS

BASARA

Story and Art by Yumi Tamura   **vol. 1**

• BASARA is great heroic *shōjo*

adventure by Yumi Tamura. Set in the fa future, a young girl has to take her dead twin brother's place as the "Boy o Destiny," even though "destiny" has already proved itself untrustworthy.

© 1991 Yumi Tamura / Shogakukan

COMPLETE OUR SURVEY AND LET US KNOW WHAT YOU THINK!

☐ Please check here if you DO NOT wish to receive information or future offers from VIZ

Name: _____

Address: _____

City: _____ State: _____ Zip: _____

E-mail: _____

☐ Male ☐ Female   Date of Birth (mm/dd/yyyy): ___ / ___ / ___   (Under 13? Parental consent required)

What race/ethnicity do you consider yourself? (please check one)

☐ Asian/Pacific Islander   ☐ Black/African American   ☐ Hispanic/Latino

☐ Native American/Alaskan Native ☐ White/Caucasian   ☐ Other: _____

What VIZ product did you purchase? (check all that apply and indicate title purchased)

☐ DVD/VHS _____

☐ Graphic Novel _____

☐ Magazines _____

☐ Merchandise _____

Reason for purchase: (check all that apply)

☐ Special offer   ☐ Favorite title   ☐ Gift

☐ Recommendation   ☐ Other _____

Where did you make your purchase? (please check one)

☐ Comic store   ☐ Bookstore   ☐ Mass/Grocery Store

☐ Newsstand   ☐ Video/Video Game Store ☐ Other: _____

☐ Online (site: _____)

What other VIZ properties have you purchased/own? _____

_____

How many anime and/or manga titles have you purchased in the last year? How many were VIZ titles? (please check one from each column)

ANIME
- ☐ None
- ☐ 1-4
- ☐ 5-10
- ☐ 11+

MANGA
- ☐ None
- ☐ 1-4
- ☐ 5-10
- ☐ 11+

VIZ
- ☐ None
- ☐ 1-4
- ☐ 5-10
- ☐ 11+

I find the pricing of VIZ products to be: (please check one)

☐ Cheap   ☐ Reasonable   ☐ Expensive

What genre of manga and anime would you like to see from VIZ? (please check two)

☐ Adventure   ☐ Comic Strip   ☐ Detective   ☐ Fighting

☐ Horror   ☐ Romance   ☐ Sci-Fi/Fantasy   ☐ Sports

What do you think of VIZ's new look?

☐ Love It   ☐ It's OK   ☐ Hate It   ☐ Didn't Notice   ☐ No Opinion

THANK YOU! Please send the completed form to:

NJW Research
42 Catharine St.
Poughkeepsie, NY 12601

All information provided will be used for internal purposes only. We promise not to sell or otherwise divulge your information.